# THE CONCEPT OF LIBERAL DEMOCRATIC LAW

This book develops a historical concept of liberal democratic law through readings of the pivotal twentieth century legal theoretical positions articulated in the work of Herbert Hart, Ronald Dworkin, Duncan Kennedy, Rudolf Smend, Hans Kelsen and Carl Schmitt.

It assesses the jurisprudential projects and positions of these theorists against the background of a long history of European metaphysics from which the modern concept of liberal democratic law emerged. Two key narratives are central to this history of European political and legal metaphysics. Both concern the historical development of the concept of *nomos* that emerged in early Greek legal and political thought. The first concerns the history of philosophical reflection on the epistemological and ontological status of legal concepts that runs from Plato to Hobbes (the realist-nominalist debate as it became known later). The second concerns the history of philosophical and political discourses on law, sovereignty and justice that starts with the *nomos*-physis debate in fifth century Athens and runs through medieval, modern and twentieth century conceptualisations of the relationship between law and power. Methodologically, the reading of the legal theoretical positions of Hart, Dworkin, Kennedy, Smend, Kelsen and Schmitt articulated in this book is presented as a distillation process that extracts the pure elements of liberal democratic law from the metaphysical narratives that not only cradled it, but also smothered and distorted its essential aspirations.

Drawing together key insights from across the fields of jurisprudence and philosophy, this book offers an important and original re-articulation of the concept of democratic law.

**Johan van der Walt** is Professor of Philosophy of Law, University of Luxembourg.

**Part of the**
**LAW AND POLITICS: CONTINENTAL PERSPECTIVES**
series

series editors
Mariano Croce
*Sapienza University of Rome, Italy*
Marco Goldoni
*University of Glasgow, UK*

For information about the series and details of previous and forthcoming titles, see
https://www.routledge.com/law/series/LPCP

# THE CONCEPT
# OF LIBERAL
# DEMOCRATIC LAW

*Johan van der Walt*

Routledge
Taylor & Francis Group
a GlassHouse Book

First published 2020
by Routledge
2 Park Square, Milton Park, Abingdon, Oxon OX14 4RN

and by Routledge
52 Vanderbilt Avenue, New York, NY 10017

a GlassHouse book

*Routledge is an imprint of the Taylor & Francis Group, an informa business*

© 2020 Johan van der Walt

The right of Johan van der Walt to be identified as author of this work
has been asserted by him in accordance with sections 77 and 78 of the
Copyright, Designs and Patents Act 1988.

*British Library Cataloguing-in-Publication Data*
A catalogue record for this book is available from the British Library

*Library of Congress Cataloging-in-Publication Data*
Names: Van der Walt, Johan Willem Gous, author.
Title: The concept of liberal democratic law/Johan van der Walt.
Description: New York, NY : Routledge, 2019. | Series: Law and politics:
    continental perspectives | Includes bibliographical references.
Identifiers: LCCN 2019020963 (print) | LCCN 2019021744 (ebook) |
    ISBN 9780429059940 (ebk) | ISBN 9780367181802 (hbk) |
    ISBN 9780367181819 (pbk)
Subjects: LCSH: Law—Political aspects. | Law—Philosophy. |
    Democracy—Philosophy. | Liberalism—Philosophy.
Classification: LCC K487.P65 (ebook) | LCC K487.P65 V36 2019 (print) |
    DDC 340/.1—dc23
LC record available at https://lccn.loc.gov/2019020963

ISBN: 978-0-367-18180-2 (hbk)
ISBN: 978-0-367-18181-9 (pbk)
ISBN: 978-0-429-05994-0 (ebk)

Typeset in Bembo
by Apex CoVantage, LLC

*For Sibylle,* . . . χιλίων ἐτῶν ἐξικνεῖται τῆι φωνῆι
διὰ τὸν θεόν
Ἡράκλειτος

# CONTENTS

# PREFACE

The era of liberal democracy is over, claimed the head of a Member State of the European Union (EU) in May 2018 on entering a fourth term of government after a landslide victory in his country's parliamentary elections.[1] Heads of several EU Member States evidently share this conviction today. The balance between EU heads of state who share this conviction and those who don't still point favourably to the latter. But for how long? Almost all the Member States of the EU that officially still consider liberal democracy the foundational idea of government and politics are exposed and vulnerable to populist movements that openly reject the essential tenets of liberal democracy. Will these states hold firm against the waves of anti-liberal populist sentiments that, evidently, not only come crashing onto their shores from the outside, but also erupt from their own bosoms?

An old undemocratic and illiberal Europe would appear to be rising from graves that liberal democrats considered soundly covered up and sealed. This book pays considerable attention to this old Europe. It relies for this purpose on the testimony of Carl Schmitt, one of its most talented and faithful spokesmen. In other words, it does not put words into its mouth. It lets old Europe speak for itself.

Schmitt's testimony is extracted from his work *Der Nomos der Erde*. There is one aspect of this formidable work to which this book does not pay attention, namely, its interpretation of the Monroe doctrine. The Monroe doctrine, claims Schmitt, was at the heart of the New World's endeavour to keep the evils of old Europe away from its innocent shores. Depending on how forgivingly one reads American history, one may want to claim that the endeavour to keep the evils of old Europe away from American soil worked for quite a while. But one cannot continue to

---

1 See https://www.dw.com/en/viktor-orban-era-of-liberal-democracy-is-over/a-43732540 (accessed April 2019).

claim today that the Monroe strategy is still intact. The outcome of the 2016 presidential elections in the United States made it clear that the Monroe doctrine was not Europe-proof. Enough seepage must have occurred in the course of two centuries for old Europe to finally break the wall of the New World's resistance against it. Illiberal conceptions of democracy inform politics on both sides of the Atlantic today. Liberal democracy is very evidently critically threatened with extinction on both the eastern and western shores of the "Occident" ocean.

It is, however, not only liberal democracy that is threatened with global extinction today. Human existence itself, at least in the forms that we have come to know it until now, appears threatened by a global collapse of the planetary ecological equilibrium that has sustained it for thousands of years. The human race may well be on the threshold of a new age in which unprecedented strategies and means of survival will turn the ideals of liberal democracy into quaint relics of a "golden age" in which the human imagination still played around with ideas of freedom and democracy, and with the principles of justice envisaged by these ideas of freedom and democracy. These ideas and principles may soon be considered as irrelevant to "our" survival and well-being (whoever or whatever will constitute the "we" that informs this "our") as the Modern Age considered witchcraft, sorcery and magic irrelevant for its future survival and well-being.

This book is informed by the concern that the age of liberal democracy is currently running the risk of coming to an end without anyone ever having understood clearly what it really was about. It is also informed by the sense that this lack of understanding may have contributed significantly to liberal democracy's demise. Had we understood it better, liberal democracy may never have been under the existential pressures that now threaten to render it a thing of the past. On the contrary, it may well have been recognised as an ingenious response to the need to alleviate the existential pressures that always burden peaceful and orderly social co-existence. This is the understanding of liberal democratic law that this book articulates. It does so in the hope that this understanding of liberal democracy may still contribute to its survival, at least in some corners of the world, however unlikely this may seem right now.

A theory of democracy that considers it a release from, instead of an instantiation of existential pressures can easily be misunderstood as an affirmation of an acquiescent politics that shies away from all revolutionary transformations of current status quos. I trust this book will not suffer the fate of such a misunderstanding. The *liberal democratic* necessity of recognising revolutionary conditions when they exist is affirmed in the early pages of this book and the chapters that follow never retreat from this affirmation. A coherent theory of liberal democracy must acknowledge the historical possibility of circumstances in which the ideals of liberal democracy demand revolutionary interventions that suspend regular institutionalisations of liberal democracy. And it would be an omission not to acknowledge that such conditions exist right now. The probability that regular political and legal reforms are going to face up to the environmental and social crises from which no corner of planet Earth is exempt today can be dismissed. The challenges that life on Earth faces today depend on the possibility and fate of revolutionary change. The human race cannot continue consuming its environment and consuming one another in the way it has been doing as long as it can remember. The future of liberal democratic arrangements of life on Earth – arrangements that might still avoid the apocalyptic reduction of life to an animalistic competition for the last available resources – depends on what one might hopefully soon begin to call the *Thunberg revolution*. Greta Thunberg sees things in "black and white".[2] In terms of the thoughts developed in this book, she is surely not a liberal democrat. Not for now, at least. She knows that it is her fate to live in exceptional times and a time of exception. She may well be or become the Antigone of the twenty-first century. She has already emerged or escaped from her personal dark cave once. And the question – upon which the future of liberal democracy depends in the first place today – is whether Creon will send her back there, knowing well that this time round there will be no Sophocles left to tell the story.

This book has two aims. The first is to put forward the argument about liberal democratic law and law-making as a technique designed for shielding societies from the existential pressures weighing down upon them, and to debunk the idea that law-making should be rooted in these pressures, or somehow embody and lay them to rest. The second is to present this argument in the language and format of a textbook that can be used in the teaching of legal and political theory. The book indeed developed over three years out of class notes that I started writing in 2016 for a first year Philosophy of Law course. This double aim inevitably burdens it with a double weakness. Readers principally interested in the central argument may find, at least at times, that they also have to read through "basic information" all too familiar to them. Readers principally interested in the book as a textbook may frequently find that it does not provide enough basic information to really work as a textbook. For instance, the book refers several times to Hobbes without once stopping to discuss his legal or political theory in detail.

I nevertheless believe both weaknesses can be dealt with easily. Readers principally interested in the central argument can easily skip or scan-read the odd paragraphs that they consider "basic information". My firm belief is that they will not want to do this very often, for "basic information" always attains a dimension of "new information" when its contextualisation is adequately innovative, as I trust is the case in this book. Readers who principally read the book as a textbook can easily supplement its "basic information" with recourse to readily available "online" encyclopaedic sources. A careful lecturer could easily instruct even first year students how to do this effectively. I would also like to add that, in my experience, the double aim of the book also provides for a very satisfactory assessment of student performance in courses where this book is used as a textbook. Students who turn out not to be particularly interested in legal theory or philosophy can be assessed

---

2  https://www.ted.com/talks/greta_thunberg_the_disarming_case_to_act_right_now_on_climate (accessed April 2019).

on their grasp of the basic information about the history of Western legal thinking that the book provides. Students who are more inspired by the subject can, in addition to their grasp of the basic information, also be assessed on their advanced grasp of the central argument of the book. I have been doing this satisfactorily for several years now and would be happy to offer guidance to anyone interested in this method of teaching.

Two other more incidental shortcomings of this book must also be mentioned. Having read it through, many readers will find it strange that it does not include chapters – or a chapter – on Rawls and Habermas. The initial plan was to include a chapter on the work of these two thinkers, considering how relevant their thoughts are for the theme that the book develops. In the end, however, I realised that this would have made the book too lengthy and therefore decided to take out the parts on Rawls and Habermas. The weakness that results from this decision will be rectified in the course of 2020/2021 with a journal article on Rawls and Habermas in which I relate their thoughts to the theme I develop in this book.

The second weakness concerns a chapter on "modern reconstructions" of Aristotle's potentiality-actuality distinction – dealing with Spinoza (leading to Deleuze and Negri), Schelling, Nietzsche and Heidegger – that I also took out to prevent the book from becoming too unwieldy. The thinkers mentioned here (with the exception of Deleuze and Negri) are mentioned prominently in a passage from Giorgio Agamben's *Homo Sacer* that plays a key role in the development of the main argument of this book. It will therefore be a useful supplement to this book to also publish an article or even a separate monograph on the "reconstruction of Aristotle's actuality-potentiality distinction" in the works of these thinkers. I will also endeavour to do this as soon as possible, but this must remain a longer term project for now.

The final chapter of this book also mentions two other monographs – respectively with the titles *Liberal Democratic Judicial Review* and *Law, Literature and Liberal Democracy* – that will follow this one. These two works will also add important supplements to the thoughts developed in this book. They are already quite well developed and should both be ready for publication in the early 2020s.

I thank Frank Michelman for many discussions and email exchanges that left clear marks on the thoughts developed in this book, and for generously reading and commenting on Chapter 8. Just before I finished off the manuscript and sent it to the publishers, Joseph Singer put a week aside to discuss the arguments that I put forward in this book from many different angles. These discussions alerted me to concerns that demand much further reflection, but which have already prompted a number of reformulations for which I am much indebted to him. I wish to thank Emilios Christodoulidis for his contribution to the reading of Sophocles' and Anouilh's *Antigone* that plays such a key role in my argument. These thoughts began to take form during inspiring classes on *Antigone* that we taught together at the University of Glasgow between 2007 and 2011. I hope he will recognise the role that *Antigone* plays in this book as a tribute to the work we did together in the course of those lectures. I also wish to thank Jean-Marc Ceci, Ricardo Spindola and

Richard Mailey for reading through an earlier draft of the whole text and providing me with first "reader's impressions" of its clarity and coherence. I also thank Richard Mailey for attention to the smallest orthographic and syntactic details that made the final text-editing much easier in the end. I thank Roila Mavrouli for helpful assistance during the last week of tying up loose ends. I dedicate this book to my wife Sibylle van der Walt. I wish to thank her for her patience with the relentless hours that I dedicated to finishing the text during especially the last six months, and for keeping me constantly alert to the fact that arguments that persuade me do not necessarily persuade others.

Johan van der Walt
April 2019

# INTRODUCTION

## 1 Law, sovereignty and justice

Let us begin our exploration of the concept of liberal democratic law with the following three statements of the Roman jurist Ulpianus:

1)  *Quod principi placuit, legis habet vigorem* (what pleases the emperor has the force of law).[1]
2)  *Princeps legibus solutus est* (the emperor is not bound by the law).[2]
3)  *Iustitia est constans et perpetua voluntas ius suum cuique tribuendi* (justice is the constant and perpetual will to give to everyone what is due to them).[3]

The first two of these three statements observe the power of the Roman emperor to make law without being bound by law. The first avers that the emperor is free to make law as he pleases. The second adds that the scope of the law-making that happens to please him is not confined or restricted by existing law. The third statement introduces a potential limit to the emperor's unlimited power to make law as he pleases. If it also pleases him to be considered a just emperor, he would need to make laws that permanently – in other words, *without exception* – guarantee to every one of his subjects that which is rightly due to each of them.

The third statement may at first glance appear to be irreconcilable with the first two, but only an overly hasty reading would lead to the conclusion that it is. Such a reading would suggest that the commitment to justice necessarily implies a commitment to be bound by existing law. However, the quite common experience that

---

1  D. 1.3.31 in Justinian 2010, p. 6
2  D. 1.4.1 in ibid, p. 7.
3  D. 1.1.10 in ibid, p. 1.

existing law is or has become unjust – the experience that it has become out of touch with contemporary social realities and all too conspicuously fails to guarantee to everyone what is rightly theirs – would necessarily demand that the emperor who aims to be just must not only *not* consider himself bound by the law, but should feel *compelled* to make new law that may succeed better in doing justice to everyone. In other words, any emperor who wants to be just would either have to justly maintain existing law, or justly take leave of it. There is nothing incoherent or disconcerting about this observation. Political actors have through the ages been moved by their understanding of the demands of justice to take leave of existing law. Some of them were reformers who changed the law to improve it. Some of them were revolutionaries who broke the law in order to destroy and replace it with more just law. What does this imply for liberal democracy and liberal democratic law?

Typical liberal democrats are generally perceived to be at least somewhat uncomfortable with revolutionary changes and more at ease with incremental reforms of law. Perhaps that is also how they perceive themselves.[4] This may be so because it seems easier to reconcile incremental law reform with the ideal of the rule of law. Incremental law reform relies on existing rules and principles of law that allow for legal change that does not break the law, as revolutions do. Essentially at stake, here, is the due application of the kind of legal rules that Herbert Hart called "secondary rules of change". These rules allow the sovereign law-maker to bring about law reform in a legal manner.[5] Legal systems usually provide for them in constitutional documents or constitutionals conventions.[6] In liberal democratic constitutional documents, these rules of change typically stipulate the parliamentary, judicial and administrative procedures required for changing "ordinary" law, and the constitutional amendment rules that allow for constitutional change. In legal systems where constitutional law is embodied in unwritten "constitutional conventions," rules of change would generally have the status of old customary practices that have been observed "as long as one can remember."[7]

Notwithstanding the typical liberal democratic discomfort with revolutionary changes that indeed *transgress* or *break* existing law, it is at least sometimes possible to consider revolutionary transformations of legal systems as re-enactments of essential principles of law that have "fallen into decay" according to the revolutionaries.[8] When one takes this construction of revolutions as one's cue, one could say that revolutionaries can, and perhaps must, always consider themselves to be acting according to law, or "under law."[9] This, in any case, is the way in which liberal democrats would want to understand revolutionary change that cannot be avoided through recourse to regular law reform.

4 See Michelman 2003.
5 See Chapter 5, Section 1 below.
6 See Michelman 2012.
7 See Pocock 1987.
8 See Arendt 1963.
9 See Michelman 1995, 1996.

But, what if the revolutionaries who move to break existing law, do so because they are motivated by ideals or sentiments that cannot be reconciled with a liberal democratic concept of justice, that is, a concept of giving to everyone what liberal democrats would consider "due to them"? According to liberal democrats, the demands of political and social justice pivot on a set of principles that can be considered the "right" principles. The essential principles of a liberal democratic constitution – John Rawls refers to them as "constitutional essentials" – are founded on principles of reason or reasonableness that everyone could reasonably be expected to endorse. Rawls calls these principles "public reason." They concern principles such as equality before the law, respect for the inviolable dignity and integrity of persons, freedom of conscience and belief of all individuals, and so forth. Taken together they constitute the "principle of reciprocity" that is central to Rawls conception of "public reason."[10] Law reform or revolutionary refoundations of law that violate Rawls' principle of reciprocity would surely no longer be reconcilable with the idea of liberal democratic law.

One can see now that liberal democrats may sometimes have a problem with reconciling Ulpianus' first and second dictum with his third dictum. They may well go along with the concession that the liberal democratic sovereign should have the freedom to make new law and should even have the liberty to do so with revolutionary acts that transgress and destroy existing law, but they will not go along with the idea that the sovereign can enact just any law he or she pleases to enact. According to them, revolutionary transformations that transgress and destroy existing law can be in order,[11] but only as long as they are motivated by the "right reasons."

## 2 Sovereignty and "correctness" or "rightness"

The idea that the sovereign cannot just enact any law did not have to wait for liberal democracy and the Modern Age before it began to burden political thought. As we shall see in Chapter 5, the view that imperial sovereignty is constrained by considerations of appropriate or correct government already informed Christian political thought from the third century onwards. This idea can also be traced to the important lines of Greek political thought developed by Plato and Aristotle. Aristotle's endeavour to articulate a political philosophy in terms of which governments are duly bound to the law or *nomos* will be one of the key focus points in this book. Aristotle's philosophy will be represented as an attempt to restore the Athenians' faith in a concept of *nomos* that not only binds the sovereign, but also elevates every aspect of Athenian life to its proper place in the harmonious order of existence to which the Greeks referred as *kosmos*. He did this in a time that this conception of

---

10 See Rawls 1996, pp. 212–254.
11 Andrew Arato's extraordinary emphasis on the need for fictions of legal continuity during revolutionary changes may make him an exception in this regard. See Arato 2010, p. 28. See nevertheless also Arato 2000, pp. 142–145 for a more ambivalent assessment of fictions of continuity against the background of revolutionary refoundations of law.

*nomos* as a reflection of *kosmos* was clearly faltering. It was being challenged by a group of philosophers called the *Sophists* who contended that the law is nothing but the rules laid down by the one who has the power to do so. Thucydides' *History of the Peloponnesian War* suggests that prominent Athenians were actually swayed by sophist teachings and responsible for Athens' descent into a ruthless politics vis-à-vis the other Greek cities. His account of the ruthlessness of the Athenian envoys sent to the island of Melos in 416 BCE is an important case in point and our engagement with Greek history and philosophy in this book will rely on this account as the essential background to Aristotle's attempt to restore a sense of correctness in Greek politics.

After Aristotle, the idea of "correct" government remained a pivotal line of thinking in the history of Western philosophy and this book will trace some of the key moments in the history of this line of thinking. However, as will soon become clear, it will also proceed to distil the concept of law from this long line of Western thinking in order to extract it from the heavy metaphysical bedrock in which this "correctness" has invariably been rooted. Liberal democracy, we shall argue, is not a pursuit of correctness. It plays out in contexts where different people typically have such different ideas of correctness that the notion of correctness can no longer inform their endeavours to find adequately common courses of action on the basis of which they can continue to live together. In such contexts, reliance on correctness gets one nowhere. Contexts of serious disagreement regarding the correct course of action to be followed demand a very different approach to the challenge of sustaining enough "common ground" to render adequately peaceful co-existence possible. That is why liberal democracy cannot be contemplated on Aristotelian foundations, and why the concept of liberal democratic law developed in this book is fundamentally non-Aristotelian.

This does not mean that the notion of correctness plays no role in the state of mind of liberal democrats. Liberal democrats have a dual relation to correctness. On the one hand, they remain squarely convinced of the need to consider all governmental decisions taken against a background of serious disagreement "groundless" and therefore immune to charges of "incorrectness." On the other hand, they cannot take part credibly and effectively in the public process of selecting common courses of action in the face of disagreement, if they do not consider the positions they take in this process "correct."

If liberal democrats were consciously to regard principles of rightness, reasonableness and equal respect faithlessly or cynically as nothing more than effective rhetorical devices, they would no longer be liberal democrats in the normative and definitive sense of the term. If they were to do so, their "liberalism" would become nothing but a ruse for yet another faithless pursuit of power, and nothing would prevent this "liberal democratic" pursuit of power to turn as ruthless as any amoral and realist pursuit of power. Indeed, not only would nothing prevent them from turning ruthless, they would more or less be committing themselves to a programme of ruthless coercion. As Hannah Arendt points out well, if you cannot convince yourself of something, you will not be able to convince others of it either.[12] When this happens, when political leaders begin to impose coercive programmes of action which they evidently do not sincerely consider correct, fair and justifiable, politics and government effectively and predictably become *nothing but* brutal and cynical suppression of dissent of the kind that took place in Athens' 416 BCE transaction with Melos. As Arendt also instructs us well, this kind of suppression has nothing to do with political power.[13] That is why Dworkin is completely correct when he contends that "those in power must believe that what they say is so."[14] But Dworkin ultimately draws conclusions from this contention that takes him right back into an Aristotelian mode of thinking about the good life from which the theory of democratic law developed in this book seeks to take leave in clear terms.

The dual relation to "correctness" that liberal democrats must maintain can be summed up as follows: By all means believe that the principles and convictions by which you act are correct. You have to do so. Your game will all too soon be up and unmasked as shallow duplicity if you do not. *But, do not succumb to the temptation to insist that those who evidently and adamantly disagree with your principles and convictions ultimately have good reasons to agree with you, good reasons that somehow just remain unbeknown to them and to which they should become enlightened. The moment you do this, you begin do betray liberalism. You then begin to descend into a dogmatic liberalism that ultimately risks becoming as illiberal as any adversary of liberal democracy imaginable.*

## 3 The symbolic and the real, conviction and opinion

In other words, the ultimate test for a realistic and truly liberal political liberalism concerns the extent to which it can resist two temptations:

1) the temptation to insist on claims of "rightness" in the face of intractable differences of opinion;
2) the temptation to think "rightness" can be *enforced*.

Liberal democrats need to remain alert to the reality that any "enforcement" prompted *by* a norm – or by faith in it – never amounts to an enforcement *of* that norm. They accordingly need to understand that "enforcement" does not constitute a *continuation*, but an *interruption* of the norm. This is the point that Ernst-Wolfgang Böckenförde captured well with the phrase that is now widely known as the *Böckenförde dictum*. Böckenförde wrote: "Liberal Democracy lives from conditions that

12 Arendt 1963, p. 103.
13 See Arendt 1970, pp. 43–56, especially at 56: "To sum up: politically speaking, it is insufficient to say that power and violence are not the same. Power and violence are opposites; where the one rules absolutely the other is absent." See also Arendt 1972, pp. 143–155 and 1958, pp. 199–207. To put it in terms that Joseph Singer emphasized while discussing this book with me, one cannot hope to persuade someone else – as opposed to simply forcing him or her – if one cannot identify reasons that persuade oneself.
14 Dworkin 2011, p. 8.

it cannot guarantee."[15] The insight contained in this dictum again came to the fore in Claude Lefort's famous statement that democracy is the only form of political power that endeavours to separate the symbolic and the real.[16]

Böckenförde articulated his dictum at the end of an historical inquiry into three key moments in the history of European secularisation, the stand-off between Henry IV of Germany and Pope Gregory VII in the eleventh century, the reign of Henry of Navarre as Henry IV of France from 1589 to 1610, and the rise of the concept of the *nation* in the wake of the French Revolution. The first two moments relate directly to the history of the relation between clergy and secular government of which we recount key developments in Chapter 5, and we return to Böckenförde's narrative then. The third deals very briefly with the outcome of the French Revolution. Of concern here is the very moment with which Lefort's essay on the theologico-political engages extensively. Chapter 6 discusses Lefort's essay at length, and it also briefly revisits Böckenförde's dictum. This books pivots on the insight it draws from Lefort and Böckenförde. The crucial instruction that it takes from them is this: Dogmatic insistence on the appropriateness or correctness of liberal democratic principles obstructs the unique mode of political praxis that these principles demand. In fact, not only does it obstruct the political praxis they demand, it also fails to realise that liberal democratic practice or the outcome of such practice actually has very little or nothing to do with liberal democratic principles, apart from being or having been inspired by them.

Lefort points out that the difference between the symbolic and the real is a different kind of difference than the difference evident in a difference of opinion. It concerns a difference beyond the difference of opinions – *une différence . . . par-delà celle des opinions*.[17] It is this *different* difference, this *other*, less manifest difference between the symbolic and the real that elicits pathos-charged resistances to every possible instantiation of political order, however much such order may actually be inspired by the very same ideal that elicits resistance to it. Let us take the ideal of freedom as an example: No concretisation of political and juridical order can embody the ideal of freedom, however much it may in fact be inspired by that very ideal. This is not just so because those who are not in power happen to have an idea of freedom that differs from the idea of freedom of those who are. It is also because no specific idea of freedom can adequately give expression to the abstract ideal of freedom. Differences of opinion are, in fact, conditioned and sustained by the irreducible difference between the ideal and any concrete idea of that ideal. It is because of the difference between the symbolic and the real that differences of opinion become possible. However, liberal democratic politics must resist the ever-present temptation to resolve the difference between the ideal and the real – or the

---

15 Böckenförde 2016, p. 60. For discussions of the dictum and its relevance today, see also Müller 2018 and Jouanjan 2018.
16 Lefort 1986a, p. 287.
17 Ibid.

symbolic and the real, as Lefort puts it – in the process of resolving differences of opinion.

Böckenförde and Lefort do of course not tell us that liberal democracy pivots on a prohibition to act. They are not suggesting that liberal democracy ends up, and must end up, devoid of any political action that responds to the principles that inform and inspire it. Liberal democracy is not an a-political passivism that allows itself to be overrun by every undemocratic threat or anti-liberal pressure (just because of its professed inability to guarantee the conditions by which it lives). On the contrary, if it is any kind of *political formation* worthy of the name, it must and will respond forcefully in the face of any threat or pressure. This response, however, never amounts to any embodiment or fulfilment of the ideals that inform it and call for it. In other words, if liberal democratic political action is to be considered an *application* of the ideals that inspire and inform it, this application should under no circumstances be considered fulfilment, embodiment or realisation of these ideals. Nor should it be considered "a completion" of the ideal, as Gadamerian hermeneutics encourages one to do.[18]

## 4 Legal positivism

Let us turn our focus now to the narrower concern that John Austin called the "province of jurisprudence." The title of this book, *The Concept of Liberal Democratic Law*, alludes conspicuously to Hart's famous book, *The Concept of Law*. The aim of this allusion is to convey the message that this book returns to Hart's rule theory of law. It should be clear from this acknowledgement that a very positivist conception of law is about to unfold on the pages that follow. This will become even clearer below when this return to Hart is supplemented with an endorsement of Hans Kelsen's "pure theory of law." There is no reason for liberal democrats to shy away from this endorsement of legal positivism. Liberal democracy cannot claim allegiance to some kind of natural law conception of law without seriously misreading its own historical narrative, to borrow a striking phrase from Lefort ([la] *difficulté . . . de la démocratie à se rendre lisible pour elle-même*).[19] Liberal democracy is the form of government that emerged from the historical recognition that divisive social pluralities disqualify everyone from claiming the capacity to glean from nature, or from "reason," rules and principles that are universally valid and bind all people in the same way. Hence the necessary positivism of liberal democracy.[20]

---

18  See Gadamer 1975, p. 315. Agamben appears to endorse Gadamer's explication of application of meaning as part and parcel of the very understanding of meaning. See Agamben 2005a, p. 40. This is surprising and puzzling in view of the position that he takes on the pages (pp. 32–39) that precede this endorsement, and his express affirmation, later, of Kafka's concern with law that is only studied but not practised (at p. 63).

19  Lefort 1986a, p. 329.

20  See in this regard Nicola Lacey's assessment of Hart's positivist response to Patrick Devlin as a stimulus for Rawls' liberalism in Lacey 2006, p. 6.

Liberal democracy is, instead, the form of government that pivots on the modern and/ or postmodern rejection of all jurisprudential claims that law comprises a-historical rules or principles that do not derive from sovereign acts of law-making that can be undone by other acts of sovereign law-making. This rejection is informed by the experience that such claims raise rather than lower the potential for deeply divisive social conflict. Liberal democrats who read their own history well know that justifications of coercion that take recourse to authoritative assessments of the course of action that "nature" or "reason" dictates, raise the stakes of conflict. They are much less likely to be met with acceptance and compromise than qualitatively and categorically more modest justifications that only invoke the contingent and reversible outcomes of political rivalry as the source and legitimation of coercion.

There are limits to this argument and liberal democrats know that. Liberal democrats would no longer be liberal democrats if they were to begin to justify atrocities with reference to contingent outcomes of political rivalry. The positivism that liberal democrats envisage is therefore limited to outcomes of political rivalry between liberal democrats, or to any other outcome of rivalry in which liberal democrats triumph. In other words, *as long as* liberal democrats win the political contest and make the law, the law they make will not permit atrocities, *as long as* they also continue to make law as liberal democrats worthy of the name. This "worthy of the name" is not a rhetorical adjective but an important condition. Liberal democrats who govern in the name of liberal democracy can of course also fail and fail dismally. But when they do so, they no longer do so *as* liberal democrats. Of concern, here, is an argument of Hans Kelsen and Ernst Kantorowicz regarding the infallibility of the state or king to which we return in Chapter 9.[21] The conceptual or religious definition of the state or the king exempts them from fallibility. The empirically observable king and the actual state can of course fail disastrously to meet the standard implied in the definition.[22] The same applies to the concept of liberal democracy and any concrete manifestation of it.

## 5 Re-reading twentieth century jurisprudence

The last chapters of this book revisit the main positions of twentieth century legal theory and jurisprudence. They nevertheless reread these positions in a way that is not typical of the debates they solicited at the time. The description and explication of liberal democratic law that will be put forward in this book demand a more incisive scrutiny of the ontological status of rules than any of the major twentieth century legal theories offered, with the exception of Hans Kelsen and Herbert Hart. The conception of liberal democracy in terms of constellations of compromises reached in the face of differences of opinion – constellations that only remain possible as long as they keep at arm's length the passionate convictions

---

21 Kelsen 2008, pp. 362–373, 581–591; 2010, pp. 440–453; Kantorowicz 1997.
22 See for instance Rawls 1999, pp. 99–103 (regarding the bombing of Dresden, Hiroshima and Nagasaki).

that nourish differences of opinion – demands that one consider every legal rule an instantiation of compromise. To repeat and rephrase more precisely: The description of liberal democratic order in terms of the distinction between the symbolic and the real demands a more careful scrutiny of the ontological status of legal rules, and more specifically of the relation between rules and their application. It demands an understanding of rule application as a compromise that simultaneously sustains, disrupts and severs the relation between the real and the ideal. It sustains the relation between the real and the ideal precisely by disrupting and severing it. The relation between the real and the ideal evaporates the moment rule application refrains from severing and disrupting this relation, the moment when rule application begins to embody this relation.

The concept of liberal democratic law that will be developed in this book takes leave of the concept of application dominant in this history of legal thought. It does so for purposes of severing "rule application" from any conception of rule application that considers it a course of action that ensures some essential normative and epistemic continuity between the ideal content and the practical realisation of a norm. We will insist, instead, that the application of norms bears *no intrinsic relation* to norms. It at most bears an extrinsic historical relation to them in the sense that a contingent historical link can usually be identified – or construed – between the moral and epistemic endorsement of the content of a norm, and the praxis of enforcement to which this endorsement gives rise. For purposes of thinking through this understanding of norm-application – thinking through what takes place in the process of application – one also needs to rethink Aristotle's *potentiality-actuality* distinction, as Agamben prompts one to do. The distinction between potentiality and actuality, and the rethinking of this distinction is for this reason one of the key focus points in this book.

## 6 Natural law

That one would yoke the two twentieth century doyens of legal positivism together should not come as a surprise to anyone. That one would also link them together as the most consistent exponents of a liberal democratic conception of law that avoids the idea that law is an instance of potentiality that can or must be actualised, must be at least somewhat surprising in view of the sweeping and enduring impact that the so-called Radbruch thesis made on legal theory after World War II. Radbruch famously argued that the collapse of the German legal system under the National-Socialist regime was a result of the positivism through which the National Socialist judiciary submitted to political authority. He accordingly therefore pleaded for a return to natural law thinking for purposes of avoiding similar judicial submissions to political authority in the future.[23]

---

23 See Radbruch 1946.

However, the Radbruch thesis no longer enjoys the unquestioning acclamation that it did during the post-War years. Evidence that the Nazi-judiciary was in general not just positivists who bowed to Nazi authorities, but active supporters of the regime who sought to advance the tenets of the Nazi ideology through the enforcement of law, is now too pervasive to accuse them of passive and deferent positivism.[24] We shall see that Carl Schmitt's theory of law became an unflinching endorsement of this actualisation of the Nazi ideology through judicial law enforcement. Undeniable evidence of pervasive Nazi judicial interpretivism and activism that is available today alerts one to the dangers that attach to all "interpretivist" theories of law that conceive of law as a potentiality that can be actualised through the judicial enforcement of law, irrespective of whether the potentiality that one has in mind would appear to tick all the boxes of a typical liberal democratic vision of law. This is why the concept of liberal democratic law developed in this book takes leave of all interpretivist theories of law, including those that evidently rely on liberal democratic concepts as the cornerstones of their interpretivist theories of law.

## 7 Critical theory and the theory of liberal democracy

The endeavour to articulate a rigorous concept of liberal democratic law could easily come across as a defence of the "capitalist status quo," considering the way in which the critical legal theory associated with especially the Critical Legal Studies movement in the United States during the 1970s and 80s considered "liberal legal theory" an uncritical endorsement of existing property and market relations averse to redistributive law reform. Many aspects of this critique of liberal legal theory remain as valid today as they were then. The same applies to associations of liberal democracy with possessive individualism and rampant capitalism of the kind C. B. Macpherson articulated in the 1960s, 70s and 80s.[25] This book does therefore not retreat one inch from the fundamental intuitions of critical legal critiques regarding the close links between liberal democracy as it is pervasively practised, and sociopathic capitalism. These links are still unsevered and must be relentlessly exposed as such. However, exposure of these links does still not provide adequate motivation for taking leave of the ideal of liberal democracy as such.

This book insists – notwithstanding this pertinent criticism – that liberal democracy remains the only plausible political position for anyone who considers the fundamental freedom of all individuals to develop autonomous lives the core value of human existence. It further insists that a critique of liberal democracy only becomes interesting and relevant if it shares with liberal democrats this basic commitment to individual freedom. Many societies that are typically considered "liberal democratic" invite the criticism of being all too individualistic, atomistic, egoistic, unacceptably unequal and, moreover, disastrous for the environment. This

---

24  See Walther 1989.
25  See Macpherson 1987, 1962, 1977.

book takes it for granted that many societies that claim to be liberal democracies indeed warrant this criticism through and through. It nevertheless insists that none of the reforms that one may wish to propose for improving these societies can be imposed on them in ways that do not comply with the basic principles of liberal democratic decision-making.

There is of course one important exception to this insistence on liberal democratic decision-making with which liberal democrats must reckon and which they must endorse when appropriate, and that is the event of revolution. There are significant historical examples of societies that became so unequal, unjust and unfree that the people who lived in them simply rose up and took power unlawfully. There is no reason to believe that such revolutions cannot occur again, or that so-called "liberal democratic" societies are immune to them. If such a revolution genuinely takes place for the sake of restoring the core value of liberal democracy in social life, liberal democrats should find themselves in the streets fighting in favour of it. Under these circumstances they should also not be so unrealistic as to think everything that happens and every decision taken in the course of a revolution will always comply with standard liberal democratic criteria for government. But they should also consider themselves under the constant duty to begin to agitate for a return to proper standards of government and decision-making as soon as circumstances appear to allow for them again. A liberal democrat can and should be able to live with a state of exception, but cannot be expected to endorse a permanent state of exception.

This recognition of the possibility of revolutionary situations that justify temporary retreats from liberal democratic principles demanded by circumstances should make it clear enough that it is not a quietist or acquiescent liberalism that is contemplated in this book. If political and legal theorists who consider themselves more "critical," "radical" or "left" would, notwithstanding this recognition, still consider this book too status quo oriented, it would have to be so because they have a problem with the basic liberal democratic principles that it endorses. In that case, however, their criticism of the thoughts developed in this book would only be interesting if they were to aim at improving the liberal democratic purport of these thoughts. They would cease to be interesting if they were to suggest the fundamental principle of liberal democracy endorsed here itself merits dismissal. In that case, the discussion would simply have to stop. We would have nothing more to say to one another.

## 8 From Böckenförde and Lefort to Agamben – a note on method and methodology

We have begun to point out the paradoxical condition of liberal democracy – the fact that it pivots on principles to which it cannot give effect – with reference to the Böckenförde dictum and Lefort's critique of the theologico-political. The line of thinking taken from Lefort and Böckenförde runs right through this book. However, it will soon become clear that the work of Giorgio Agamben is the key influence for another central line of thinking that we will be developing, namely, the critique of Aristotle's potentiality-actuality distinction that begins to take clear shape in Chapter 4. This critique is fundamentally inspired by a key passage in *Homo Sacer* that calls for a fundamental rethinking of Aristotle's potentiality-actuality distinction. Aspects of Agamben's *State of Exception* and *The Time that Remains* are also central to the concept of liberal democratic law that will emerge towards the end of this book.

It is likely that readers of Agamben will be dismayed by any reliance on his work for purposes of explaining the concept of liberal democracy. Agamben's concern is vastly different from the one pursued in this book, they are likely to say. This complaint may constitute a problem for readers who entertain "original intention" conceptions of textual interpretation and correct reading, but such conceptions play no part in this book. Care has been taken to offer a plausible and well-informed reading of Agamben's texts, but no claim is made here to an expert reading that grasps *the* true meaning or his own understanding of his texts correctly. This of course also applies to all the other authors with whom this book engages, especially those with vast and multi-faceted oeuvres. It should nevertheless become clear enough that a diligent effort has been made throughout to present respectful, coherent and plausible readings of their texts.

Serious readers of Hart, Dworkin and Kelsen typically do not read Agamben, just as readers of Agamben and of other comparable thinkers from the tradition of "continental" philosophy do not typically engage with the works of Hart, Dworkin and Kelsen. Both these groups of readers may well, from both their respective positions, consider the attempt to engage with these vastly different orientations of scholarship ill-conceived, considering that all these different authors develop thoughts that are hardly comparable to one another. This typical division of readership in the world of philosophy of law and politics is regrettable, for it condemns the insights of political and legal philosophy to "two halves" that never come together. This book will indeed be an attempt to bring these "two halves" together in an instructive way. It will seek to supplement analytical jurisprudence with an ontological and historical mode of inquiry that may reopen "deeper" levels of reflection which the analytical tradition simply closes off. However, it will also retain an adequately analytical mode of inquiry to prevent it from going so deeply into onto-theological or post-onto-theological modes of inquiry that it begins to lose touch with the exigencies of concrete institutional analysis and critique.

The strategy that will be employed to keep these two halves closely enough together to keep them "speaking" to one another will consist of linking them both to a third line. This third line will comprise a rudimentary record of relatively well-known historical examples of institutional failure that came to pass in ancient Greece and Rome, as well as medieval, modern and especially twentieth century Europe. The "historical narrative" that emerges from connecting a number of conspicuous dots found in ancient Athens and Rome, and medieval and modern Europe, will indeed be the backbone of this book that will hopefully hold all its limbs together. In this respect, the theory of liberal democracy developed in this book also offers some redress regarding the typical unhistorical profile of Anglo-American analytical jurisprudence that historically minded theorists tend to find frustrating.[26]

## 9 Outline

The central argument of this book is modelled on the metaphor of distillation. It begins with the heavy brew of an ancient manner of thinking that mixed the conception of law into an ambiguous metaphysics of nature, a metaphysics that always remained burdened by the clamouring of two competing concepts of nature that raged on in its breast, nature conceived as cosmos or order, and nature conceived as *physis* or anarchical force. The argument proceeds by bringing both these conceptions of nature to the boil, so as to extract from them, through a process of conceptual distillation, the ethereal substance of liberal democratic law. The early chapters of the book begin by heating up the ancient ingredients of a non-transparent and heavy metaphysical soup. The last chapters move to separate and render transparent – through careful evaporation and condensation – a pure concept of liberal democratic law.

The philosophical narrative through which this evaporation and condensation is pursued begins with the two histories of the notion of *nomos* on which ancient Greek culture pivoted until the fifth century BCE. The first history concerns the epistemological mutation and decay of the concept of *nomos* that can be traced from the end of the fifth century BCE to the fourteenth century CE in Western metaphysics. In the course of this mutation and decay the realist cosmological philosophies of Aristotle and St. Thomas eventually gave way to the nominalist thinking of William of Ockham, which, in turn, led to the subjectivist and positivist political and legal theories of modernity, represented par excellence by Thomas Hobbes and Hugo Grotius. The second history concerns the displacement of ancient, medieval and early modern notions of *nomos* – conceived either as *natural law* or *naturalised institutional* arrangements – by the rise of positivist legislation as the main source of law towards the end of the nineteenth century.

This first history will be related in Chapter 1 under the heading "The Villey thesis," in recognition of the extent to which this history is taken from Michel Villey's seminal work *La formation de la pensée juridique moderne* (1975). It will largely but not exclusively be based on a concise summary presentation of the six hundred page narrative that Villey developed in this colossal piece of scholarship. This exposition of Villey's thesis serves a double purpose. First, it provides a framework of analysis from the perspective of which the nature of legal language can be assessed. And secondly, it facilitates an opportunity to put a serious question mark behind the democratic credentials of natural law theories. Villey's thesis provides one with a distinction between realist and nominalist conceptions of law that is crucial for a

---

26 See Horwitz 1997.

proper understanding of liberal democratic law as an essentially nominalist conception of law. Natural law thinking belongs to the tradition of realist metaphysics that is foreign to the liberal democratic understanding of law.

Chapter 2 begins to trace the second history pointed out above with recourse to Carl Schmitt's portrayal of the *Jus Publicum Europaeum* in *Der Nomos der Erde*. This narrative portrays the international legal order that conditioned European law and legal systems through the Middle and Modern Ages. Schmitt's portrait of the legal orders of medieval and modern Europe, we shall see, differs fundamentally from Villey's portrayal of these legal orders. Evidence that throws light on the respective levels of accuracy of these two accounts will emerge in Chapter 5. However, the point of these chapters is not just to stage a debate between Schmitt and Villey. They also offer a telling record of institutional failures that underline the failure of the Western metaphysical tradition to provide firm foundations for politics and law during the Middle and Modern Ages. It is from this failed metaphysics of law and politics that the concept of liberal democratic law pursued in this book will be carefully distilled so as to rid it of all metaphysical elements.

A third historical narrative emerges from Chapters 3–7. Building on insights already gained from the narratives developed in Chapters 1 and 2, this third narrative takes a closer look at the theoretical and institutional quest for persuasive definitions of law, justice and political order that commences in the *nomos-physis* debate in fifth and fourth century Athenian politics and philosophy, and continues until the major debates about law, history, society and justice of the nineteenth and early twentieth centuries. We trace key moments of this history from its fifth century Athenian beginnings, through its Roman-Christian transmutations and up to the emergence of modern conceptions of legitimate political order, agency and representation in the eighteenth, nineteenth and twentieth centuries. This is a very long history and the idea is not at all to "cover" it. The purpose of these chapters is to highlight a selection of key institutional and theoretical developments that allows one an adequate comprehension of the history of ideas and events that informed the development of modern liberal democratic ideals.

With the background of the three narratives outlined above firmly behind it, Chapters 8–10 then turn to take stock of the major jurisprudential debates of the twentieth century. Chapter 8 focuses on the debate between H. L. A. Hart and Ronald Dworkin in Anglo-American jurisprudence. Chapter 9 turns to two Weimar legal theorists, Rudolf Smend and Hans Kelsen. Chapter 10 then compares the work of Carl Schmitt and Duncan Kennedy. The distillation process started in the early chapters of this book continues in these chapters. They heat up twentieth century legal thought with the aim of separating and extracting a pure concept of liberal democratic law from the metaphysical elements that this century inherited from a long history of philosophy and legal thought and continued to cultivate right into the twenty-first century. Chapter 11 concludes the whole narrative with all its sub-narratives by listing and clarifying the key elements of the pure concept of liberal democratic law that emerge from this long distillation process.

# 1

# *NOMOS* AND NOMINALISM –
# THE VILLEY THESIS

## 1 Philosophical beginnings: Plato and Aristotle

The narrative that Villey develops in *La formation de la pensée juridique moderne* – a text that grew out of his lectures in the Faculty of Law of Paris from 1961 to 1966 – begins in ancient Greece. The two great Greek philosophers, Plato and Aristotle, responded to a major socio-political crisis that raised its head in fifth century Athens. The crisis concerned the collapse of the *cult of nomos* that until then provided the Athenians with the measure of appropriateness for everything they did. *Nomos*, explains Villey in the opening pages of the book, consisted in the ensemble of customary rules and practices that informed every aspect of Greek life and law from the seventh to the fifth century BCE. It comprised the ethics that gave form to daily routines of Greek citizens during this time, as well as the wisdom, prudence and jurisprudence that informed the political decisions of their governors and leaders. Pericles' famous "Funeral Oration," as recounted by Thucydides,[1] can be regarded as a confident reflection of one of Athens' great political leaders on the *nomos* of the Athenians. The irony of the Pericles' oration should nevertheless not be missed. It eulogised the Athenian way of life – the Athenian *nomos* – just when it was about to fall apart.

Athenian democracy lost its way in the last years of the fifth century BCE. The Athenians waged war on other Greek cities for twenty seven years (431–404 BCE) and became swayed by ambitious demagogues to commit atrocities during the war that eventually shook their confidence in the sense of virtue that Pericles' "Funeral Oration" still extolled with eloquence after the first year of the war. Five years after the end of the war (399 BCE), it convicted Socrates of concocted crimes never committed and sentenced him to death. The death of Socrates at the hands

1 See Thucydides 1928, II 34–46.

of democracy spawned a philosophy that had no faith in democracy, no faith in
deliberative politics and no faith in the ability of citizens to generally live their lives
wisely and virtuously without being instructed how to do so – and ordered to do
so – by a philosopher who had superior insight into the nature of all things. This
philosophy was Plato's. Its cornerstone was a tripartite division of the ideal city into
three classes of citizens – ruling, military and peasant – who co-exist in orderly
fashion under the command of a philosopher king who possesses rational insight
into the demands of justice. The philosopher king also safeguards the justice and
rationality of the city by preventing poets (through banning them) from seducing
its citizens to succumb to irrational emotions.[2]

Plato, observes Villey, evidently had no appreciation of *nomos* as a product of
practical norms and practices that develop organically (like the growth of a plant or
living being) so that no one gets to experience the law as imposed rules that must
be "obeyed." Plato believed order could be imposed on a city by someone with
superior insight into the truth of things. He was an authoritarian political thinker
who entertained the idea that the law could enforce the correct way of life. This
understanding is surely the polar opposite of the concept of liberal democratic
law that is contemplated in this book. The aim of this book is indeed to explain
liberal democracy as a form of society and government that resists the Western or
European history of the politics of truth that began with Plato and resurfaced again
and again after him, often with bitter and bloody consequences. And even when
Western philosophy endeavoured to retreat from Plato's harsh philosophy of truth,
it would almost invariably end up repeating it. Aristotle's philosophy was the first
case in point, as we shall see in Chapter 4, but this is not how Villey sees the matter.
According to him, Aristotle's philosophy constituted a formidable critique of Plato
and in some respects he is surely correct. Aristotle responded to Plato's idealism
with a good dose of realism. The law, or *nomos*, he argued, is a reflection of how
things are *intrinsically*. It is not something that can be imposed on existence from
the outside, after abstract reflection on how things ought to be. It is something that
can and must be observed through careful inquiry into the way things already are.[3]

All that is required to sustain or restore *nomos* in a city, argued Aristotle, is to be
more observant of how things work, and to teach the citizens to be more observant
of how they work. This teaching – *paideia* – was a key feature of Aristotle's philosophical vision.[4] This vision was evidently more modest and forgiving regarding

2 See Plato 1930, III 415–417 (on the three classes of the ideal republic), V 473d (on the philosopher
king), and 1935, X 605e–607b (on the banning of poets).
3 Villey 2003, pp. 85–99.
4 See in this regard Jaeger 1936, 1944 and 1947. Unfortunately Jaeger's formidable work ends with
Plato and does not come round to discuss Aristotle's views on education as the formation of the
Greek person (*Formung des griechischen Menschen*). However, Alasdair Macintyre's works engage almost
constantly with education, formation and tutoring as the king pin on which his whole metaphysics
of potentiality and actuality hinges as far as the actualisation of human potential is concerned. See
Macintyre 1985, 52–53 for this concise but comprehensive statement of the problematic: "The desires
and emotions which we possess are to be put in order and educated by the use of such precepts and by
the cultivation of those habits of action which the study of ethics prescribes; reason instructs us both as

the "imperfections" of human arrangements. In comparison to Plato, Aristotle was evidently more at ease with earthly imperfection. In fact, he incorporated it into his conception of perfection by developing a cosmological vision of *eternal becoming*. Things are imperfect, he argued, because they are always in a state of development. They are always in transition, always *in medias res*, always still in the process of ful-filling their ultimate goal or end (*telos*). Aristotle thus articulated a philosophy of an eternal flow. Everything is in flux. *Panta rei*, to use the expression of the earlier Greek philosopher, Heraclitus. But, Aristotle's "flux" is very different from that of Heraclitus. His flux is a tame or tamed flux, an ordered flux. He arrives at this con-ception of a tamed or ordered flux through a philosophy of *potentiality and actuality* according to which everything is destined to fulfil or *actualise* its own ideal potential or *potentiality*. This philosophy ultimately retains more of Plato's idealism than Villey suggests. Villey paints the picture of a much clearer break between the two thinkers. Chapter 4 will show more carefully that this portrait is not quite accurate. Suffice it to only observe here that the Platonic elements in Aristotle's thinking also commit him to a concept of law that is hardly reconcilable with the idea of democracy, let alone liberal democracy. To begin with, he suspects democracy very Platonically of being prone to demagoguery. But, even when he does contemplate the possibility that democracy could be a good form of government for a virtuous polity, he does so on the assumption that the virtue of such a community is effectively in place in advance of any practices of democratic deliberation in which they may come to engage. His thinking ultimately entertains a concept of law that is not up for politi-cal deliberation. On the contrary, democratic deliberation is subject to law, subject to *nomos*. A key passage from Aristotle's *Politics* makes this very clear:

> [A]nother kind of democracy is for all the citizens that are not open to chal-lenge to have a share in office, but for the law to rule; and another kind of democracy is for all to share in the offices on the mere qualification of being a citizen, but for the law to rule. Another kind of democracy is where all the other regulations are the same, but the multitude is sovereign and not the law; and this comes about when the decrees of the assembly over-ride the law. This state of things is brought about by the demagogues; for in the states under democratic government guided by law a demagogue does not arise, but the best classes of citizens are in the most prominent position; but where the laws are not sovereign, then demagogues arise; for the common people become a single composite monarch, since the many are sovereign not as individuals but collectively. . . . However, a people of this sort, as being monarch, seeks

---

to what our true end is and as to how to reach it. We thus have a threefold scheme in which human-nature-as-it-happens-to-be (human nature in its untutored state) is initially discrepant and discordant with the precepts of ethics and needs to be transformed by the instruction of practical reason and experience into human-nature-as-it-could-be-if-it-realised-its-*telos*. Each of the three elements of the scheme—the conception of untutored human nature, the conception of the precepts of rational ethics and the conception of human-nature-as-it-could-be-if-it-realised its *telos*—requires reference to the other two if its status and function are to be intelligible."

to exercise monarchic rule through not being ruled by the law, and becomes despotic, so that flatterers are held in honour. And a democracy of this nature is comparable to the tyrannical form of monarchy. . . .[5]

Villey does not cite this passage, but puts forward instead Aristotle's vision of a dialectic between *nomos* and democracy, or between natural law (*nomos*) and positive law (legislation and judicial decisions), in terms of which the latter is bound to the former and the purpose of the latter is only to complete the former. The principles of natural law reflect the way all things hang together properly, but they are broad and abstract and for this reason "incomplete" as far as concrete disputations about "applicable law" are concerned. Democratic decisions that lay down legislation and judicial decisions that apply this legislation must therefore be considered the practical wisdom or *phronesis* that completes natural law.[6]

This dialectic vision of legislation and judicial application that facilitate all things and persons in becoming what they already potentially are is certainly less disconcerting to liberal democracy than Plato's vision of governmental and judicial imposition of alien truths on everyone and everything. It is, however, still vastly at odds with the concept of liberal democracy that will emerge from the chapters of this book. At stake in this book is a concept of democracy that liberates itself completely from all conceptions of *nomos* and natural law, and which does so in response to the exigencies of an age in which invocations of *nomos* and natural law no longer enjoy the authority with which Aristotle endowed them to bring fourth century Athens to its senses.

It turned out, however, that Aristotle was already too late in any case. The end of the war spelled the end of Athens' glorious years. The Athenians never got a chance to try out Aristotle's *paideia* and to restore the old *nomos* of the city. Alexander the Great intervened and largely deprived the Greek cities of the political autonomy they enjoyed until the middle of the fourth century BCE. Political philosophy consequently lost much of its significance for them. After Aristotle, the prominent Greek philosophers turned to a new kind of moral philosophy for purposes of sustaining a personal intellectual concern with the meaning of life as such, as opposed to the meaning of citizenship, or the meaning of life in this or that city. This new philosophy would become known as Stoicism.[7]

## 2 Aristotle and Roman law

This is where the Stoic philosophers should have entered Villey's narrative, but Villey clearly does not have much appetite for them. He postpones their story till much later in the semester when he turns to the humanist philosophers and jurists

---

5 Aristotle 1932, IV 4 1292a.

6 Villey 2003, pp. 91–92. Villey does not refer expressly to phronesis or practical wisdom in *La formation* but he undoubtedly has the dialectic between general principle and particular application in mind that Aristotle discusses under the rubric of practical wisdom in the *Nicomachean Ethics*. See Aristotle 1989, VI 5.

7 This point is made more expressly by Macintyre, but it is also implicit in Villey's treatment of the Stoics. See Macintyre 1967, p. 8; 1985, pp. 168–170; Villey 2003, pp. 101–103.

of the sixteenth century and consequently can no longer avoid addressing them. So he moves, instead, directly from Aristotle to Roman law with the insistence that Roman law was a true embodiment of Aristotle's philosophy and wisdom. Roman law, he asserts, pivoted on Aristotelian cosmological vision of the intrinsic ways of the world and the need to observe these ways well so as to embody them in the written laws of the city and in jurisprudential decisions when necessary. Roman law was not based on Stoic philosophy, he insists, quite to the contrary of many who argue that Roman law is well permeated with Stoic wisdom.[8] No, not permeated, maintains Villey adamantly, only edified and embellished with phrases taken from Stoic philosophy. The essentials of Roman law are undoubtedly Aristotelian. Thus, in any case, continues his narrative.[9]

The Aristotelian essentials of Roman law that Villey stresses concern the principles of justice elaborated in Book V of *Nicomachean Ethics*. Roman law was not about the personal or private morality of the Stoics, insists Villey. It pivoted on the two categories of public justice developed in the *Nicomachean Ethics*, distributive and corrective justice. It is highly doubtful, however, whether Roman law ever came close to the equitable public law distribution and redistribution of social goods that Villey attributes to it. The socio-economic history of Rome surely does not leave one with this impression.[10] This is nevertheless the picture of Roman law justice that Villey puts forward throughout his thesis on the formation of modern legal thought and the rise of positivist legal systems devoid of the redistributive principles of Roman law. Villey's picture of Roman law's redistributive wisdom may well be more accurate when it comes to the principles of natural law on which Saint Thomas would insist many centuries later,[11] but by this time, these principles will have become significantly more Christian, and significantly less Aristotelian.

8  For a careful engagement with and response to the long record of scholarship on the relation between the Aristotelian and Stoic influences on Roman law, see Kroger 2004. See, however, also Watson 1995, pp. 158–165 for the view that the substance of Roman law was not significantly influenced by Greek philosophy.

9  Villey 2003, pp. 100–106.

10  The endless problems with debt, debt-bondage and basic scarcity of food from which the poor especially suffered throughout the history of ancient Rome tell the story of severe and unforgiving social relations and attitudes between Patricians and Plebeians that were invariably only softened by legal reforms concomitant to the gradual increase of the power of the Plebeians. See Forsythe 2005, pp. 217–219, 314–315, Raaflaub 2005, pp. 189–194, Eder 2005, pp. 257–259, and Martin 2017, 106–111. The problem of scarcity of food continued until 27 BCE when Augustus began to resolve it. And when he did so, it was not through recourse to Aristotelian Roman law principles of redistribution, but with a visionary act of statesmanship. See Martin 2012, 120: "Augustus's most important service to the urban masses was to assure them adequate and affordable food. By using his personal fortune to pay for imported grain to feed the hungry, he prevented food riots and demonstrated his respect for the Roman value of patrons supporting their clients." This governmental distribution of food in Rome was not new, but the scale of it was unprecedented under Augustus' reign. It nevertheless bears repeating that no "natural law" redistribution of goods of the kind that Villey imagines was at stake here, only a very subject or agency based governmental response to crisis.

11  Saint Thomas famously argued that a loaf of bread stolen in need is not theft, and rather considered the hoarding of unneeded wealth theft. See Aquinas 1975, 2a 2ae 66 7. One has, of course, no reason to believe that medieval law ever lived up to this vision of distributive justice.

The conception of justice that Villey identifies as the heart of Roman law was underpinned, according to him, by another feature of Aristotle's philosophy that ultimately becomes the central plot of his thesis about the formation of modern law. The central narrative of the book concerns the cosmological conception of law as a reflection of the natural order of just relations between all things and persons. This natural order generally prevails and only calls for express deliberations and applications of law to rectify and redress rare cases of deviation. This ancient Greek and Roman conception of human or positive law as a reflection and occasional restoration of the natural order of things, argues Villey, gave way to the modern conception of law as a voluntarist imposition of an abstract system of legal norms on the natural condition of things and persons. In the process of this transformation, claims Villey, the Roman concept of *ius* mutated into the modern conception of *subjective rights*. Whereas the former referred to an objective state of affairs that literally constituted a thing or *res* on the basis of which individuals were entitled to a proportional sharing of benefits, the latter referred to the power or *potestas* that law, conceived as a system of norms created and enforced by a sovereign ruler, allowed one person to wield over another.[12]

This development, contends Villey, led to the general acceptance of the word "right" as a suitable translation for the Roman legal concept "*ius*." This translation is nevertheless highly misleading, he argues. It encouraged the misconception of "*ius*" as a legally guaranteed personal or subjective power, whereas in Roman law, it denoted a *res* or thing. It was of course an *immaterial* thing that was of concern here, but nonetheless a thing, *une chose* in French, something that is as much part of an objective state of affairs as a tree may be part of a wood or a plantation.[13] The

---

12 Villey 2003, pp. 244–248, 1946, pp. 201–227.

13 Villey 2003, p. 247: [L]e *jus* romain soit toujours une chose, et non la maîtrise sur une chose." See also Villey 1946. For a view that is diametrically opposed to Villey's, see Donald Kelley's insistence that the modern concept of subjective rights can be traced all the way back to Gaius' trichotomic foundation of Roman law relations in terms of persons, things and actions. Kelly insists that Roman legal science broke away from the naturalistic tradition of Greek philosophy. According to him, the Roman understanding of law and legal relations did not begin with cosmology, but with the human subject, and more specifically the subject of consciousness and of rights. See Kelley 1979, p. 624 and 1990, p. 49. Kelley does not take issue with Villey and does not even refer to him. For views of Roman law scholars who are expressly critical of Villey's thesis regarding the medieval origin of subjective rights, see Pugliese 1954 and Tierney 1988. However, over the years, Romanists and civil law historians have expressed enough qualified support for Villey's thesis (or a thesis similar to his – not all of them refer to him) regarding the non-existence of a subjective right in Roman law to make one duly hesitant to simply dismiss it. See Coing 1962, pp. 30–36, Kaser 1971, p. 195, Schrage 1977, pp. 21–24. There is also no wish or need to dismiss it here. It suffices to observe that it cannot do all the work that Villey wants it to do. His ultimate claim is that the objective legal relations – the things or *res* – recognised by Roman law were adequately shielded from the arena of power relations and domination (*dominium*) outside the law to ensure that the law always or predominantly reflected a conception of objective order (the very *cosmos* that Kelley denies) duly informed by Aristotelian principles. This claim is simply too rich to be credible. Kelley's submission that the Greek cosmological vision played no role in Roman law thinking also appears to overstate his case, but Villey's thesis regarding the non-existence of subjective rights in Roman law is bothering on two counts: It ignores the role that power relations played in the development and practice of Roman law and

specificity of Roman law in comparison to modern law that Villey seeks to point out, concerns the way in which the ensemble of immaterial things that constituted Roman law was part and parcel of the global order of all things, a global order of things, moreover, that no one, not even the Consul – the highest official in the time of the Roman republic – could change at will.

The matter became more complicated, however, when emperors began to rule Rome again from 27 BCE onwards, as will become clear in Chapter·5, but the endeavour to consider even the emperor bound to law that he cannot change would remain a central concern of Roman law, notwithstanding Ulpianus' famous dictum *princeps legibus solutus est*. One can grant Villey the point that the method of the Roman jurists generally consisted in identifying the presence of a *ius* and inferring from this *ius* whatever benefits and burdens would accrue to all parties involved in a dispute. One can also grant to him that this *ius* was a thing or *res*, an immaterial thing that formed no less part of an objective state of affairs than any material thing. There is adequate support for this view from legendary Romanists on this point.[14] Putting it directly into Aristotelian terms, one can refer to this *ius* as a *universal*, a secondary form or category of existence that can be attributed to all things of the same kind.[15] The time was certainly not ripe yet for the idea that an emperor could change a category of existence by fiat. In fact, the time was not even ripe yet for the idea that God could change a category of existence by fiat. That idea had to wait until the fifth century CE to gain currency, as we shall see presently.

The concern of Roman law with things *as they are*, does of course not mean that the law never changed according to them, it only rendered it inconceivable that human beings could intervene to bring about such change wilfully. The Romans clearly recognised changes that altered the order of things and demanded law reform. Roman procedural law made provision for the hearing of unprecedented cases with institutions such as the *actio utilis* and *actio in factum*.[16] Students of Roman law have also been taught for generations how the *actio legis aquilia* changed slowly but surely to make provision for compensation of damages that were not considered actionable earlier.[17] But things generally changed slowly, not only because of technological constraints typical of the time, but also because of a pervasive consciousness that nothing could be changed at will. No consul or emperor could be

---

it fails to recognise the extent to which Aristotle's metaphysics, political theory and ethics were also not immune to, but indeed permeated by realities of power and dominance in Greek societies. In this latter regard, Macintyre surely offers one a more realistic picture of Aristotelian ethics. See Macintyre 1988, 105: "Aristotle's mistake, and the mistake of others whatever reason similarly, was not to understand how domination of a certain kind is in fact the cause of those characteristics of the dominated which are then invoked to justify unjustified domination." For a much more realistic view of the relation between Roman law and social power struggles in ancient Rome, see Watson 1995, pp. 33–41.

14  See again the previous footnote.

15  Aristotle 1938, 2a11–a18.

16  These two actions were often used where the typically applicable or original action could not be applied to a case. See Schultz 1992, pp. 31–32.

17  See ibid, p. 588.

lobbied to change things for the sake of pursuing some new advantage or benefit, without invoking the ancient order of things.

This, in any case, was the theory of Roman law. The reality may well have departed from it frequently, but perhaps also just rarely enough for the Romans to remain confident that their law was the reflection of how things are and how the gods ordained them to be. That their sense of the good order of things was indeed still deeply informed by faith in the ordinances of their gods is surely underlined by the fact that many of them would blame the eventual disintegration of public order in Rome on the rise of Christianity, the new religion that lured increasing numbers of citizens away from the rituals of worship with which they used to secure the favour of their old gods. This is indeed the main charge against the Christian religion that Saint Augustine fended off in the fifth century CE by simply throwing it back at the Romans: Rome is falling into decay, he said, because of the worship of false gods and the failure to recognise Christianity as the true religion.[18]

Christianity eventually triumphed over the old pagan religions of Rome, and, from the third century on – that is, since the reign of the first Christian emperor – it introduced one thousand five hundred years of political endeavours to anchor justice and the law in the articles of Christian faith. Only then – towards the end of the eighteenth century – was a first attempt made to dispense with the need to anchor the law in religion. Only then did liberal or *free* democracy receive its first chance in the history of mankind. It nevertheless failed again, and with little delay, as we shall see in Chapter 6. However, before this short-lived but real experiment with liberal democracy towards the end of the eighteenth century, Western politics remained fundamentally tied to religious justifications of government that continued to claim decisive links between law and politics, on the one hand, and the natural order of things or the will of God, on the other. A significant change nevertheless took place in the fifth century. This change concerned the remarkable shift in emphasis from the notion of the natural order of things to the will of God that resulted from the rise of Christian thinking. It is to this remarkable shift of emphasis that we now turn.

## 3 From Roman law to Saint Augustine

Aristotle's wisdom began to fade when ancient Roman law fell into decay and gave way to codifications of Roman emperors influenced by Christian religion and philosophy. This development came to a head in the fifth century CE when Saint Augustine, Bishop of Hippo, became the dominant philosopher of the time. Saint Augustine's philosophy was based on Christian faith. He expressly dismissed conceptions of natural law informed by notions of the intrinsic order of things. He

---

18 See Villey 2003, pp. 111–117, referring to Augustine's *Retractiones*, but especially to the key passage in the *City of God* where Augustine denounces the fundamental injustice on which Roman law is founded, because of the false religion on which the whole Roman state was founded. See Augustine 1960, XIX pp. 69–71, 81, 189.

postulated, instead, the absolute freedom of God to create and recreate the world as he deems fit. His followers – they later became known as Nominalists – soon began to argue that the absolute freedom of God's will renders the idea of natural essences and the intrinsic ways of things completely implausible.[19]

The order of things is not intrinsic but extrinsic to them, claimed the Augustinians.[20] Things are what they are because of the way God's will provisionally determine their existence. God can change the essential facts of nature, they argued. He turned water into wine at the wedding at Canaan and fed a whole crowd of people with two fishes and five loaves of bread, and so forth. These examples, argued these philosophers of the "new way," showed that no one can know the world. Our concepts are not epistemic reflections of the world as it is in itself, as Aristotle claimed, but an expression of how we have become familiar with it. They are habits of thought, as David Hume would put it many centuries later. For the Augustinian philosophers of the "new way," constant observation was necessary to ascertain whether existing knowledge of the world was still valid. In stressing this, they indeed were forerunners of the empiricist philosophy that would come to a head in the works of John Locke, George Berkeley and David Hume.[21]

In addition to paving the way for a philosophy that renders enduring knowledge of nature unattainable, Saint Augustine also started to spread a philosophy that any decent pagan would, at the time, consider an invitation to act *unnaturally*. He preached a philosophy of love, giving and forgiveness, and taught the Christian emperors and kings that the way to God's glory leads through imitating his infinite grace. From the fifth century on, asserts Villey, the Christian world lost all sense of just proportions, and of law and politics as the proportional administration of finite

---

19  The debate between the Nominalists and the Realists can be traced back to the early Middle Ages. One of the early sources of the debate was Boethius' late fifth or early sixth century discussion of universals (concepts with general application as opposed to proper names that only pertain to particular entities) and his contention that the Aristotelian categories were only words and did not apply to things themselves. Already in the ninth century we encounter the realist responses of Fredegisius of Tours and Remigius of Auxerre who argued that universal concepts apply to and actually inhere in universal substances. In the early Middle Ages this ultra-realism was referred to as the ancient doctrine as opposed to the "modern" view that only individual or particular entities exist. The dispute came to a head with the famous debate between William of Champeaux and Abelard in which Abelard succeeded in making the "ancient" doctrine of William appear rather foolish. Thomas of Aquinas' thirteenth century Aristotelianism was considered a return to the ancient way (*via antiqua*), whereas positions held by Dun Scotus and William of Ockham were taken to be representative of the "modern way" associated with Abelard. See Coplestone 1972, pp. 69–71, 81, 189. For an instructive discussion of the profound and far-reaching impact of this Augustinian turn in European thinking and the rise of modernity, see Oakley 1961a and 1961b.

20  The interior light of the soul, must nevertheless be excluded from this exteriority, for this interior truth is directly related to God's truth, according to Saint Augustine. See Augustine (1962), XXXXIX.72: "Noli foras ire, in te ipsum redi. In interiore homini habitat veritas." Charles Taylor (1989, p. 129) quotes in English: "Do not go outward; return within yourself. In the inward man dwells the truth."

21  See Priest 2007 for a good discussion of the development of "British Empiricist" epistemology from John Locke to George Berkeley to David Hume.

concerns and resources. Hence, according to him, the transformation of political power during this time into capricious exertion of force, on the one hand, and pretentious displays of religious piety and glory, on the other.

These two sides of medieval power actually conditioned one another, as Villey notes in passing, and as Macintyre observes particularly pertinently. Christian morality concerned an ethics of the inner self that cannot be judged or sanctioned on earth, they maintain. It effectively unties the hands of the Christian ruler to pursue power on earth in whatever way he or she deems fit. The Machiavellian prince is not conceivable, writes Macintyre, without these fundamental precepts of Christian morality being well established.[22] Chapter 5 will cast more light on this mutual conditioning of capricious power struggles and religious piety. Suffice it to observe for now that Christian political and legal thinking neglected the study of both natural and Roman law for several centuries after the Augustinian revolution, according to Villey, and consequently lost all sense of government as the art of just and proportional redistribution of social goods. This remained the case until Aristotelian philosophy made a comeback in the twelfth century, and until Saint Thomas finally led the Christian spirit back to Aristotle's ancient wisdom, in the thirteenth.[23] But this revival of Aristotle remained little more than a flash in the pan in the greater course of things, as we shall see. Aquinas' philosophy was all too soon discredited by the Church and from then on the way was wide open once again for the new philosophy of Saint Augustine and his late medieval followers – now properly called Nominalists and Voluntarists – to lay the foundations for the modern age.

## 4  Saint Thomas and William of Ockham

A very Aristotelian Saint Thomas becomes the would-be saviour of the world in Villey's narrative, at least for a while. God does not change the ways of the world like a capricious child-king argued Saint Thomas. God's will is surely the origin and principle of all things, as Saint Augustine preached, but he entrenched his will in a comprehensive set of "second causes" that henceforth spared him the trouble of an undignified micromanagement of all things. Thus, contends Villey, did Saint Thomas manage to secure knowledge of the world again and to rehabilitate, for a while, an understanding of natural law, natural rights and judicious juridical proportions that are based on a profound understanding of the ways of the world. He did so by a neat division between religion and society and between clerical and secular government. The administration of matters relating to grace and salvation he entrusted to canonical law and the Church. Concerns of worldly justice he reserved for secular law and government. Villey refers to Saint Thomas's "modernity" in this regard.[24]

---

22  See Villey 2003, pp. 127–130, Macintyre 1967, pp. 121–145.
23  See Villey 2003, pp. 132–148.
24  Villey 2003, pp. 188–201.

It is, however, not Saint Thomas's "modernity" but a very different modernity that dawned on Europe in the end – *[quelle] que soit la dette du droit moderne envers saint Thomas, il reste que les caractères spécifiques de la pensée juridique moderne sont dérivés d'une autre École.*[25] This sentence warrants full citation here, for it goes to the heart of Villey's thesis on the development of modern law and legal thinking. His hero, or two heroes – Aristotle and Saint Thomas – did not triumph in the end.[26] They did not halt the dismal formation or rather malformation of modern juridical thought that Villey laments. The Nominalists swept the field after Saint Thomas, and laid the foundations for the positivist legal systems of the Modern Age. They inaugurated a world in which terrestrial sovereigns bent the foundations of law to their will whenever it pleased them, and in which nothing would ever rest again in the settled peace that Aristotle discerned behind the daily travails of mortal existence. Chapter 5 will take a closer look at the bottomless turmoil into which this new world descended frequently during the Middle Ages. For now, let us follow the rest of Villey's narrative regarding the demise of the old world of Aristotle and Saint Thomas and the rise of the new world of Grotius and Hobbes.

Saint Thomas's philosophy fell out of favour with the Church towards the end of his life. In 1277, three years after his death, the Bishop of Paris condemned many of the Aristotelian elements of his philosophy for the second time (the first time was in 1270) because of the way they seemed to undermine the omnipotence and free will of God stressed in the theology of Saint Augustine. The condemnations of Saint Thomas' Aristotelianism coincided with the prominence of an Averroist movement (followers of the twelfth century Andalusian philosopher Averroes who advocated a radical Aristotelianism[27]) that the Church considered particularly threatening to the Christian faith at the time. Saint Thomas's Aristotelian ideas – which he always sought to reconcile with Christian dogma – may therefore have been wrongly associated at the time with the philosophy of Averroes.[28] However, the condemnations of his philosophy also coincided with the rise of the Franciscan Order in which Augustinian theology enjoyed particular prominence. Two Franciscan theologians, Duns Scotus and William of Ockham, stepped into the scholastic limelight during this time. Both of them belonged to the Augustinian school of thinking that stressed the freedom of God's will.

Not both of them were pure Nominalists though. Scotus developed a subtle epistemology in terms of which universals – categories of existence with universal characteristics – are possible because of the human being's capacity for perception. Ockham, however, went down in the history of philosophy as the leading

---

25 Villey 2003, p. 202.

26 In his fine little book on Villey, Stéphane Rials portrays Villey's thinking as constantly and consistently against any kind of idolizing thinking, constantly *contre les idols*. See Rials 2000, p. 17–18. However, the whole narrative in Villey 2003 leaves the reader with the impression of a rather unsubtle idolization of Aristotle and Aquinas.

27 See Van Steenberghen 1980.

28 See Thijssen 2013.

nominalist philosopher of the time. He considered language a system of signs that named particular observations and stressed the impossibility of knowing or articulating general categories of existence. Ockham was a theologian and a philosopher. He was no jurist. But as we shall see presently, circumstances compelled him to put forward juridical arguments to which Villey attaches decisive importance. In the process, he came to articulate a conception of law that took leave of the method of Roman jurisprudence. The Roman jurists claimed the capacity to identify and interpret the category or categories of existence correctly, hence their ability to identify the *ius* or *iura* relevant to any dispute in law. Ockham dismissed this claim. And in doing so, he was one of the first to articulate the grand transfer that marked the advent of the Modern Age: the transfer of God's authority to make law, to the law-making capacity of terrestrial sovereigns.[29]

According to Villey, Ockham also articulated the first concept of subjective rights in the history of modern law and legal thought. Villey's account of Ockham's inaugural articulation of the concept of subjective rights in the history of Western law starts with the thirteenth and fourteenth century dispute between the Franciscan and Dominican Orders that eventually became known as the "poverty debate." The Franciscans claimed that they lived, following the instructions of Saint Francis, without owning property. At first, their teachings were approved and protected by the Church. However, they eventually became a very successful order that commanded considerable wealth and influence, and this earned them the contempt of the Dominicans particularly. For a while, several Papal bulls came to their avail by acknowledging that they only used their assets, reserving the ownership of these assets for the Church. However, the discrepancy between the wealth they commanded and their claim that they owned no property eventually became too difficult for the Church to defend. In 1323 Pope John XXII passed the bull *Ad Conditorem Canonum* that clearly recognised the property rights of the Franciscans in the vast assets under their control.[30]

The Franciscans mostly abided by the bull and Saint Bonaventure, a later general of the Franciscans, actually took the decision to have the legends regarding the life of Saint Frances burned. But a radical Franciscan movement continued to claim that they lived without property. They claimed that they were following the example of Jesus and the disciples who never owned property. John XXII rejected the argument and accused them of heresy. To say that Christ and the disciples did not own the goods that they used and consumed was to accuse them of theft, he argued on advice from Béranger Fredol, Cardinal-Bishop of Frascati and renowned canon lawyer of the time. One cannot have rights of usage over fungible goods, was the essence of Béranger's advice to John XXIII.[31] According to Villey, this was one of the most critical hours in the millennial formation of modern legal thinking.

---

29 Villey 2003, pp. 265–266.
30 Villey 2003, pp. 218, 254.
31 The finding of the bull pivots on the arguments that 1) rights of usage must eventually go back to the owner of the goods, so one cannot retain rights of usage perpetually, and 2) one cannot have

Ockham came to the defence of the Franciscans with an argument in which he articulated, as Villey insists, the first definition of subjective rights in the history of Western legal thought.

Ockham's argument is recorded in his work *Opus Nonaginta Dierum*.[32] The argument begins with a distinction between two kinds of law, the *ius fori* and the *ius poli*. The *ius fori* is the law that applies in the secular fora of law where legal disputes about earthly matters can be heard and resolved with reference to secular law. It derives from positive or human law – *ordinatione humana* – and concerns the powers that positive law grants individuals to defend and vindicate their rights in a court of law – the *potestas vendicandi et defendendi in humano judicio*. The *ius poli* concerns the law of the heavens. Secular law does not apply to it. It concerns gifts and benefits received from God that have no relevance to earthly law. The clothes worn and food consumed by Jesus and the disciples were evidently gifts bestowed upon them by God, for they were never challenged to defend their usage and consumption of these goods in a secular forum of law. Secular law and categories of secular law such as property do for this reason not apply to them. It is therefore quite correct and coherent to argue that Jesus and the disciples never owned any property, argued Ockham.[33]

## 5 An anti-democratic thesis?

This is the end of a truly remarkable story. According to Villey, it is also the beginning of a formidable history. By putting forward the idea of a right as a power to vindicate one's rights in a human court of law, the *potestas vendicandi et defendendi in humano judicio*, Ockham provided the history of Western law with the first conceptualisation of the subjective rights on which modern legal systems would come to pivot. This, in any case, is Villey's claim. Not everyone agreed with him subsequently,[34] but he was probably correct enough to accept the basic point he was making. Ockham's phrase was a decisive moment in the history of Western legal thinking. Villey evidently admired the ingenuity of Ockham's argument – *ce jeu dialectique aboutit à renverser victorieusement les conclusions de Jean XXII*[35] – but lamented the way in which it dealt a deathblow to the old understanding of Roman law. To the students who attended Villey's classes from 1961 to 1966, the whole course of lectures that later became the formidable six hundred pages of *La formation de la pensée juridique moderne* must have come across as one long lamentation of Ockham's ingenious phrase and the consequences that followed from it.

Liberal democrats, however, should find no cause for lamentation here. They do not sit easy with the idea of juridical assessment of natural essences. They are

---

rights of usage over consumable goods, given that they cannot be returned to the owner after having been consumed.

32  Ockham 1974, 2, p. 306.
33  See Villey 2003, pp. 240–268.
34  See Tierney 1988.
35  Villey 2003, p. 260.

much more comfortable with the conception of law that Villey finds so abominable; much more at ease with an understanding of law as a system of rights and duties that are clearly defined by a contingently elected democratic majority. The culturally conservative juridical mindset that the liberal democrat detects in Villey's thesis has illustrious precursors. The resistance of Friedrich Carl von Savigny and the Pandectists to the codification of German law in the nineteenth century to which Chapter 7 pays extensive attention is perhaps the most well-known case in point. The irony of Savigny's and the Pandectists' stance – at least from the perspective of Villey's thesis – must not be missed. Ockham's definition of a subjective right as a power or *potestas* eventually became the cornerstone of the Pandectist systems of law. Savigny led the way by defining subjective rights in terms of the "power that a person wields in the legal sphere" – "*diese Macht nennen wir ein Recht dieser Person . . . Manche nennen es das Recht im subjectiven Sinn.*"[36] All the other Pandectists followed with similar definitions.[37] However, unlike Villey, the Pandectists did not consider this conception of the subjective right a deviation or rupture with Roman law. As the term "Pandectist" indicates, they all considered themselves Romanists and faithful readers of Justinian's *Digest*, faithful modernisers of the ageless wisdom of Roman law. Savigny and Puchta both referred to their work as "contemporary Roman law" – "*heutiges romisches Recht*" as if no significant break had ever occurred between ancient Rome and nineteenth century Germany that rendered this expression somewhat rich to digest.

Be that as it may, it was this new Roman law that the Pandectists wanted to shield from democratic legislation and codification. This new Roman law, claimed Savigny, was the contemporary manifestation of the *Volksgeist*. We return to this claim in Chapter 7. Suffice it to just observe now that the Pandectists basically endeavoured to bury the distributions of subjective rights current in nineteenth century Germany in the mists of an ancient legal system so that no democratic decision could revisit or revise them. In this respect, nineteenth century German science indeed produced the non- or anti-redistributive positivist legal systems that Villey maligns with good reason. The irony is that they did so under the banner of Villey's beloved Roman law.

---

36  Savigny 1840a, p. 7 (§ 4).
37  See Puchta 1862, p. 56 (§ 22), Jehring 1894, p. 140 (§ 31), Windscheid 1963, p. 156 (§ 37).

# 2

# *NOMOS* OF THE EARTH – BETWEEN VILLEY AND SCHMITT

## 1 Pindar's poem: *nomos* as *physis*

In the first section of Chapter 1 we described *nomos* as the "ensemble of custom-ary rules and practices that informed every aspect of Greek life and law from at least the seventh to the fifth century BCE." We also said "it comprised the ethics that gave form to daily routines of Greek citizens during this time, as well as the wisdom, prudence and jurisprudence that informed the political decisions of their governors and leaders." These two sentences summarised the half page that Michel Villey dedicates to the cult of *nomos* that prevailed in Greece during the archaic period of ancient Greek civilisation before moving on to a brief discussion of the crisis in which *nomos* ends up in fifth century Athens. However, Villey offers no explanation of how *nomos* came into existence in the first place. He moves very quickly to the crisis of *nomos* and emphasises in this regard the positivist spirit that comes to the fore in the positions taken by the Sophists in the debates with Plato. Considering the way in which his whole narrative eventually comes to focus on the displacement of the Aristotelian conception of *nomos* by the rise of the modern positivist conception of law, and how this narrative actually becomes the expression of a melancholic yearning for the lost Aristotelian *nomos*, his discussion of the rise and demise of the Athenian *nomos* actually passes remarkably quickly over this criti-cal moment in Greek history.

The narrative of *nomos* that Carl Schmitt develops in *Der Nomos der Erde* is much more instructive in this regard.[1] Schmitt's narrative of *nomos* will be the main focus of this chapter. In the final analysis, we shall see, Schmitt's narrative becomes another melancholic lamentation of a lost world that is in many respects compara-ble to Villey's narrative. The last section of this chapter will therefore indeed turn

---

1 Schmitt 1997.

to a brief comparison of Schmitt's and Villey's melancholic narratives of "*nomos* lost." Let us begin, however, by working our way into Schmitt's story of *nomos*. This "working our way in to" will involve some important detours in this section and the next. We begin with Schmitt now, but it is only in Section 3 that we turn squarely to his own narrative.

The *nomos-physis* opposition in fifth century Athens, writes Schmitt, concerns the destruction of the original meaning of *nomos* that severs it from existence or Being (*Sein*) and reduces it to an arbitrarily imposed "ought" (*Sollen*) – "*durch [die Entgegensetzung von Nomos und Physis] wird der Nomos zu einem auferlegten Sollen, das sich vom Sein absetzt.*"[2] In the discourse of the sophist Calicles – as related in Plato's *Gorgias* – *nomos* ends up being nothing more than the arbitrary law imposed by the strongest, continues Schmitt, "*nichts anderes als das beliebige Recht des Stärkeren.*"[3]

In the passage from the *Gorgias* to which Schmitt refers here, Calicles cites Pindar's invocation of *nomos* as the "king of everything and everyone, both mortal and immortal . . . that justifies utmost force." Here is the part of Pindar's poem at stake here:

| | |
|---|---|
| νόμος ὁ πάντων βασιλεὺς | Law is the sovereign of all, |
| θνατῶν τε καὶ ἀθανάτων | Of mortals and immortals, |
| ἄγει δικαιῶν τὸ βιαιότατον | It leads with the strongest hand, |
| ὑπερτάτᾳ χειρί τεκμαίρομαι | And may justify the greatest violence.[4] |

It is important to pause for a moment to point out what happens in his poem. It is clear that the poem does not oppose νόμος to, but associates it with force in these lines, as the words τὸ βιαιότατον (the greatest force or violence) and ὑπερτάτᾳ χειρί (the strongest hand) underline. Pindar's poem evidently effects an association between νόμος and natural force or φύσις, and it is this association that becomes the trademark of the philosophers associated with the Sophists. It is important to note, here, the way in which an absence of a clear distinction between νόμος and φύσις actually leads to an equation of νόμος with φύσις. The opposition between *nomos* and *physis* that is commonly invoked to mark the different stances of Plato (and/or Socrates), on the one hand, and the Sophists, on the other, does therefore not really concern an opposition between νόμος and φύσις, but an opposition between two different understandings of νόμος. The Sophists understood νόμος as the law of nature – νόμος as φύσις – in the sense of the law of the strongest force. They anticipate the way Hobbes would come to understand nature more than two thousand years later. This reduction of *nomos* to the natural law of the strongest force is also exactly what is at work in the Thucydides' portrayal of the discourse of the Athenian envoys to the island of Melos. We pay more attention to the discourse

---

2 Ibid, p. 38.
3 Ibid, p. 42.
4 Pindar, fragment 169a, quoted in Plato 1925, 484.

of the Athenian envoys to Melos in Chapter 3. Let us nevertheless already quote it in full here while we are still in close proximity to Pindar:

> For of the gods we hold the belief (ἡγούμεθα γὰρ τό τε θεῖον δόξῃ), and of men we know (ἀνθρώπειόν τε σαφῶς διὰ), that by a necessity of their nature (διὰ παντὸς ὑπὸ φύσεως ἀναγκαίας), wherever they have power they always rule (οὗ ἂν κρατῇ, ἄρχειν). And so in our case since we neither enacted this law (καὶ ἡμεῖς οὔτε θέντες τὸν νόμον) nor when it was enacted were the first to use it (οὔτε κειμένῳ πρῶτοι χρησάμενοι), but found it in existence for all time (ὄντα δὲ παραλαβόντες καὶ ἐσόμενον ἐς αἰεὶ καταλείψοντες), so we make use of it (χρώμεθα αὐτῷ), well aware that both you and others (εἰδότες καὶ ὑμᾶς ἂν καὶ ἄλλους), if clothed with the same power as we are (ἐν τῇ αὐτῇ δυνάμει ἡμῖν), would do the same thing (γενομένους δρῶντας ἂν ταὐτό).[5]

We see in these lines of Thucydides a veritable concatenation of φύσις (ὑπὸ φύσεως – by nature), κρατος (ἂν κρατῇ – when having power), ἄρχειν (to rule) and νόμος (τὸν νόμον – the object or accusative form of νόμος). This concatenation is highly significant as regards the debate between the Sophists and philosophers of Athens towards the end of the fifth and the beginning of the fourth century. It will become clearer in Chapter 3 that the *nomos-physis* debate concerns a mutation of the understanding of nature itself in fifth century Athens. This mutation gives rise to two different understandings of *nomos* or law: 1) *nomos* understood as *kosmos* (or *logos*), that is, the meaningful and appropriate order in which every individual element of existence has or finds its proper place, and 2) *nomos* understood as *physis* or natural force that ultimately respects no established order.

It is not necessary to determine conclusively (assuming that it is actually possible) the meaning that Pindar attributed to *nomos* in the lines of his poem that Callicles quotes. The key question for us is whether he understood *nomos* as an order that exists independently of power and only relies on power to become effective, or whether he considered it so closely linked to power that he ultimately drew no significant distinction between *nomos* and power. Pindar – a poet from Thebes who died seven years before the Peloponnesian War – was forty-two years old when the Ephesian philosopher Heraclitus died at the age of sixty. As a contemporary of the great philosopher of the eternal flux of physical forces, his understanding of *nomos* may well have been more in line with this earlier age of Greek philosophy, than the one represented by Plato and Aristotle.[6] This may also indicate that Callicles' understanding of Pindar's invocation of *nomos* <u>as</u> power may indeed be in line with how the poet himself understood this invocation. As will be suggested in Chapter 4, Aristotle probably understood the Sophists' invocation of the law of the strongest

5 Thucydides 1921,V, CV 2.
6 Schmitt also makes this link between Pindar and Heraclitus – see Schmitt 1997, p. 47.

as a disconcerting relapse into an earlier version of Greek "natural law" philosophy at a time to which that philosophy was no longer suited. Aristotle's philosophy, we shall argue then, is a quest for a stabilising conception of *nomos* on the basis of which urban settlements can establish orderly and peaceful routines of economic and cultural exchange. A philosophy of the eternal flux of things is not exactly reassuring when the need for settled order is at stake.

The problem that fifth century Athens and fourth century Athenian philosophy came to face concerned a period-specific exacerbation of the eternal difficulty of reconciling the desire for orderly and peaceful existence in settled urban societies with yearnings for excellence – and for the savouring of the natural forces of existence concomitant with it – that always threaten to disrupt and unsettle settled order. This difficulty kept Europe and European philosophers of law and politics busy for another two and a half millennia. Schmitt's narrative in *Nomos der Erde* is perhaps one of the most disconcerting but also most telling testimonies of this eternal tension in the history of European law and politics. Before we turn more squarely to Schmitt's narrative, however, let us first look again at Villey's failure to explain the more felicitous period of the *nomos* cult – assuming that there actually was such a period – in terms that cast adequate light on the drama of its eventual decline.

## 2 *Nomos* as *kosmos*

*Nomos*, avers Villey, should not be translated as "law." It does not refer to anything that one would associate with law in the modern sense of the word, that is, with written law or legislation. It refers, instead, to the proper customs of a city, and thus to its social order – *plutôt que par loi écrite, [nomos] doit être très longtemps traduit: coutume propre à une cité; ordre social, droit.*[7] In other words, the "*ordre social*" or "*droit*" invoked here concerned ancient customs that are not subject to any arbitrary or voluntarist legislative interventions of political rulers. Villey briefly refers to the stories of Themis, Dike, Eudonomie, Eirene, Nemisis and Erinues in Hesiod's *Theogony*. These stories or myths constituted a literary reflection of this early sense of "just customs and orders of existence."[8] Plato sometimes still invoked this mythological idiom, but the philosophers soon turned this notion into a secular conception of the natural order of things.

However, the question of how customs – conventional ways of doing – could be elevated to the natural order of things, the question of how and why *nomos* was amenable to an elevation that would turn it into *kosmos* (the Greek word for "order"), is one to which Villey pays much less attention than one would expect from someone who attaches so much importance to *law* as a *transcendent order*, that is, as an order that transcends the arbitrary and contingent preferences of humans,

---

7 Villey 2003, p. 61–62.
8 Ibid.

however conventional or customary these preferences may have become in the course of time. "Conventional" or "customary" does not mean "cosmological," but that is what it comes to mean for the Greeks, as the philosophy of Aristotle makes clear, and Villey does not pause to explain this transformation.[9]

In other words, Villey pays little attention to the question of how the poets and philosophers of ancient Greece managed to graft *nomos* onto *kosmos* so effectively that they soon became indistinguishable. The question is surely a weighty one. At issue here is nothing less than the precondition for Aristotle's teleological philosophy according to which everything pursues an intrinsic goal proper to itself. This teleological philosophy pivoted on an elevation of *nomos* to *kosmos*. Why did Aristotle consider this elevation convincing, to himself in the first place, and to others for whom he wrote it down? We need to address this question in two steps. Why was it still possible for philosophers to have faith in this elevation up to the middle of the fifth century BCE, and why was it still plausible for Aristotle to pursue its rehabilitation in the fourth, after its evident demise towards the end of the fifth? This essential elevation of *nomos* to *kosmos* – apparently still possible in fifth and fourth century Athens – would become impossible in the Modern Age. One of the key features of liberal democratic law, we shall see later, concerns the very fact that it is fundamentally conditioned by modernity's inability to elevate *nomos* to *kosmos*. So why was this elevation still possible in fifth and fourth century Athens, and no longer in the Modern Age?

Parmenides, the sixth century Eleatic philosopher, assertively postulated the oneness of human thinking and existence: τὸ γὰρ αὐτὸ νοεῖν ἐστίν τε καὶ εἶναι.[10] The concern that human custom, convention and practice may be at odds with existence – that is, not well-aligned with "nature," – may well have bothered him when he articulated this thought. In other words, one can assume Parmenides was not just stating what he considered obvious. He would surely not have articulated the sameness of thinking and being – or thought and existence – with such solemnity had he not felt the need to respond to the disconcerting perception that thought and existence were indeed, or just perhaps, misaligned. It is fair to read an element of purposeful reassurance into his statement. Confirmation of the alignment of thinking and being is surely a precondition for any confidence that *nomos* and nature are well attuned.

Is it fair to move so quickly from *nous* to *nomos*, that is, from thought to custom? It is not difficult to imagine the possibility of considerable slippage or overlap in early Greek usage between statements regarding the unity of *nous* and *einai*

---

9 Villey's short discussion of *nomos* relies principally on the formidable work of Rudolf Hirzel. He would have done well to dig a little deeper into Hirzel here, given the latter's express attention to the question of how custom eventually attained the status of nature (*zweite Natur . . . statt etwas Widernatürliches*) and natural justice (*Gerechtigkeit/dikē*) among the ancient Greeks. See Hirzel 1907, pp. 359–386. For a likewise formidable work on the "birth of nomos," see Zartaloudis 2018. I am indebted to Ricardo Spindola for bringing this publication to my attention.

10 Parmenides, fragment 3 in Diels 1912, I, p. 152.

(thought and existence), on the one hand, and the unity of *nomos* and *einai* (custom and existence), on the other. It should be noted that the distinction between *nomos* and *nous* was apparently infirm enough in early Greek to give rise to considerable difficulties or uncertainties of interpretation among future specialist readers of ancient Greek texts, especially pre-classical texts. Schmitt cites a key passage from Homer's *Odyssey* from which it is not entirely clear whether Homer meant *nomos* or *nous*.[11] He nevertheless rejects the dominant version of the passage that opts for *nous* instead of *nomos* with a sarcastic confidence capable of leaving any philologist astounded.[12] Why this remarkably confident rejection?

## 3 *Nomos* as concrete political space and order

Well, Schmitt is not one for accepting easy idealistic equations of spirit and matter, or thinking and being, it seems. Marx famously criticized Hegel for just thinking or interpreting the opposition between subject and object or spirit and nature away.[13] One needs at least one decent revolution for these divisions to go away, he insisted. Schmitt's central thesis in *Der Nomos der Erde* reminds one at least in one respect of this materialist or Marxian critique of Hegel's idealism. Some real historical work – *ein geschichtlicher Vorgang* or even *Grundvorgang* (a historical or fundamental act of commencement)[14] – needs to be accomplished before this grafting of concept and custom onto cosmos can be made to stick, he claims. His whole narrative in *Der Nomos der Erde* pivots on an understanding of *nomos* that relates it to an original taking and sharing of land, and to the concrete spatial order that results from this taking and sharing. The following is the key passage:

> *Nomos* comes from *nemein* – a Greek word that means both "to divide" and "to pasture." Thus *nomos* is the immediate form in which the political and social order of a people becomes spatially visible – the initial measure and division of a pasture-land, i.e., the land appropriation as well as the concrete order contained in it and following from it.[15]

If there is anything that might explain why Parmenides could think the thought of the unity of thinking and being so confidently in the sixth century AD, and why

11  Schmitt 1997, p. 46.
12  Ibid, chiding those who accept the *nous* version for turning Odysseus into a social-psychologist–[als wäre der listenreiche Held] so etwas wie der erste Sozialpsychologe gewesen. . . ."
13  See Marx 1978, p. 7: "Die Philosophen haben die Welt nur verschieden interpretiert; es kommt darauf an, sie zu verändern."
14  Schmitt 1997, pp. 40, 47.
15  Schmitt 2006b, p. 70. The original German (Schmitt 1997, pp. 39–40) reads: Nomos dagegen kommt von *nemein*, einem Wort, das sowohl "Teilen" wie auch "Weiden" bedeutet. Der nomos ist demnach die unmittelbare Gestalt, in der die politische und soziale Ordnung eines Volkes raumhaft sichtbar wird, die erste Messung und Teilung der Weide, d.h. die Landnahme und die sowohl in ihr liegende wie aus ihr folgende konkrete Ordnung.

Aristotle could so easily return to it in the fourth, it is the ancient blood and sweat that went into the taking and sharing of land. This, in any case, is what Schmitt suggests. *Der Nomos der Erde*, published just ten years before Villey started to give his lectures on the formation of modern legal thought in Paris, actually claims remarkable insight into the essential grafting process that allowed for the elevation of *nomos* to *cosmos* which could have served Villey's lectures well. Like Villey – in fact much more so than Villey – Schmitt takes care to show that *nomos* does not concern "legislation" or the act of "laying down the law." If there is an element of legislation or law-making at work in this original "taking" and "sharing" denoted by *nemein*, it is the consequence of the way in which the sharing of land eventually permeates the soil and literally becomes the "law of the land." *Nemein*/sharing thus brings forth an accomplished geography, a writing (*graphein*) into the earth (*geo*) that becomes a writing of the earth. It brings about a critical and fundamental nexus between order and place – *Ordnung* and *Ort*. *Nemein* is the act of creating a space – *ein Raumordnungsakt*[16] – that founds the critical nexus between the creation of space and the creation of order, *der entscheidende Zusammenhang von Ortung* and *Ordnung.*[17] The taking of land – *Landnahme* – that orders space and inaugurates the nexus between place and order concerns a great historical event and not just a mental construction – *ein großes historisches Ereignis und nicht . . . eine bloß gedankliche Konstruktion.*[18]

So, if Parmenides could still contemplate the unity of thinking and existence in the sixth century, if Athens could still believe itself to live by this unity well into the fifth and if Aristotle could revive it again – or at least consider it plausible to attempt such a revival – in the fourth, it would all appear to have been possible because of some fundamental taking and sharing of land through which the human spirit and the material world became attuned to one another. This fundamental attunement, suggests Schmitt, was effectively restored or re-accomplished in the wake of the major cultural transitions from ancient Greek to ancient Roman, medieval Christian and modern European societies. The last of these fundamental attunements, contends Schmitt, remained intact until the end of the nineteenth century. In other words, Schmitt evidently disputes the impossibility of the *nomos-kosmos* elevation that the last chapters of this book will consider an essential condition of liberal democracy. It is therefore important to look carefully into the cogency of his claims in this regard.

Schmitt extends this practice of original and epochal land-taking and land-sharing to the early modern politics of cartography through which European powers divided up and shared the earth.[19] He continues to employ the ancient word *nomos* to denote this division and sharing of the world by the sovereigns of modern Europe right up to the end of the nineteenth century. It is with regard to the

---

16 Schmitt 1997, p. 40.
17 Ibid, p. 39.
18 Ibid, p. 17.
19 Ibid, pp. 54–69.

division and sharing of the Earth between European sovereigns that his narrative in *Der Nomos der Erde* invokes *the law of peoples of the Jus Publicum Europaeum – das Völkerrecht des Jus Publicum Europaeum*. The book recounts the story of the three major phases of this *Jus Publicum Europaeum*: the medieval phase that ends in the sixteenth century; the modern phase that lasts from the sixteenth to the nineteenth century and the new era – the age of nihilism – that raises its head in the twentieth century.

During the Middle Ages, the *Jus Publicum Europaeum* pivoted on the idea of the *katechon*, that is, the place holding or holding-in-place that postpones the appearance of the anti-Christ to the end of time when God will finally reckon with it. The political and legal order of this Christian Roman Empire was fundamentally structured by this idea of postponing the end of time by holding the world in place. The space and order or *Ortung* and *Ordnung* of this Christian Empire pivoted on the division between *imperium* and *sacerdotum*, that is, between the secular power or *potestas* of the Emperor (or king) and his magistrates, on the one hand, and the clerical authority or *auctoritas* of the Pope and the clergy, on the other.[20] The struggles between the Emperor and the Pope that resulted from this division were nevertheless not struggles between two alien societies, stresses Schmitt. These struggles never threatened the unity of the *Respublica Christiana*. They all took place under the auspices of the single guiding motive of the *katechon*. Never did the conflicts between the Emperor and the Pope turn into an offensive of the Emperor against Rome. The quests of the Emperor always remained offensives in the name of Rome and never against Rome, *ein Kampf um Rom . . . nicht . . . gegen Rom*, insists Schmitt.[21] They never upset the fundamental order, space and concrete institutions of Rome as *katechon*.

The same applies to all conflicts between Christian kings. Hostilities were never undertaken outside the fundamental order of Rome, but always in the name of that order. They took place as vindications of rights – *Rechtsbehauptungen [und] Rechtsverwirklichungen* – claimed in the name of the order instituted and symbolised by Rome. The wars fought between the kings were accordingly ordered and contained – *umhegten* – wars guided by papal authority. They never threatened this authority and never threatened the unity of the Christian order, avers Schmitt repeatedly in *Der Nomos der Erde*.[22] The concept of the contained war – *umhegter Krieg* – that never threatens but in fact sustains the fundamental order of the world, becomes an ongoing refrain in the book. It also applies – *especially* applies, we shall see – to modern wars between European powers, at least up to the end of the nineteenth century. Only at the beginning of the twentieth century did the order of the *Jus Publicum Europaeum* finally fall apart, he contends. Chapter 5 will put forward another perspective on this fundamental "*Ortung* and *Ordnung*" of the Middle and

20 Ibid, pp. 30–34.
21 Ibid, p. 29.
22 Ibid, p. 28.

Modern Ages. Let us nevertheless follow Schmitt's narrative of *nomos* further to see where it leads him.

The great achievement of the Modern Age, argues Schmitt, consisted in the rise of modern sovereignty and of modern Europe as a constellation of horizontally ordered territorial states – *Flachenstaten* – that considered one another equal. In the framework of the strict equality between these European states, the concept of the just war or *bellum iustus* received a new meaning. It no longer reflected the just pursuit of a right supported by clerical authority, as it did throughout the Middle Ages. After the seventeenth century the phrase "just war" began to apply to any hostility between two sovereign states that complied with the proper form of war. In other words, the concept of the just war became severed from all questions regarding the soundness or justness of the reason for starting a war. It only concerned the formal requirements that the war be properly declared between two states that consider one another equal, and that the manner and extent of the hostilities do not destroy the global legal order. The latter requirement demanded that the equality and sovereignty of the enemy as a just enemy – *iustus hostis* – remained respected at all times. The just enemy was not a criminal or outlaw. He could therefore not be destroyed or in the slightest sense disrespected. The peace treaty that ended the hostilities therefore also had to embody this fundamental respect for the enemy as a just enemy. The sovereignty of neither of the warring states was to be disrespected or jeopardized by the terms of peace.[23]

The logic that Schmitt attributes to this understanding of war between the modern states of Europe seems impeccable. Two equal partners cannot judge one another without assuming a superiority for which the constellation of strict equality does not allow. Third parties can also not act as judges. The modern *Jus Publicum Europaeum* demanded that one either joined in the hostilities, or kept out of them. A third state could also declare war on one of the two warring states when it considered it in its interest to do so. When it did so, it entered the constellation of strict equality and could then no longer judge the substantive justness of the war. When it did not, it could also not express judgement, because doing so would terminate the neutrality it claimed. The logic of the scheme thus excluded the possibility of a third party judgement that remained neutral. Strict logic, however, does not seem to render this possibility inapplicable. Why does neutrality require that one does not judge? For a certain kind of jurisprudence – one that is widely considered representative of the ideal and symbol of Western law – neutrality is the precondition for sound judgement. But this understanding of judgement and neutrality requires slipping into the deck of cards of the modern *Jus Publicum Europaeum,* a card that Schmitt has carefully removed from it. That card is the card of transcendent knowledge in matters of justice and just causes. Without that card in the deck, judgement necessarily becomes interested, non-neutral judgement.

The removal of the trump card of transcendent knowledge from the game of politics is the great merit of modernity, according to Schmitt. It is also the heart

---

23 Ibid, pp. 114, 121.

of the "concrete order" thinking or *Ortungsdenken* that he contrasts with – and endorses at the cost of – the normative thinking that underpins much of modern jurisprudence.[24] Schmitt understands the scheme of the modern *Jus Publicum Europaeum* in terms of the concrete institutional nexus between place and order or *Ortung* and *Ordnung* pointed out above. The two developments that came to affect the nexus of *Ortung* and *Ordnung* with the advent of modernity are the opening up of the high seas and the discovery of the New World. From the perspective of the *Jus Publicum Europaeum*, both these "new" geographical spaces – the sea and the New World – remained "foreign" elements to which the rules of the *Jus Publicum Europaeum* did not apply. The established wisdom of the old world held that the sea is not chartable and not subject to the nexus of *Ortung* and *Ordnung*. The high seas were accordingly not governed by law. They constituted a completely free expanse – not really a space or place – where the daring pirate could in good conscience try his luck. Even the states of Europe – bound as they were to the rules of the *Jus Publicum Europaeum* on European soil – were free to do as they pleased on the high seas. The sea remained ungoverned in this way until the age of maritime law finally dawned in the nineteenth century. Until then, it remained an open arena of a boundless free-for-all in which the European powers could also act like pirates and attack one another's ships without entering into the formalities of war and without any legal consequences.[25]

The European powers were permitted to act in this unconstrained fashion beyond the line where the application of the *Jus Publicum Europaeum* ended, a line that was known as the amity line, the *Freundschaftslinie*. The amity line became a key concept of the modern *Jus Publicum Europaeum*. And it also has a pivotal organising function in Schmitt's narrative. He presents the amity line as the last guardrail that shielded both the old and the modern world from the sheer nihilism that ensued when the line snapped and the planet became a semantic void, an undifferentiated expanse devoid of place and order, devoid of *Ortung* and *Ordnung*. Schmitt is adamant that the demise of the old European world order signalled the dawn of a fundamentally lawless age, notwithstanding the plethora of positive laws and legislation through which this new age would seek to keep its fundamental lack of order at bay. Hence his reference to this age as the age of nihilism.[26]

The somewhat misleading irony of the name "amity line" must not be missed. It did not denote a line between a zone of lawless warfare, on the one hand, and lawful peace, on the other. It concerned instead a line that separated a zone of lawless violence and looting, on the one hand, and orderly and lawful warfare, on the

24 See Schmitt 2006c, pp. 10–20.
25 It is worthwhile to note that even Grotius, considered (in typical denouncing fashion) one of the historically most prominent normative legal theorists by Schmitt, also made use of this argument in his legal opinion written for the Dutch East India Company in defence of the Dutch piracy of the *Santa Catarina* – a Portuguese ship with a huge bounty – in 1603. The opinion was later published as *De Iure Praedae*. See Grotius 1886.
26 Schmitt 1997, p. 36.

other. The "amity" or "friendship" to which the name of the line refers concerned the unique heroic friendship between nations that only waged war on one another when the conditions of the *ius bellum* prevailed. As we saw, these conditions had nothing and could have nothing to do with substantive reasons for declaring war. It only concerned the formal requirements of declaring war properly and preventing its inevitable violence from erupting into an annihilation of the enemy or yielding to practices no longer characteristic of a respectful duel between gentlemen.[27] The enemy, we saw, was not to be annihilated, for he or she remained and had to remain an equal for the nexus of *Ortung* and *Ordnung* to remain in place. That is why the line that created the order of the Old World was called the "amity" line. In this old world, on the law side of the line, the enemy remained a "friend" in the sense that he or she was considered just, a *iustus hostis* worthy of respect.

The distinction between the public and the private enemy that Schmitt already drew in *Der Begriff des Politischen* in 1922 evidently still underpins the refrain of the *iustus hostis* that rings from the first to the last page of *Der Nomos der Erde* in 1951.[28] However, when one met this same just or public enemy on the other side of the amity line, a different order prevailed. The friend-enemy then became the enemy-enemy or criminal enemy that could be annihilated without consequences if whim or expedience would so demand. Schmitt offers a remarkable explanation of this enigmatic change of status of the enemy that results from traversing the amity line to which we come back below.[29] For now, let us first take a closer look at what he seeks to achieve with this astounding description of the *Jus Publicum Europaeum* that ended with the Treaty of Versailles in 1919.

Schmitt's description of the Medieval and Modern frameworks of the *Jus Publicum Europaeum* endeavours to articulate a conception of political order that accomplishes a seemingly impossible reconciliation between the quest for a stable framework of orderly co-existence, on the one hand, with the irresistible and irrepressible allure of wielding power for the sake of wielding power, on the other. The wielding of power of concern here is not at all aimed at gains in property or material wealth. If a gain in wealth of some kind is at stake in the taking of land or *Landnahme* envisaged in his narrative, it is definitely not the private wealth embodied in property. The sovereign that took the land of another sovereign on the *Jus Publicum Europaeum* side of the amity line, was strictly subject to the rule that this taking of land may not interfere with the private law rights of the subjects of the sovereign from whom the land is taken. In this respect, the freedom of the sovereign to declare war against a fellow sovereign was not at all irreconcilable with settled private property relations. Some collateral harm and damage could occur to private lives and property, granted, but the sovereign that conducted a just war – in the sense described above – did not in the least intend to harm private life and damage property and would always gladly pay reparations for any such harm or damage

27  Ibid, pp. 115–121.
28  See Schmitt 1996a and 1994, pp. 278–285.
29  Schmitt 1997, p. 66.

caused. The sovereign conducted war for the sake of testing and experiencing his strength and power, and not for the sake of acquiring material wealth. That was the goal of imperial expansion, nothing else. This is the picture painted in *Der Nomos der Erde*.[30]

A different picture emerges on the other side of the amity line and Schmitt paints that picture astoundingly honestly, too honestly, some would say. He does not seem to understand or recognise just what he is saying, some will observe. He introduces his portrayal of land-taking on the other side of the amity line with a close reading of Vitoria's sixteenth century justification of Cortes' treatment of the American Indians and his taking of their land. Vitoria chided the Spanish conquerors for treating the Indians as sub-human beings unworthy of respect. He took a line of Christian thinking – traceable all the way back to Saint Augustine – according to which barbarian and savage peoples (this distinction denoted an important hierarchy during the Middle and early Modern Ages) had souls and were worthy of respect.

With this theological argument, Vitoria already took a significant step towards the abstract, neutral and universalist normativity with which modern philosophy broke away from the historical and concrete institutional normativity – the *Ortung-Ordnung* nexus – of the Middle Ages. However, Vitoria himself did not yet make the complete transition to modernity, avers Schmitt. His thinking was in the final analysis still sufficiently rooted in the medieval institutional framework to justify the Spanish conquest on the basis of a medieval Christian just war argument. The Indians obstructed the missionary, propaganda and commercial freedom of the Spaniards, argued Vitoria. They therefore precipitated a just war in the medieval sense of the term, a war conducted on the basis of a just cause or reason. The taking of their land was a further consequence of the war and therefore justified and just.[31]

This "just war" argument lost its institutional justification in the sixteenth century and the conquest of land beyond the amity line acquired a new justification in the seventeenth. Hugo Grotius led the new way by taking recourse to Roman private law concepts for purposes of developing a "discovery-based" justification of land-takings beyond the amity line. No real discovery was of concern here, of course, for the land "discovered" was already discovered and duly inhabited by indigenous peoples. His argument pivoted on the idea that the land inhabited by these indigenous peoples was not effectively governed and occupied by them. The European powers were for this reason free to take it. Not only were they free to govern these territories, they were also free to dispossess land from groups or individuals who actually lived on the land, given that their "informal" possession or use of land did not constitute property rights that the discoverer needed to respect.[32] The just war argument was no longer operative or needed in this new context, but Grotius furnished this new scheme of land-taking with a new justification. The new justification for the taking and dispossession of land inhabited by non-European

30 Ibid, p. 159.
31 Ibid, pp. 78–80.
32 Ibid, p. 171.

peoples turned on the idea of the educational mission of the civilised world. By taking and occupying the land of non-Europeans, Europeans brought civilisation to them. That this indeed became modern Europe's justification of land-taking in the New World became abundantly clear at the time of the Congo Conference of 1885. Schmitt cites in this regard the words pronounced by King Leopold of Belgium during the conference: "Civilization opens up the only part of the globe it has not yet reached, piercing the darkness, enveloping [entire populations]. That is, I wager to say, a crusade worthy of this century of progress."[33]

The Congo Act was for Schmitt the last endorsement of the *Jus Publicum Europaeum* before its final demise at the beginning of the twentieth century. It was a "last relic of another time, when Europe still was the sacral centre of the earth" – *ein letztes Relikt aus einer andern Zeit, in der Europa noch die sakrale Mitte der Erde war.* It reflected the "last bloom of the *Jus Publicum Europaeum*" – *diese Zeit der letzten Blüte des jus publicum Europaeum.*[34] However, it soon also emerged as the first nail in its coffin, the coffin that became fully nailed down in the Treaty of Versailles. Conceived as an endeavour to draw a new amity line between the states of Europe, it became the death knell of the earlier amity line that sustained the old *Jus Publicum Europaeum* with the fundamental distinction between Europe, on the one hand, and non-Europe (the high seas and New World), on the other. The Congo Act itself had already blurred this line by recognising the Congo as an independent state (a prerogative until then reserved for European sovereigns), but it still aimed at sustaining the crucial difference between European and non-European soil. This difference, however, was finally erased by Belgium's subsequent annexation of the Congo on the basis of its "effective control" and "occupation" over it. This annexation of the Congo removed the last pillar that sustained the old spatial world order between Europe and non-Europe.

For the first time in the history of the world, European and non-European soils were put on an equal footing. This erasure of the distinction between European and non-European soil was complemented by an erasure of the distinction between sea and soil as such. The rise of England as a maritime power in the sixteenth century and the rise of modern maritime law in the seventeenth culminated towards the end of the nineteenth and beginning of the twentieth century in "a general international law" – *ein allgemeines "international law,"* as Schmitt's German text refers to it with tangible disdain – that dissolved European public law.[35] From this equation of European and non-European soils, and of soil and sea as such, resulted a complete erasure of ordered space and place, argues Schmitt, a complete *Entortung* that turned the world into an undefined expanse with no *Ortung* and *Ordnung.*[36]

The scene was thus duly set for the world to take leave of the arrangements with which the states of old Europe governed relations between themselves, on the one

---

33  Schmitt 2006b, p. 216; 1997, p. 190.
34  Schmitt 1997, pp. 188, 190.
35  Schmitt 1997, p. 155.
36  Ibid, p. 194.

hand, and governed – or just possessed – the rest of the world, on the other. The most critical casualty of this process, as far as old Europe and Schmitt are concerned, are the notions of the just war and just enemy that allowed European sovereigns to freely measure their strengths without raising discriminating questions with regard to "who started the war" and "for what reason." A war began between the states of Europe in 1914 with the old European public law conception of just and innocent wars between European sovereigns still in place, but it ended in 1918 under a cloud of international politics that raised questions regarding the aggressor who commenced the war and the absence of reasons for doing so. And thus began the elevation of the notion of the unjust and criminal war to the foundational principle of a new international order. The Treaty of Versailles of 1919 culminated in declaring the German emperor criminally responsible for the war and forcing him to seek refuge from personal prosecution in the Netherlands.[37]

The reader of *Der Nomos der Erde* can be forgiven for getting the impression that this – the criminal conviction of the German sovereign – is the bitter pill that Schmitt is struggling to swallow with his grand narrative of a noble and profoundly wise old European world order that ended in 1919. What was the essential achievement of this old European world order, this old European *nomos* of the earth? Its achievement, according to Schmitt, concerned the way it resolved for almost twenty centuries a problem that raised its head two and a half millennia ago, in Mytilene and Melos. In any case, this is how we shall construct Schmitt's assessment of the *Jus Publicum Europaeum* that disintegrated so dismally, according to him, with the Treaty of Versailles. For the purpose of doing so, however, we shall first take a short detour again through ancient Greece.

## 4 *Nomos* from Mytilene and Melos to Versailles

Alasdair Macintyre explains the excesses of Athenian brutality during the Peloponnesian War in terms of the foundering of Athens' *nomos* and *ethos* of moderation. The Athenians began to understand their virtue – the virtue of Athens as a city – in terms of the competitive and agonistic spirit of the Homeric warrior-king and hence came to consider the virtue of *sophrosune* (moderation) irrelevant in their conduct vis-à-vis other cities.[38] Macintyre's explanation is complemented by H. D. F. Kitto's narrative of the Peloponnesian War.[39] Kitto relates in detail how the city of Mytilene narrowly escaped the fate that would later befall Melos. During the deliberations of the action to be taken with regard to Mytilene – the capital city of the island of Lesbos that revolted against Athenian rule in 428 – Cleon swayed the Athenian Assembly to decide that all the men of Mytilene should be put to death and the women be sold into slavery, and towards the evening a ship was sent to Lesbos to instruct the Athenian commander accordingly. Remorse gripped

---

37  Ibid, pp. 235–237.
38  Macintyre 1967, pp. 11–12, 1988, pp. 47–68.
39  For the exposition that follows, see Kitto 1951, pp. 143–152.

the Athenians the following day and after further debate Diodotus persuaded the Assembly to spare the city and to put only the ringleaders of the rebellion on trial. A second ship with the new instruction reached Mytilene just in time to avoid the massacre.

Twelve years later, however, the island of Melos was not so fortunate. Diodotus' voice of civil moderation was evidently no longer around when the Athenians decided its fate in 416. The rhetoric that presented Athens as a Homeric hero and warrior-king had already begun with Pericles, but both Kitto and Macintyre stress that Pericles always maintained and cultivated a certain moderation of spirit and always put the interests of Athens first.[40] After Pericles, however, an unrestrained competitive spirit took hold of the Athenian leaders which evidently served their own ambitions more than it served the interests of Athens. Pericles still stressed the Athenian regard for "those laws which are enacted for the advantage of those to whom injustice has been done and those unwritten laws the breach of which incurs shameful disgrace,"[41] but this regard was evidently lost by the time the Athenians decided the fate of Melos. Using Schmitt's terminology, Melos became the non-place, or the destruction of place – the *Entortung* where the Athenian *nomos* gave way to the blind vicissitudes of natural force, that is, of *physis*. Thucydides' narration of the discourse between the Athenian envoys and the Melesians quoted above is the literary record of this *Entortung* that would echo for centuries to come. Let us quote this fateful sentence once again:

[W]e neither enacted this law (καὶ ἡμεῖς οὔτε θεντες τὸν νόμον) nor when it was enacted were the first to use it (οὔτε κειμένῳ πρῶτοι χρησάμενοι), but found it in existence for all time (ὄντα δὲ παραλαβόντες καὶ ἐσόμενον ἐς αἰεὶ καταλείψοντες).[42]

The key phrases in these lines that underline the destruction of place or *Entortung* that they describe are "we neither enacted this law" and "[we] found it in existence for all time." Thucydides' message is clear. It is not just the Athenians who did not enact this law. A law that is "found in existence for all time" is not enacted at all. And a law "found in existence for all time" is not related to place or a place. It turns place into endless space, and time into endless time, the time of eternal vicissitudes of natural forces that ultimately undo all aspirations to draw boundaries and construct place, or a place; the eternal ups and downs of Heraclitus that are ultimately one and the same, ὁδὸς ἄνω κάτω μία καὶ ωὐτή.[43]

Schmitt, we saw above, attributes the *nomos-physis* debate in fifth century Athens to the dawning sense among many Athenians that the *nomos* of Athens was just arbitrarily posited law. It posed no constraint on *physis* and came across as an incidental

---

40 Kitto 1951, p. 143, Macintyre 1988, p. 65.
41 Macintyre 1988, pp. 61–62.
42 Thucydides 1921, V, CV 2.
43 Heraclitus, fragment 60 in Diels 1912, I, p. 89. See also Laertius 1925, p. 417.

and fleeting manifestation of *physis* itself. For all its pretensions to establish *kosmos* and *xora*, order and place, *nomos* remained *physis*, it remained nothing but a temporary manifestation of the ageless flux of physical force. This is the devastating experience of reality that the "weeping philosopher" articulated in Ephesus in the sixth century BCE. It is the experience from which Athenian civilisation and democracy endeavoured to offer respite and sanctuary in the fifth century, only to be swept away by it again when the ageless sun set on that brief and briefly beautiful century.

The seemingly futile dream of lawful respite from physical force is a resilient one, though. Aristotle started to dream it forthwith again in fourth century Athens. But fourth century Athens was itself soon swept away by the *physis and nomos* or *nomos-physis* of an alien emperor. Only two centuries later, and a thousand kilometres to the west, did Rome again begin to dream of severing and shielding *nomos* from *physis*, and law from sheer natural force. The Romans dreamt this dream forcefully enough and long enough to leave the Western world with another formidable legacy.

Indeed, the Roman Empire itself came and went, but it bequeathed to Europe the idealistic conception of law as something definitively different from sheer force, and different from the incidental commands of powerful sovereigns. This legacy became an essential ingredient of the European culture that imposed itself – forcefully no doubt – in many corners of an increasingly colonised planet. This legacy of Rome also continued to inspire Western jurisprudence and theories of law right up to the beginning of the twenty first century, notwithstanding the performative contradiction from which it never managed to escape, that is, the contradiction between the idea that law is not sheer force, and the sheer force required to give effect to this idea. Western jurisprudence would never manage to extract Rome's legacy from this contradiction. Pindar's poem never ceased to haunt Western law.[44]

But where exactly does Schmitt stand in this history of jurisprudence and legal theory? Does his concern with *nomos* as a nexus of *Ortung* and *Ordnung* constitute an endeavour to contemplate law as something different from the arbitrary will of a powerful sovereign? This is surely what his negative assessment of the *nomos-physis* debate in Athens suggests. His recognition of the extent to which the *nomos* of Athens had deteriorated into mere *nomoi* surely contains a denouncement. This denouncement is also evident in his imputation of "artificial negotiation theses spawned from theoretical and tactical grounds" – *eine künstliche, theoretische [und] aus taktischen Gründen vorgebrachte Verhandlungsthese* – to the French and Portuguese negotiators during the Congo Conference,[45] and in his attribution of "merely positive or positivist contractual concerns of foreign law" – *vertragspositivistischen Einzelfrage des Aussenrechts* – to Belgium after the conference.[46] These are all examples

---

44  See Kyriakou 2002 for a markedly more expert interpretation of Pindar's poem which nevertheless also ends up underlining the deep ambiguity (between the fateful and sovereign violence of *nomos* and the justice of Zeus that often relies on this violence) reflected in these lines. I am indebted to Ricardo Spindola for pointing out Kyriakou's essay to me.

45  Schmitt 1997, p. 194.

46  Ibid, p. 197.

of arbitrary subjective interventions that have no sense of the spatial structure of concrete order – *[keinen] Sinn für die Raumsruktur einer konkreter Ordnung* – he insists.[47] The Congo Conference and its aftermath were for Schmitt the beginning of the end of the European *nomos* that became fully manifest with the Treaty of Versailles.

The narrative of *Der Nomos der Erde* is a melancholic reflection on the loss of *nomos*, the loss of an "objectively" perceivable nexus of place and order, *Ortung and Ordnung*. As such, it is clearly concerned with something akin to the transcendental cosmological order that Aristotle contemplated. It is in this respect that the narrative in *Der Nomos der Erde* resonates – notwithstanding its ambiguities to which we return below – firmly with Villey's narrative in *La Formation de la pensée juridique moderne*. We shall presently turn more squarely to the resonance and dissonance between these two narratives. Let us first take a closer look at the nexus of *Ortung* and *Ordnung* that Schmitt claims to observe in the *Jus Publicum Europaeum* of the Middle and Modern Ages so that we can determine where he really stands.

## 5 *Nomos*, force and violence under the *Jus Publicum Europaeum*

The idea that the Middle Ages were anarchical is a widely spread mistake – *es ist eine weitverbreitete Irrtum, von der Anarchie des Mittelalters zu sprechen.*[48] According to Schmitt, the seemingly disorderly feuds and conflicts of this time were fully recognised institutions and methods through which disputes about rights were settled – *[anerkannte] Einrichtungen und Methoden der Behauptung und Verteidigung des Rechts.*[49] The same applied to the wars between European states from the seventeenth to the twentieth century. These wars were orderly, properly contained and lawful processes – *geordnete, von den neutralen Grosßmächten eingehegte, rechterfüllte Vorgänge.*[50]

Schmitt simply dismisses the pacifist conception of war as anarchy. He concedes that anarchical wars do occur, but the formal state wars between European sovereigns that took place after the Peace of Westphalia were the opposite of such anarchical wars, according to him. "They were, in fact, the highest form of order of which human force is capable." – *[Diese] Kriege sind das Gegenteil von Unordnung. In ihnen liegt die höchste Form der Ordnung, deren menschliche Kraft fähig ist.*[51] To this observation he adds another: "Containment, and not abolition of war has thus far been the real success of law ... [and] the only achievement of the law of peoples" – *Eine Einhegung, nicht die Abschaffung des Krieges war bisher der eigentliche Erfolg des Rechts ... [und] die einzige Leistung des Völkerrechts.*[52]

47  Ibid, p. 194.
48  Ibid, p. 158.
49  Ibid.
50  Ibid.
51  Ibid, pp. 158–159.
52  Ibid, p. 159.

These extraordinary and extraordinarily confident statements surely invite the following assessment: Schmitt saves and secures the distinction between *nomos* and *physis*, or law and physical force, upon which he insists throughout *Der Nomos der Erde*, by integrating characteristic aspects of *physis* into *nomos*. What others consider the anarchic clash of physical forces, he calls order, the highest kind of order, in fact, of which human strength is capable – *die höchste Form der Ordnung, deren menschliche Kraft fähig ist*. The question that this move elicits must surely be: Does Schmitt not in fact erase the distinction between *nomos* and *physis* disingenuously while artfully claiming to secure it? A simple positive answer to this question must be avoided for it will only obscure what is essentially at stake here. Let us rather follow Schmitt's argument more closely to determine precisely what he is getting at.

The key to the puzzle that *Der Nomos der Erde* is creating here relates very specifically and precisely to this startling invocation of the "highest kind of order of which human strength is capable" – the *höchste Form der Ordnung, deren menschliche Kraft fähig ist*. One misses the key point if one takes this phrase to simply refer generically to the limits of human capability. We often say "this is the best I can do" to communicate the simple statement "I have done all I can." This is not how Schmitt should be read here. He is saying something more. He is saying much more pointedly: Given that humans rely on force or power to create order (recall Pindar), this is the highest order of which they are capable. Or more precisely: Given that physical force is an undeniable feature of human existence which not only conditions, but also constantly threatens all order, this is the highest form of order of which humans are capable. At issue in this sentence is nothing less than the key move that underpins the whole narrative of *Der Nomos der Erde*. A close reading of this narrative shows that Schmitt is very honestly – too honestly, we already noted above – proposing a way of preserving the notion of law in the face of what he considers the inevitable fact and factor of physical force in the relations between human beings. He is proposing a conception of *nomos* that resolves the problem that the human being's taste for heroic competition poses to the idea of peaceful law and order. This, we saw, is the problem that Macintyre and Kitto detect in their reading of the Peloponnesian War: The Greeks were obsessed with excellence and force and they lost the ability to contain this obsession sufficiently to sustain an adequate degree of civil order towards the end of the fifth century. *Der Nomos der Erde* can therefore be read as a response to the seemingly ageless predicament that the fascination with physical force creates for all endeavours to sustain law and civil order between humans.

In the cultural memory of Europe and the West, this predicament raised its first terrifying head in fifth century Athens. It did not raise its head in the eighth and seventh century Greece of Homer, for the Greece of Homer was still fundamentally and heroically *accustomed* – with all the trappings of a stable *nomos* or custom – to the experience that the rise and demise of physical force dictate the law of all things. Even in the sixth century, the tears of the weeping philosopher were not a protest, but an elegiac affirmation akin to the tears of the mother who wept when her brave son died in the full beauty of youth on the battlefields of the seventh century, "knowing" that it cannot be otherwise. This is underlined by his Fragment 20 which considers death on the battlefield the only worthy fame to which mortals can aspire. We return to this fragment in the final pages of this book where we cite it in full. It is the decay and demise of Heraclitus' elegiac knowledge – and the modern resistance to this knowledge – that Hegel articulated when he invoked the twilight in which philosophy paints its dreary grey in dreary grey.[53] We return to Hegel's twilight in Chapter 7. It is in the twilight of fifth century Athens that we must seek to understand Schmitt better.

The solution to the problem that Schmitt proposes, however, does not only consist in finding a way in which the physical force of humans can be harnessed in the format of formal wars between political sovereigns that largely leave civil relations – property and private law relations – undisturbed. This is surely part of the sweeping solution that *Der Nomos der Erde* offers in response to the predicament that the ageless allure of physical force creates among humans. But, there is more to this solution than that. The problem that the allure of physical force poses for the endeavour to establish and sustain the "highest kind of order of which human strength is capable" is ultimately a darker one that demands a darker solution, darker than any solution that the gentlemanly and well-ordered measuring of strength between equal sovereigns can offer. In fact, this well-ordered measuring of strength between equal sovereigns is itself dependent on this darker solution. It is itself exposed to the darker problem that lurks in the ageless allure of physical force. This darker problem and darker solution concern the human being's apparent taste for sheer cruelty and limitless violence that is bound to turn, not only civil order, but also orderly and gentlemanly wars into orgies of utter destruction if it does not find an outlet elsewhere. The *Jus Publicum Europaeum* had a solution for this problem until the end of the nineteenth century, argues Schmitt. That solution was the *amity line*. No violence and no destruction were barred beyond the amity line, and this freedom of unconstrained violence and destruction beyond the amity line, he contends, relieved the wars on European soil from the pressures of the human being's undeniable taste for unconstrained violence and destruction. Two passages that contain some of the most startling lines in *Der Nomos der Erde* articulate this contention unflinchingly:

> [The amity] line set aside an area where force could be used freely and ruthlessly. It was understood, however, that only Christian-European princes and peoples could share in the land appropriation of New World and be parties to such treaties. But the commonality of Christian princes and nations contained neither a common, concrete, and legitimating arbitrational authority, nor any principle of distribution other than the law of the stronger and, ultimately, of effective occupation. Everything that occurred "beyond the line" remained outside the legal, moral and political values recognised on this side

---

53 See Hegel 1970, vol. 7, pp. 11–28.

of the line. This was a tremendous [unburdening] of the internal European problematic. The significance in international law of the famous and notorious expression "beyond the line" lies precisely in this [unburdening].[54]

The significance of amity lines in 16th and 17th century international law was that great areas of freedom were designated as conflict zones in the struggle over the distribution over a new world. As a practical justification, one could argue that the designation of a conflict zone at once [unburdened] the area on this side of the line – a sphere of peace and order ruled by European public law – from the immediate threat of those events "beyond the line," which would not have been the case had there not been such a zone. The designation of a conflict zone outside Europe contributed also to the [containment] of European wars, which is its meaning and justification in international law.[55]

It should be clear now why the line between public and private law – which prevented the land-taking sovereign on European soil from terminating private law rights – made no sense in this zone beyond the law. European land-taking beyond the amity line did not respect local land use practices of indigenous peoples who occupied the land before the land takers came. It was self-evident to the European conquerors that private or personal use of the land taken could be terminated unscrupulously and in good conscience, for this was a truly lawless zone that catered for every cruel appetite imaginable.

This then, is how the *Jus Publicum Europaeum* of the sixteenth till nineteenth century ensured the "highest kind of order of which human strength is capable." It exported the darker potential of human strength to zones of existence that simply did not matter to this *Jus Publicum*. This is how it managed to secure the distinction between law and physical force that the legacy of Rome bequeathed to it. Towards the end of the nineteenth century, we saw above, the spokesmen of Europe began to invoke the civilising function of this ruthless and violent land-taking beyond the amity line. This was how civilisation was to be exported to the New World, claimed the leaders of Europe at the end of the nineteenth century. *Der Nomos der Erde* ultimately tells a different story. If there was any civilisation and civilising process at stake in the *Jus Publicum Europaeum*, it had a very different trajectory. If it existed at all, it consisted in exorcising the worst incivility and cruelty "of which human strength is capable" and sending it off to zones where they did not matter. But this potential for sheer incivility and utter cruelty ultimately also came round to erasing the amity line, thus allowing itself to return to Europe with a fury that the human being had never seen before. Wars of utter destruction erupted on "European soil" in quick succession in the first half of the twentieth century and

---

54 Schmitt 2006b, p. 94.
55 Schmitt 2006b, pp. 97–98. I have inserted the words "unburden" and "unburdening" into the English translation quoted above, because it reflects much more accurately the words "*entlasten*" and "*Entlastung*" that Schmitt employs in these lines.

deprived Europe and the world of all the confidence it may have had in the idea of civilisation.

It is against this background that the legacy of Rome nevertheless raised its head again, and continued to do so. In the course of the twentieth century, and especially in the second half of that century, devastating images of a complete collapse of the distinction between law and physical force reached every corner of the world and seemed to signal the final collapse of the millennial European endeavour to civilise *menschliche Kraft* with recourse to notions of *nomos* that transcend the sheer anarchy and caprice of *physis*. It is against this background that the question of liberal demo-cratic law absurdly raised its head once more – or perhaps for the very first time – in yet another attempt to secure the distinction between law and physical force.

Absurdly? Well, by this time, it would have been a sign of simple realism had Western legal theory simply abandoned the endeavour to sustain a distinction between law and physical force. But some strands of legal theory persisted with the endeavour to sustain this distinction. These strands of post-war legal theory will be the focus of attention in the last chapters of this book. For now, let us conclude this chapter by highlighting both the commonalities between Schmitt's and Villey's narratives, and the way in which these very commonalities undermine one another.

## 6 Villey and Schmitt

Villey's and Schmitt's respective narratives in *La Formation de la pensée juridique moderne* and *Der Nomos der Erde* resonate in many respects, but they also highlight weaknesses in one another that warrant closer scrutiny. Both narratives put forward formidable theoretical concerns with the concrete founding nexus between legal order and specificities of place. Schmitt contemplates an *Ortungsdenken* – a think-ing of concrete space and order. Villey invokes natural law, not just any natural law, though, and certainly not modern theories of natural law based on principles of human reason (*Vernunftrecht*). He has in mind Aristotelian and Thomist natural law within the framework of which concrete exigencies of spatial or geographic belonging determine legal obligations and entitlements. The Aristotle and Saint Thomas whom Villey contemplates fit well into Schmitt's narrative, and the Aristo-telian conception of *nomos* that Schmitt invokes fits perfectly into Villey's.[56]

Both narratives repeatedly stress the importance of the Aristotelian distinction between *nomos* and positive legislation. And both narrators are purists with regard to this Aristotelian conception of *nomos* as concrete order. Both dismiss the impure revivals of natural law or *nomos* in the sixteenth century. Both consider these revivals already too deeply implicated in the abstract universalist normativity that especially Grotius will make salient in the seventeenth century. Francisco Vitoria is the telling figure for both of them. Vitoria's scathing "Christian" critique of Cortes' treatment

---

56 See again Schmitt's reference to Aristotle's distinction between legislation and law in Schmitt 1997, pp. 37–38.

of the American Indians is for Schmitt a clear signal of the extent to which Vitoria has already exchanged the concrete Christian order of the Catholic Church for the abstract and universalist normativity of the new age.[57] The dismissal of Aristotle's pagan distinction between peoples who are slaves by nature and peoples who are by nature free, and his insistence on the equal dignity of Christians and non-Christians, are for Schmitt the telling signs of the abstract, neutral, impartial and unhistorical focus – *[die] allzu abstrakt neutrale, teilnahmslose und daher auch ungeschichtliche Zuspitzung* – of Vitoria's thinking. Only in his ultimate justification of the Spanish conquest in terms of the Papal missionary decree does Schmitt find a last remnant of the concrete Christian thinking of medieval Europe.[58] Villey, on the other hand, is not completely ungrateful to the Spanish Scholastics – and to Vitoria among them – for their last ditch resistance to the contractualist, positivist and individualist normativity of an advancing modernity, but he ultimately also considers Vitoria fragrantly culpable of betraying the *Summa Theologiae* to his contractualist and individualist adversaries – *en flagrant délit de trahir la Somme théologique en faveur de ses adversaires.*[59]

The most significant differences between the two narratives concern the respective ways in which they explain and comprehend the beginning and end of the reign of *nomos*. As we saw above, Schmitt explains the primal origins of *nomos* meticulously with reference to an initial taking and sharing of land, whereas Villey largely glosses them over. Villey briefly mentions the origins of the notion of *nomos* in Greek poetry and myths, but basically turns from myth to Plato and Aristotle without delay. In the process, he leaves many questions unanswered, among them the key question regarding the material conditions that render *nomos* possible. From a Schmittian point of view, Villey's narrative could be considered too philosophical and metaphysical. Villey does not pay attention to the material grafting process of *nomos* onto *nature*, the material grafting that establishes the link between law and nature which plays such a key role throughout his narrative of Aristotelian and Roman natural law. The mortal blood and sweat that stain the taking and sharing of soil perform this grafting of *nomos* onto nature for Schmitt. The law becomes real, it becomes the *law of the land*, we saw above, through this original labour.

However, having highlighted this initial grafting process of land-taking and sharing, how can Schmitt "neutralise" it sufficiently for it to truly become "one with the land" again, so that it does not remain remembered as some arbitrary intervention that could be terminated and replaced by any other such intervention that is physically forceful enough to do so? Expressed in terms borrowed very loosely from Pocock, the question of concern here is that of reconciling the "Machiavellian moment" with the "ancient constitution."[60] Having highlighted the fact that *nomos* is not just naturally there, but must be given through an adequately significant

---

57 Ibid, p. 84.
58 Ibid, pp. 76, 80.
59 Villey, 2003, p. 346. For Schmitt's parallel formulation see Schmitt 1997, p. 84.
60 See Pocock 1987 and 1975.

historical act, what guarantee can Schmitt give that this giving of *nomos* is qualitatively different from "artificial negotiating theses motivated by tactical theoretical grounds" that he imputes to the French and Portuguese delegations during the Congo Conference,[61] or from the positivist contractual foreign law concerns of Belgium in the wake of that same conference.[62] According to Schmitt, interventions like these destroy rather than give and sustain the spatial order intrinsic to *nomos,* or at best leave them unaltered. As he himself observes, not all attempts at foundational acts produce *Nomos* – *nicht jede Invasion oder jede vorübergehende Okkupation ist schon eine Ordnung begründende Landnahme.*[63] *Nomos* must not be confused with every contingent and passing historical status quo – *jede zufälligen [und] jeweilige territorialen status quo.*[64] But what distinguishes these *nomos*-destructive or at best *nomos*-ineffective politics from the concrete historical intervention – *konkret historischer Vorgang* – of a truly *nomos*-producing politics? Only their lack of force or power? If so, Schmitt would surely be left at pains to distinguish the *nomos*-giving politics – *raum-teilenden Grundvorgang* – from the mere positing-positivism – *Setzungspositivismus* – that he dismisses with barely camouflaged disdain.[65]

One might argue on behalf of Schmitt that *nomos*-giving politics possesses the profound power to become naturalised, that is, to become forgotten in the mists of time while remaining effectively present as the enduring definition of space and place of an entire epoch. But for how long and till exactly when can one continue to confidently assume the endurance of an epoch? This question becomes pertinent when one begins to read *Der Nomos der Erde* through the lens of *La Formation de la pensée juridique moderne.* The unremitting refrain in the latter is the demise of Aristotelian and ancient Roman natural law that gives way, towards the fourteenth century, to a conception of law that corresponds in all important respects with the *nomos*-empty contractualist and positing positivism – *Vertragspositivismus, Setzungspositivismus* – that Schmitt maligns from the first till the last page of *Der Nomos der Erde.* It is this parallel development of the two narratives that makes Vitoria their common cause of contempt. Villey's entire thesis about the transformation of the meaning of the word right or *ius* is of key concern here. For the Roman jurists, he insists, the word *ius* referred to a thing, *une chose.* It is an immaterial thing that is intrinsically related to material things, that is, to the way things hang together, to the "lay of the land," so to speak. Human agency had little or no impact on such assessments of "the lay of the land" and in this respect ancient Roman law could be claimed to be the veritable "law of the land." This is Villey's story.

Voluntarist interventions into the way things are only entered Roman law when the Augustinian and nominalist turn in medieval scholasticism commenced to relativize invocations of "the way things are." Increasingly, "the way things are" became

---

61  Schmitt 1997, p. 194.
62  Ibid, p. 197.
63  Ibid, p. 48.
64  Ibid, p. 157.
65  Ibid, pp. 45, 48.

understood as the way in which God and his terrestrial representatives ordained them for the time being. The power or *potestas* to determine the way things are, "the lay of the land" included, thus became the determining factor in deliberations of rights and duties. Hence Villey's insistence on the significance of Ockham's fourteenth century definition of *ius* in terms of *potestas*. Ockham's definition reflected the way in which the meaning of *ius* changed from a thing – or the relation between things – to a subjective power that the law – itself laid down by a sovereign power – allowed one to impose on someone else. Thus did the law end up, according to Villey, as the product of that which Schmitt calls *Setzungspositivismus*. To be sure, Villey does not see this development as the outcome of scholastic debates. He considered it the outcome of the chaotic reality of medieval power relations. These relations were no longer properly arranged by existing law. They increasingly reflected a reality in which arbitrary interventions of powerful individuals remade the law at will and gave rise to incessantly conflicting rights claims.[66] Ockham's definition of *ius* as a *potestas* was just the scholarly confirmation of a new social reality that had displaced the old Aristotelian formations of Roman law.

This chapter of Villey's narrative evidently tells a different story than the one told in the corresponding chapter of Schmitt's narrative. Schmitt, we saw above, also considers the feuds and conflicts between medieval princes ways in which they vindicated rights claims. But unlike Villey, he does not consider this development a descent into chaos. He views it as the ongoing instantiation of the *nomos*, *Ortung* and *Ordnung* of the medieval *Jus Publicum Europaeum*. Schmitt makes passing reference to Hobbes' characterisation of late medieval Europe as a state of nature,[67] but this reference does not detain him for long, and surely does not prevent him from confidently affirming the enduring *nomos* of the *Jus Publicum Europaeum*. It is a mistake to talk about the anarchy of the Middle Ages, he insists – *es ist ein Irrtum von der Anarchie des Mittelalters zu sprechen*.[68] It would appear that Villey and Schmitt have decidedly different views of the instantiation and continuity of *nomos* and well-founded order during the Middle Ages. It is, however, not the first time in the history of European political thinking that one person's sense of good order differs fundamentally from that of another. The history of such deep perspectival differences regarding the prevalence or not of "good order" can be traced all the way back to Thucydides' portrayal of the discourse between Melos and Athenians. The differences between Schmitt's and Villey's discourses are nevertheless particularly intriguing for they derive from practically the same premises.

We return to medieval political and legal history in Chapter 5. We shall then explore evidence with reference to which one might determine which of these two discourses is the more accurate. The answer is nevertheless not that important. The long reflection on these two discourses in this and the previous chapter has already

66 Villey 2003, p. 262, cited in full towards the end of Chapter 5, at fn. 54.
67 Schmitt 1997, p. 65. Just here – on this briefly mentioned point regarding Hobbes – does his narrative regarding the *nomos* of medieval Europe concur with Villey's.
68 Ibid, p. 158.

been highly instructive. Both discourses provide a vivid record of the historical odds that any concern with the ideal of liberal democratic law has to face. It is the long shadow of Thucydides that evidently hangs over Schmitt and Villey, and also hangs over the long history of Western legal theoretical and philosophical attempts to come to terms with the relation between nature and law, and life and law. It is this long history to which we return once more in Chapter 5. Suffice it to observe now that it is to this long history – and this long shadow of Thucydides – that any historically convincing concept of liberal democratic law must answer. The task of articulating a historically convincing concept of liberal democratic law has up to now largely been avoided in favour of a-historical logical constructions of how democratic law works. The few pertinent clues that we have received in this regard from twentieth century jurisprudence – most notably from Hart and Kelsen – have largely remained misread. The last chapters of this book will endeavour to improve this record.

# 3

# *NOMOS* AND *PHYSIS*

## 1 Two conceptions of nature

The ancient and medieval narratives regarding *nomos* traced in Chapters 1 and 2 through the work of Villey and Schmitt tell the story of early European endeavours to come to terms with the irreducibly problematic relation between law and life. These endeavours, we saw, ultimately produced two concepts of nature, nature conceived as *kosmos* and nature conceived as *physis*. The former conception suggested law is founded on the good order of nature. Plato, Aristotle and Saint Thomas are principally associated with this position. According to the latter conception, law was an arbitrary outcome of clashes between physical forces. The Sophists in general, but also Heraclitus, Pindar and Thucydides can be considered exponents of this position.

Chapter 2 paid extensive attention to Carl Schmitt's narrative in *Der Nomos der Erde*. What makes this narrative especially interesting is its startlingly candid suggestion that the shift from a physicalist to a cosmological (or quasi-cosmological) conception of order is fundamentally dependent on a parasitic unburdening – *Entlastung* – of *nomos* that frees it sufficiently from *physis* for it to become *kosmos*, or something closely akin to *kosmos*. The setting free of *physis* on the other side of the amity line, suggests Schmitt, constituted an unburdening of *nomos* on this side of the line, and thus created a space that allowed for a stable sense of order on this side of the line. It allowed *nomos* to reflect an order that transcended human convention and intervention. It turned it into a register of the way things are, and should be, that is clearly distinguishable from any subjective imposition of order on things by means of positive legislation.

The significance of this argument concerns the insight that something must be done with *physis* to transform it into *nomos*. In Schmitt's portrayal of the *Jus Publicum Europaeum*, orderly physical contests between equal sovereigns through the mechanism of the just war were not only reconcilable with the profound order of this *Jus Publicum*, but also crucial to sustain it. This mechanism, however, could only perform this constitutive and sustaining role because the amity line consistently relieved it of the disorderly excesses – cruelty and lust for violence – of untempered and unrefined *physis*. This aspect of Schmitt's narrative reflects his clear sense that something must be done with *physis* before it becomes reconcilable with, and constitutive of, *nomos*. To put it in terms made salient by Giorgio Agamben: Something must be done to bare life – *zoē* – before civil life – *bios* – becomes possible.[1]

Both Schmitt and Agamben consider this fundamental act that makes civil life possible in structurally similar terms of export, exile or banishment. *Nomos* becomes possible on this side of the amity line, argues Schmitt, because of the way the line allows for an exportation of unconstrained physical conflict and violence to a far off region where it no longer matters. *Bios* becomes possible, according to Agamben, because the sovereign ban creates boundaries of civil life by sending bare life into exile. It banishes bare life to a zone of existence that is of no concern to civil life. What makes the cosmological visions of Aristotle and Saint Thomas so markedly *metaphysical* concerns the way in which they both make the transition from life to law and the transformation of *physis* into *nomos* too easy. They both make the metaphysical assumption that this transition and transformation is always and already in principle accomplished. They pay no attention to the fundamental constitutive act or decision that renders *physis* amenable to *nomos*. Plato can no longer be counted with them in this regard. The act of banning or banishment is written all over his unique brand of performative idealism. His is a different kind of metaphysics. If one were to refer to Aristotle's and Saint Thomas' metaphysics as a metaphysics of *integration*, Plato's would need to be called a metaphysics of *separation*.

As we shall see in Chapter 4, the metaphysical assumption through which Aristotle makes *physis* amenable to *nomos* pivots on the concepts of *dunamis, energeia* and *entelecheia* – potentiality, actuality and actualisation. According to Agamben, it is this conceptual constellation – or a misreading of it – that more or less dooms the whole history of Western political thought to a disastrous course of thinking that invariably fails to articulate and sustain a stable distinction between potentiality and actuality, and, thus, invariably fails to articulate and sustain a stable relation between life and law. The only exception to this constant failure of Western political thought, the only promise of a sustainable relation between potentiality and actuality, and between life and law, claims Agamben, is offered by Pauline theology. We turn to Agamben's response to Aristotle in Chapter 4. In the rest of this chapter we will take a closer look at the ways in which the two concepts of life and/or nature invoked, here, came to frame the metaphysical imagination of the Greeks.

## 2  An irreversible fall from innocence

How did these two concepts of nature and natural order come to compete in fifth century Greek society? And why would this initial competition between two concepts of natural justice become so fateful? Why did it bequeath to the Western imagination of justice a binary opposition from which it seems unable to escape?

---

1  See Agamben 1998, p. 8.

In his eighteenth century response to these questions, Jean Jacques Rousseau draws a distinction between the corrupted and uncorrupted state of nature, the former corresponding to *kosmos*, and the latter to *physis*.[2] Contemporary social science no longer gives much credence to "histories of the fall" that attribute the imperfections and woes of current societies to the loss of a true human nature that long ago allowed humans to live together in peace and harmony. The realistic acceptance that human societies have always had to contend with excessive levels of competition is more current today. From this more realistic perspective, the tensions that the Greeks experienced between conceptions of *nomos* and *physis* or *kosmos* and *physis* would probably need to be explained with reference to an observation that these concepts invariably compete in the minds of most human beings.

Few humans are impervious to the fascination with strength, superior intelligence and talent. Rousseau himself was no exception. If there ever was a time when humans were docile creatures who always cooperated and only aimed their spears to fend off the threats of ferocious animals,[3] he surely did not want to return to it. The allure of advanced culture was too strong. The task that he sets for himself in *The Social Contract*, we shall see in Chapter 6, is to articulate the principles of civil liberty – as opposed to natural liberty – that would allow societies to enjoy the full benefits and beauty of competitive freedom, without allowing this freedom to destroy the conditions of civil cooperation and order.

The ancient Greeks were very definitely not impervious to the beauty of strength, superior intelligence and talent. Excellence in competition and rivalry and the cruellest displays of this excellence played a significant role in their social and political imagination, long before the fifth century BCE. In fact, one may venture to consider the celebration of cruel excellence the only or dominant concern in the centuries that preceded the fifth. This is especially true of the time that is still known as the heroic period of ancient Greek history, the time of the great battles and adventures described in the Homeric epics (roughly associated with the seventh century BCE). However, during the sixth century, a transformation of Greek societies took place in the course of which the ethics and aesthetics of the warrior became increasingly displaced by an ethics and aesthetics of peaceful urban life.

It would not be wrong to invoke a certain fall from innocence in this regard, but the innocence of concern here is not that of the docile spear carrier that Rousseau seems to contemplate with his "noble savage." It is an innocence that regarded the most brutal and skilful launching of a spear at the throat or heart of an enemy with delight and admiration.[4] In the course of the sixth century transformation of the

---

2 Rousseau 1992, p. 254.

3 Ibid, pp. 176, 215.

4 Consider the visceral descriptions of brutal killing on the battlefield in Book V (Diomedes fights the Gods) of the *Iliad*. For those who have forgotten these descriptions, or who have never read them, here is a taste: "Meges the mighty spear man caught up with Pedaeus and struck him with his sharp lance on the nape of the neck. The point came through between his jaws and severed his tongue at the root. He fell down in the dust and bit the cold bronze with his teeth." See Homer 1950, V 65–95.

Greek ethos, however, two different ethics came to compete with one another, and it is this competition that henceforth rendered the festive indulgence in cruel excellence deeply problematic. The new ethic that gained ground in the sixth century put great emphasis on the merit of orderly civil relations and transactions that were perceived to cause no harm. For this new ethic, moderation was the key operative term, not excellence.

The crisis in late fifth century Athens was arguably the result of the failure of the Athenians to reconcile their disparate concerns with both moderation and excellence, *sophrosune* and *arete*, as Chapter 2 already noted with reference to Mac-intyre and Kitto. For a while at least, the Greeks, especially the Athenians, seemed to have found a way of reconciling these two very different forms of life. They could celebrate and exult in the excellence displayed in athletic competition. It is from this celebration of athletic excellence that we inherited the Olympic Games. They continued to admire the courage of their soldiers in battle, but took pride in the fact that they were not only soldiers, but also citizens who could savour the pleasures of urban and sedentary life.[5] And their poets could compete and excel in the cruellest beauty of artistic expression in ways that allowed citizens to taste this cruelty – indeed savour it and become drenched in it – without having to give vent to it in urban life. Athletics, war and poetry were the channels through which the Greeks effectively channelled the human yearning for extreme experiences of life into realms of existence that prevented this yearning from ruining the peaceful order of urban co-existence.[6] This was a crucial achievement, for this yearning always threatens established orders of institutionalised life with disaster.

Athletics and poetry routinely cleansed the Greeks of this yearning. In the case of poetry they called this cleansing catharsis. In other words, the Greeks found a way of "writing the disaster" or "staging a theatre of cruelty," to put it in terms Blanchot and Artaud would make salient in literary circles in the course of the twentieth century.[7] They wrote and staged the disaster in order not to literally live through it, and to cope with no longer being able to live through it as frequently as it was still possible to do in the time of Homer and the great warriors. To put it in terms that Castoriadis employs with regard to the tragic poets: The tragedies staged the primal chaos of the world – *[l]a tragédie affirme constamment, non pas d'une façon discursive ou raisonnante mais par la présentation de la chose, elle donne à voir à tous que l'être, c'est le chaos.*[8] Note, however, that the tragedies did not *represent* this chaos, but *presented* it. A presentation and not a representation is at stake here. The tragedies rendered present the primal chaos, present enough to be cured from the yearning for it, at least for a while.

The same must have applied to athletics, their great fictionalisation of war and battle.[9] The yearning to engage in battle – which is always pervasive enough to

---

5 See again Thucydides 1928, II 34–46.
6 See Huizinga 2016. I am most grateful to Jean-Marc Ceci for reminding me of this important text.
7 See Blanchot 1980, Artaud 1964, pp. 131–198.
8 Castoriadis 2008, p. 139.
9 Huizinga 2016, p. 102.

consider it a political predicament – concerns the yearning to *literally live or relive the disaster*. For the Greeks, athletics was another way of staging the disaster fictionally. It turned it into a literary or poetic experience of the limits of existence, the limits of existence that only battles of life and death would render tangible otherwise. Cutting anthropologies of athletics would most likely emphasize the surreptitious death drive – the drive to experience viscerally the very limits and ends of one's powers (that unleash the endorphins, the happiness hormones!) – that animates this manifestly beautiful celebration of bodily perfection. Athletics: Not quite living the disaster, but surely playing with it, coming close enough to it to sense its taste on the tongue and its brush on the skin.[10]

One should reflect carefully on the deeper reasons that persuaded Plato to banish the poets from his ideal state.[11] Perhaps he was well aware, beyond his manifest concern with poetry as flattery and seduction,[12] that poets are the ultimate warriors. They do not fight for just this or that cause, against this or that city. They engage in the most frightening of battles against urban order as such. Poetry, Paul Celan would write late in the twentieth century, is the endeavour to thrust language back into the absurdity from which it emerges, and to break through the confines of urban coinage.[13] Celan evidently articulated with this thought the obsession of the poet to break out of the flabby exchange of common persuasions and common places that is the very condition of urban order. He, too, was evidently contemplating a writing of the disaster.

What Plato did not seem to appreciate, however, is that it is precisely by keeping the poets in the city that one may effectively spare urban order some of the human being's mad and cruel obsession with disastrous absurdity. He did not comprehend that this mad obsession could inflame the tamed hearts of the most bourgeois of citizens, were it not to have its due day and time and place in the city. That is what the Greeks seemed to have grasped for a brief moment in the short history of *classical* Greek civilisation. They managed to prevent their citizen soldiers, to whom Pericles referred with conviction and praise, from hardening into mercenaries who constantly crave disaster in unmitigated fashion. They did so by including in the

---

10 See Brophy 1978 and Brophy and Brophy 1985 for illuminating evidence of the exposure of athletics to fatality in ancient Greece. Risk was a crucial element of the athletic contest. Without it, the athletic feat, however excellent, was devoid of honour among men and hollow ships, Pindar tells us in his sixth Olympian Ode – ἀκίνδυνοι δ' ἀρεταί οὔτε παρ' ἀνδράσιν οὔτε ἐν ναυσὶ κοίλαις. See Pindar 2012, O vi. 9–10. See also Gardiner 1930, p. 70. It is also important to note in this regard the nexus between some athletic contests and ancient forms of blood or human sacrifice (ritual murder). The link was especially clear in the case of the Funeral Games held in honour of the agrarian god Pelops. See Drees 1968, p. 30–31. It is here – in its relation to ancient concerns with sacrifice, however remote – that athletics also becomes manifest as a practice that, just like poetry, answers to the human being's apparent desire (or need) to sustain contact with the primal chaos of the universe.
11 See again Plato 1935, Book X 605e–607b (pp. 456–465) where Plato insists that poets should not be admitted to the well-ordered republic.
12 See in addition to the previous note also Plato 1925, pp. 464–466, 502.
13 See Celan 1983, p. 199: *das Gedicht wäre somit der Ort, wo alle Tropen und Metaphern ad absurdum geführt werden wollen.*

organisation of urban life a passion for poetry and athletics. Thus were their warriors able, for a brief moment in their history, to be poets when they were called to be poets, just like their poets became able warriors when called upon to defend their city. And, most important of all, they were also able not to confuse the one call with the other. Aeschylus was their walking example.

Was the ancient Greek passion for poetry and athletics the embodiment of something akin to the *Entlastung* function that Schmitt discerns in the amity line of the *Jus Publicum Europaeum*? Was it a way of containing excessive belligerence among the Greeks, at least for a while? If so, it surely constituted a mode of *Entlastung* or unburdening that a theory of liberal democracy could contemplate more comfortably as a constitutive element of liberal democratic law. The amity line that facilitated Schmitt's *Jus Publicum Europaeum* so brutally is something that liberal democracy surely cannot contemplate consciously as a condition of possibility. There is no point in cultivating a condition of possibility that renders the possibility contemplated pointless. But one could use Schmitt's insight to question liberal democracy's own conditions of possibility. Are the liberal democracies of our time not in fact relying on hidden amity lines that indeed render the whole project of liberal democracy pointless?[14] And if so, should they not explore the possibility of such hidden amity lines relentlessly, for the sake of replacing them with modes of unburdening such as poetry and athletics that are more reconcilable with the ideals of liberal democracy?

We return to these thoughts right at the end of this book. Suffice it now to just point out provisionally the crucial observation to which they will lead us: Liberal democracy may well be critically conditioned by cultural conditions that manage to keep soldiers away from cities. Schmitt's disturbing 1951 interpretation of the amity line as an unburdening of the *Jus Publicum Europaeum* also reflects this insight. As we saw in Chapter 2, he considers the amity line a crucial condition for keeping European warfare away from civil society. A European sovereign that emerged victoriously from just war with another European sovereign was prohibited from interfering with the system of private law rights of his vanquished opponent. The likelihood of any savage yearning to do so was lowered by the exportation of cruelty that the amity line rendered possible.

Keeping armies away from cities was a critical concern in ancient politics, as the ancient law prohibiting Roman generals from entering Italy with their armies underlined. It was this law that Julius Caesar decided to ignore when he crossed the Rubicon and triggered the chain of events that soon led to the end of republican and the beginning of imperial rule in Rome. In other words, Caesar's entry into Rome with an army of soldiers spelled the end of Roman democracy. Agamben's reflections on the purple toga of the Roman emperors as the symbol of the way in which military command – the togas of the Roman generals were purple – terminated republican politics in Rome are highly instructive in this regard.[15]

---

14  See Gündoğdu 2015 for a probing study into the ways in which contemporary human rights discourses give rise to new lines of exclusion, notwithstanding their normative claims to inclusiveness.
15  See Agamben 2011, pp. 177–178.

It is plausible to consider the capacity of soldiers to disarm and become citizens again when they approach the city – the very idea of a citizens' army, in other words – key to the democracies that Athens and Rome managed to cultivate and sustain for a while. Poetry and athletics may well have been the crucial cultural achievements with which they managed, for a brief moment in history, to prevent armed soldiers from entering the walls of their cities. The unique imagination that sustained this capacity did not last for long, though. Rome's failure to do so soon spelled the end of the Roman republic. Athens failure to keep soldiers out of the cities and to sustain their capacity to become citizens again when they returned from the front, became manifest during the Peloponnesian War.

The Greek Civil War may have been a war between cities, but it ultimately became a war against the very principle of the city, for it ended up disrespecting and destroying the urbane order that conditions the idea of the city and the citizen soldier. Thucydides' description of the Athenian destruction of the city of Melos underlines this, and it should not be forgotten that the destruction of Melos was also a reflection of the extent to which the merciless military and mercenary rhetoric of *physis* – the law of the strongest – had already displaced urban and urbane politics in Athens itself (see the discussion of Macintyre and Kitto in Chapter 2). The trajectory of Athens' demise may well have been a function of the tempo with which sound political debate gave way to practices of merciless mercenary persuasion towards the end of the fifth century. There must have been good reasons for an able and gifted philosopher such as Plato to select oratory as one of the main targets of his philosophical critique of politics. The theory of liberal democracy cannot learn much from Plato, but it can learn much from the circumstances that turned him into the opponent of democracy that he evidently was.

## 3 Antigone

Sophocles' tragedy *Antigone* has for a long time been considered a quasi-Platonic reprimand of sovereign action that violates the inviolable laws of God or nature. Generations of law students have been instructed by the idea that Antigone's resistance to Creon's decree must be understood as a reflection of Sophocles' conviction that the positive law of earthly sovereigns are subject to eternal principles of natural law. They have been taught that Antigone is "right" and Creon "wrong." We take a different instruction from Sophocles in this book. We shall read his *Antigone* as a statement that the right principle of government and law-making is invariably impossible to determine. In a 1955 lecture on the future of tragedy, most likely with Jean Anouilh's "modern Antigone" in mind, Albert Camus assessed the conflict between Creon and Antigone as follows: "Antigone is right, but Creon is not wrong."[16] Cornelius Castoriadis underlined Camus' insight in a 1983 seminar at the Collège de France with the observation that an understanding of Sophocles'

---

16  See Barbara Bray's introduction to Anouilh 2000, p. xlv.

*Antigone* that considers Antigone "right" and Creon simply "wrong" ignores exactly that which makes the work a tragedy and not an idiotic literary portrayal of a modern moralistic distinction between right and wrong – *[b]ien entendu, si Créon avait unilatéralement tort, one ne serait plus dans la tragédie, mais dans un univers de héros positifs et négatifs, c'est-à-dire, dans la stupidité moderne.*[17]

These observations of Camus and Castoriadis reflect their regard for the irreducible aporia that informs and conditions all conflicting appeals to justice. This is the first of two insights from Antigone's story that we shall salvage for the concept of liberal democratic law. We shall turn to the second presently. It is important to first consider Camus' reading of the *Antigone* more closely. Due recognition of the frequent if not constant impossibility of selecting the uniquely correct and just principle of law has all along been an invitation for non-normative conceptions of justice to dispense with the idea of the "right" principle of law and justice. This non-normative stance with regard to claims of justice is characteristic of a "realistic" tradition of political thought that is generally associated with Niccolò Machiavelli, Thomas Hobbes and Carl Schmitt, and can be traced all the way back to the ruthless manifestation of political realism that Thucydides attributed to the Athenian envoys to the island of Melos.[18]

For this realist tradition of political thought, the sovereign's will cannot be considered subject to any sovereignty-independent principle of justice. On the contrary, political realists typically insist that justice is conditioned by the superior power of the sovereign. They accordingly contend without any difficulty that there is no tension between the first, second and third statements of Ulpianus quoted in the Introduction above. Whatever justice is possible under whatever circumstances, they typically insist, is always conditioned by the scope and limits of sovereign power, that is, by the scope of what the sovereign is willing and able to do. The sovereign's freedom to change the law is accordingly also not limited or subordinate to "right reasons" that exist beyond the reach of the sovereign will. Neither is it subject to secondary "rules of change," as some liberal democrats would arguably want to maintain (see Introduction, Sections 1 and 2).

---

17  See Castoriadis 2008, p. 144. Castoriadis continues on the next page: "Si Créon était un monstre, il n'y aurait pas de tragédie, mais du Grand-Guignol. Sa décision est politique, elle repose sur des raisons extrêmement solides." As regards the common interpretation of the *Antigone* as the portrayal of a conflict between the laws of the city and the laws of the gods, and the old natural law argument that the former should yield to the latter, he points out that the protection of the city was no less a heavenly or religious duty than the duty to bury the dead. Creon's problem is that he is as fixated on his duty and his reasons for doing what he is doing, as Antigone is. The tragedy results from the inability of both to see beyond their own convictions. It is important to note that this understanding of Antigone and Creon as both significantly "right" and "wrong" can be traced all the way back to Hegel's reading of the tragedy as a conflict between two heroes who are both equally right and wrong – *beide [haben] gleiches Recht und . . . gleiches Unrecht*. See Hegel 1970, vol. 3, p. 539. For in-depth discussions of this "controversial" and even "scandalous" aspect of Hegel's reading of the Greek tragedies, see Menke 1996, pp. 79–82 and Schulte 1992, pp. 368–369.

18  This position has not received pervasive endorsement since World War II, but is still evident in Martin Loughlin's invocation of *droit politique*. See Loughlin 2010, pp. 396–402.

A reading of the *Antigone* that maintains that both Antigone and Creon are both "right" and "wrong" appears to endorse this realistic strand of political thought. It certainly underlines the insight that sovereignty concerns the capacity to decide matters under circumstances that do not afford any inference of a clearly correct answer. This does not mean, however, that Sophocles offered no critical comment on Creon's sovereign action. On the contrary, his *Antigone* is evidently a very critical engagement with both Creon's and Antigone's respective insistences that they are exclusively right. As such, it dissociates itself clearly from a realist conception that the sovereign cannot be judged. However, it does more than just this. It also dissociates itself from normative political stances that claim the ability to identify the "correctness" with which sovereign action must comply.

Liberal democrats have much to learn from Sophocles in this regard, provided they can avoid succumbing to Platonic interpretations of his *Antigone*. They can learn from the *Antigone* that circumstances may require and justify the imposition of one's opinion on others, but they never require or justify imposing one's sense of rightness on anyone. Of concern is again the programmatic statement spelled out more completely in the introduction above: *By all means believe that the principles and convictions by which you act are correct. You have to do so if you wish to be taken seriously. But do not succumb to the temptation to insist that those who evidently and adamantly disagree with your principles and convictions ultimately have good reasons to agree with you.* Castoriadis' observation regarding Creon (but it also applies to Antigone) goes to the heart of the matter: Even if you happen to be right about what you think is right, thinking only about your own sense of rightness already makes you wrong – *"[m]ême si l'on a raison, n'écouter que la raison qu'on a, c'est déjà avoir tort."* [19]

Whence the illiberal temptation to impose one's "sense of being right" on others who do not share this sense? And whence the concomitant temptation to think the "rightness" in which one believes can be realised through enforcement? An answer to these questions can be drawn from the second instruction that this book draws from Antigone's resistance to Creon's decree. This second lesson pivots on the observation that there is more to Antigone's resistance to Creon than just being "right." Antigone may be "right," or may have good reasons to feel she is right, but her course of action is not inspired by just this "sense of rightness". There is a surplus of "motive" that moves her, and that surplus can be described in terms of a pathos that is obscure and forceful enough to be deemed "pathological."

Antigone may well have a point that makes her "right." Yes, granted, *dike* (justice) demands that Polyneices be buried. However, Sophocles suggests clearly that Antigone is also moved by another impulse, a darker impulse. She is also moved by a "necrophiliac" or even "incestuous necrophiliac" obsession with her dead brother.[20]

---

19  2008, p. 145.
20  Castoriadis' assessment of Antigone's position also moves in this direction. He refers to her "bizarre" argument regarding her irreplaceable brother that turns her sense of duty to bury the dead into some pathological attachment to or passion for her dead brother – *"appelez-la incestueuse ou non"* – that fixates on his irreplaceability. See Castoriadis 2008, pp. 143–144. This assessment – originally

Had this dark impulse in her not been so forceful, she may well have understood that Creon needs to restore order in Thebes and that his excesses could be pardoned under the circumstances. This is all the more the case when one considers the fact that she has already "complied" with the rites of burial that the gods impose on her. She has already covered Polyneices' corpse with a layer of soil. Everything considered, she could reason in this level-headed fashion: "Well, I have buried Polyneices. The gods can surely see that I have done what I had to do. If there is someone who has to answer to them now, it is Creon, not me. He ordered the body to be uncovered again. It is he who must cover him up now, or take responsibility for not doing so."

Antigone's state of mind, however, is completely alien to this dispassionate juridical reasoning (this very modern mode of juridical reasoning, one must add). She is consumed by a passion that cannot be further away and more different from level-headed juridical reasoning. She is consumed by an obsession that no longer has anything to do with the quite correct and reasonable conviction that some rites of burial must be performed here, however imperfect they may have to be under these exceptional circumstances. Hers is a pathos that resists all forms of compromise that would allow the turmoil to stop and permit the restoration of civil order. What does liberal democracy stand to learn from this obsessed resistance to any compromise that may lead to the restoration of civil order? It can learn from it that resistance to civil order is not only the result of different conceptions of civil order that compete with one another. It is not only about the *Tragödie im Sittlichen* that Hegel identified in Sophocles' Antigone, that is, the fragmentation or splitting of the normative framework that underpins the common morality of the city.[21] It is not just about Creon's and Antigone's irreconcilable conceptions of what should be done to restore order in Thebes. It is not just about "her being right and him not wrong." At issue is not just an irresolvable epistemic and normative conflict. Antigone's obsession with her dead brother also signifies a melancholic (in the psychoanalytical sense of the term that denotes an obsessive "clinging to one's sense of loss") resistance to *any* return to order. In other words, it becomes a resistance to order as such. From a realistic conception of politics, "order as such" is nothing but a constellation of compromises. Such a constellation of compromises becomes possible because of the ability of everyone involved to let go of ultimate and "non-negotiable" convictions and to replace them with opinions amenable to compromise, however strong these opinions may be. Antigone cannot make this switch from conviction to opinion. Her melancholy prevents her from doing so.

Liberal democracy can learn from Antigone that moral conflict is not just about *differences of opinion*. It also concerns *differences of conviction* that are fatefully rooted in

---

articulated during a lecture at the Collège de France in 1983 – also corresponds with elements of Martha Nussbaum's analysis of Antigone's obsession. Nussbaum refers to Antigone's remarkable coldness towards the living – towards her husband, but also her sister – and her heated passion for the dead. See Nussbaum 1986, pp. 64–65.

21 See Hegel 1970, vol. 2, p. 495. For in-depth discussions of Hegel's concept of Greek tragedy and "the tragedy of the ethical" (*Tragödie im Sittlichen*), see Menke 1996 and Schulte 1992.

another difference that haunts the human psyche, namely, the irreducible difference between the infinite potentiality of symbolic ideals, and all actualisations of ideals that compromise with finite circumstances. It is this difference beyond difference of opinion – *une différence . . . par-delà celle des opinions* – to which Lefort alerts us in his essay on the permanence of the theologico-political (see Introduction, Section 3, as well as Chapter 6, Section 2). The conflict between Antigone and Creon becomes excessive because the concrete difference of conviction between them mutates into two uncompromising obsessions that unleash the full force of the respective ideals that motivate them. The force of neither of these ideals can be accommodated under the finite circumstances that call for action. Conflict inevitably becomes carnage when this happens.

This then is the second lesson that this book takes from the *Antigone*: Conflict invariably turns into carnage when it is fuelled by the desire or obsession to erase the distinction between the ideal and the real, or between *potentiality* and *actuality*, as we shall now also begin to refer to it. Liberal democracy is the organisation of political power that severs political differences from all conflicting convictions regarding proper relations between the real and the ideal. It is the organisation of political power that limits political differences to differences of opinion. And in doing so, we shall see, it is also the organisation of political power that severs political potentiality from political actuality. Liberal democracy thus conceived may well depend on the ability of political leaders to convince citizens to suspend all convictions for the sake of opinions that allow compromise. John Rawls came close to saying just this when he advised liberal leadership "to urge citizens not to ruin public reason" when public reason fails or frustrates their deeper convictions.[22]

## 4 Protagoras

The anti-Platonic reading of Sophocles' *Antigone* as an engagement with the tragedy that results from antagonists who both consider themselves exclusively right finds much resonance in the theoretical position associated with the fifth century Athenian sophist Protagoras. The characterisation of Protagoras as a Sophist is not unproblematic. The unique theoretical stance of Protagoras in the debates of his time demands a suspension of the standard sophist-philosopher opposition in the *nomos-physis* debate. Protagoras cannot simply be considered a Sophist who countered the *nomos* arguments of the philosophers with a simplistic *physis* argument. He was not one for simplistic oppositions. Diogenes Laertius referred to him as the one who insisted that on "every subject there are two *logoi* [arguments] opposed to one another."[23] It is this assessment of Protagoras' position that guides the portrayal of his thinking that follows. In comparison to his open argumentative approach to disputation, the philosophical insistence on "correct" arguments comes across as an

22 Rawls 1996, pp. 240–241.
23 Laertius 1925, p. 463.

unforgiving "Creon-like" approach to truth.[24] In other words, the philosophical concern with demonstrable "correctness" turns the concern with truth into yet another strategy of force and power – *physis* – as Nietzsche and Foucault would argue later. Thus do the tables get turned between the Sophists and philosophers in the *nomos-physis* debate in the case of Protagoras.

Protagoras is the one thinker of his time who avoided both the cosmological and the physiological naturalisation of politics respectively at work on the two sides of the *nomos-physis* debate.[25] Generally considered a Sophist, Protagoras typically stressed the importance of the skills of rhetoric and oratory in politics. However, his emphasis on the importance of rhetoric did not serve a mercenary pursuit of predefined ends for the sake of effective self-promotion. He was the one party in the philosophical debates of the time who squarely addressed the political crisis at hand without using it to his own advantage.[26]

As long as a society remains confident that its way of life is good and virtuous, it can comfortably assume that its traditional ways of doing correspond to the way things really are and should be. That is why it was possible for the Greeks, at least until well into the fifth century, to consider their long-established customs an ontological assessment of how things are. In other words, that is why it was possible for them to elevate the notion of *nomos* – which today would generally signify contingent conventionality – to *kosmos*, that is, to the eternal order of nature (see Chapter 2, Section 2). But the crisis that fifth century Athens came to face – the deep loss of confidence in the virtue that Pericles' *Funeral Oration* still invoked so confidently – changed this situation fundamentally. Aristotle more or less ignored the problem, as we shall soon see, but Protagoras already knew in the fifth century that it was no longer possible to elevate ancient custom to the natural order of things as Aristotle continued to do in the fourth. He knew that the time of self-evident equations of *nomos* and *kosmos* was evidently over.

The crisis that Protagoras perceived was *immense*. It confronted the Greeks with nothing less than the *immeasurable* as such, the immeasurability of existence. For

24 See the fine exposition of Thucydides' caution regarding the expedience and even murderous intolerance of philosophical argument, as opposed to the tolerance for many perspectives in rhetorical debate, in Boyarin 2012. For an earlier statement of a similar position, see Havelock 1957.

25 For the anti-naturalistic and humanistic (in the sense of accepting how limited human perspectives condition perception and understanding of things) purport of Protagoras' reliance on the myth of Epimetheus, see Kerferd 1953, and especially Versenyi 1962. Versenyi concludes his argument (p. 184) with the following statement: "It is Protagoras' historical position, i.e. that he radicalized and unified these views in the midst of and in opposition to natural philosophy's search for absolute, unchanging, universal first principles and substances, which gives his relativism the status of a much needed reform. While natural philosophy wanted – and thought itself capable of – getting away from what is merely human, relative, and conditioned, Protagoras in effect declared that this attempt is neither fruitful nor desirable. The world we live in and are able to know is the world of our relative, conditioned, human experience, and so instead of framing abstract hypotheses about the theoretical nature of the universe we had better return to everyday life and try to solve the problems that confront us here and now."

26 See for instance O'Sullivan 1995.

those thinkers courageous enough to face the bottomless void that opened up right in front of them, the Parmenidean faith in the unity of *logos* and existence (see Chapter 2 again) was simply shaken too deeply to continue as if nothing had happened. Plato reverted to the Parmenidean assertion of the unity of *logos* and *physis*, but could only do so by turning *physis* into *eidos*, that is, into a transcendent *idea* that has nothing to do with the realm of empirical reality, a realm that he dismissed as mere *doxa*, mere opinion. The task of the philosopher, Plato accordingly insisted, was to dedicate a lifetime of research into the true nature of things. Only thus – by finally attaining a wisdom that would allow comprehension and effective contemplation of the Idea of the good – could the mind – *nous* – become *one* with *physis* again. Plato articulated a dictatorial and totalitarian political philosophy from this idealist and transcendentalist position, but this philosophy evidently had little to offer in response to the political crisis that Athens was facing. Aristotle saw this and had the good common sense to bring philosophy back to earth, but he only managed to do so, it seems, by ignoring the depth of the crisis that precipitated Plato's flight from the world. He believed the crisis could be overcome. He believed *nomos* could again be elevated to *kosmos* by good educational practices that would firmly re-establish the virtues that conditioned orderly social and political existence. An awareness that the civil virtues of moderation had become deeply questionable and could not just be invoked again without offering cogent arguments as to how they might be restored convincingly, is not detectable in his texts.[27]

Protagoras –almost a century before Aristotle wrote the *Nicomachean Ethics* – evidently had little hope that the crucial elevation of *nomos* to *kosmos* that underpinned earlier Greek societies was still an option for fifth century Athens. On the contrary, the way in which *nomos* ended up being unmasked in his time (the way in which its cosmological pretensions became reduced to arbitrary convention), convinced him that *kosmos* was all along a product of *nomos* and that *nomos* could claim no independent anchorage in existence that would afford it self-evident validation. This was what Protagoras' *homo mensura* argument was ultimately about. The human being is the ultimate measure of all things (πάντων χρημάτων μέτρον ἄνθρωπον εἶναι), he claimed, of the existence of things that exist (τῶν μὲν ὄντων, ὡς ἔστι), as well as the non-existence of things that do not exist (τῶν δὲ μὴ ὄντων, ὡς οὐκ ἔστιν).[28] Humans decide the nature of the reality in which they live, and

---

27 See the reference to Macintyre's assessment of Aristotle's ethics in Chapter 1, fn. 13.

28 Diels 1912, II, p. 228. See also Plato 1921, 152a and Laertius 1925, IX 51 for two of the key quotations that preserved Protagoras' statement for posterity. The Diels version quoted in the text above is taken from Plato's *Theaetetus*. Diogenes Laertius' quotation differs only slightly, which is remarkable when one considers the history of the statement that Neumann points out below. No pretention is staged here that we know exactly what Protagoras meant to say with the statement. After thorough reflection on the long debates between philologists and historians of philosophy regarding the exact meaning of the statement, Alfred Neumann insisted in 1938 that the debate cannot be concluded and laid to rest. See Neumann 1938, p. 378. Not that the debate would stop after 1938 or cease to be meaningful, as Versenyi's 1962 contribution (see fn. 25 above) underlines. The two main hermeneutic questions regarding the fragment concern the meaning of the world ὡς (whether

they do so without access to any objective measure that would save them from arbitrariness.

However, Protagoras did not turn this insight into an argument for expediency and sheer self-promotion. He developed the *homo mensura* insight into an argument for democratic practices and a democratic ethic that would allow the citizens of a city to cope with the void which they cannot avoid facing every day.[29] The myth of *Epimetheus* to which he took recourse to argue his case for democracy – the myth which held that a sense of justice was given to all men so that they may live together peacefully – was not offered as an "answer" that filled the void.[30] Had he interpreted the myth to mean that the sense of justice inscribed in the hearts of humans could be invoked to restore *kosmos*, that is, to restore an objective – cosmological – criterion for proper civil relations, he would not have insisted that the opinions of all citizens had to be asked when important decisions were to be made. If he understood the myth to offer an "objective" or "substantive" answer to the question of justice, it would have sufficed to ask one or just a few citizens for their opinion – thus justifying a monarchy, oligarchy or aristocracy. But his insistence that every citizen should be consulted surely testifies to his conviction that a common measure was not given to humans, but had to be established between them through good political practices, practices in which rhetoric – the art of persuasion – indeed played a crucial role.

If this understanding of Protagoras' position is cogent, he surely comes across as an early forerunner of Claude Lefort. Lefort, we saw in the Introduction above, considered democracy the only arrangement of power that engages with the insight that politics is held in an opening that it does not create itself.[31] Politics proceeds from the opening up of a historical precipice from where it must leap. The precipice provides no measure, and fundamentally denies the possibility of measurement. The precipice of the political is the very experience of the immeasurable, and of

---

it meant "that" or "how") and whether ἄνθρωπον referred to the individual person (thus implying the statement represents a radical relativism and subjectivism) or human beings collectively (thus allowing for an interpretation of the statement as a "pragmatist" or "humanist" pursuit of the "good" through collective decision-making). The apology of Protagoras in Plato's *Theaetetus* provides good textual evidence for the pragmatist or humanist interpretation (at 166d: "whatever practices seem just and laudable to each city, are so for the city as long as it holds them"), but the *Theaetetus* can also be read to refer to both individual and collective convictions. In the dialogue *Protagoras*, Plato seems to be contemplating individual rather than collective perception. See Levi 1940 and Versenyi 1962, pp. 178–179. For more recent contributions to the debate, see Zilioli 2007 and Lee 2005. The uncertainty or ambiguity of the text will most likely never be fully resolved, considering that one has to rely on restatements of the *homo mensura* statement – with all the problems of *representation* and *re-presentation* attendant upon restatements – by Plato, Sextus Empiricus, Aristotle, Diogenes Laertes, and Cicero as one's sources, for Protagoras himself probably never penned down the statement in written form, as Neumann points out (at p. 378).

29  For a careful engagement with how Protagoras engaged with the two different meanings of *arete* (virtue) that competed with one another in his time – *arete* as competitive excellence and *arete* as excellence in civil cooperation – see Adkins 1973.

30  See Plato 1924, pp. 322–323.

31  See Lefort 1986a, pp. 287, 329.

irreducible incommensurability. Yet, it demands measurement. It demands that the human being brings measure to the immeasurable. This is the insight that Protagoras articulated with his *homo mensura* statement. In doing so, he resisted the two great naturalisations of the politics of his time, the physicalist and the cosmological. The theory of liberal democracy stands to gain much from him.

## 5 The poetic and the political

The link between Protagoras and Lefort proposed here may sound rather poetic. It may come across as a contemplation of a very "poetic politics." It is, however, the inverse of the poetic that is at stake in this Lefortian-Protagorasian understanding of the political. The fact that politics and poetry both rely on rhetoric and a creative employment of words does not make them the same thing, and it is important to understand the difference between them, and to understand how this difference is constitutive of both.

It was the achievement of the great poets of Greece – and also their task, we shall argue towards the end of this book – to expose the Greeks to the abyssal void from which all human concerns proceed. They took the Greeks back to this void so as to satisfy their appetite and yearning for it sufficiently to enable them to retreat from it again. And it is with this retreat from the void that politics begins, not from the yearning to enter or re-enter it, as Schmitt evidently thought.[32] Poetry – catastrophically cathartic poetry, as described with reference to Sophocles above – exposes the human being to the abyssal void from which the human world springs, as Castoriadis tells us. In doing so, it may just satisfy – there is of course no guarantee – the human appetite for this abyss sufficiently to also allow a retreat from it. It is for this reason that poetry is a crucial companion of the political (here lies Plato's biggest error). It should nevertheless not be confused with the political. The political begins with a careful retreat from the abyss. It thus moves exactly in the opposite direction than the direction in which great poetry moves.

Protagoras told the Greeks that the human being has no readily or constantly available measure at hand when the counter-poetical trajectory of politics begins. It has to find a measure, as good a measure as possible. It must do so in exchanges of argument in which as many voices as possible must partake. If the measure appeals to a good majority of the partakers as fitting enough, the procedure can be considered felicitous (its outcome not necessarily so). Nothing more should be expected. Pretensions of perfection – and thus of justice – are impermissible, for they belie the reality that the precipice of the political is an encounter with the immeasurable.

These are the instructions that the theory of liberal democratic law takes from Protagoras. It is the most enduring instruction that it takes from the Greeks. It is ironic but not surprising that the instruction should come from one considered a

32 See Preuss 1993, p. 133: "[Schmitt] ist einer der Intellektuellen, die sich theoretisch und praktisch von den Abgründigkeiten der Politik haben fesseln lassen und das in ihr enthaltene humane Rationalisierungspotential ausgeschlagen haben."

"Sophist," and not a philosopher. The philosophers, with the possible exception of Socrates and the pre-Socratic philosophers, have always shown themselves irremediably partial to the cosmological conception of measurable politics and measurable law. As we shall see in Chapter 4, Aristotle would take recourse to this cosmological faith again, hard on the heels of Protagoras. He would do so with recourse to confident notions of proportional justice, practical wisdom, due moderation and equity, none of which would have made any sense in the absence of an overarching organisational scheme of actuality, potentiality and teleological fulfilment. With this firm cosmological constellation firmly established, the critical questions of whether our "justice" is really "proportional," whether our pragmatism or practices are really wise and whether our moderation is really due and equitable, just could not strike him with the same force that it struck Protagoras.

Perhaps Aristotle just did not have the nerve to walk the tight rope between the political and the poetic that Protagoras and the great tragic poets had drawn tight for him. He could not accept that the little order that exists in the world is nothing more than the effect of a temporary triumph of one opinion over another. He preferred to ignore the bottomless chaos that always lurks under the frail fabric of civil order. It is to this tight rope – and its frail fabric of fragile threads – that the theory of liberal democratic law needs to return. Its task is to show how every legal rule and every legal decision subsumed under the notion of liberal democratic law traverse this tight rope and the abyss beneath it. This is the understanding of liberal democracy that will emerge from its distillation from Western metaphysics on which we have embarked. Let us now take an incisive look at the formidable cornerstone that Aristotle laid for this metaphysics. Let us take a good look, in other words, at the way in which Aristotle restored the language of secure foundations. As we shall see, he not only brought the West's understanding of politics back to earth after Plato's endeavour to secure it in a celestial sphere of pure ideas, as Raphaël's famous portrait of the two philosophers suggests. He also endeavoured to secure it in the very lay of the land and in the way things are.

# 4

# POTENTIALITY AND ACTUALITY

## 1 Aristotle's potentiality – actuality distinction

In a fine 1936 study on the way in which the pre-Socratic philosophers conceived of fate, good and evil, William Chase Greene observes:

> [I]t is a commonplace that both Plato, . . . mouth of Socrates, and Aristotle went out of their way to declare that the pre-Socratics had no real idea of causality. . . . What both Plato and Aristotle really mean . . . is that the forerunners of Socrates did not conceive of Nature as teleological, as Socrates and as they themselves did, and moreover that without such a conception (Aristotle's final cause) there is no room in the world for ethical distinctions. In terms of our problem, they attribute to the pre-Socratics a conception of Fate, but not of Good and Evil.[1]

Greene's observation is consistently confirmed in studies of the difference between the pre-and post-Socratic philosophers. The general consensus among scholars of ancient philosophy converges on the view that the pre-Socratic philosophers, most notably Heraclitus and Anaxagoras, had an impoverished understanding of causal relations according to which things came into existence and perished again as particular instances of matter, without ever manifesting enduring essences or lasting – not to mention eternal – forms that could be identified as underlying or final causes.[2] According to Aristotle, the causal developments contemplated by

---

1 Greene 1936, pp. 88–89.
2 Shorey 1922, p. 352. Shorey asserts that according to Aristotle, the pre-Socratics did not have any concept of qualitative change, genesis or coming into existence (at pp. 339–340). Solmsen (1960, p 21) refers to Plato and Aristotle's "rehabilitation of genesis" in this regard. Heidel 1910, pp. 95–96 writes: "There are, strictly speaking, only two periods in the history of occidental philosophy, the

the pre-Socratics manifested no more than an eternal "up and down" of which the only constancy was this blind change itself.[3] It is ultimately for purposes of reconceiving and transforming this blind change into qualitative change that Aristotle introduces the distinction between *potentiality* and *actuality* – ἡ δύναμις and ἡ ἐντελεχεία. Here is the key statement at the beginning of Book IX of the *Metaphysics*:

> And since the senses of being are analysable not only into substance or quality or quantity (ἐπεὶ δὲ λέγεται τὸ ὄν τὸ μὲν τὸ τὶ ἢ ποιὸν ἢ ποσόν), but also in accordance with potentiality and actuality and function (τὸ δὲ κατὰ δύναμιν καὶ ἐντελέχειαν καὶ κατὰ τὸ ἔργον), let us also gain a clear understanding [of] potentiality and actuality (διορίσωηεν καὶ περὶ δυνάμεως καὶ ἐντελεχείας . . .).[4]

Aristotle introduced this distinction within a framework of a teleological philosophy according to which everything was in a constant process of striving to realise its intrinsic end by moving from *potentiality* to *actuality*. The introduction of the word ἔργον – function or purpose – directly after ἐντελεχεία already alerts one to the essential link between actuality, purpose and end – τέλος – in his philosophy. Once should also note that the adjective τέλειος in ancient Greek denoted the state of being fully-grown, perfect or complete. Hence, then, the role of actualisation and the potentiality-actuality distinction in Aristotle's teleological metaphysics. It is the essential dynamic in the development that leads from the seed to the fully mature plant, from the infant and uneducated human individual to the politically conscious and articulate citizen, and, ultimately, to the philosopher as the highest end of human existence and of existence as such.[5] It is important to note, however, that Aristotle never uses the word τέλος or τέλειος in Books IX and XII of the *Metaphysics* where he discusses the relation between potentiality and actuality. He always uses either ἐντελεχεία or ἐνέργεια.

In his reading of Book IX of the *Metaphysics* in which Aristotle articulates the distinction between potentiality and actuality, John Watson understands Aristotle as

---

pre-Socratic and the Socratic. The first took external Nature as its point of departure, and fixed for all time the fundamental conceptions of physical processes. Even where it considered biological and intellectual processes, it started with mechanical notions and arrived in the end at materialistic conclusions. We may, if we choose, speak of the ethics or metaphysics of the pre-Socratics; but every careful student will be conscious of a fundamental difference. Socrates, by introducing the logical method of definition, based upon induction and employed in the interest of deduction, discovered a new order of existence, which was subject not to mechanical, but to teleological laws. Teleological facts were known from the beginning of time ... but teleology, considered as a method of explanation, was a discovery of the Socratics. ... Henceforth the world is definitively divided into two spheres, one subject to mechanical, the other subject to final, causes." Recognition of this discovery of qualitative change in Socratic philosophy abounds in the literature. See also, for instance, Lacey 1965.

3 See Chapter 2, fn. 43.

4 Aristotle 1933, IX I 1045b.

5 See Aristotle 1935, XII 1072b.

arguing against the Megarians that we "cannot deny the distinction of 'potential' and 'actual' reality without making the facts of experience inexplicable."[6] He then continues to explain the central role of the distinction in Aristotle's philosophy as follows.

> What Aristotle . . . is contending for, is that the transition from 'possibility' to 'actuality' must take place in certain fixed and unchanging ways, in which the true nature of the real is manifested. Thus we get, as the meaning of the 'potential,' the persistent tendency towards the 'actual.' The world is not a chaos but a cosmos, and there can be no cosmos, if reality is conceived as the infinite possibility of any actuality whatever. The acorn is the possibility of the oak, but not of the fir; the child is the possibility of the man, but not of the horse or dog; and so in all cases. We can thus understand why, in the case of 'natural' things, 'moving principle,' 'form,' and 'end' become identical. The principle which determines the transition from 'potentiality' to 'actuality' is the 'end' or determinate mode of 'actuality' which a thing is capable of becoming, i.e., its 'form;' and the 'end' is therefore involved in the 'potentiality.' The distinction and the correlation of 'potentiality' and 'actuality' is therefore a fundamental principle in the Aristotelian philosophy.[7]

Watson's explanation of the role of the potentiality/actuality distinction in Aristotle's "cosmological" theory of meaningful and orderly changes – in a world that, in the final analysis, remains fundamentally unchanging – goes to the heart of Aristotle's philosophy. It also reflects an accurate reading of Book IX of the *Metaphysics* in which Aristotle draws the distinction and expounds it at length. This is the essence of the ingenious metaphysical system with which Aristotle "saved the phenomena" from the pointless perishing to which the pre-Socratics condemned

---

6 Watson 1898, p. 338.
7 Watson 1898, p. 339. This concise and lucid statement of Aristotle's key metaphysical tenets provides an excellent summary statement of the main lines of thinking that can be traced in Books IX to XII of the *Metaphysics*. One should nevertheless remain cautious with regard to the simplification that it also brings about. Anyone who is reasonably familiar with Aristotle's work will know that such a clear picture is hardly forthcoming from the *Metaphysics* as a whole. This is not surprising in view of the challenges that the posthumous editing of Aristotle's writings on metaphysics had to overcome to forge out of them a relatively coherent text. Werner Jaeger's classic book on Aristotle provides one with profound insight into this editing process and the lack of systematic synthesis in which it culminated. The surviving texts with which the editors worked were the products of different phases of a long process in the course of which Aristotle, after having been a Platonist himself at first, slowly distanced himself from Plato and only eventually began to put forward views that were significantly independent and critical of Plato's position. See Jaeger 1948. Macintyre's association of Jaeger with the period of Aristotle scholarship that read a too clear opposition to Plato into his works before G. E. L. Owen commenced to highlight a much more complex relation between the two philosophers is not quite accurate. It was Owen who insisted on a clearer separation between Plato and Aristotle from the beginning, and who criticised Jaeger for considering Aristotle a mere disciple of Plato at first who only later developed critical independence from his master. See Macintyre 1988, p. 94 and Owen 1966, p. 128, 130, 150.

it.[8] It is important to grasp the Herculean task that the potentiality-actuality distinction performs in Aristotle's thinking. The whole weight of world order is made to rest on it. If the potentiality-actuality distinction is to carry this weight, it is crucial that it remains an adequate filter that prevents actuality from simply flooding into potentiality or vice versa. Another careful articulation of Watson shows clearly what is at stake here:

> Change, therefore, implies that there is some underlying basis, which persists in the change, or which is capable of existing in contrary states, though not at the same time. This underlying basis or "matter" is, therefore, the "permanent possibility" of contrary states. We can thus see that sensible things are necessarily finite or transitory, just because the mode in which they exist at any given time does not express all that is implied in them. The plant passes through a succession of states, but in no one of them is its whole nature realized; in each phase, only part of its reality is "actual," and, therefore, its "matter" and its "form," what it is "potentially" and what it is "actually," do not coincide.[9]

Aristotle insisted on this filter between actuality and potentiality, which allowed them to effect one another without changing into one another. This insistence informed his objections against the Megarian school of thought. According to Aristotle, the Megarians failed to recognise the actuality-potentiality distinction properly for reasons of not understanding that something had a potential even when that potential was latent and therefore not immediately evident. In other words, for the Megarians, potentiality was only observable when it was adequately actualised already, or in the process of being actualised. The importance of noting this critique of the Megarians here concerns the way it underlines a key difference between Aristotle and Protagoras. Aristotle expressly contends that the Megarians endorse Protagoras' *homo mensura* statement.[10] It is important to note this, for it also helps one to understand that it would not be accurate to consider Protagoras' concern with the civil education – which he sought to promote through teaching the art of rhetoric – as an actualisation of the potential of civic virtue.[11] In Protagoras' treatment of the Epimetheus myth, the partial vision of civic justice that individuals received from Epimetheus is not a natural potentiality that requires actualisation, but a post-natural remedy for a defect or lack.[12]

---

8  See, for instance, Shorey 1922, pp. 347–348, and especially this statement at p. 347: "This ingenious scheme saves the phenomena and explains the transmutation of all the elements into one another. . . ."

9  Watson 1898, p. 342. The caveat in fn. 7 again applies here.

10  Aristotle 1933, IX 1047a7.

11  Adolfo Levi does this quite literally. See Levi 1940, at p. 294: "Here we have a general outline of a theory of education and its elements, which are treated also in some Protagorian fragments. A state of pure *physis*, namely of a human nature which has not made its ethical potentialities actual, is a state of absence of morality, because it is only through society and its νόμος that they are revealed."

12  See Chapter 3, fn. 25.

As a fragment of knowledge, the partial insight into civil justice that the individual receives according to the myth is not a unique potential that can be fulfilled. What comes out of the civic process of communicating these partial insights for purposes of reaching a common measure is something different from any one of them. The process can therefore not be considered an actualisation of any specific potential. It is thus unlikely that Protagoras understood the civic realisation of virtue as an actualisation of potentiality, and it is definitely not how Aristotle understood Protagoras, as his critique of the Megarians makes clear. Aristotle considered the potentiality of beings a constant and repeatedly actualisable presence that secured the whole process of teleological development, irrespective of whether it is manifestly present or not. Protagoras' civic process of human measuring did not offer Aristotle the ontological security that he found in the potentiality-actuality distinction. The *homo mensura* statement made the human measure too hazardous, he must have thought, hence his express inclusion of Protagoras in his critique of the Megarians. It is on this point, we shall see later, that the concept of liberal democratic law that will emerge from this book sides with Protagoras and not with Aristotle. And it is precisely for this reason that the theory of liberal democracy should commence with a fundamental questioning of the tenability of the potentiality-actuality distinction in the concerns of law and politics. Giorgio Agamben's reflections on this distinction, and on the role it plays in the constitution of sovereignty, we shall soon see, offers the theory of liberal democracy a highly instructive lead in this regard.

Let us nevertheless first take stock of the gain Aristotle claims to make with the potentiality-actuality distinction. The teleological understanding of existence – both human and non-human – that it makes possible evidently communicates a conception of a *sustaining* flux in which all things find and re-find themselves at all times. One may want to attribute a profound restlessness to the totality of existence because of the constant state of flux – the unremitting pursuit of itself – to which Aristotle's teleological metaphysics appears to sentence it. This is nevertheless not how Aristotle saw the matter. It never occurred to him that the evident busyness of a universe in constant self-pursuit – that is, in constant pursuit of its intrinsic ends – could pose a threat to the overarching order – *kosmos* – in which everything ultimately comes to nest and rest in the end. Aristotle's world was never fundamentally at odds with itself. It rested in itself, despite its constant movement and therefore could not be conceived in terms of a relentless restlessness.

That this was indeed how he perceived things is evident from his conception of the mover of all things – the ultimate goal or *telos* of all things – that did not move itself.[13] For a metaphysical regard that stressed the pointless restlessness of existence, the very pointlessness of which conditioned its restlessness (considering that the slightest invocation of an overarching end necessarily begins to restore calm), one has to return to a time well before Aristotle, when thinkers such as Heraclitus and

13 Aristotle 1935, XI–XII.

Anaximander still considered the universe in terms of an endless and blind antago-nism – *polemos* – war – that has no identifiable end or orientation, either intrinsic or extrinsic to itself. Indeed, for Anaximander, justice – *dikē* – is ultimately nothing more than the serial termination of an endless sequence of injustices.[14] To be sure, the invocation of the word *dikē* or justice with regard to this blind process shows that the pre-Socratic philosophers commenced to perceive some "order" in it, or at least endeavoured to do so. They can and are in this sense duly regarded as the first "cosmologists."[15] But the "cosmos" they perceived in the physical processes of nature was rudimentary. It pivoted on the idea of a bare equilibrium that prevailed against a backdrop of relentless evanescence. This understanding of justice as bare equilibrium evidently had no lasting repose on offer. The Greeks had to wait for the Stagarite to show them the picture of a calmer universe before the word "jus-tice" could begin to signify the governmental sustenance of enduring relationships between citizens that duly recognised their respective merits. It is only in such a world that Aristotle could confidently put forward his distinctions between general and specific justice, distributive and restorative justice, equity, due moderation and practical wisdom.

This staggeringly ingenious philosophical scheme can be considered an endeav-our to lay to rest again the world of the Greeks that appeared to have lost its equi-librium towards the end of the fifth century. From the perspective of this scheme, the *physis* argument of the Sophists may well have come across as a throwback to the time of the pre-Socratic philosophers, a time during which the fleeting evanescence of all things, weak and strong, was the only constancy perceivable in an elementary and endless antagonism. Expiry was the only enduring relief this universe offered, and it may also for this reason have earned the name justice – *dikē* – for itself. Aristotle may well have considered the Sophists advocates for the return to this pre-Socratic world, this world in which the elements just burned off and allowed nothing to anticipate or pursue, let alone attain, fruition. Again, he countered this advocacy with profound and unparalleled ingenuity that eventually came to sustain more than two millennia of metaphysics and metaphysical political theory. And the essence of his ingenious resistance to the return of the pre-Socratic

---

14 See Heraclitus, Fragment 53 and Anaximander, Fragment 9 in Diels 1912, I, pp. 15, 88. Fragment 53 contains Heraclitus' famous statement about war as the father and king (of all things who points out some to be gods and others to be men, and who makes some slaves and others free – Πόλεμος πάντων μὲν πατήρ ἐστι, πάντων δὲ βασιλεύς, καὶ τοὺς μὲν θεοὺς ἔδειξε τοὺς δὲ ἀνθρώπους. τοὺς μὲν δούλους ἐποίσε τοὺς δὲ ἐλευθέρους. Fragment 9 contains Anaximander's statement about the infinite as the origin of all things from which they are born and into which they die again accord-ing to necessity, because they pay to one another the penalty and receive the punishment for their injustice in the order of time – καὶ μαθητὴς ἀρχήν τε καὶ στοιχεῖον εἴρηκε τῶν ὄντων τὸ ἄπειρον, πρῶτος τοῦτο τοὔνομα κομίσας τῆς ἀρχῆς. λέγει δ' αὐτὴν μήτε ὕδωρ μήτε ἄλλο τι τῶν καλουμένων εἶναι στοιχείων, ἀλλ᾽ ἑτέραν τινὰ φύσιν ἄπειρον ἐξ ἧς ἅπαντας γίνεσθαι τοὺς οὐρανοὺς καὶ τοὺς ἐν αὐτοῖς κόσμους ἐξ ὧν δὲ ἡ γένεσίς ἐστι τοῖς οὖσι, καὶ τὴν φθορὰν εἰς ταῦτα γίνεσθαι κατὰ τὸ χρεών. διδόναι γὰρ αὐτὰ δίκην καὶ τίσιν ἀλλήλοις τῆς ἀδικίας κατὰ τὴν ἢ τοῦ χρόνου τάξιν.…
15 See the assessment of the pre-Socratic philosophers as the discoverers of the cosmos – in Jaeger 1936, pp. 206–248.

world was to consider this world doomed to a perennial potentiality incapable of actualisation – "ἦν ὁμοῦ πάντα δυνάμει, ἐνεργείᾳ δ' οὔ."[16]

In the end, however, Aristotle's ingenuity neither halted the politics of pointless perishing, nor escaped its own evanescence. Having already disappeared twice from the terrestrial register of philosophy, once in the fifth century, and once again in the fourteenth after a brief revival in the twelfth, the twentieth century finally came to destroy the foundations of Aristotle's ontological scheme. The twentieth century – the most murderous in the history of mankind[17] – destroyed all realistic hope that the world will ever appear amenable again to visions of stable and meaningful rhythms of genesis, fruition and repose. And today, this no longer applies only to the vicissitudes of political environments that never quite lived up to this three step rhythm. The human being's natural environment now also appears to have fallen badly out of step and threatens to do catastrophically worse. The teleological waltz of the world finally appears wastefully broken on both fronts.[18] If ever there was a time in which politics had to recognise that it is not rooted in nature, that it is, in fact, a non-natural or indeed *unnatural* endeavour that has nothing to do with the actualisation of potentialities, it is now.

Athens is standing at the gates of Mytilene and Melos again, but with the consequences of the decisions that stand to be taken apocalyptically exponentialised. The questions that the human race is facing today will have to be decided without anyone being able to stage cogent philosophical or scientific claims regarding the "good life." The essential condition that underpins the notion of the good life, Aristotle's potentiality-actuality distinction, has unravelled so obviously that only those who opt for a veritable state of denial can deny this epochal unravelling with conviction. Let us take a closer look now at this unravelling and at the reasons why it was destined from the start to happen sooner or later.

## 2 The unravelling of the potentiality-actuality distinction

It was already clear from Watson's invocation of the "non-coincidence" of potentiality and actuality that something very enigmatic and precarious is at stake in this "non-coincidence." The non-coincidence of concern here is not like the non-coincidence evident in the distinction between, say, a cat and a dog. There is "mammalness" in both, but absolutely no incidence of "catness" in "dog" or "dogness" in "cat." The same cannot be said about the distinction between potentiality and actuality. In the way Aristotle draws the distinction, actuality must at least be partly operative and present in potentiality for potentiality to be the potentiality for some

16 Aristotle 1935, XII, 1069b.
17 This remains the case, I believe, notwithstanding Steven Pinker's attempt to deny this with references to "lower averages", so to speak. See Pinker 2012, p. 233.
18 These idioms are taken – with some slippage between waist and waste – from Federico García Lorca's *Little Viennese Waltz* and Leonard Cohen's interpretation of it in 'This waltz', from the album *I'm Your Man* 1988.

kind of future actualisation. The non-coincidence between potentiality and actuality that is at stake for Aristotle must therefore be a partial non-coincidence. It concerns, in fact, only the moment of "pure actuality" in which potentiality no longer plays any role in the ontological condition of some instance of existence. For the rest, there must be some overlap between actuality and potentiality. The precariousness of this whole metaphysical undertaking concerns the instability of the distinction that results from this overlap.

The problem exists for Aristotle in a way it does not for Plato. Plato effects a complete separation of potentiality and actuality by means of his categorical distinction between the phenomenal and the ideal, *doxa* and *eidos*. We need not go into the problems Plato created for himself with this strict separation of potentiality and actuality, but it is worthwhile noting that they all converge on the question of the relevance of the phenomenal world in his philosophical or metaphysical project, or rather, the relevance of his philosophical and metaphysical project for the phenomenal world. How the two worlds are to relate and communicate with one another across the divide that results from this rigorous dualism was the key question Aristotle put to Plato.[19] But, by posing this question, and by ultimately finding an answer to it through recourse to the conception of a teleologically organised universe, Aristotle created a different set of problems for himself. These problems concern the stability of the potentiality-actuality distinction and the possibility of assessing the level of transcendent truth or actualisation that the phenomenal world, or any element of it, can claim to embody. Aristotle's problem results from his ambitious wish to have his piece of heavenly Platonic cake while making a sumptuous banquet out of it on Earth.

The enigma and precariousness that result from this ingenious metaphysical endeavour concern the conceptual coherence and accuracy that the potentiality-actuality distinction requires to serve as a criterion of meaningful classification. Aristotle's metaphysics does not concern a simple descent from the ideal to the phenomenal world. It pivots on an importation of the ideal into the phenomenal world that turns the latter into a mix of ideality and phenomenality within which the ideal and the phenomenal elements can no longer be distinguished and identified. Under these circumstances, the distinction between potentiality and actuality simply does not enjoy the self-evidence that Aristotle attributes to it. This is true with regard to both "fronts" invoked above, that is, both the natural and political environment.

A moment of careful reflection almost immediately leads one to conclude that the identification of the merely potential *phases* and the fully actualised *forms* of

---

19 See Aristotle 1933, I, 991a–991b. This key passage contains Aristotle's crucial question to Plato regarding the relation between the ideas and the phenomenal world. Plato avers that the ideas are the substances that cause the existence of all things in the physical or phenomenal world, says Aristotle, but he offers no explanation – no principle of generative movement – as to how the ideas, which exist in a separate sphere, generate the phenomenal world – καίτοι τῶν εἰδῶν ὄντων ὅμως οὐ γίγνεται τὰ μετέχοντα ἂν μὴ ᾖ τὸ κινῆσον.

the natural world is a thoroughly arbitrary exercise. Why would one consider the acorn the potentiality of the majestic oak, instead of the oak the potential of the acorn? The question would appear unanswerable without selecting some or other extrinsic consideration from an infinite range of such considerations. Suppose we assume the majestic oak full of well-formed and ripened acorns is the full actualisation of this particular plant species because it represents its full life cycle. Would this assumption necessarily be uniquely correct? Not quite. There is nothing disturbingly counter-intuitive about a number of alternative assumptions. One could also assume that the life cycle of the species is only fully actualised when a fallen acorn has germinated and has turned into a healthy sapling as yet untouched by adverse environmental conditions. Who knows, those acorns hanging from the beautiful old oak may just be worm-infested and incapable of germination. Or the acorns may be fine but the tree itself may show signs of periodic droughts that stinted growth some years, etc. We can continue like this, but it is not necessary. It is evident enough that it is impossible to single out the unique moment that any empirical tree is fully actualised. And, if we infer too glibly from this impossibility that actualisation only concerns the comprehensive idea of the full presence of the specimen of concern, then we evidently slip back into Platonic idealism. This is the difficulty from which Aristotle's metaphysical taxonomy – straddling as it does Plato's ideal and phenomenal world – cannot escape.

However, the predicament of coherent conceptual classification is aggravated exponentially in the context of politics, given that this context is burdened with the additional factor of arbitrary intervention. The growth of an oak tree generally takes place independently of human intervention (ignoring for the moment that this is not quite true either, considering that biological technologies, enhanced cultivation practices and common pollution invariably alter "natural" growth cycles incisively enough to raise ethical and political questions), but political and social "growth" is predominantly the result of arbitrary intervention. Categorical classifications of actuality and potentiality are therefore significantly less possible and plausible in the sphere of politics and society than they are in the natural environment. The resolution of this problem was of course the very aim of Aristotle's naturalisation of politics. This naturalisation allowed him to invoke ideas of natural law and natural virtues that rendered human potentiality as classifiable as any other natural potentiality, or at least similarly so.

Historical processes and developments, however, are invariably processes of denaturalisation. They expose the arbitrary and non-natural status of all attempts at – or pretensions to – naturalisation. History invariably unmasks all naturalisation as false or pseudo-naturalisation. Claims to naturalisation only endure as long as history can be ignored or denied, and it was the fate of the Aristotelian worldview to be succeeded by successive epochs of increasing historicisation. The Christian age that followed in the wake of Greek and Roman antiquity consciously considered itself an age of historical consciousness. Up to the end of the Middle Ages, this historical consciousness was still rooted in Saint Augustine's grand narrative of creation, sin, judgement and redemption (see Chapter 1). The historical consciousness of the Modern Age, however, was rooted in the idea of freedom from nature and natural constraints. Aristotle's naturalistic view of the world was still reconcilable with the Christian idea of history, for this idea of history still accommodated nature as a set of secondary causes that remain relatively stable, as Saint Thomas argued (see Chapter 1), and its grand narrative itself still retained elements of eschatological fruition and actualisation. The self-understanding of Modernity, however, came to pivot on the conception of freedom as the overcoming of natural constraints. Hobbes' understanding of civil order as an exit from the state of nature and Kant's conception of morality as the overcoming of natural inclination underlined this new understanding of history and freedom, and history as freedom, unequivocally.

Modern science again came to understand nature in terms of symbolically unconstrained concatenations of elementary forces, and not in terms of the actualisation of natural essences or forms, as Aristotle did. It considered the natural environment, as it exists at any particular moment in time, the outcome of physical forces held in check only by other such forces. This modern understanding of nature is in significant respects not fundamentally different from the physicalist conception of nature of the pre-Socratic philosophers that Aristotle endeavoured to replace with his teleological cosmology. And, as in the case of the pre-Socratics, this modern conception of nature as anarchic *physis* again came to serve as a foundational framework for a naturalised conception of anarchical politics. We return to this physicalist – as opposed to cosmological – naturalisation of modern politics towards the end of Chapter 5. It is nevertheless important to note now that it is this physicalist naturalisation of politics that ultimately informs the reconstruction of Aristotle's potentiality-actuality distinction that is evident in key texts of the Italian philosopher Giorgio Agamben. It is to this reconstruction that we now turn.

## 3  Agamben's Pauline reconstruction of the potentiality-actuality distinction

Giorgio Agamben articulated an enigmatic call for a radical rethinking of Aristotle's potentiality-actuality distinction in the following passage from *Homo Sacer*:

> Only an entirely new conjunction of possibility and reality, contingency and necessity, and the other *pathē tou ontos*, will make it possible to cut the knot that binds sovereignty to constituting power. And only if it is possible to think the relation between potentiality and actuality differently – and even to think beyond this relation – will it be possible to think a constituting power wholly released from the sovereign ban. Until a new and coherent ontology of potentiality (beyond the steps that have made in this direction by Spinoza, Schelling, Nietzsche, and Heidegger) has replaced the ontology founded on the primacy of actuality and its relation to potentiality, a political theory freed from the aporias of sovereignty remains unthinkable.[20]

20  Agamben 1998, p. 44.

We shall restrict our engagement with this dense passage to three of the statements it makes. The first concerns the need to think about potentiality and actuality differently. The second concerns the need to find or develop a new ontology of potentiality that can replace the ontology founded on the primacy of actuality and its relation to potentiality. The second must be considered a specification of the first and they will be addressed together. The third concerns the claim that, as long as we cannot manage to rethink the relation of actuality to potentiality in the way contemplated in the first two statements, "a political theory freed from the aporias of sovereignty will remain unthinkable." This third statement will also be considered a restatement of the reference to "cut[ting] the knot that binds sovereignty to constituting power" in the second line. Any attempt to get to the bottom of the other dense lines in this passage – notably the references to Schelling, Nietzsche and Heidegger – will lead us too far away from our immediate concern with Agamben's reconstruction or rethinking of the actuality-potentiality distinction. We shall therefore only concern ourselves with two questions in what follows: 1) How does Agamben reconstruct the actuality-potentiality distinction? 2) How might this reconstruction free us from the aporias of sovereignty and cut the link between sovereignty and constituting power? The first question will be addressed in the remainder of this last section of Chapter 4. The second will be addressed in the first section of Chapter 5.

Agamben's reconstruction of Aristotle's potentiality-actuality distinction finds its most incisive expression in his book *The Time that Remains*. This is so notwithstanding the fact that an express engagement with Aristotle's actuality-potentiality occurs only twice in the text, and very briefly at that.[21] The main focus of the book and the central thought that runs through it (the messianic suspension of the law) must nevertheless be understood in terms of the definitive "weakness" or "lack" (which distinguishes potentiality from actuality) that deprives the law of actualization and renders it "inoperative."[22]

The essential move that Agamben makes in this book consists of turning away from Greek metaphysics and turning towards Saint Paul's Judaic messianic thinking. The move consists of turning to a very Jewish Saint Paul, the Saint Paul who "[wrote in Greek, but thought in Yiddish]."[23] The title of the book clearly announces the key thought it pursues. At issue in the book is an incisive and extensive reading of Saint Paul's instruction to the early Christian communities to live through the rest of the time on Earth in constant anticipation of the return of Christ and of God's final judgement. The instruction encourages the Christian communities (*ecclesia*) not to make themselves at home in this world. This world is nothing but a passing phase of existence and the only meaning that can be attributed to it is to consider it nothing more than a time of anticipation and preparation. Christians are called to live on in *the time that remains* as if they are no longer living in this world, but

21 See Agamben 2005b, p. 65, 136–137.
22 See ibid, 136–137. For a more express and extended engagement with this distinctive lack or weakness of potentiality, see Agamben 1999, pp. 185–204.
23 Agamben 2005b, 3–4.

are already in the world to come. And this instruction takes specific issue with the question of the role that the law must play in their lives. Saint Paul instructs the Christians to live under the law as if not (*hōs mē*) under the law. In other words, the law as it manifests itself in this world should not be considered the law of God.

Considered against the background of the need for "a new and coherent ontology of potentiality" that Agamben articulates in *Homo Sacer*, the significance of the thoughts that he develops in *The Time that Remains* is this: For the Christian, this world is no more than an anticipation of the glory of God that will be revealed at the end of time, and it will never be anything but this anticipation. The Christian can also not do anything to realise the glory of God in this world and should not attempt to do so. Christ will come in his own time. God will reveal his final plan with the universe in his own time. Christian faith stoically resigns itself to the reality that this world is not *the* world.

The early Christians were indeed deeply influenced by Stoic thinking.[24] And through this Stoic mind-set, they managed to stabilise the relation between potentiality and actuality by clearly separating the one from the other. This world is but the potentiality of the actuality of God's will, and humans can not intervene to precipitate the transition from potentiality to actuality. This also means that the law as it manifests itself on Earth – the positive law enacted by earthly sovereigns – should in no way be confused with the actualisation of God's will. Christians must live under this law as if not (*hōs mē*) under the law. Agamben nevertheless clearly suggests that the essential thoughts at stake here resulted from the Jewish messianism that formed his thinking, rather than any Hellenic influences. It is therefore important to note that the Aristotelian terms in which we have cast this messianism here are fundamentally foreign to it.

The law of the earthly sovereign – the emperor – is not the actualisation of the law of God. Saint Paul famously instructed the Christians in Rome to obey the emperor's law and to consider it part of God's plan. He nevertheless also instructed them to consider it nothing more than a provisional arrangement that God will terminate in his own time. The Christian community should therefore not rebel against the law in the hope of making it conform to God's will and the demands of His justice. It should simply live under it as if it is not the law. One can already sense how these messianic thoughts answer Agamben's call in *Homo Sacer* to separate potentiality from actuality in a way that may free "political theory . . . from the aporias of sovereignty" and "disconnect the idea of law from the idea of Being." However, the full significance of this turn to the Yiddish Saint Paul in *The Time that Remains* will only come to the fore after a proper engagement with the second question that we extracted from the dense passage from *Homo Sacer* quoted above: How might this messianic reconstruction of Aristotle's actuality-potentiality distinction free us from the aporias of sovereignty and cut the link between sovereignty and constituting power? It is to this question that the engagement with Agamben's *State of Exception* in Chapter 8 will now respond.

---

24  See Everett 2003, p. 368.

# 5

# *AUCTORITAS* AND *POTESTAS*

## 1 The state or exception

The themes that Agamben elaborates in *State of Exception* relate directly to the key concepts of *abandonment* and the *ban* that he develops in *Homo Sacer*. It is indeed crucial to understand the continuity between these two works. *Homo Sacer* is already squarely concerned with the state of exception and it is precisely with reference to the state of exception that it elaborates the relation between sovereignty and the *ban*. The first part of *Homo Sacer* explains the concept of sovereignty in terms of the sovereign power to create and sustain a civil sphere through excluding from this civil sphere – *banning* from the civil sphere – instances of life that then, through this exclusion or *banning*, become bare life. Sovereignty, in other words, is the capacity to establish a realm of civil life, also called *bios* by the Greeks, by excluding from it bare life, that which the Greeks called *zoē*. The sovereign establishes the civil sphere by abandoning bare life and banning it from the civil sphere.

Agamben's explanation of sovereignty hinges on the idea that the protection of life in the civil sphere – through law and the recognition of legal rights – only becomes possible in the wake of a sovereign decision that draws a line between life that is protected by law, and life that is not so protected. It is for this reason that he identifies *homo sacer* – the figure in Roman law who could be killed without recourse to legal sanction[1] – as a telling instantiation of the sovereign distinction between life and bare life. Only by banning some life – indeed *sacred life* – from the legal protection of civil life can the sovereign guarantee a sphere of life that will be protected by law. Seen from this perspective, the humanistic idea (central to a pervasive understanding of human rights today) that human life is always protected by law is spurious.[2] The right to life, the right to the legal protection of life, pivots on a

---

1 Agamben 1998, pp. 71–74.
2 See Chapter 3, fn. 14.

crucial exception, a crucial exception (and exclusion) of some life from the right to life. It is important to also note here Agamben's express observation in *Homo Sacer* that this sovereign exception of some life from the protection of life is an enduring feature of the sovereign power that constitutes and sustains a legal order. It does not concern a specific period or a one-off event that constitutes civil order once and for all for as long as that sovereignty endures. It concerns the essential operation at work in the ongoing process of constituting and sustaining civil order.[3]

Agamben's explanation of the sovereign ban in *Homo Sacer* is key to his analysis of the Roman law conception of the state of exception in *State of Exception*.[4] This is particularly the case in the pivotal passage in *State of Exception* in which he assesses the Roman law distinction between *auctoritas* and *potestas* – and the institution of the *senatus consultum ultimum* that turned on this distinction – as the Greco-Roman fiction with which the Romans navigated the precarious link between law and life.[5] The distinction between *auctoritas* and *potestas* demarcated the spheres of legitimate action of the Roman senators, on the one hand, and the magistrates on the other. *Auctoritas* denoted the governmental authority of the senators. *Potestas* denoted the governmental power of the magistrates. *Potestas* was constrained by the limits of existing law. It was defined by law. The magistrates were not allowed to take any action for which there was no clear legal provision. *Auctoritas*, on the other hand, could not be defined by law. It concerned an extra-legal governmental authority which could be invoked to deal with governmental needs for which the law made no provision. When circumstances appeared to demand governmental action for which the law did not allow, the magistrates first had to consult and obtain the *auctoritas* of the senate. The senate would then issue an opinion – a *senatus consultum* – that would either allow or disallow the course of action which the magistrates deemed necessary. In cases of social unrest that threatened the breakdown of civil order, the magistrates could ask the senate to issue a *senatus consultum ultimum* that declared a *tumultus* and therefore a *iustitium* (suspension of law). Only once the *iustitium* had been properly declared by the senate could the magistrates proceed to restore law and order through recourse to emergency powers for which normal law did not allow.

This is the way, avers Agamben, in which the Romans navigated the link between life and law.[6] This contention must be understood against the background of the sovereign ban analysed in *Homo Sacer*. The precarious link between life and law invoked in *State of Exception* concerns the distinction that *Homer Sacer* draws between bare life and civil life. The distinction between *auctoritas* and *potestas* and the institution of the *senatus consultum*, contends Agamben, is a reflection of the Greco-Roman insistence on the two phases through which all political action should pass in order to accomplish and sustain an effective transition from life to law, or bare life to civil life. When this process of political creation collapses into

---

3  Agamben 1998, p. 36.
4  Agamben 2005a.
5  Ibid, p. 73.
6  Ibid, pp. 84–86.

one single sweep of action, something that happens when *auctoritas* and *potestas* are consolidated in one and the same person, as they were in the case of the totalitarian political systems of the twentieth century, the result is a killing machine.[7] The relation between law and life then becomes murderous.

It is important to note now that the distinction between the *potestas* of the magistrates and the *auctoritas* of the senate that Agamben elaborates in *States of Exception* are features of the Roman Republican framework of government that came to an end when Augustus was crowned as the first emperor of Rome in 27 BCE. From then on, a new framework of law-making prevailed in Europe for almost two millennia before it commenced to give way to the transition from imperial to democratic government from the end of the eighteenth century onwards. In the course of this long history of imperial or monarchical rule, the political imagination of Europe attempted to reinstate the separation of *auctoritas* and *potestas* in a number of different ways. We turn to more details of this history in the next two sections of this chapter. Suffice it to observe, however, that the clear distinction between sovereignty and law that appeared to allow for two separate and distinct phases of political action during the time of the Roman Republic, at least according to Agamben, was displaced for a long time in Europe by conceptual theories of imperial and monarchical rule that left the distinctions between sovereignty and law, and *auctoritas* and *potestas*, less clear and institutionally significantly less stable.

The main reason for this lack of clarity and institutional instability was the almost constant endeavour during this time to unite *auctoritas* and *potestas* in one person. As we shall see in the next section of this chapter, *auctoritas* and *potestas* came to be united in the person of the Roman emperor, and later in the kings of Europe, after the demise of republican rule in Rome in the last decades before the birth of Christ. The problem of the unification of *auctoritas* and *potestas* with reference to which Agamben explains the murderousness of twentieth century totalitarian regimes, was therefore not unique to the disastrous beginning of the twentieth century. By that time, it had already been haunting Europe for more or less two millennia. As will also become clear below, all the theoretical and theological endeavours in imperial Rome and medieval Europe to restore the distinction between *auctoritas* and *potestas* remained highly precarious as long as the key figure of the emperor or monarch dominated political imagination.

Should one then consider the Roman Republic an instantiation – or a significant precursor – of the "coherent ontology of potentiality" that successfully avoided the "primacy of actuality," and thus prevented potentiality from turning into actuality, to which Agamben alludes in the passage from *Homo Sacer* cited in Chapter 4? Did the Roman Republic manage to avoid the "aporias of sovereignty"?[8] If so, should one also consider Agamben's remarkable turn to Saint Paul in search of a different constellation of potentiality and actuality a response to the fateful loss of

---

7 Ibid, p. 86.
8 Agamben (2005a, p. 86) appears to suggest this.

republican government in ancient Rome? And should one then also consider it a response to a fatal loss from which European and Western governmental institutions never really recovered, notwithstanding the ostensible return to republican frameworks of government in at least some parts of Europe and the United States from the eighteenth century onwards? Is Agamben's point that throughout this long history, Western political thought and institutions never again managed to separate the question of *Being* – the *Being* of abandonment – from the question of law, in the way the Roman Republic once managed to do? These are the questions that surely raise their heads when one takes a closer look at the vicissitudes of the potentiality-actuality and *auctoritas-potestas* distinctions in imperial Rome, as well as medieval and modern Europe, as we shall now do in Sections 2 and 3 of this chapter.

## 2 Emperor, Pope And king

Let us begin our exploration of the *auctoritas-potestas* constellations in the course of ancient Roman imperial and medieval monarchical rule with the three statements of the Roman jurist Ulpianus with which the Introduction to this book also began:

1) *Quod principi placuit, legis habet vigorem.*[9]
2) *Princeps legibus solutus est.*[10]
3) *Iustitia est constans et perpetua voluntas ius suum cuique tribuendi.*[11]

As has already been pointed out on the first pages of this book, the three statements of Ulpianus cited here need not reflect a deep or irresolvable tension between the extra-legal power of the king or emperor, on the one hand, and the demands of justice of the other. They actually demand a clear understanding of the inseparable link between the extra-legal power of the sovereign, and any justice that the sovereign may want to pursue through law (see Introduction, pp. 1–3). If the three statements indeed raise a question, it rather concerns the difficulties that could arise if the king or emperor's conception of justice were to come to deviate significantly from the conception of justice shared by those who are subject to his power. The question, in other words, is strictly speaking not about how the king or emperor could be bound to the law, but how he could be bound to the conception of justice that prevailed among the people he governed. But, as we shall see presently, during the Middle Ages this question to a large extent boiled down to whether the king or emperor should be bound to the law, for the people's sense of justice was largely reflected by their customs and law. Under these circumstances, a contradiction or tension between Ulpianus' first two statements and the third indeed raised its head. A king or emperor that is *legibus solutus* evidently poses a real problem if *lex* and *iustitia* are as

9 D. 1.3.31 in Justinian 2010, p. 6.
10 D. 1.4.1 in ibid, p. 7.
11 D. 1.1.10 in ibid, p. 10.

intrinsically connected as they were in ancient Rome and medieval Europe. All the theoretical and theological conceptions of emperorship or kingship that emerged during this period reflected an ongoing endeavour to deal with this problem.

Ulpianus' idea of the emperor's unlimited power to make law as he pleases, and his unlimited freedom not to be bound by any of his own laws, was corroborated by the Eusebian conception of the emperor as a representative of God on Earth. Eusebius of Caesarea (263–339 AD) developed this idea during the reign of the Emperor Constantine (306–337 AD). Joseph Canning, whose fine book on medieval political thought we shall follow closely in this section, explains this conception as follows:

> Eusebius believed that Constantine's establishment of the Christian empire marked a crucial turning-point in human history, nothing less than the fulfilment of God's promise to Abraham. This view interpreted Roman History as being determined by divine providence: that the empire was founded under Augustus, in whose reign Christ was born, in order to facilitate the spread of the Christian religion, a development culminating in the conversion of the emperor himself.[12]

Eusebius was also influenced by pagan – Hellenistic and Neoplatonic – ideas that considered the king or ruler divine – "lord and God" (*dominus et deus*). This conception of the divinity of the emperor had pagan roots, but Eusebius Christianised the idea by replacing the divinity of the ruler with a unique closeness to God that made him God's vicegerent or representative on earth.[13] This theocratic conception of the Roman emperor dominates the *Corpus Iuris Civilis*, Justinian's sixth century codification of Roman law, in the first part of which – the *Digesta* – one finds Ulpianus' three statements about the emperor, law and justice. The conception of emperorship reflected in the *Corpus Iuris* is predominantly monarchical and theocratic. At the beginning of the *Digesta*, Justinian also expressly describes himself as "at God's command governing our empire, which has been entrusted to us by heavenly majesty" – *Deo auctore nostrum gubernantes imperium, quod nobis a caelesti maiestate traditum est.*[14] This understanding of the divine source of imperial authority also runs through the third and fourth parts of the *Corpus Iuris*, the *Codex* and *Novellae*.[15] However, the *Corpus Iuris* – especially the *Digest* and *Institutes* – also contains conceptions of law, and constitutional law in particular, that evidently derive from the time of the Roman Republic. The *Corpus Iuris* could therefore be relied on in support of both monarchical and republican theories of government from the sixth century onwards.[16]

---

12 Canning 1996, p. 4.
13 Ibid, pp. 4–5.
14 Justinian 2010, p. XIII; Canning 1996, p. 7.
15 Canning 1996, pp. 6–7.
16 Ibid, p. 7.

Two of the statements of Ulpianus cited above – *[q]uod principi placuit, legis habet vigorem* and *[p]rinceps legibus solutus est* – evidently reflected the theocratic and auto-cratic conception of emperorship. It is not evident from what we have said thus far, but it will become clearer presently, that the third statement – *[i]ustitia est constans et perpetua voluntas ius suum cuique tribuendi* – could be understood as an expression of the idea of government by the people, or at least *for* the people. Two other notions also played an important role in this theoretical and juridical endeavour to bind the emperor's rule to the good of the people. The first was the "royal law" or *lex regia*. The second was the notion of custom and customary law.

The *lex regia* was a construction on which later classical jurists relied to explain the transition from the republic to the empire. It did not exist, but was invoked to explain the transfer of sovereignty from the Roman people to Augustus, the first *princeps*.[17] It was also identified by some jurists with the *leges de imperio* by which the popular assembly gave power to each emperor at the beginning of his reign. Justinian himself invoked an ancient law (*lex antiqua*) to explain this transfer of sovereignty.[18] Be that as it may, these constructions evidently introduced views regarding popular sovereignty into the *Corpus Iuris* that are hardly reconcilable with the theocratic and autocratic endorsements of imperial sovereignty evident in the text. The text of the *Corpus Iuris* also offers no suggestion as to how these two notions could be reconciled. It simply leaves them juxtaposed. At the time of Justinian's reign, however, the theocratic view had become so dominant that the idea of popular involvement in the election and appointment of the emperor – who was practically always chosen by his predecessor – was already fully displaced by the conception that the emperor was selected by God and received his power directly from him.[19]

The people's will as the sovereign source of law nevertheless continued to find significant support in a conception of customary law that remained current dur-ing the Middle Ages. The *Digesta* contains a statement by the second century jurist Julian that considered the will of the people the source of customary law. The pas-sage states expressly that custom, as unwritten law, can override written legislation. The Emperor Constantine expressly dismissed this view and Justinian also main-tained that the emperor was the sole source of law. The idea nevertheless remained an argument for theories of popular sovereignty during the Middle Ages. It was also not without substance at that time. The legal codes of the kings that governed in the various regions of the Western Roman Empire after the fall of Rome often consisted of little more than express confirmations of vast areas of well-established customary law that was already in place. In the twelfth century the Glossators

---

17 Ibid, p. 8,
18 See C 1.17.1,7 in Justinian 2010, p. 70. See Canning 1996, pp. 8, 189 n. 20.
19 Canning 1996, p. 9. See also Lee 2016, pp. 27–31 and Ullmann 1975, pp. 62–63. See further also Ullmann 1946, pp. 50–51 for the fourteenth century theocratic views of imperial power among the Post-Glossators.

also firmly re-established the idea that the historical development of custom could abrogate the written legislation of a king.[20]

Be that as it may, throughout late antiquity and the Middle Ages, the theocratic conception of emperial rule and kingship evidently endowed the emperors and kings of these periods with the power to make law and depart from law freely. In practice however, these emperors and kings largely considered themselves bound by existing law and custom and generally created new law that confirmed custom rather than breaking with it. It is also important to note – especially from the perspective of the Greek elevation of *nomos* to *kosmos* discussed in Chapters 1 and 2 – that the conception of custom as an expression of the nature of things and an embodiment of natural law would again gain prominence with the rise of feudal law in the late Middle Ages.[21]

The conception of natural law as superior to positive law was nevertheless a later development. The idea that contraventions of the former by the latter would render the latter invalid only became fully fledged normative principles during the late phases of medieval kingship. Only then did the conviction that the emperor or king was bound by principles of natural law become pervasive. The Roman emperor was evidently not considered bound by natural law.[22] In late antiquity and the early Middle Ages, the big question regarding transcendent constraints on the emperor's or king's power to make law concerned his compliance with the articles of Christian faith and the teachings of the Church. These articles of faith and teachings of the Church certainly also remained the most significant definitions and limitations of imperial and monarchical sovereignty during the later Middle Ages, until sovereignty finally attained the character of absoluteness with the rise of Modernity. In other words, Christian faith and clerical dogma, represented by the Pope and clergy, remained the most significant constraints on imperial and monarchical power until the Early Modern consolidation of monarchical power removed the Pope and clergy from the scene of secular government. It is only in the wake of this demise of papal and clerical power that Jean Bodin's sixteenth century and Thomas Hobbes' seventeenth century affirmations of undivided and unlimited sovereignty could be articulated coherently.[23]

The significance of Bodin's sixteenth century insistence that sovereignty cannot be divided becomes especially clear when one takes into consideration the many centuries during which the claims of emperors or kings to be the ultimate (and therefore unitary) sovereign remained adamantly contested by several popes. Justinian officially articulated the relation between the emperor and clergy in his *Novellae*. He drew a distinction between emperorship and priesthood (*imperium* and *sacerdotum*) and asserted that both derived directly from God. The *Corpus Iuris*, notably the *Codex* and *Novellae*, affirmed the emperor's right to regulate religion

---

20  Canning 1996, pp. 10, 23, 24, 117.
21  Ibid, pp. 162–163.
22  Ibid, pp. 12.
23  See Bodin 1986, 10 (p. 306); Hobbes 1839, pp. 167–168.

and the priesthood. This was in line with the traditional Roman view that matters of religion were matters of public law.[24] The views reflected in the *Corpus Iuris* nevertheless also reflected a long standing Byzantine compromise between imperial and priestly powers in terms of which the emperor could call Church councils, preside over them and take part in the discussions, but had to respect the exclusive authority of the priesthood to articulate the doctrine of the Church.[25]

However, the compromise between religious and secular power articulated in the *Corpus Iuris* remained unstable throughout the Middle Ages. The claim to ultimate sovereignty with regard to both secular and religious affairs remained a source of vehement contestation between emperors or kings, on the one hand, and the clergy, on the other, until the dawn of Modernity finally laid the dispute to rest (by simply rendering obsolete the claim of clergy and the Pope to ultimate sovereignty in both secular and religious affairs). The debates had their origins in the early Byzantine "Caesaropapist" claims of the emperor to be both priest and emperor. The Byzantine relation between the emperor and the Church nevertheless remained relatively stable and thus laid the foundation for a new conceptualisation of the relation between *auctoritas* and *potestas*.[26] The emperor wielded ultimate power with regard to all affairs of secular government, which included the regulation of many institutional aspects of the Church, while the patriarch remained the ultimate authority with regard to questions of truth and faith. It was with regard to the emperors and kings that came to rule in the Western Empire after the fall of Rome that the clergy and Pope increasingly claimed ultimate authority/*auctoritas* in both secular and religious affairs, and insisted that the power of the king was given to him by the Pope.

Pope Gelasius addressed a letter to the Emperor Anastasius I in 494, arguing that the *auctoritas* of the bishops was so much higher than the *potestas* of the emperor that it actually limited the *potestas* of the earthly ruler incisively enough to consider the bishops co-rulers of the Roman world. The papacy retreated from this extreme position in the sixth century, notably under Pope Leo I.[27] But the claims of clergy and the Pope again gained confidence during the ninth century with regard to the Carolingian dynasty. During this time, both clergy and the Pope resorted to the Byzantine idea of the emperor as both emperor and priest. They did not do so, however, to recognise the ultimate supremacy of the emperor. On the contrary, they did so to effectively subsume the powers of the emperor under the powers of the clergy and thus to subordinate imperial power to the power of the Church. Especially prominent in this regard were ideas developed by Archbishop Hincmar of Rheims during the second half of the ninth century. By developing the ritual of the anointment of kings recorded in the Old Testament into a veritable episcopal consecration of the king that bound him to the episcopacy, Hincmar managed to

---

24  See Ullmann 1975, pp. 36–37.
25  Canning 1996, pp. 12–13.
26  Ibid, pp. 14–15.
27  Ibid, pp. 35–36.

subject the king to all constraints and implications of subordination attendant upon becoming part of the order of the Church.

This was his theory, and it enjoyed much influence at the time, so much so that King Charles the Bald even seemed to have accepted it. But would it have worked in practice, for long? Could the king henceforth be deposed by the Church because of insubordination? Hincmar never went so far as to make this claim.[28] But the idea that the emperor was created by the Church and the Pope became the lasting legacy of the Carolingian period. During this time the famous document known as the *Donation of Constantine* also began to feature in debates on the relation between secular and religious power. According to the document, the ultimate governmental superiority in both secular and religious matters derived from the Emperor Constantine's transfer of the government of Rome to Pope Silvester and his successors, after Silvester had baptised him and cured him of leprosy.[29]

Suffice it to say that the emperors understood the matter differently, as was evident from the events that came to pass between Pope John II and Emperor Otto I. After Otto's coronation in 962, John XII expected Otto would act as the safeguarding arm of the papacy. For Otto, however, his coronation signalled the subordination of the Pope to his imperial authority. His successor, Otto III, continued to believe this and expressly claimed the ultimate authority and power in both secular and spiritual matters as well as complete control over the Church. He also denounced the *Donation of Constantine* as a forged document. The Ottonian emperors evidently used their status as vicar of Christ, devised by Hincmar to subordinate the emperor to the order of the Church, to return to the Byzantine Caesaropapist conception of the emperor as priest, thereby making him both the secular and spiritual ruler of the empire.[30]

Considering these developments, it was only a matter of time before a head-on clash between an emperor and the Pope would lead to a real constitutional and institutional crisis, and this happened when King Henry IV of Germany and Pope Gregory VII both refused to back down in a conflict that became known as the Investiture Contest. Before his ordination as Pope in 1073, Gregory, in his capacity as the Sub-deacon and later the Archdeacon Hildebrand, played a leading and radical role in Church reforms that led to renewed claims to papal and clerical supremacy in both secular and religious matters. The direct background of the conflict between Henry and Gregory was a dispute concerning the right of the emperor to invest his own candidates in ecclesiastical offices. The dispute came to a head between 1075 and 1122 with regard to the appointment of the Archbishop of Milan. Henry invested Godfrey in the position in 1072, but Pope Alexander II recognised another candidate, Atto, as canonically elected. Alexander subsequently excommunicated five of Henry's counsellors for their role in the appointment of Godfrey. Henry, however, did not renounce the excommunicated counsellors and

28 Ibid, pp. 52–59.
29 Ibid, p. 73.
30 Ibid, p. 77.

proceeded to nominate a third candidate as Archbishop of Milan, as well as two other candidates as Bishops of Spoleto and Fermo. Gregory VII, then just recently ordained as Pope, wrote to Henry and demanded that he dissociate himself from his excommunicated counsellors, and also complained about the investiture of his candidates in the episcopacies of Fermo and Speleto and the archiepiscopacy of Milan. Henry wrote back, addressing Gregory as "Hildebrand, now not pope, but false monk."[31]

Gregory responded by excommunicating Henry and suspending his kingship. Henry's standoff with Gregory and his excommunication caused him to lose support among his princes. They made continued loyalty to him conditional upon a reconciliation with Gregory that would include three elements: an oath of obedience by Henry to Gregory, a revocation of Gregory's deposition from the papacy by Henry and the reversal of Henry's excommunication by Gregory. Henry complied and Gregory freed him from excommunication, but failed to reinstate him as king without further delay. The princes therefore also began to lose faith in the Pope's ability to resolve the situation. Among the princes, those opposed to Henry consequently elected a new king, Rudolf of Rheinfelden. The subsequent events spiralled into civil war in Germany between the supporters of Henry and those of Rudolf. Gregory then re-imposed Henry's excommunication and declared Rudolf king. In response, Henry, with the support of most of his German bishops, again declared Gregory "deposed" and elected Wibert of Ravenna as anti-Pope. The critical turn in these events came with the Battle of the Elster on 14 October 1080. Henry lost the battle decisively, but Rudolf got fatally wounded (his right hand was cut off and his stomach run through with a sword) and died one day after the battle. Henry's position commenced to improve again, but it took him till March 1084 to fight his way through to Rome and get Wibert elected as Pope Clement III.[32] Gregory had to flee Rome and died an exile at Salerno in 1085.

The Investiture Contest was only resolved almost forty years later with the Concordant of Worms of 1122. The Concordant stipulated Henry V's forfeiture of the power to invest bishops and Pope Calixtus II's acceptance that the election of bishops would take place in the presence of the king. The bishops would accordingly also receive their regalia from the king, before their consecration. However, the history of the unstable constellation between monarchy and papacy did not end there. A very similar contest for supreme power over both secular and spiritual affairs came to a head in the conflict between Philip IV of France and Pope Boniface VIII. Boniface had again claimed the ultimate supremacy of the papacy in his *Unam sanctam* bull of 1302, but he completely misread the times. He achieved nothing with the bull. France had by now consolidated significant territorial sovereignty and the status of the king as the supreme ruler of earthly affairs was generally recognised by everyone who understood the context, the clergy included. Philip was

---

31 Ibid, p. 90.
32 Ibid, pp. 87–91.

also in no mood to tolerate dissemination of ideas that seemed to challenge this order. Boniface died some weeks after having been manhandled and imprisoned by Philip's forces and Pope Clement V moved very quickly in 1306, under pressure from the crown, to decree expressly that the *Unam sanctum* bull contained no prejudice to the king and the kingdom.[33]

Several prominent scholarly defences of exclusive secular sovereignty articulated in the wake of the showdown between Philip and Boniface – notably in the writings of John of Paris, Dante and Marsilius of Padua, with which Ockham's position also resonated in many respects – reflected the sense that a new political reality was dawning in the course of the fourteenth century. The morally unquestionable territorial sovereignty of kings that John Figgis described in his work *The Theory of the Divine Right of Kings* had taken its first confident steps.[34] Europe's political imagination was now clearly on its way to the conception of undivided sovereignty that Jean Bodin would articulate in the sixteenth century. This consolidation of the earthly sovereignty of the king would soon lead to the perception of the need to split this sovereignty once again. The late Middle Ages and Early Modernity responded to this need by giving the king a "second body." Let us take a closer look at this "divine right" and "second body" of the late medieval and Early Modern kings.

Figgis explains the notion of the "Divine Right of Kings" in terms of the consolidation of the king's freedom to govern without recognising any supervision by the Church or Pope, or any limitation by parliament or law. The complete freedom that late medieval kings began to assume vis-à-vis the Pope, parliament and established law was considered a logical consequence of his status as the representative of God on Earth. According to Figgis, the publication of John Wycliffe's *De Officio Regis* (1378), the reign of Richard III of England (1452–1485) and the reign of Henry III of France (1551–1589) constituted crucial moments in the historical development that led to the confidence of kings to assume absolute power.[35] However, this status of absolute sovereignty – directly rooted as it was in God's sovereignty – was evidently too much of a claim for any mortal being to make. A need soon announced itself in medieval institutions and practices of royalty to distinguish between the king as a mortal person with evident imperfections, and the king as an immortal bearer of God's sovereignty who "could do no wrong," as Kelsen later put it.[36] From this need to split the king into two persons – one mortal, the other immortal – derived the ritual institution of the king's two bodies.[37] The institution entailed a visual symbolisation of the king's two bodies through the construction of a funeral effigy. The practice dates back to the death of Edward II of England in 1327 and was transplanted to France with the death of Charles VI in 1422.[38]

33  Ibid, pp. 139–140.
34  Figgis 1896.
35  See ibid, pp. 66–80, 118.
36  See Introduction, fn. 21.
37  Kantorowicz 1997.
38  See ibid, pp. 420–421.

Whether this artful ritualization of the distinction between the king as a mortal person and the immortal office of the king as representative of God managed to rehabilitate a significant separation of *auctoritas* and *potestas* in the late Middle Ages is doubtful, but it is a question that need not be addressed further. Modernity was well on its way by the time the late Middle Ages staged this last quaint effort to separate *auctoritas* from *potestas*. Modern political theorists remained intrigued by this separation, and by the questions that informed it. Scholarly attempts to sustain it persisted until the twentieth century, but they dispensed with the notion of the two bodies of the sovereign and replaced it with the idea of two fundamental modes of government, as we shall see below. It is nevertheless remarkable that modern political theory sought to sustain the *auctoritas-potestas* distinction at all. By that time, the distinction evidently already had a long record of calamitous instability. Why the persistent fascination with it?

The way in which the medieval inability to establish a coherent and stable constellation of *auctoritas* and *potestas* ultimately spiralled into a bloody civil war between king and Pope and anti-king and anti-Pope in the eleventh century, surely tells a story of how the crucial distinction between civil life and bare life – the condition of all civilisation or civilian order, as Agamben tells us – collapsed completely during this time. In the process, the most elementary concepts of civilisation lost all substance. No king and no Pope who emerge from an event such as the Battle of the Elster can continue to lay claim to "true" kingship or "true" papacy. Instead of securing civilian order, these crucial moorings of medieval civil order themselves drifted off into the squelchy lowlands of the Elster in 1080, thus allowing for bare life to re-emerge from the marsh of existence. It was not only the *auctoritas-potestas* constellation that got torn up in the process. The very framework of kingship and papacy on which it pivoted became a farce. This is literally what happened on that fateful 14 October, a day that must count among the most un-sovereign moments in the history of Europe. A breach of bare existence opened up so widely on that day that not only two, but effectively four Monty Python-like characters – two Popes and two kings – waded into muddy lowlands from which neither they, nor their successors for centuries to come, would emerge again.

This is what happened when king and anti-king joined battle in the name of Pope and anti-Pope in the marshlands of the Elster. The concepts of kingship and papacy became completely empty notions when their "terms of engagement" regressed to a free for all in the course of which the vanquished triumphed because the victor happened to get killed. There can only be one sovereign, asserted Jean Bodin five centuries later. It should be clear that this concept of sovereignty cannot support constellations of kings and anti-kings, Popes and anti-Popes, for it turns on a deeper or more primordial banishment or abandonment that ultimately must leave only one king on stage. If this abandonment does not take place effectively, everything returns to the blind contingency under the sway of which the incidental depth and murkiness of muddy marshlands determine which frogs get to procreate and which get spiked by herons before they manage to do so. The fourteenth century fracas between Philip IV of France and Boniface VIII underlines the reality that the marshlands of the Elster effectively continued to determine the terms of engagement between king and Pope long after the Concordant of Worms in 1122.

"It is a widespread error to speak of the anarchy of the Middle Ages" – "*Es ist eine weitverbreitete Irrtum, von der Anarchie des Mittelalters zu sprechen.*" When one recalls these words of Carl Schmitt (see Chapter 2, Section 5) against this background of the investiture debacle and the transaction between Philip and Boniface two centuries later, one could be forgiven for considering Schmitt's invocation of the unity of *Ort* and *Ortung* (place and order) during the Middle Ages somewhat farcical. Perhaps his own equivocation on this count is the telling sign of one who knew that his presentation of the medieval *nomos* hovered on the threshold of forgery. Or did Schmitt just forget that he himself invoked the "anarchy" of the Middle Ages twice in the early pages of *Der Nomos der Erde?* In the first sections of the book, he conceded the frequent anarchy of medieval politics, but adamantly distinguished it categorically from "nihilism," the term he reserved for the epoch that would begin towards the end of the nineteenth century.[39]

Anyone who adamantly finds meaningful order – order distinguishable from the nothingness of nihilism – in the kind of anarchy that came to a head in the investiture debacle, and later in the transaction between Philip IV and Boniface VIII, will also predictably consider this meaningful order still manifest in the constellation of power that panned out between General Von Hindenburg and Adolf Hitler, and later between Hitler and Hitler himself. The next section of this chapter takes a closer look at this modern history of the *auctoritas-potestas* distinction in Schmitt's work. Let us nevertheless first conclude this section by taking a look at the different emphasis that Ernst-Wolfgang Böckenförde – arguably the most influential legal scholar associated with Schmitt in post-war Germany – puts on the investiture debacle and the ultimate outcome of the struggle between clergy and secular government in the wake of the Reformation.

Böckenforde, we saw in the Introduction to this book (Section 8), considers the events that came to pass between Henry IV and Gregory VII as one of three important moments in the secularisation of Europe. Unlike Schmitt, he considers Henry's road to Canossa – the castle in Italy where Gregory reversed Henry's first excommunication after having made him wait for three days in front of the gate in a raging blizzard – as the end of the medieval *katechon*. Gregory reversed Henry's excommunication, but he did not bother to restore him to the throne, so as to also restore the idea of the common *katechon* which the clerical and secular powers of the *Respublica Christiana* had to sustain together. Gregory's failure to reinstate Henry as king, contends Böckenförde, was a clear sign that secular government was no longer his concern. He had won the contest and rested content that Henry subjected himself as a person to the order of the Church. He could not care less about Henry's or anyone else's kingship afterwards. This, then, was the critical moment that split the *Respublica Christiana* for the first time and untied secular from clerical government.[40] And this was also when the Christian devaluation of secular

39 Schmitt 1997, pp. 26, 36.
40 Böckenförde 2016, p. 46.

government paved the way for its emancipation from Christian religious demands. As Böckenförde observes poignantly: *was als Entwertung gedacht war . . . wurde . . . zur Emanzipation.*[41]

The second moment came five centuries later with Henry of Navarre's 1593 conversion to the Catholic faith in order to become Henry IV of France. At first glance, Henry's conversion may have looked like another epochal triumph for the Church over secular power, but the reality was a complete reversal of the eleventh century exchange between Henry and Gregory, contends Böckenförde. According to him, the remarkable mirror images of the two kings, Henry IV of Germany and Henry IV of France, reveal the extent to which their respective relations to the Church had reversed. Henry IV of France converted, not out of conviction or religious subordination to the Church, but because he wanted to restore peace and proper secular government. Just as Gregory's failure to restore Henry IV as the German king in 1077 showed his supercilious lack of concern for the future of secular government, the conversion of Henry IV of France basically amounted to an expedient bow to the Church to get it out of his way. This was underlined by his passing of the Edict of Nantes in 1598, four years after ascending the throne. He could not have stated the future irrelevance of matters of faith in the affairs of secular government in clearer terms, and Pope Clement VIII fully understood that Henry's reign was a disaster for the Church.[42]

Louis XIV revoked the Edict of Nantes in 1685 and thus inaugurated a new era of religious persecution in France. The "conclusive" secularisation of France only came in the wake of the French Revolution in 1789. In an important respect, however, the Revolution was also a failed secularisation. The recognition of religious freedom in the Edict of Nantes revealed the split or torn condition to which modern society was irrevocably heading, the irreversible state-society split that terminated the Aristotelian tradition of the unitary polis, as Böckenförde observes well.[43] The Edict suspended the state's authority in matters of personal conviction, thus creating a separate sphere of society over which it had no authority. This separate sphere of society, however, carried in its bosom new seeds of destructive social division and conflict. Post-revolution France sought to overcome this threat of division and conflict with recourse to the notion of the Nation, or the deified People, as we shall see in Chapter 6 where Böckenförde's historical narrative links up with Lefort's. We shall briefly return to it then. The meaning of the famous *Böckenförde dictum* – "the liberal democratic state lives from presuppositions that it cannot guarantee" – will also become clear then.

The split condition of society, we shall see in Chapter 7, also became the central concern of the nineteenth century philosopher Hegel, whom Böckenförde singles out as the profoundest thinker of the modern condition.[44] Hegel considered

41  Ibid.
42  Ibid, pp. 52, 63 n. 29.
43  Ibid, p.60.
44  Ibid, p. 61, 63 fn. 50.

the modern state the guardian of social unity, but his view of statal unity, we shall see, was, at least at times, fundamentally premised on the idea of sustainable division and sustainable conflict, not the overcoming of division and conflict. This idea of sustainable conflict and division became a pillar of liberal democratic thinking in the twentieth century, but only after it had fallen disastrously apart in the first half of the century at the hands of a social movement – a pure movement– that endeavoured to restore social and political unity at a cost that Aristotle would not have been able to imagine in his worst nightmare. It is to this early twentieth century history that we now turn.

## 3 President, chancellor, *Führer*

The *auctoritas-potestas* distinction again came to the fore in the eighteenth century in writings of Benjamin Constant. Constant drew a distinction between two different governmental functions, *reigning* and *governing*. It is evident from his explanation of these terms that he meant by them the distinction between *auctoritas* and *potestas*, or something very similar to it, reigning being the equivalent of *auctoritas*, and governing the equivalent of *potestas*. Schmitt took over Constant's distinction between reigning and governing in 1931 to put forward an argument that the imperial president, General Paul von Hindenburg, did not govern but reigned over Germany. As such, he was able to occupy a neutral position that transcended the political factions of the time, and could therefore be trusted with the activation of emergency powers – for which Article 48 of the Weimar Constitution made provision – if he considered the future of the German state at risk. In other words, Schmitt argued that General von Hindenburg should be considered the protector of the German Constitution (*Hüter der Verfassung*).[45] Schmitt invoked the distinction between reigning and governing again when Adolf Hitler became Chancellor of Germany. He did so to articulate the point once more that Hindenburg was the president who reigned over Germany, while Hitler governed Germany. At that point in time, however, the argument was evidently no longer about Hindenburg's emergency powers to protect the constitution. It effectively amounted to a statement that Hindenburg could not interfere with Hitler's government.[46] And when Hindenburg died not long after that, Schmitt appeared to accept unperturbedly that Hitler had assumed both the function of governing Germany, and reigning over it.[47]

We know that this collapse of the *auctoritas-postestas* distinction and the consolidation of both powers in one person became the killing machine to which Agamben alludes in *State of Exception*. In this respect, Agamben articulates a profound understanding of the totalitarian regime that the National Socialist movement became. However, his interpretation of Schmitt's position in this development

---

45 See Schmitt 1996b, pp. 132–140.
46 See Schmitt 1933, pp. 9–10.
47 See Schmitt 1994, pp. 227–232.

is remarkably inaccurate. He portrays Schmitt in *State of Exception* as the theorist who sustained the *auctoritas-potestas* distinction, in contrast to Benjamin, who basically collapsed this distinction with his notion of *divine violence* that terminates the circle of law-making and law-enforcing violence. We need not go into the details of the remarkable debate that Agamben constructs between Schmitt and Benjamin.[48] Suffice it to simply observe that his portrayal of Schmitt as a theorist who rigorously sustained the *auctoritas-potestas* separation in his work is far from accurate. This inaccuracy is not restricted to the texts Schmitt wrote and published after 1933, it also applies to key elements of his *Verfassungslehre* of 1928 and his *Der Begriff des Politischen* of 1932.

Schmitt's 1921 text *Die Diktatur* describes the legal order as a commissioned or relative dictatorship that is ultimately created by a sovereign dictatorship.[49] The *Verfassungslehre* of 1928 also does not shy away from defining constituent power as a sovereign dictatorship.[50] Agamben recognises this briefly in *State of Exception*, but he then goes on to portray Schmitt as the one who insists on the apparatus that separates the state of exception and the normal rule of law, the one who knows the apparatus cannot function when "the exception becomes the rule."[51] From 1933 onwards, however, Schmitt was quite content to endorse a totalitarian governmental arrangement in which the exception indeed became the rule and the distinction between *auctoritas* and *potestas* collapsed completely. The absolute unity of the people on which this post 1933 erasure of the *auctoritas-potestas* distinction hinged was nevertheless already central to his *Verfassungslehre* of 1928 and *Der Begriff des Politischen* of 1932.[52] In this respect, his post-1933 texts constituted no break with the texts of 1932 and 1928. We return to more aspects of this unitary conception of the political in these works in Chapter 10. Suffice it to conclude these reflections on Schmitt and Agamben with an observation of the obvious link between the concern with political unity that Schmitt articulated in the 1920s and 1930s and the political development in Germany after 1933. What became manifest in Germany between 1933 and 1945 was a pure political movement – *Bewegung* – that virtually displayed the complete liberty of permanent self-constitution that Schmitt's *Verfassungslehre* modelled on Spinoza's *natura naturans*. It was a movement that ceaselessly dissociated itself from any specific form that it happened to take at any particular moment in time. In this respect, as we shall see, German politics effectively became one with the ageless force of *physis* that the Athenians invoked in their transaction with the Melesians in 416 BCE.

48 I have done so elsewhere. See Van der Walt 2015b.
49 See Schmitt 2006a, pp. 127–149.
50 Schmitt 2003, p. 59.
51 Agamben 2005a, p. 58.
52 The discussion of constituent power in the *Verfassungslehre* begins with a long footnote on the *auctoritas-potestas* distinction, but it gives no indication of the division of institutional functions that might separate *auctoritas* from *potestas* effectively under the *pouvoir constituant/pouvoir constitué* constellation put forward in the *Verfassungslehre*. See Schmitt 2003, p. 75 n.1.

## 4 *Nomos* and *physis*

National Socialism styled itself as *Being* or *physis*, that is, as a natural force with regard to which government is nothing but an embodiment of a sweeping movement in which the ruler and ruled become one, to use Schmitt's phrase from the *Verfassungslehre*. This is confirmed by Hitler's assertion that he himself is nothing but the incarnation of a cosmological law to which mankind is as subject as any particle of the universe:

> In a world in which planets and suns follow circular trajectories, moons revolve round planets, and force reigns everywhere and supreme over weakness, which it either compels to serve it docilely or else crushes out of existence, Man cannot be subject to special laws of his own.[53]

The sulphurous dungeon of the beast had been long in the making. It is the words of the Athenian envoys to Melos that Hitler repeated here, whether he was aware of it or not. As we have already pointed out above, the discourse of the Athenian envoys did not only reflect a conception of *nomos* as *physis* (see Chapter 2, Section 1), but also a conception of *nomos* as *kosmos* (see Chapter 2, Section 1). Hitler's words, referring as they do to planetary regularities alongside the reign of force over weakness, touch upon the very weakness of the distinction between the conception of nature as *kosmos* and nature as *physis* that Aristotle, and a whole history of metaphysics after him endeavoured to sustain. As we saw, Aristotle's endeavour to secure the distinction between *kosmos* and *physis* pivoted on the additional distinction between potentiality and actuality. In Chapter 4 we also noted Agamben's invocation of a whole history of modern philosophy that endeavoured to rethink Aristotle's potentiality-actuality distinction. He pointed out the steps taken by Spinoza, Schelling, Nietzsche and Heidegger in this regard. We did not engage with these thinkers then, but the need to do so is evident, for it would appear that all these additional attempts to secure the potentiality-actuality distinction just worked like an erosion that hollowed out the deep recesses of the metaphysical cave even further, instead of facilitating an escape from them. It was Plato's sincere aim to prepare an exit from the dungeon, but the history of metaphysics that he founded ultimately just dug it deeper and deeper.

Aristotle was the threshold figure. He got caught up at the entrance, unable to let go of either the inside or the outside. Did he go wrong somewhere, or did he just select a task the accomplishment of which was impossible from the very beginning? Would any conception of nature as *kosmos* ever have been able to convincingly silence the realistic observation that *kosmos* is ultimately itself conditioned by *physis*, that is, by natural forces that come and go, displace others and get displaced by others? Would it ever have been able to present itself as immune to the Heraclitian and Anaximandrian conceptions of natural equilibrium to which Nietzsche desired so

---

much to return two thousand years later? Consider for a moment the phenomenon of a pack of wild dogs savagely tearing apart some other animal whilst still alive. On what grounds can one say this "savagery" violates the cosmological order of nature? And on what foundation can anyone firmly claim that human nature and human *life* is categorically exempt from this "savagery" of "other" animal life?

This is, of course, the inescapable question with which Hobbes left modern political and legal thought. This question, however, cuts deeper than the suggestion that the human being is, after all, nothing but a wolf among wolves. It confronts us with the broader question of whether there is any substance in the distinction between *kosmos* and *physis*, after all. This is the question that Michel Foucault raised again, in Nietzschean fashion, in the second half of the twentieth century, when he proceeded to analyse all social and epistemological arrangements as strategies of power. It is on the shoulders of this Nietzschean-Foucaultian mode of enquiry that one should ultimately assess Villey's and Schmitt's respective contentions regarding the expiry date or dates of the European *nomos*. Villey, we saw, discerned the expiry date of this *nomos* in the fourteenth century when the rise of the modern subjective right, fatefully defined by William of Ockham, began to displace the Aristotelian conception of *ius* in Roman law. It is this development, contends Villey, that reduced modern law to positivist systems of sovereign regulation that condoned power struggles between individuals or groups of individuals while keeping them in check. The fourteenth century was therefore the beginning of the end of the European *nomos*, according to Villey. He was, of course, not as naive as to think that this development was the result of the scholastic debates of the time, and of a theologian's incidental articulation of the first definition of the modern concept of subjective rights. He attributed it to the crude regime of kings, lords and vassals constructed on the ruins of the Roman Empire – *sur les ruines de l'Etat romain ils reconstruisent grossièrement un régime social fait des maîtrises individuelles, de la combinaison des pouvoirs des rois, des seigneurs, de leur vassaux*.[54]

Schmitt, we saw, perceived this *nomos* as having come to an end at the end of the nineteenth century and the beginning of the twentieth. He considered it definitely expired by the time of the Treaty of Versailles in 1919. Perhaps this narrative contained an argument of doom: there was no *nomos* left in Europe after 1919 that prevented the complete unleashing of *physis*, that is, the *physis* that the *Jus Publicum Europaeum* had managed to expel for four centuries to the far side of the amity line. Perhaps this was his point: there was no *nomos* left that prevented the return of *physis* to European soil. We know from Schmitt's own candid confirmations at what cost to the New World this expulsion of *physis* from Europe's civilian neighbourhoods and civil battlefields was bought. Anyone who finds solace in this "gentlemanly" response to the eternal tension between physical force and civil order must either be desperate or deeply cynical. Perhaps Schmitt was both, but this is not our concern, for neither cynicism nor desperation precludes one from being accurate, albeit

---

54 Villey 2003, p. 262.

"accurate" in a rather twisted way. Villey's assessment of the political "system" of the Middle Ages as a crude arrangement of power relations between individuals – *des maîtrises individuelles* – is surely more convincing than Schmitt's construal of this system as an example of a well-established *nomos* that reflected a deep unity of place and order or *Ortung* and *Ordnung* (see Chapter 2). Schmitt's accuracy, however, lies elsewhere. It relates to the way in which a deep equivocation in his thinking matches the deep equivocation of the metaphysical tradition in which it is rooted.

In a most amicable article about his former *Doktorvater*'s work, Ernst Rudolf Huber observed that Schmitt never made a clear choice between *Ortungsdenken* and the grand interventionism which his concern with the sovereign decision required.[55] Huber's observation can for all practical purposes be taken as an acute assessment of Schmitt's refusal to choose between *nomos* and *physis*, or rather, between *nomos* as *kosmos* and *nomos* as *physis*. In this respect his thinking matched the undecided tension between the conception of nature as *kosmos* and the conception of nature as *physis* that underpins the whole tradition of Western metaphysics, pointed out above (see Chapter 3, Section 1). This tension, and the deep equivocations to which it gave rise over two and a half millennia of Western metaphysics, may well be rooted in the deep ambivalence between the concern with stable order and the concern with the destabilising power that characterises and burdens life itself.

Any concept of law that is rooted in life is therefore likely to reiterate the old equivocations regarding *physis* and *kosmos* in Western metaphysics. Schmitt's concept of law surely showed clear signs of being rooted in life. Rudolf Smend – a relatively close friend of Schmitt for many years – referred poignantly to Schmitt's *vitalistischen Dezisionismus* (vitalistic decisionism), as we shall see in Chapter 9. Schmitt's invocation of the *Lebensrecht* of the German people in his 1934 essay *Der Führer schutzt das Recht* is deeply instructive in this regard.[56] He did not have "the right of the German people to life" in mind when he employed this term *Lebensrecht*, although it could perhaps also be understood in this way. What he did want to denote was the idea that law was rooted and embodied in the very life of the German people. In the final analysis it is this link between law and life that the theory of liberal democratic law seeks to sever and destroy, for this link lies at the heart of the naturalisation of law – or at least an essential aspect of it – that a whole history of metaphysics and natural law theories bequeathed to the Western legal imagination.

---

55 Huber 1951, pp. 4–5.
56 Schmitt 1994, p. 229: "Alles Recht stammt aus dem Lebensrecht des Volkes."

# 6

# FROM *NOMOS* TO *DEMOS*

## 1 The people?

And the people? Where were they amidst all these stories of emperors, kings and Popes, presidents, chancellors and *Führers*? The people are hard to find, it seems, regardless of the times.[1] The Roman Republic was in name government by the people, but the name "republic" was already then a rather empty notion, unless one is content to equate "the people" with a small number of senior patricians who managed to retain power over a vast majority of plebeians for the first two hundred years of the republic. And, when the plebeians finally succeeded in establishing themselves as an equal political force alongside the patricians – with the passing of the *lex Hortensa* in 287 BCE – it was still not the people, but a small number of wealthy plebeian families who ascended to power in Rome. These plebeian elites cared little for the plight of the vast numbers of common citizens who increasingly experienced debilitating economic hardship. It was only under the imperial rule of Augustus from 27 BCE onwards that the general welfare of common citizens was significantly improved.[2] But by that time, the role of the people in Roman politics was at best fictional and/or oblique. *Fictional?* Fictional in the sense that the people came to be "constructed" by a handful of jurists in the form of the *lex regia*. The *lex regia*, we saw above, was the fictional law with reference to which the Roman jurists explained the transfer of power from the republican institutions to the emperor. It was the law, they argued, with which the Roman assembly transferred power to Augustus. *Oblique?* Oblique in the sense that the people, or at least the people's interests, would henceforth be represented or mediated by God through the myth of the emperor or king as the representative of God on Earth.

1 See Rosanvallon 1998.
2 See Chapter 1, fn. 10.

The myth of the people's involvement in the selection of the emperor persisted throughout the Middle Ages with regard to the medieval kings of Europe. The idea was largely based on Germanic customs which suggested that the Germanic tribes elected their kings and that the kings thus elected were answerable to their popular assemblies. Hand in hand with this idea of the popular basis of kingship went the idea that the king, as representative of God, was a servant of God's people. Early in the seventh century, Isidore of Seville articulated the latter principle concisely with a play on the words *rex* and *recte*. The king would only be king, *rex*, if he acted correctly, *recte*,[3] "*recte*" meaning "for the benefit of the welfare and salvation of his subjects." The combination of the two ideas of popular and theocratic kingship led Walter Ullmann to observe tension in medieval conceptions of monarchy which he described in terms of an antithesis between the "ascending" and "descending" conceptions of kingship, that is, between the understanding of the power of the king as ascending from below, that is from the people, or descending from above, that is, from God.[4] The institutional reality probably reflected a complex mixture of both elements in terms of which the king's popular support would depend on whether the people could continue to consider him a representative of God. The events that came to pass between Henry IV of Germany and Gregory VII related in Chapter 5 seem to underline this interdependence of the two conceptions of kingship. As we saw, Henry lost the support of his princes while excommunicated by Gregory, and the princes insisted on Henry making his peace with Gregory and having his excommunication reversed before giving him their support again.

Be that as it may, the story of Henry IV and Gregory VII also focuses our attention on another aspect of popular representation at the time. Popular kingship evidently did not entail election by the people themselves, but by the princes to whom the people had sworn allegiance. The people were evidently not directly involved in the selection of their kings, but very indirectly so, through their allegiance to their princes. In other words, a doubly oblique relation existed between the people and their king. Only through God, who demanded government on behalf of their welfare and salvation, and through their princes, who demanded evidence of government on behalf of God, were the common people the source and legitimation of the king's power. To this complex configuration one should add a third element. The sign that assured the princes that the king was a representative of God depended on the favour of the Pope – who evidently also had his own agenda. The people were indeed difficult to find in this double or triple constellation of medieval kingship, if not indeed unfindable, *introuvable*, to use Rosanvallon's expression.

The fictionality and/or fictitiousness of this whole constellation was unmasked in sixteenth century Germany when the peasants finally began to revolt against the German princes. However, their claim to be the people of God, and therefore entitled to the justice of their kings and princes, could evidently not be invoked for

3 Isidore wrote in his *Etymologiae*: "Rex eris si recte facies, si non facias, non eris." See Canning 1996, pp. 20, 191 n. 62.
4 Ullmann 1975, pp. 30–32, 62–63, Canning 1996, p. 19.

purposes of earthly welfare. This soon became very clear to them. Martin Luther, the man of the Church in whom they saw some promise of the idea that the grace of God would finally come to them through the benevolence and wisdom of their kings, communicated their delusion to them in no uncertain terms.[5] It was only when kings began to use royal justice – justice at the court of the king – to undermine and eventually sever the direct bonds between the people and the princes that the people began to enter the scene of power more directly. This turn in the destiny of the people is often associated with the founding of the Imperial Court or *Reichskammergericht* by Maxmillian I in 1495, but its significance was not yet evident at the time of the peasant wars that broke out in 1525.

The founding of the Imperial Court represented an important milestone in the effective territorial centralisation of royal power, the development that also allowed the kings of Europe to eventually establish the unitary and undivided sovereignty that Jean Bodin and Thomas Hobbes began to contemplate in the sixteenth and seventeenth centuries.[6] The people nevertheless remained difficult to find during this time. They entered the scene of power only to the extent that their demands and needs increasingly became a concern of their monarchs. They were not yet stepping up onto the stage of power as *a* people or *the* people. They were just people, people whom the king came to recognise as a factor to be taken into account for purposes of effective government. But this recognition was far from insignificant, for it contributed to the creation of territorially extended and stable infrastructures that eventually empowered a commercial class of people to stage popular revolutions, beginning with the French Revolution in 1789. This was the moment at which the people seemed to step up from just being recognised as an important consideration and object of power, to becoming the veritable subject of sovereign power.

This French Revolution, however, soon also turned into just another substitution in the history of substitutions of the people. The bourgeoisie that established itself as the sovereign then, first in France and then in larger parts of Europe, was evidently not yet "the people." More than a century of further struggle and revolution – key milestones of which were 1848 and 1918 – made it abundantly clear that the people had not yet been found, or had not yet found themselves. The years 1848 and 1918 were important dates in the history of "the people," but they were also not years in which "the people" finally came to find themselves, either in France, Germany or anywhere else. They were ultimately just dates that marked an increasingly exasperated search. Somehow, the people remained unfindable and continued to remain so, for yet another long and bitter century. By the beginning of the twenty first century, they had clearly become the figure of something irremediably unfindable, notwithstanding the efforts of rising populist movements to once again extract extinct metaphors from the labyrinths of transnational bureaucracies and global supply chains.

5  See MacIntyre 1967, p. 122; Villey 2003, pp. 281–302.
6  See Thornhill 2011, pp. 77–80.

The big "democratic" revolution in France towards the end of the eighteenth century failed to give political and legal history its "people." It did not furnish history with the subject, soul or spirit that Hegel attributed to it, as we shall see in Chapter 7. As time passed, it became increasingly clear that history was just a passage of time. The French Revolution, too, failed to give history the people it needed for purposes of transcending rudimentary time, or at least surviving it. Did it at least liberate this passage of time from the political myths of old Europe, that is, from its divine emperors, kings and Popes, some of them double-bodied to boot? No, not even that. For instead of giving history its people, it gave it the myth of the people. In this respect, the French Revolution and modernity constituted not a liberation from mythology, but a mythological exchange. It substituted one myth for another, and kept on doing so in several forms or variations. This exchange, and some or its more prominent variations, are the key concerns of this chapter.

## 2 The revolutionary deification of the people

Chapter 5 (Section 2) noted Böckenförde's identification of the idea of the Nation that arose in the wake of the French Revolution as the third important moment in the secularisation of Europe. The rise of the idea of the Nation, contends Böckenförde, reflected the response of post-revolutionary France to the threat of social division and fragmentation. The response failed. Even at the beginning of the Modern Age the idea of the Nation proved itself incapable of rising above the conflicting interests of individuals, observes Böckenförde, and it will continue to do so in future, he insists. The concept and consciousness of individual rights that became the cornerstone of modernity legitimise individual interests and therefore sustain the conflict between them at the expense of any prospect of significant social unity. It is on the back of these reflections that Böckenförde moves directly to his famous dictum that the liberal democratic state lives from conditions that it cannot guarantee.[7] The themes that Böckenförde raises in this regard resurface in Claude Lefort's seminal 1986 essay *Permanence du théologico-politique* and the paradox that Böckenförde articulates in his *dictum* is also the key focus of Lefort's essay. It is to this essay that we now turn. As we shall see, the essay probes the depths of the predicament of modernity that Böckenförde has only begun to explore.

Lefort's essay begins with the observation that one cannot assess accurately what appears, disappears or reappears in a major social transformation such as the French Revolution without interrogating the religious significance of the old and the new.[8] Of concern, here, he continues, are not the works of jurists and theologians that debate the relation between the authority of the emperor or king, and that of the Pope. Such works are situated inside the horizon of a theologico-political experience of the world. What interests Lefort is the persistence of deeply religious

---

7 Böckenförde 2016, p. 60.
8 Lefort 1986a, p. 275.

imaginary constructs in the secular understanding of social transformation and civil order that came to the fore in the sixteenth century and culminated in the nineteenth century rhetoric of the French Revolution. In other words, Lefort is interested in the persistence of questions regarding the religious significance of social transformations in an era that consciously denies ecclesiastic authority in affairs of secular government.[9]

The rise of princely and demise of ecclesiastic authority in secular government constitutes a rupture that does not take place *in time*, asserts Lefort. It establishes a relation with time as such and precipitates a sense of the mystery of history.[10] What comes to the fore with this sense of the mystery of history, he continues, is nothing less than a new faith that is simultaneously political, religious and philosophical. Taking these elements apart and separating them – that is, not regarding their interrelatedness – would be a huge mistake, he cautions his readers with reference to the epochal warning that Hegel articulated in his *Enzyklopedie*.[11] Our time, he continues, is making the very mistake against which Hegel warned.

Lefort's aim in *Permanence du théologico-politique* is to interrogate the thinking of those who lived and thought in the crack that opened up with the departure of the ancient and the arrival of the new during the French Revolution. Did these thinkers not still have the power of symbolic thinking, the thinking that holds together (Greek: *sym-ballein*) that which should be held together – religion, politics and philosophy – in any attempt to comprehend significant social change, asks Lefort.[12] We shall return to his engagement with this question presently. Let us first observe a number of key aspects of his concern with the symbolic thinking that holds politics, religion and philosophy together in the quest to understand the true significance of incisive social transformation.

The first aspect concerns his observation that the need to contemplate the symbolic does not necessarily imply an insoluble link between politics and religion. The need for symbolic thinking concerns the need to understand the inspiration that prompted this link in the past, that is, in the long history that preceded the apparent uncoupling or delinking of politics and religion that occurred during the French Revolution.[13] The second aspect concerns the way this symbolic thinking also allows one to discern and contemplate a *secret element* of social life, the very element that remained obfuscated by the operational effectiveness of the link between politics and religion in earlier times. In other words, this *secret element* concerns the hidden process that allows for effective adherence to the political regime that conditions a form of social existence (literally: a way of existing socially/ *une manière d'être en société*) and thus ensures this regime adequate endurance in time (literally:

---

9 Ibid.
10 Ibid.
11 Ibid, p. 276.
12 Ibid, p. 277.
13 Ibid, p. 278.

a permanence that remains independent of any contingent events that affect it/*une permanence dans le temps, indépendamment des événements qui les affectent).*[14]

Lefort proceeds to scrutinise this secret operation by distinguishing between the two different meanings for which the word for "politics" in French allows. French allows for a distinction between *le politique* and *la politique*. The former is usually translated as "*the political*" in English, and the latter as "*politics.*" The former, explains Lefort, concerns the secret operation that is at stake here, namely, the very staging of a *form of social existence* that allows for an array of adequately coherent social practices that can, therefore, be said to belong together. The latter – *la politique* – concerns politics as one of the many social practices that become possible once a social form has been staged. Politics in the latter sense prevails as a specific and distinct social practice among other such practices such as economics, law, religion, etc. It is the task of political science to study and define the distinctions and relations between politics and these other social practices, argues Lefort. Political philosophy, on the other hand, can be distinguished from political science because of the way it seeks to compre-hend *the political*. In other words, political philosophy seeks to comprehend the way in which a social form with its array of different social practices – amongst them politics – comes into the world. It seeks to comprehend the very formation (*mise en forme*) through which a social world is staged or made visible (*mise en scène*) and rendered intelligible (*mise en sens*).[15] To neglect this distinction between politics and the political and between political science and political philosophy, insists Lefort, is to surrender to the positivistic fiction that the social is preceded by the social – *la fiction positiviste [qui met] la société avant la société.*[16] Political philosophy accordingly concerns a contemplation of the way a world comes into existence and becomes knowable as a world. It is therefore an engagement with Being as such (*l'Être comme tels*).[17]

Lefort refers only to Husserl's distinction between world and lifeworld on the pages where he expounds these thoughts, but it is clear that he is also moving very close to Heidegger's distinction between Being (*Sein*) and beings (*Seienden*).[18] A cru-cial passage that follows shortly after his invocation of "Being as such" suggests that he is rearticulating Heidegger's ontological difference as the political difference that conditions the formation of the social, that is, the "primary" difference that precipi-tates the arrival of a world of shared familiarities and meanings after which, or on the basis of which, politics (*la politique*), as the "secondary" encounter of differences of opinion, becomes possible.[19] Lefort writes:

> What philosophical thought strives to preserve is the experience of a dif-ference that goes beyond differences of opinion (and the recognition of the

14 Ibid, p. 278.
15 Ibid, pp. 279–282.
16 Ibid, p. 281.
17 Ibid, p. 283.
18 See Heidegger 1979, p. 6, 1978, pp. 123–173.
19 The proximity between Lefort's political difference and Heidegger's ontological difference is noted by Marchart 2007, pp. 93, 98.

relativity of points of view that this implies); the experience of a difference that is not at the disposal of human beings, whose advent does not take place *within* human history, and that cannot be abolished therein; the experience of a difference that relates human beings to their humanity, and that means that their humanity cannot be self-contained, that it cannot set its owns limits, and that it cannot absorb its origins and ends into those limits. Every religion states in its own way that human society can only open to itself by being held in an opening it did not create. Philosophy says the same thing, but religion said it first, albeit in terms that philosophy cannot accept.[20]

This passage performs two tasks for Lefort. The first puts forward the idea of political difference. The second underlines the need for a mode of philosophical thinking that continues to pay attention to a force that religion once had, but no longer appears to have in the wake of the French Revolution. Let us first take a look at the second task. At issue here is the concern with a symbolic thinking that holds together the political, the religious and the philosophical. These three dimensions of inquiry must be considered together if significant social transformations are to be understood incisively. The democratic revolution appears to have disqualified religion from taking part in the new political discourse that took centre stage after the Revolution. It appears to have effected a separation between politics and religion that has relegated religion to a matter of private opinion that would henceforth have no standing in public or political discourse. But, had it really done that, that is, had the Revolution really relegated religion to a private matter, to a matter of *private differences* of opinion, politics would also have lost the only voice that, at the time, could have communicated the thought of *political difference*. It would have lost the only way of articulating the irreducible difference that derives from the opening that society does not create, but in which it is held, that is, the opening that allows it to open up to itself, to have a relationship with itself, to sustain an irreducible difference to itself, and which thus prevents it from collapsing onto itself. Political difference, in contrast to private differences of opinion, concerns this opening which holds society open, that is, holds it in a state of irreducible difference to and from itself. This is the message that religion was first to communicate, says Lefort, albeit in terms that philosophy cannot accept. This is the message that philosophy nevertheless seeks to retrieve from religion in order to preserve it in terms that it can accept.

The language and age of Christianity that prevailed for eighteen centuries before the democratic revolution put a stop to them always communicated the message that the language of the secular sovereign and the law that he or she creates at will or pleasure (*quod principi placuit legis habet vigorem*) is answerable to an authority beyond the will or pleasure of the sovereign. This was the way in which ancient and medieval Christianity held secular sovereignty in an opening – in a relation to something beyond itself – that it did not create, but to which it must answer. It is

20  Lefort 1986b, p. 157. See Lefort 1986a, p. 287 for the original French text.

this history of secular sovereignty (*potestas*) and Christian authority (*auctoritas*) that we recounted above. Why is this language unacceptable to philosophy? Lefort does not answer this question directly, but the following answer can be parsed from the last pages of his essay. The opening that ancient and medieval Christianity offered to politics was not really an opening, but a closure in its own right. The language of Christianity, in other words, closed down the political because of the way that it simply confronted the closure of politics with another closure. Christian dogma and symbolism effectively closed up the very language that should have sustained society's opening to itself. Hence the struggle and conflict that ensued between secular and religious power. Instead of offering society a passage to an opening beyond itself, Christian religion became a competing society. It became a doubling of society, or the sign of a society doubling up and folding back onto itself, the sign of a society that posits and absorbs its own limits, as Lefort puts it in the passage quoted above. Another passage closer to the end of the essay underlines this. At issue in the clashes between kings and Popes, he states, was not a conflict between politics and theology, but between politics that was already theological, and theology that was already political. He writes:

> That which one would discover again here, is a dynamic scheme that expresses itself in this complex game of schisms, that Ernst Kantorowicz has analysed so subtly; schisms, let us repeat, not between theology and politics, as his own formulations sometimes prompts one to suppose, but . . . between a theology already politicised and a politics already theologised.[21]

This is Lefort's articulation of the observation we made with regard to Canning's concise account of this history. The clashes between the Popes and kings that Canning recounts did not stem from conflicts between *potestas* and *auctoritas*, but from conflicts between two conflations of *potestas* and *auctoritas*, one by the king and one by the Pope. At issue was not a limitation of the political by the theological and vice versa, but a doubling of the theologico-political that obliterated and absorbed the limits that medieval society endeavoured to lay down for itself. From this obliteration and absorption of the limits of the social must follow the threat of complete social disintegration, a complete disintegration of the civility of society. A society that posits and absorbs its own limits evidently loses the very boundaries that define it as a society. That society is doomed to diffuse and disintegrate into the bare life, and the struggles of bare life, that evidently surfaced again in the lowlands of the Elster in 1080 when king and anti-king, and Pope and anti-Pope, came to face one another in a bogged-up enclave effectively closed off from any opening that would allow it to appeal to an authority beyond itself.

Lefort tells us at the beginning of his essay that his aim is not to return to the old battles between kings and Popes, but this is how one might reread this history

---

21 Translated from Lefort 1986a, p. 322.

in the light of his essay on the permanence of the theologico-political. When this history finally closed down the appeal to the Pope as a way of appealing to authority, it resorted to the notion of the king's second body to create a passage (an opening) and a possibility of an appeal to something beyond the closures of empirical sovereignty. Whether this second body of the king opened up a channel of appeal to a beyond that it could not assimilate and which therefore remained a limit, or whether it simply became the last plug that effectively sealed off the closure of sovereignty so that sovereignty became the depositor of its own re-absorbable limit, is a question that we need not pursue further here. More important is to ask whether the democratic revolution that ostensibly terminated the narrative of popes and kings, and double-bodied kings, succeeded in opening up a channel of appeal to something beyond itself. Did democracy simply confirm the permanence of the theological political, or did it manage to open up a *different* register, one in which the difference of democracy to itself became a sustainable framework?

Democracy, argues Lefort, is the first form of the political that endeavoured to grasp and sustain the "[opening in which it is held but which it did not create]." It was the first endeavour to sustain the "difference beyond the difference of opinion" we pointed out above. As he puts it:

> [M]odern democracy [is] of all political regimes . . . the only one to have represented power in such a way as to show that power is an *empty place* and to have thereby maintained a gap between the symbolic and the real . . . by virtue of a discourse which reveals that power belongs to no one.[22]

This understanding of democracy, however, was not recognised by the great thinkers of the French Revolution who endeavoured to assess its achievement. Lefort meticulously points out how the writings of Michelet reintroduced the imagery of ancient and medieval political theology, thus allowing it to once more permeate the self-understanding of democracy at the beginning of the modern age. He shows how early modern democratic thinking soon found itself compelled to return to the key concepts of Christian monarchy *and* imperial government to safeguard the unity of the social. The "*and*" is stressed here to point out the paradox of the particular and the universal that informed monarchical government in the wake (or even under the last rests) of imperial rule. Of concern here is the late medieval maxim that the king was an emperor in his own kingdom – *imperator in suo regno*. The maxim reflected the post-imperial reality that the king was but a king among many kings, with all the implications of the particularity of kingship that this implied. And yet, the maxim also stressed the imperial aspiration of kingship, that is, the claim of the king that his rule – and his law – is the embodiment of a universal humanity and universal reason.[23]

22  Lefort 1986b, p. 159. For the French text, see Lefort 1986a, p. 291. See also Lefort 1994, p. 92.
23  Lefort 1986a, pp. 326–328.

This notion of imperial kingship "filled" the place of power. It replenished it with the claim to an embodied spirituality that unites the universal and the particular and the symbolic and the real. The essence of the theologico-political lies in this royal monarchical-imperial spirituality – this *Royauté de l'Esprit*, as Michelet called it – that claims the unity of particular rule and universal reason.[24] Modern democracy would assume this spiritual royalty every time it would claim the ability to embody – through territorially particular law and legislation – the universal claims of humanity. And by doing so it would reflect time and again its inability to read its own history – *une difficulté, sans doute incontournable, sans doute ontologique, de la démocratie à se rendre lisible pour elle-même.*[25]

Lefort refers in the very last line of his essay to the difficulty of political thought and philosophy to face up to the tragedy of modernity without betraying or perverting it – *à assumer, sans travestissements, le tragique de la condition moderne.*[26] The tragedy at issue here relates directly to Rosanvallon's reference to the unfindable people – *le people introuvable* – invoked above (Section 1). We can now explain this "unfindable" status of the people more incisively in view of the key thoughts of Lefort that we have examined in this section. If philosophy, and philosophy of law in particular, is to avoid returning surreptitiously to the medieval conceptions of the theologico-political, if it would want to steadfastly adhere to the democratic imperative to sustain the empty space of power, it would have to accept that this empty space severs the link between the symbolic and the real irredeemably and irretrievably. And this would also imply an acceptance that all references to "the people" must remain empty. The people *must* remain unfindable because "the people" is an empty notion. This also applies to the notion of the "will of the people," and to any law that is considered the "will of the people." The tragedy of modernity is therefore well expressed by Hans Kelsen's assertion that "the people" is nothing but a construct of law.[27] We will return to Kelsen in Chapter 9. For now, let us take a closer look at the way in which this notion of the "the people" raised its head in nineteenth century political thought.

Lefort's reading of Michelet recounts the way in which Michelet's glorification of the French Revolution takes over the very symbolism of Christian monarchy which the Revolution wanted to terminate. Michelet, Lefort shows, reinstituted the medieval theologico-political discourse with which the Revolution wanted to break, by reintroducing the Christian "scene of sacrifice" into the symbolism of the Revolution. The people become Christ in the theologico-political discourse that Michelet puts forward. The sacrifices that the people made during the Revolution replaced the sacrifice of Christ. The blood of Christ that redeems humanity in Christian theology now becomes the blood of the people who put their lives on the line for one another. It is the blood offering that the people made during

24 Ibid, p. 328.
25 Ibid, p. 329.
26 Ibid.
27 See Kelsen 1981.

the Revolution that will sustain them as a people in the future. It is this blood, in other words, that will sustain them as *a people* and which will give them a symbolic permanence or endurance in time that transcends the varying vicissitudes of different historical periods. Empirically observable people or persons will always be immersed in these varying vicissitudes of time, but *the people* will always survive and transcend these vicissitudes because of the founding act of sacrifice that united them and constituted them as *the people*. In what follows we shall take recourse to the capitalised P when we refer to this symbolic *People*, in order to distinguish it clearly from the people as a group or mass of individuals who just happen to live together in the same time and space. In other words, we shall use the capital P to distinguish the People as a symbolic ideal from the people as a sociological reality (when neither the symbolic ideal nor the sociological reality is specifically at issue in a phrase, usual rules regarding usage of capitals or lower case will continue to apply).

Michelet's text, contends Lefort, contemplates a doubling of time and a doubling of the People/people that mirror the doubling of the king in medieval political theology. At stake in this doubling of time is the introduction of a register of transcendental time that is not outside time, but also not in time – *une référence à un temps qui, sans être hors du temps, n'est pas dans le temps*.[28] The people taken as a group of people – a gathering of individuals – that is empirically observable at any moment *in time*, thus comes to be accompanied by *a symbolical People* that exists, not outside time, but also not in time. The two temporal registers of the existence of the People/people endow them with the two aspects of monarchy that medieval times symbolised with the ritual institution of the king's two bodies. Michelet, contends Lefort, did not shy away from rehabilitating the symbolism of monarchy to explain this dual nature of the people/People. He expressly portrayed the people as the real king – "le vrai roi, qui est le peuple."[29] It is important to understand the exigencies of the time that moved Michelet to rehabilitate the old political theological symbolism of Christian monarchy. The re-invocation of this symbolism in a time that was consumed by a sweeping desire to break away from it only becomes comprehensible when one takes into consideration the crisis that threatened after the revolutionary destruction of this symbolism. The revolutionary dismantling of the institutions of medieval political theology destroyed the essential institutional mechanism that up to the time of the Revolution managed to unite the people.

The Christian king, with or without the Pope, symbolised the unity of the people (and legitimated whatever levels of coercion were necessary to enforce this unity) for many centuries before the Revolution removed him from the scene of power. Now that he was removed, the people seriously risked turning into a sociological reality of competing groups and individuals. Now that social competition – between citizens and between groups of citizens – was no longer bridled by a loyalty to the king that was rooted in religious conviction and faith, it seriously threatened to tear

28　Lefort 1986a, p. 309.
29　Ibid, p. 311.

society apart. It did not do so during the tumultuous days of the Revolution. For a time, the heady experience of acting in unison and sacrificing together to destroy the *ancien régime* suppressed the competitive drive that generally compelled them to distinguish themselves from one another at the cost of social unity. However, the post-revolutionary society soon faced a real menace of dissolution, and post-revolutionary thinkers of all colours – conservatives, liberals and socialists – turned to religious symbolism to dispel this threat.[30]

Sustaining faith in this symbolism nevertheless was and remained a real problem. Amidst the competition and conflict that became increasingly visible between the citizens in the years after the Revolution, *the People* that was supposed to bind them into a unity became increasingly invisible. The reality of *the People* and the real sense of unity between them were highly visible and tangible during the Revolution when they were literally shedding their blood together on the streets like one body. The question was how to turn the bloody event of the Revolution into something with enduring significance and force. The question was how to turn the *People as event* into *the People as an enduring reality* that transcends the contingent tensions and conflicts between its members and allows them to overcome these conflicts and remain united.

At stake was nothing less than a question of faith and faithfulness. The post-revolutionary thinkers soon saw that their Christ had departed again, the Christ whom the people themselves had become through common bloodshed, the Christ in whom they were united, at least for a brief moment in time. The question was how the holy spirit of this Messiah could be sustained among them, now that He was no longer physically with them. The challenge was to sustain a time or temporal register of unity that exceeded the register of empirical time under which the people were evidently no longer united. In order to sustain the faith in the continuing or enduring unity of *the People* in the face of evident division and fragmentation among *the people*, they needed to create a time or temporal register for an *invisible People* that awaited its final re-incarnation – *[le temps] du Peuple, d'un Peuple, en attente de son incarnation et, de quelque manière, toujours invisible, quoiqu'il se soit fait voir un moment dans l'histoire. . . .*[31] But such a vision of an invisible people that awaits its own incarnation demands faith – *[elle] demande la foi.*[32]

## 3 The unfindable People

Pierre Rosanvallon's *Le Peuple introuvable – histoire de la représentation démocratique en France* vividly recounts the difficulties and challenges that the revolutionary and post-revolutionary generations faced as far as this question of enduring faith in the People was concerned. For purposes of sustaining the sense of unity that was tangibly, visibly and viscerally evident when they shed their blood together in the

30  Ibid, p. 321.
31  Ibid, p. 309.
32  Ibid.

streets of revolt, they organised national feasts and contemplated works of art that might sustain the memory of those grand days of the Revolution. Uniquely telling in this regard was the proposal of the revolutionary artist Jacques-Louis David to erect a giant public sculpture representing the People. The sculpture had to be cast out of bronze obtained by melting the canons captured from the enemy. The figure had to carry a massive hammer in one hand to symbolise the power of the People. In the other it had to hold figures representing equality and liberty and thus symbolised the values of the republic. The base of the sculpture had to be adorned with reproductions of the text of the Constitution and the Declaration of Rights, as well as medals that recalled the great events of the Revolution. But, as if knowing that all of this would still not suffice to produce a visceral enough experience, David also proposed that the words *lumière, nature, vérité, force* and *courage* be written in large letters on the forehead, chest and arms of the statute. This hyperbolism only underlined the futility and desperation of the endeavour to represent the miraculous unity of the People that once revealed itself briefly on the blood-stained streets of Paris. As Rosanvallon observes:

> Everything happened as if it was necessary to add words to the signs so as to really make the people visible, the work of the imagination alone proving to be somehow incapable of grasping it.[33]

The difficulty or futility of any attempt to represent in art and through festivities a People that could no longer be felt and sensed as it was felt and sensed during the Revolution would soon come to haunt the question of political representation. In the minds of the post-revolutionary leaders, there was much more at stake in the question of political representation than a mere mandate to communicate particular and factional interests of the people to the National Assembly. As a decision-making platform, the National Assembly itself had to be a veritable embodiment of the virtues and ideals of the People and this gave rise to perplexing questions regarding the criteria for electing the deputies. The election of the representatives of the People had to comply with several crucial criteria. The first was that the representatives were not to be elected *by* the people in their ordinary capacity as a group of individuals. The *sociological reality of the people* – that is, of a group or mass of individuals who happen to live together in the same time and space and invariably compete with one another for survival, wealth and honour – had no significant relation to the *symbolical ideal of the People* that the representatives had to represent. In other words, the representatives had to represent the People, not the people.

At issue here again is the split between the people as an empirically observable sociological reality, on the one hand, and the People as a symbolical projection, on the other. In other words, the conceptualisation of the People/people in terms of a doubling that echoed the symbolism of the two bodies of the king, again played

---

33 Translated from Rosanvallon 1988, p. 37.

a key role when the question of national representation came to a head. The selection of the representatives therefore entailed *an election* with a veritable theological or spiritual dimension, just as the kings of former times were considered elected by God.[34] The fact that the representatives of the People were not and could not be elected by the people also meant that their candidacy could not be organised at all. The question then was how the potential representatives were to come to the fore so as to become the elect.

The second criterion concerned the rejection of any kind of elitism. The radically egalitarian spirit of the revolutionaries proscribed any form of hierarchy. This proscription of hierarchy ruled out the possibility of "candidates" or "candidacy," for in the very notion of "candidacy" lurked the germ of hierarchy. It should become clear that the double proscription of any kind of organisation by the people and any kind of candidacy turned the election of the representatives into a highly mystical or theological affair. The candidates were to be elected on the basis of a moral nobility that made itself known by a kind of electricity – literally a moral electricity –*électricité morale*[35] – that immediately inspired confidence and made possible a perception of pure merit that had no sociological link or connotation.[36] In other words, the election of the representatives was to become evident through a moral purity that severed them from all sociological particularity and from all considerations of merit – such as wealth or education – related to such particularity. These pure individuals were to come to the fore to represent the People in the way a sublime work of art may have endeavoured to represent the People. The true will of the People had to shine through the representatives. This lustre would educate the people and inspire them to take leave of the sociological particularity and the personal or factional interests that divided and separated them from one another. The representatives of the People would in this way allow the people – all those who did not have their moral purity – to also retain some recollection of the true unity and virtue of the People that prevailed during the sublime days of the Revolution when they acted and shed their blood together.

Well, this was the idea and the philosophy of representation in the years after the Revolution. But the sociological reality of difference, distinction and notability started to weigh down these lofty ideals with little delay. It was not long before social standing and wealth turned these ideals into a common bourgeois meritocracy. It only took a couple of years before the same Guizot who made the term "moral electricity" salient, began to promote wealth and property as the key indicators of the social qualities expected from the representatives of the People (to resort for a moment, not inappropriately, it seems, to the managerial language of today).[37]

---

34  Rosanvallon 1988, p. 59.
35  This was an expression made popular by Guizot, but it was already used during the Revolution. See Rosanvallon 1988, p. 63 n. 2.
36  Ibid, p. 62–63.
37  Ibid, pp. 69–70.

The irony could not be greater. Jean-Jacques Rousseau, whose thought was a main source of inspiration for the revolutionary generation, specifically identified property as the source of all social competition and conflict. The fact that property had by 1830 become the sign of the moral purity of the representatives of the People that was to remind the people of the sublime unity that transcended their common divisions, was a clear indication of how far the revolutionary imagination – if one can still call it that – had strayed from its initial inspirations and ideals. Let us turn to Rousseau now, for there is another element of his thinking that is quite remarkable when one compares it to the post-revolutionary endeavour to symbolise and represent the unity of the People that evaporated so quickly after the Revolution. Rousseau evidently did not consider symbolic representation a key element of the unitary will of the people. He simply replaced it with a *conceptual assumption* that the unity of the People must have existed at least once. This one-off unity, he argued, cannot be invoked or enacted – let alone re-enacted – to overcome the divisions that soon followed in its wake. It can at best be invoked as a source of legitimation. It can and must be invoked, argued Rousseau, to legitimise the coercive rules to which a society takes recourse to manage its divisions and conflicts. Let us take a closer look at this argument.

## 4 The general will of the People

Now that we have seen just how difficult it is to find or establish a People, we have also developed a good vantage point from where the ingenious "contractual" sub-stitution of the people in Jean-Jacques Rousseau's *Du Contrat social* can be grasped. Rousseau evidently did not entertain the idea that people ever existed as *a* People or *the* People. He consequently also did not participate in the search for such a People. He did not try to give an enduring substance to the people in the way the revolutionary thinkers of the nineteenth century did, ironically, often with recourse to his thinking. As is clear from his *Discours sur l'origine et les fondements de l'inégalité parmi les hommes,* he had no illusions about the irredeemable lack of actual social solidarity between individuals that came to prevail ever since they emerged from the absolute and non-reflective need to collaborate that conditioned their exist-ence in the state of nature. Sentiments of solidarity, or the lack of them, simply did not enter the consciousness of a group of "spear carriers" who constantly sensed the threat of pouncing wild beasts. They either collaborated or perished. How-ever, when settled communities eventually began to afford them a more sedentary existence – that is, when they emerged from the state of nature – the potential for reflective solidarity between these former spear carriers was soon ruined by the mimetic competition that resulted from the institution of property. Henceforth, the need to distinguish oneself materially and socially that resulted from the first claims to ownership would invariably displace all sentiments of solidarity that might have been. Thus proceeds the argument in the *Discours sur . . . l'inégalité parmi les hommes.*[38]

---

38 Rousseau 1992, p. 222.

To identify a People from this association of individuals competing for honour and property is evidently a hopeless matter if one means by "a People" a collective entity with a symbolic significance of togetherness and solidarity that transcends the bare sociological fact of a group of individuals who cohabitate in space and time. Rousseau evidently knew this and steered clear of any suggestion that such a People could actually be identified as an empirical reality. The theory of the people as *a People* that he put forward in *Du Contrat social* therefore pivots on a very different basis. It turns on *an assumption, an assumption* that a general consensus regarding the basic terms of communal existence must have existed at least once. In other words, it turns on the assumption that the members of any society must have agreed on terms on which future disagreements and conflicts between them would be managed. These terms, Rousseau argued, can be assumed to have issued from a one-off consensus that he called the general will – *la volonté générale*. This is key statement in the *Du Contrat social* at issue here:

> In fact, if there were no anterior convention at all, from what does the obligation derive that the minority must submit themselves to the choice of the major- ity, given that the decision was not taken unanimously. And why do a hundred citizens who vote for a leader have the right to impose that choice of leader on ten who do not want him as leader? The law concerning the binding nature of majority votes is itself established by a convention with regard to which a once off unanimity must be supposed [*suppose au moins une fois l'unanimité*].[39]

This passage from Book I of the *Du Contrat social* states clearly that the notion of the *volonté générale* that the ensuing chapters postulate and explain does not concern a substantive unity between individuals that makes them "a People." It concerns instead a formal presupposition on the basis of which any conflicts and disagree- ments that arise between them – precisely because they are not "a People" – can be managed. This is reiterated and underlined poignantly by two later passages from *Du Contrat social*, one also from Book I, and the other from Book II. The first concerns Rousseau's infamously brazen statement that the general will simply has to be imposed on anyone who begs to disagree with it. The second concerns his observation that a real or empirical agreement or consensus between the people is not necessarily an expression of the general will and may even be at odds with the general will. Let us take a closer look at both passages in turn.

Real or empirical disagreements *with* the general will can evidently be antici- pated, according to Rousseau, but they will not be tolerated *by* the general will. The general will is not the embodiment of a factual unity of the people, but the embodiment of foundational arrangements that guarantee them their freedom. These foundational arrangements (which they are assumed to have endorsed at least once) can be understood to guarantee all members of society their freedom,

---

39 Translated from Rousseau 1964, p. 181.

precisely because the constraints imposed by these arrangements have been freely endorsed by everyone (as they are assumed or *supposed* to have done – see the last line of the passage quoted above). The constraints embodied in the general will are, in other words, not curtailments of freedom, but conditions of freedom. Any act that would reject or resist them, would not be an act of freedom, but a rejection of freedom. So, if anyone who can be assumed to have freely endorsed the constraints imposed by the general will – at least once – should later refuse to be constrained by these constraints, that person will simply be constrained by force. He or she would thus, as Rousseau put it, be forced to be free, forced to re-endorse the freedom that he or she once endorsed:

> In order then that the social pact is not a pointless formula, it tacitly also includes the agreement that renders the rest of the agreements enforceable, namely, that whoever refuses to obey the general will will be forced to do so by the whole social body. This means nothing else but forcing him to be free [*ce qui ne signifie autre chose sinon qu'on le forcera d'être libre*].[40]

Forcing someone to be free – *le forcera d'être libre* – is something that free societies do whenever they enforce the freely endorsed constraints of law against anyone in that society who happens to resist or transgress the law. Hegel later expressed the same principle even more dramatically than Rousseau did, as we shall see in Chapter 7. Suffice it to say here that both Rousseau and Hegel considered criminal punishment a confirmation of the liberty of the convicted criminal. The principle that motivated them is one that the most exemplary of liberal democracies endorse routinely. Punishment is generally considered the legitimate promotion of the liberty of the punished because the punished, too, can be considered to have endorsed, without later revocation of this endorsement, the penal code of the society with which he or she continued to associate.

This principle applies irrespectively whether it is only one, only a couple or everyone, who is resisting the constraints of the *volonté générale*. This becomes abundantly clear in the other passage from *Du Contract social* that we referred to above. In this passage, Rousseau draws a clear distinction between any empirically observable expression of the will of the people, on the one hand, and the *volonté générale*, on the other. Let us take a closer look at this passage now. Rousseau writes:

> There is often a difference between the will of everyone [*la volonté de tous*] and the general will [*la volonté générale*]. The latter only pertains to the interests truly held in common, whereas the other pertains to private interest, and amounts to nothing but the total sum of particular wills [*n'est qu'une somme de volontés particulières*].[41]

---

40 Translated from Rousseau 1964, p. 186.
41 Translated from ibid, p. 193.

This statement makes it clear that the *volonté générale* should not be confused with either the empirically observable will of a majority of the citizens, or the unanimous will of all citizens. What is the *volonté générale* then? It is, according to Rousseau, the expression of a norm that complies strictly with the requirement of reciprocity. It is not just a reflection of something to which a majority or everyone may have agreed under the exigencies of specific circumstances (which could, for instance, include the agreement between those who wish to enslave and those who are prepared to accept enslavement as a means to avoid death), but a reflection of the norm that would be endorsed when everyone concerned decides, whatever needs to be decided, strictly with regard to the equal concerns of everyone as understood by everyone. Rousseau writes:

> Why is the general always right, and why does everyone constantly want the happiness of each one among them, if it is not because there is no person who does not appropriate these words "each one" for himself and who is not thinking of himself when he is voting for everyone [*qui ne s'approprie ce mot chacun, et qui ne songe à lui-même en votant pour tous*]? This proves that equality before the law and the notion of justice that it produces derive from the preference that everyone gives to himself and therefore from human nature [*de la nature de l'homme*]. It also proves that the general will, in order to really be the general will, must be it in its aim and its essence, and that it must come from everyone and apply to everyone [*qu'elle doit partir de tous pour s'appliquer à tous*].[42]

The thoughts of Rousseau that we have traced thus far allow us to make a key observation regarding the status of the *volonté générale*: The *volonté générale* can in no way be understood to refer to the historical or sociological embodiment of the will of any people. In this respect, the *volonté générale* can for all practical purposes be considered a forerunner of the principle of universalisation that Kant articulated with his categorical imperative.[43] In other words, it is a normative principle and not a historical or sociological fact. It is not the historical or sociological realisation of the will or identity of a people that happens to live together in a society. Rousseau makes it very clear that the general will concerns a normative principle of strict equality and reciprocity that is *imputed* to the individuals who form a society. They are assumed to have endorsed this principle of reciprocity and equality at least once and it is this assumption or imputation that turns them into a People who have a general will or can be considered to have one.

The significance of the move that Rousseau makes here lies in the way it reverses the temporal relation that a common sense understanding is likely to identify between a People and the norms endorsed by this People. A common sense

---

42 Translated from ibid, p. 195.
43 Kant 1983, vol. 6, pp. 51, 140 (§ 7).

understanding of this relation may well insist that a People precedes the norms that it endorses. Rousseau would seem to suggest the contrary. He seems to suggest that the People follow the norm or follow from the norm. It is the norm itself that constitutes a free People, not their historical existence, or their historical endorsement of the norm. There is no knowledge available of such a historical endorsement. The endorsement of the norm is one that can at best be assumed to have taken place, or presupposed, as Hans Kelsen would argue later (see Chapter 9). In this regard, Rousseau may well be considered a forerunner of Kelsen.

The invocation of "human nature" in the last passage quoted above must be understood accordingly. Of concern there cannot be real human nature, but an assumed or supposed human nature that has its origin in *the assumption* of a decision taken by everyone who applies to everyone. If Rousseau actually considered this passage as an articulation of a real correspondence between law and human nature, he cannot be exempted from the history of the metaphysics of life and law that we have been analysing since the beginning of this book. There is, however, good reason to believe – in view of the first passage quoted from *Du Contrat social* above, that he was a forerunner of the Kantian and Kelsenian constructivism that effectively severed the link between life and law.[44]

## 5 Universal and particular – key coordinates of a bourgeois century

Multiple social tensions came to a head in France in the years after the French Revolution. On the one hand, struggles between Royalists and Republicans gave rise to alternating republican, monarchical and imperial forms of government which only came to an end with the founding of the Third Republic in 1870. On the other hand, the century is also deeply marked by rising tensions between the bourgeoisie and the working class. These tensions culminated in the development that Rosanvallon calls "*la séparation ouvrière*," that is, the opening up of a gap or split within the citizenry because of an increasing consciousness among the workers that they are not really part of the People as it came to be represented by the bourgeoisie. Not only were French workers – basically all citizens without property – excluded from the right to vote from 1792 to 1848,[45] even after regaining the vote in 1848 they continued to consider themselves excluded from the People because the list of "candidates" or potential representatives of the People for whom they could vote were all selected from a class of property owners with whom they did not identify. After 1848 participation of workers in the representation of the People became a major concern in French politics.

---

44 This "Kantian" reading of Rousseau is also evident in Mauss 1992 (see especially pp. 185, 220–221) but it is not shared by everyone. See Volk 2015, p. 85.
45 The initial inclusion of all citizens to the right to vote in 1792 was terminated by the reinstitution of the *suffrage censitaire* (suffrage conditioned by compliance with a minimum tax duty called the *cens*) by the *Directoire* of 1795 to 1799. See Rosanvallon 1988, pp. 73–74.

The separation of the workers from the bourgeois conception of the citizenry was highly significant because of the way it shattered the universalistic pretentions of the bourgeois class. The claim that the unique moral integrity of representatives elected exclusively from the propertied bourgeoisie would adequately represent the unitary and universal will of the People, and not only the interests of the bourgeoisie (or, ideally, *not at all* the interests of the bourgeoisie – see the discussion above of the idea that representation of the *volonté générale* did *not at all* concern class or social interests) was no longer credible after 1848. It had by then become abundantly clear that the French citizenry was deeply divided and split, and that a core aspiration of the revolutionary imagination – the idea of one united People – had completely run out of steam. Three workers – Jean-Jacques Blanc, Henri Tolain and Coutant (apparently known only as Coutant) – stepped forward as candidates to represent the workers among the representatives of the People in the elections of 1863, but they were massively outvoted. However, their defeat could not erase the historical significance of their candidacy. As Rosanvallon observes poignantly:

> It would be wrong to evaluate the significance of these first workers candidacies on the basis of their modest results. In fact, they constituted a double historical rupture. They testified to the deepening split that opened up between the world of the workers and the republican universe. But they also rendered evident the fragmentation of the universalistic political culture that emerged from the French Revolution.[46]

The bourgeois electorate – both Republicans and Liberals – accused the workers of wanting to retreat from the universalism of the Revolution and for wanting to reintroduce into French politics the particularities of the old corporatism that the Revolution came to destroy. They were accused of undoing the unitary *People* that the Revolution had come to forge out of a mere multitude of *people* with conflicting interests.[47] This accusation was evidently very blind to the flagrant way in which the universalism it claimed had become a vehicle for particular class interests. One may well want to suspect this false universalism of having been nothing more than a cynical lie, but one should not jump to the simple conclusion that it was. Had it just been a cynical lie, it surely would have been up for easy exposure and rapid obsolescence. But something with much more profound historical significance was at stake here than a mere lie could ever have. Of concern was nothing less than an epochal demise of the capacity to draw self-evident distinctions between the universal and the particular that the revolutionary generation still claimed so confidently. Rosanvallon observes with regard to France: "The candidacies of the workers and the reactions they solicited clearly showed that French politics struggled to contemplate social diversity and civic universalism simultaneously."[48]

46 Translated from ibid, pp. 93–94.
47 Ibid, pp. 117–119.
48 Translated from ibid, p. 113.

The problem was not exclusive to France. A similar drama unfolded in England in the context of the English Reform Bill of 1867. The bill – which increased the number of English voters from 1,634,000 to 2,445.000 – was vehemently opposed by conservatives who had an organic view of society according to which specific groups were to be represented in Parliament, and not individuals. In his argument against this Conservative opposition to the bill, John Stuart Mill turned their own arguments against them. He insisted that the bill was effectively about class and argued that the workers should be included as a specific class. If those who opposed the bill did not want to include worker representation in terms of individual rights, they should, he said, completely in keeping with their own philosophy, endorse the representation of the workers as a group, for they were the only group in society that enjoyed no representation.[49] Here too, the instability and paradoxes of the universal-particular distinction were no longer deniable. They just became manifest in an inverse fashion. The English Conservatives endorsed an organic vision of society that stressed particularity. They stressed the need to distinguish and recognise the particular interests of the diverse components of society, but they, too, were surreptitiously sustaining a false universal that claimed to speak on behalf of millions of people who were prevented from speaking for themselves.

What was unfolding here – both in France and England – was nothing less than the failure to come to terms with the tragic condition of modernity that Lefort invokes in his essay on the permanence of the theologico-political.[50] The concept of the universal as reflected in notions of universal interests, universal rights and universal representation may well be considered the empty space of power that modern democracy aspired to keep empty. Having taken leave of all medieval endeavours to fill this space with final authority and a complete capacity for truth, modern democracy sought to keep it empty and open, and thus aspired to sustain the difference between the real and the symbolical. In other words, the universal should be understood as a symbolic notion that must not be confused with any reality. The universal cannot be realised without making it party to some particularity and thereby turning it into a transparent misrepresentation of reality. The difference between this misrepresentation and a cynical lie will always depend on a range of specific circumstances that need not be elaborated here. Suffice it just to observe the epistemic link between them that will always render the former very predictably vulnerable to accusations of the latter.

A certain negative instantiation (not embodiment because a certain disembodiment is exactly what is at stake in this instantiation) of the universal is at stake in the aspiration of modern democracy. This negative instantiation becomes possible when the pursuit of a symbolic ideal puts every aspect of particularity – that is, the sum of all conceivable particular concerns – on the line. This is what the Revolutionaries did when they put their own bodies in the line of fire. When a particular

---

49  Ibid, p. 121.
50  See the discussion of Lefort above.

quest for the universal becomes as selfless as it does when it puts itself – and the very life that sustains it – completely on the line for the sake of this universal, it enters a zone of transmutation where the particular and the universal become one. But, the universal evaporates the moment that it is hinged to the pursuit and promotion of any enduring positive interest, be this interest expansive or minimal. Both the French bourgeoisie – who only later stepped into the shoes of Revolutionaries who had indeed put themselves directly in the line of fire when the Revolution erupted – and the English Conservatives were for this reason false universalists. They both claimed the commitment to afford to every group what is due to it, but they were surreptitiously promoting particular interests at the cost of other such interests.

It may appear odd to refer to the English Conservatives as "universalists." Were they not, quite to the contrary, insisting on the recognition of particular class claims? They were, indeed, but they presented their particularistic claims in the name of *all* particular concerns in contention, not only their own. One need not make typically universalistic claims to become a false universalist. One only needs to present one's particular concern under the umbrella of a universal concern and leave the task of excluding certain particular concerns to the surreptitious limits of the umbrella. Epochal examples of such spurious universalisms abound. Mill was effectively accusing the corporatist arguments of the English Conservatives of such a spurious universalism. He saw right through their traditionalist claims that English democracy was based on group and not individual representation. He saw all too well that they were claiming political representation for "all" social groups while silently excluding the one that posed a threat to their own interests.

In the second half of the twentieth century the apartheid regime in South Africa (1948–1994) claimed that the policies of apartheid pursued the "separate development" of all groups in South Africa, not just of whites. One would have to partake in cynicism not to recognise the cynicism of this "separate development" ruse, and the cynicism of the Reagans and Thatchers who lent support to it till late in the century. But the motive for misrepresenting reality among those who opposed the English Reform Bill of 1867 is open to some doubt. Resistance to the bill may or may not have been cynical self-preservation and self-promotion. The honestly critical and self-critical moral and political reflection that one associates with the ideals of the Enlightenment were still standing in baby shoes then. The English Conservatives, or some among them, may still have been very blind to the exclusions they were perpetrating, blind to the fact that the Industrial Revolution had created a new and as yet voiceless class of people. This excuse may or may not have held some water at the time. One has to leave this assessment open, considering that the French bourgeoisie, who inherited a truly universalist revolution, did no better in its wake.

It is important to attain a clear grasp of the ideological confusions, conflations and obfuscations that nineteenth century Europe was still bound to perpetrate. Not only was the nineteenth century the century in which the universalist ideals of the French Revolution were attacked from both left and right (workers and social movements who considered themselves excluded from the bourgeois conception of political representation attacking it from the left, Royalists and supporters of the *ancien régime* attacking it from the right). The nineteenth was also the first century in which moral reflection and political deliberation became philosophically articulated in terms of the problematic relation between the universal and the particular. Towards the end of the eighteenth century, Immanuel Kant re-cast the foundations of Western moral thinking with two seminal works, the *Grundlegung der Metaphysik der Sitten* of 1785 and the *Kritik der praktischen Vernunft* of 1788. Both these works severed the problematic link between the universal and the particular that had been the key assumption of Aristotelian ethics throughout.

Aristotle articulated a principle of ethical deliberation in his *Nicomachean Ethics* that turned on a *dialectic between the universal and the particular*. At issue for him was a notion of practical reason or *phronesis* that required particular applications of general virtues that responded appropriately to the specificity of concrete circumstances.[51] The conception of moral deliberation articulated by Kant severed this link between the general or the universal, on the one hand, and the particular, on the other. According to Kant, the compliance with the demands of universality stipulated by the categorical imperative (act so that the maxim of your conduct can be considered a universal law) *cannot* be achieved with any particular instance of ethical conduct. Such compliance would only become possible in the course of an infinite pursuit of moral perfection.[52] Kantian moral perfection is, in other words, subject to a condition that no particular moral action can claim or hope to fulfil.

It should be clear from the way in which Kant articulated the categorical imperative that he considered it a transcendental condition that rendered moral conduct possible as a pursuit, but not as an achievement. In other words, the categorical imperative does not concern a criterion with which any specific instance of moral conduct can hope to comply. Understood in this way, the Kantian conception of moral duty underpins the separation of the symbolic and the real that Lefort articulated two centuries later. The categorical imperative entails a symbolic articulation of moral perfection that remains irreducibly external to any actual attempt at moral perfection. Seen from this perspective, the categorical imperative envisages a moral potentiality that never enters any attempt to actualise this potentiality. Kant's moral philosophy can therefore also be considered a precursor of Agamben's call for a distinction between potentiality and actuality that disallows the transformation of potentiality into actuality. A meticulous reading of Kant's moral philosophy confirms that this is exactly what Kant is arguing for, notwithstanding Kant's own occasional failures to grasp this.

One of the most striking examples of Kant's misunderstanding of the significance of his rigorous distinction between the demands of the categorical imperative and any particular instance of moral conduct concerns his facile conflation of moral

---

51 See the discussion of Aristotle's conception of practical wisdom in Chapter 1, p. 18.
52 Kant 1983, vol. 6, pp. 252–254.

perfection and truthfulness. Kant failed to see that moral reflection can come to turn on a morally sincere distinction between circumstances under which a lie is ethically justified, and even required, and circumstances under which it is ethically reprehensible. Hence his argument that one should honestly disclose the hiding place of a person to persecutors who threaten him or her with unjust harm, because any dishonest attempt to protect that person may easily backfire and actually contribute to the harm instead of preventing it.[53] This argument is so contrived that any person seriously concerned with moral integrity under circumstances such as these would not give it a moment's consideration. One should consider morally incompetent anyone who would, under the circumstances sketched by Kant, be painfully burdened by the question of whether a lie would be morally acceptable or not. It is not the morality of the lie that counts here, but its efficiency. Whether or not the lie will save the situation is surely the only question that a morally sound person should ask under the dire circumstances Kant puts up for consideration. Anyone burdened by the question of the morality of a lie under these circumstances is surely descending into a petty moralism that has nothing to do with sound moral reflection.[54]

Be that as it may, Kant's practical philosophy is ultimately not significantly impaired by the petty bourgeois moralism to which he evidently appeared to be partial. The separation of the symbolic and the real which his conception of the categorical imperative articulated became a cornerstone of the ideal of liberal democratic deliberation and should remain so for two reasons: It provides one with a conception of moral reflection that resonates closely with Lefort's conception of democracy as the only political form that endeavours to keep the symbolic and real apart and the place of power empty. And it stabilises the potentiality-actuality distinction. Both these considerations are key to the liberal democratic resistance to modern relapses into medieval conflations of power and authority which, predictably, lead to the worst of totalitarianisms, as Agamben points out. The effective separation of potentiality and actuality, and *auctoritas* and *potestas*, is the essence of Kant's philosophical achievement. This achievement became the main target of the formidable critique of Kant that Hegel began to articulate soon after his death in 1804. We turn to Hegel in Chapter 7. It will become clear then that his gigantic philosophical endeavour pivoted on an erasure of the essential separation of potentiality from actuality with which Kant articulated the theoretical foundations of Modernity, foundations without which liberal democracy is hardly thinkable. Much irony attached to this erasure. As we shall see, it largely undermined the very aspiration that motivated it.

---

53  See Kant 1983, vol. 7, pp. 637–643.
54  Kant indeed showed more signs of such a petty bourgeois moralism in his letter exchange with Maria von Herbert. See Van der Walt 2018, pp. 56–60.

# 7

# ECONOMY, SOCIETY AND SPIRITUAL HISTORY

## 1 The utilitarian and economic unity of the people

John Austin published *The Province of Jurisprudence Determined* in 1832. The book was crucial for the development of modern jurisprudence and theory of law in at least two respects. On the one hand, it was a major stimulus for Herbert Hart's *The Concept of Law* (1961) which became a pivotal work in the tradition of analytical jurisprudence. On the other, it articulated a utilitarian theory of law that could be considered a forerunner of economic theories of law associated with the Chicago School of economic thinking. In what follows, we will only consider the latter legacy. We turn to Hart in Chapter 8.

The opening pages of *The Province of Jurisprudence Determined* define law as a habitually obeyed command of a sovereign.[1] In other words, Austin once more endorsed Ulpianus' maxim *quod principi placuit legis habet vigorem*. However, he did not consider the law-making capacity of the emperor arbitrary. The law of the sovereign, Austin claimed, must reflect the eternal law of God.[2] Up to this point of his argument, his thinking was still very much in line with the theocratic conception of sovereignty of ancient Rome and medieval Europe. However, he then made a move that clearly took leave of the Roman conception of sovereignty. He simply equated the law of God with the greatest happiness of the greatest number of people.[3]

As we saw in Chapter 5, the constraints that ancient and medieval political theologies imposed on sovereign law-making were motivated by conceptions of the "good of the people." These conceptions of the "good of the people" were, however, not amenable to the flattening of the concept of happiness that became evident in

1 Austin 1861, pp. 5, 13.
2 Austin 1861, pp. 46–47.
3 Austin 1861, pp. 32.

Austin's conception of "the greatest happiness for the greatest number of people," notwithstanding the theocratic connection between God and happiness that he ostensibly sustained. It is very likely that Austin took over this maxim from the work of Jeremy Bentham. Bentham was a mentor and friend with whom he closely associated. He may also have been influenced later by John Mill, the other great utilitarian thinker of the time who was also a contemporary and friend. However, Mill was only in his mid-twenties when *The Province of Jurisprudence Determined* was published in 1832, whereas Austin was already forty-two by this time. It is therefore safe to assume that Bentham (forty-two years Austin's senior) was the main influence on the utilitarian principle that found its way into *The Province of Jurisprudence Determined*. Whereas Mill developed a much more nuanced concept of utility in his book *Utilitarianism* (published in 1863) that accommodated a whole range of spiritual and intellectual values, Bentham's utilitarian thinking purposefully pursued a flattening of the concept of utility so as to turn it into a *pleasure/absence of pain* heuristic. This flattening of the concept of utility was part and parcel of his anti-metaphysical and "adequately empirical" theory of law and government that expressly rejected the notion of abstract or natural rights which inspired the French Revolutionaries at the time. Bentham considered natural rights "simple nonsense: natural and imprescriptible rights, rhetorical nonsense, nonsense upon stilts."[4] The purpose of law and government, he argued, turned strictly on the principle of utility.

> It has been shown that the happiness of the individuals, of whom a community is composed, that is their pleasure and their security, is the end and the sole end which the legislator should have in view: the sole standard, in conformity with which each individual ought, as far as depends upon the legislator, to be made to fashion his behaviour.[5]

Bentham's determined endeavour to strip the concerns of law and legislation of all metaphysical ideas was corroborated by his express avoidance of religious ideas in the contemplation of law and politics. The critique of William Blackstone's *Commentaries on the Laws of England* – which Bentham articulated in two closely related texts, *A Comment on the Commentaries* and *A Fragment on Government* – is exemplary in this regard. The idea of God is of no use if it is not linked to considerations of utility, he argued in response to Blackstone's invocations of God as the ultimate author of law. And if it can be linked to considerations of utility, he added, there is no need to do so, for the principle of utility can stand very well on its own two feet and "admits of no rival . . . or associate."[6]

We saw above that Austin did not join in Bentham's proscription of theological concepts in jurisprudence. It is unlikely that Austin knew nothing of Bentham's views in this regard, considering the close association between them. He may not

---

4 Bentham 2002, p. 330.
5 Bentham 1948, 147.
6 Bentham 2008, pp. 26–27.

have had full knowledge of the sharp anti-religious statements of the *Comment on the Commentaries*, given that Bentham had abandoned it after the publication of the *Fragment on Government* in 1776 and it was only published in 1928, long after Austin's death in 1859. The *Fragment* was not completely silent as far as Bentham's rejection of religious ideas was concerned,[7] but not nearly as vociferous as the *Comment*. Be that as it may, it is clear that Austin still clung to the religious symbolism of pre-modernity at a time when Bentham was already rejecting it expressly.[8] Considered in the terms of Lefort with whom we engaged above, Bentham completely rejected the significance of a distinction between the real and the symbolic. In fact, it was his avowed endeavour to rid the human mind of the need for religious symbolism. As James Crimmins puts it: "Between 1809 and 1823 Jeremy Bentham carried out an exhaustive examination of religion with the declared aim of extirpating religious beliefs, even the idea of religion itself, from the minds of men."[9]

Bentham's extirpation project did not succeed, as the reference to God in Austin's *The Province of Jurisprudence Determined* makes clear. Had it succeeded, however, it would have left the consciousness of his time with just one register for making sense of its physical and social environment, namely, the register of "real" and empirically observable pleasure and pain. Would this reduction of the two separate registers of the symbolic *and* the real to only one register – the strictly empirical register of the "real" – ever have stood a chance of succeeding? How, might one ask, would a common or shared understanding of place and time and purpose of conduct have survived the loss of the second register? Phrased differently, how would a single register of "pain and pleasure" have provided for a common "framework of reference"?

A framework of reference only becomes possible in the wake of a division of registers that renders reference between registers possible. Common or communal meaning only becomes possible through a referential relation between at least two different registers. A flattened pain/pleasure heuristic does not provide for this referential play between two or more registers. The experience of pain or pleasure – Bentham's one and only register – can only attain normative meaning in a second register that renders it meaningful or meaningless. This is surely the first insight that one should draw from the destruction of medieval and ancient registers of religious transcendence during the French Revolution discussed in Chapter 6. Instead of engendering a single register of universal humanity, the destruction of religious transcendence almost immediately precipitated a search for a new source of transcendence. It was this new or renewed need for referential transcendence that demanded the splitting of the post-revolutionary social condition into a sociological fact of competitive and divisive co-existence, on the one hand, and a unifying

7  Ibid, p. 450.
8  Crimmins (1990, p. 285) cites Austin (along with Mill and other utilitarian thinkers) as one of the "English moralists . . . who resumed the effort to find a place for religion within their thought" in "the period that followed Bentham's death."
9  See *Crimmins 1986, p. 95, as well as Crimmins 1990, pp. 50–65, 271, 275.*

political aspiration, on the other. How else would the post-revolutionary society have been able to refer to itself? This renewed doubling of registers was the only way in which a vantage point could be construed from the perspective of which the sociological fact of divisive competition could be assessed in either negative (e.g.: the competition is excessive, destructive and debilitating) or positive terms (e.g.: the competition is adequate and incentivising).

Perhaps this is exactly what Mill sensed when he supplemented Bentham's pleasure/pain register with multiple registers of utility from the respective vantage points of which both pleasure and pain could be assessed in positive or negative terms (and vice versa, of course: the pleasure/pain register can also become a vantage point from which the pertinence of other utility registers can be relativised). However, utility as such – even when developed into a refined hierarchy of utilities – ultimately becomes a dull instrument when it is not situated in a framework of reflection that may, or may not, render every imaginable register of utility irrelevant in view of a non-utilitarian concern. This is why expansive modes of economic imagination culminate predictably in simplifying and over-simplifying reductions of social reality that effectively turn "the social" into an object that is assessable in only one utility register, namely, economic efficiency.

The utility principle has often been presented in highly reductive forms such as this one: Social utility requires that one kill an innocent person if that is the only way to save the lives of ten others. An uncompromising adherence to the maxim of the greatest happiness for the biggest number of people would indeed require this bleak prospect. John Rawls and Bernard Williams articulate forceful critiques of this reductive understanding of utility that demand careful consideration here. Williams makes this point in this regard: The utility principle becomes spurious when it is presented as a complete formula for moral reasoning that requires no further information extrinsic to it. Whether someone is morally required to kill an innocent person in order to save ten others depends on the life-project of that person and the values that inform that project. A person may have religious convictions that oblige him or her never to harm another person, but do not demand that all harm to other persons should actively be prevented, especially when such prevention would itself require actively harming someone. The argument that more harm can be prevented by actively doing harm is one that this person will neither find nor need to find compelling, argues Williams. Someone else may well feel that this person has regrettably simple moral and religious convictions, but there is no universally applicable moral principle that demands him or her to take leave of a whole life project or a conscious set of moral convictions for purposes of doing something that he or she believes is wrong to do.[10]

To subject someone to the normative cogency of a simple utility calculation, avers Rawls in a similar argument, is to tie that person to a society or group of people to

10  Williams 1973, pp. 96–100; 110–117.

which he or she does not belong.[11] The person of concern here just does not belong to a facile utilitarian society where the meaning of life can be assessed in terms of a numerical relation between lives saved and lives abandoned. Much more than just numbers and units of utility may be at stake for this person. Not to see and acknowledge this is not to recognise "the separateness of persons." As Rawls puts it: "Utilitarianism does not take seriously the distinctions between people."[12] Utilitarianism only becomes possible, he argues, when one takes the position of an impartial spectator that "fuses" all members of a society "into one."[13]

That a significant element of modern economic reasoning turns on exactly this fusion of people into one that Rawls has in mind is very evident from the reasoning that Ronald Coase put forward in his seminal 1960 article, "The Problem of Social Cost."[14] The article takes the concepts of economic efficiency generally known as Pareto and Kaldor-Hicks efficiency as its point of departure. According to the principle of Pareto efficiency, a transaction between any number of people is efficient when the transaction leaves one person better off, without leaving another worse off, under circumstances where the transaction costs are zero. However, the fact that real life transactions between people often leave one or more persons worse off soon led to the realisation among economists that Pareto efficiency disqualifies too many transactions as inefficient, thus leaving economic systems with an excessively narrow range of economic activity that could be considered efficient. This insight led the economists Nicolas Kaldor and John Hicks to develop a broader concept of efficiency that is now known as Kaldor-Hicks efficiency. According to the Kaldor-Hicks efficiency, a transaction is efficient if it can compensate all loss resulting from it, while leaving at least one person better off under circumstances where transaction costs are zero. It is important to note that there is no redistribution consideration at stake here. The benefit that results from the transaction must make the disadvantage in principle compensable, the compensation need not actually take place. If the total gain that results from a transaction is x, where x equals A's benefit y and B's disadvantage z, the transaction is Kaldor-Hicks efficient irrespective of whether A retains both y and z and B is left to suffer a loss of z. The point is strictly that the gain that results from the transaction is big enough to offset all loss and create a benefit, irrespective of how the benefit and loss are allocated.

Coase essentially relied on the idea of Kaldor-Hicks efficiency to explain the problem of "social cost," thereby basically reducing the question of "social cost" to "economic cost." For this purpose, he took recourse to the case of a cattle farmer Smith and a corn farmer Jones who farm on two adjacent stretches of land to explain and resolve this "problem of social cost." With every head of cattle that Smith raises, he causes an amount of damage to Jones' cornfields. Suppose now that Jones takes legal action to prevent Smith from causing the damage. The question

11 Rawls 1973, pp. 26–27.
12 Ibid.
13 Ibid.
14 Coase 1960, pp. 1–44.

that the court faces is whether Smith can be constrained by law not to cause damage to Jones' cornfields. Kaldor-Hicks efficiency would require the court to allow Smith to carry on with his cattle farming as long as he can continue to make a profit *and* (in principle) compensate Jones for all the damage to his cornfields. By doing so, the court would also assume that there are no other legitimate costs involved that render the transaction inefficient. All legitimate transaction costs must be treated as either part of the loss that must be compensated, or as a negative factor that diminishes gain, so that it can be considered to be zero. And all illegitimate transaction costs must be ignored as if they did not exist. This brings one to the crux of the problem at hand. How does one make sure that illegitimate transaction costs do not enter the calculation and ruin the deal? More precisely, how does one distinguish between legitimate and illegitimate transaction costs?

Let us first see how Jones might increase the transaction costs illegitimately. Jones could tell Smith that he would allow him to carry on with his cattle farming as long as he not only compensates him for all his damages, but also lets him share in half of Smith's profits. In this case Smith may well decide that the effort involved in cattle farming is not worth it. Jones would thus obstruct the transaction and destroy the benefit that Smith's cattle farming could have brought to the society to which they both belong. So the question that a court of law could predictably be asked to consider under these circumstances is whether these or similar demands of Jones should be allowed to raise the transactions costs in ways that frustrate economic activity, or whether it should disqualify all such extra demands in order to lower the transactions costs and make the transaction go through.

How must the court do this? Coase's answer is that Smith and Jones must be considered to be the same person. They must become (or be ordered by law or government to become) the "firm" Smith-Jones.[15] Smith-Jones will simply consider how much income he can raise with cattle and how much he can earn with corn. And, if it then turns out that cattle farming is more lucrative than corn farming, the solution is simple: Give up the corn farming and raise cattle on all the land available. By putting itself as an impartial observer into Smith-Jones' four shoes, the court will have no qualms in simply awarding Smith the liberty to carry on cattle farming as long as he compensates Jones for all his real damages, even if this would require Jones to stop farming and rest content with receiving damages from Smith that replace the income that he would have earned with corn.

If it were to do this, it would be clear that the court was effectively structuring the transaction between Smith and Jones so as to promote economic efficiency and economic efficiency only. Higher economic efficiency, it would be argued, would leave the whole society to which Smith and Jones belong better off. The idea that law structures the transactions between individuals in a way that renders society as a whole better off is central to the economic analysis of law developed by Guido Calabresi and Douglas Melamed. However, Calabresi and Melamed's analyses of law

---

15 See ibid, p. 16. For an instructive discussion of this move in Coase's argument, see Coleman 1984.

are not exclusively guided by efficiency considerations. They take into account significant constraints on economic efficiency that many contemporary societies generally consider legitimate. According to them, a legal system basically facilitates two kinds of transactions and proscribes a third.[16] The first kind of transaction that the law makes possible can be labelled *property transactions*. When property is the basis of a transaction, the court will not allow any diminishing of the property right against the owner's will, even if such diminishing would raise economic efficiency. A court that did that in the case of Smith and Jones discussed above would grant Jones an interdict that prohibits Smith from continuing with his cattle farming, if this was the only way that damage to Jones' cornfields could be stopped. It would do so notwithstanding the fact that Smith could easily compensate Jones for his damages and make a decent profit. The only way that Smith would be able to carry on with his cattle farming would be to offer Jones a purchase or rental price for his land that Jones, as owner of the land, would be ready to accept voluntarily. In other words, the only transaction that would be possible would be the lease or purchase of property.

However, one can well imagine that a legal system may want to inhibit or even prohibit transactions that so easily frustrate economic activity, prevent industrious individuals from earning well deserved incomes and create jobs down the line, etc. Everyone would be better off and no one worse off, it would consider, if the law were to allow Smith to raise his cattle and pay Jones for all the damage caused to his land, assuming that corn farming cannot do this equally well (assuming, in other words, that current market indicators are in favour of cattle and against corn farming under all circumstances where the two compete). The country that finds itself in this situation would then create rules of law that would turn the transaction between Smith and Jones into one that is not based on property, but on tort (wrongful causation of damage). Jones would then be able to file a claim for damages against Smith, but he would not be able to prevent Smith from raising cattle. Modern legal systems regulate many aspects of society on the basis of such tort transactions. Had they not done so, the scope of economic activity in modern societies would have been far too restricted to sustain the entrepreneurial economies that they consider essential for the wealth that they aspire to create. No dangerous manufacturing process, no high speed means of transport and no other potentially harmful but economically lucrative activity would be possible if owners of property could turn to courts to absolutely interdict all foreseeable instances of harm being caused to them without their consent.[17] That is why vast areas of social co-existence are today governed by tort or civil delict rules that promote economic activity. They first permit non-consensual harm and secondly restrict compensability of such harm sufficiently to encourage entrepreneurship effectively.

Roman law provided for a category of goods that could not be bought or sold. These goods were called *res extra commercium* – things that are not subject to

---

16  Calabresi and Melamed 1972, pp. 1089–1128.
17  See Horwitz 1977, pp. 32–34, 80–84.

any commerce. Modern societies still keep certain concerns completely free from commercial exchange by strictly prohibiting any kind of activity that would lead to such exchange. They do so by rules which Calabresi and Melamed call "inalienability rules."[18] This is where criminal law – combined with fundamental rights law – begins to organise a crucial aspect of a society's transaction scheme. Criminal law ensures that some social exchanges remain completely out of bounds, even out of bounds of agreements between consenting owners. The most common example that comes to mind concerns commercial exchanges of bodily organs. Most modern legal systems limit exchanges of bodily organs to voluntary and altruistic donations. Although known instances of abuse in the regulatory systems that organise such donations frequently cast an ominous shadow over the "extra commercial character" of these transactions, they still reflect the normative concern that some commercial exchanges between individuals remain inadmissible. As such, they represent a certain closure of prevailing transaction schemes in a society. In other words, inalienability rules turn the range of transactions allowed in a society at any given time into a *numerus clausus* that cannot be exceeded.

This closure, however, does not necessarily testify to the existence of a non-utilitarian dimension of human coexistence. On the contrary, the proscription of certain transactions may well reflect the extraordinary utility of some goods or concerns. This raises the question of whether anything like a purely non-utilitarian exchange between human individuals is at all possible. Mill argued that all social exchanges are underpinned by a framework of utility concerns that range from basic pleasure/pain considerations to higher order spiritual or intellectual utilities.[19] Were one to accept this argument, it would not disrupt but effectively corroborate the unifying and fusing effect that utilitarian frameworks of social analyses produce in any society. However refined and elaborate the full range of utility concerns of any society may be, they would still bring about the fundamental social fusion that Rawls invokes in the argument pointed out above. They would still suspend or even terminate the separateness of individuals. Whatever the value considered, it would still fit into the common framework of utilities that all humans share. And even the most differentiated and sophisticated utilitarian framework would still fuse all the Smiths and Joneses into Smith-Joneses, and Calabresi and Melamed's inalienability rules would not change this at all.

This would also seem to suggest that any recognition of any individual as significantly different from all others would depend on the possibility of a completely non-utilitarian encounter with that person. Whether this is at all conceivable is a question that has occupied twentieth century thinkers like George Battaille, Emmanuel Levinas and Jacques Derrida. We cannot engage here with the formidable resistance to the economic organisation of society that these thinkers contemplated.[20] Suffice it just to note that the slightest acceptance of binding utility

18 Calabresi & Melamed 1972, pp. 1111–1115.
19 Mill 1996, pp. 1–43.
20 I have endeavoured to do so in Van der Walt 2018.

considerations between persons unites them in a way that terminates or drastically weakens the separateness or otherness between them. The adoption of an exclusively utilitarian perspective on social exchanges thus brings about a complete fusion between people, as Rawls says. Coase's explication of social cost basically confirms and explains this fusion par excellence, given its reliance on a procedure that essentially reduces any number of parties to a transaction into one party, a procedure that turns all Smiths and Joneses into Smith-Joneses.

The utility or economic principle would seem, then, to provide a mechanism with which the *people* can be turned into one *People*. It would seem to promise a transubstantiation that is similar to the transubstantiation contemplated by the revolutionary leaders in France after the Revolution, that is, in the wake of the divine transubstantiation that took place momentarily on the streets of Paris during the heady first days of revolt (see Chapter 6, Section 2). If this were indeed the case, it would have to be considered the greatest of ironies, for it would mean that particular interests, the very source of social division that the revolutionary concern with transubstantiation sought to transcend, became the new source of social unity and cohesion in the years after the Revolution. Perhaps that is exactly what the post-revolutionary leaders – Guizot in particular – contemplated; hence the introduction of property as the mark of the moral merit that rendered some citizens worthy of representing the People politically, and others not.

In a debate with Jürgen Habermas in 1995, Dieter Grimm argued that Europe cannot have a constitution because it does not have a *demos*. In other words, it does not have a People with a capital P, it only has people.[21] However, the thinking that has been guiding European Union (EU) elites and law-makers ever since the early enthusiasm for political union started to wane evidently suggests Europe does not need a People. It only needs a market for purposes of bringing about the "ever closer union of the peoples of Europe" envisaged in the EU treaties (TEU, Article 1 and TFEU, Preamble). What these elites and law-makers appear to have in mind is not just a market, but nothing less than a Market with a capital M. They seem to have a veritable transubstantiation process in mind that is structurally highly comparable to the transubstantiation of the people into a People that the revolutionary leadership contemplated in the wake of the Messianic moment of the Revolution.

This may be an exaggerated way of putting the matter to which these EU elites and law-makers would most likely object, but any attempt to reject it as devoid of any element of truth will certainly leave many social theorists concerned about a better balance between political and economic integration in Europe unconvinced. A widely read and influential contribution to the debate on European integration by Fritz Scharpf underlines the imbalance between political and economic integration in the EU.[22] Utilitarian analysts and economists may well still be hoping that the utilitarian and economic transubstantiation of the peoples of Europe into the

---

21  See Grimm 1995.
22  Scharpf 2010.

People of Europe may still materialise, but the odds look more than formidable. Europe abounds today with people and peoples who are again turning to nationalist and populist visions of political transubstantiation into Peoplehood. The EU appears to be less and less a candidate for political transubstantiation and the only question that remains compelling in this regard is whether or for how long the common market, which the EU has essentially or predominantly remained, will survive the political fragmentation and disintegration that the market itself promotes so fervently.[23]

The reason why economic integration on its own is unlikely to bring about the socio-political unification that it envisages, be this in the EU or elsewhere, may well relate to its inclination to present itself as a social dimension of integration that neither needs nor tolerates contextualisation. Market integration invariably considers itself unrelated to any outside that is not of its own making. It does not consider itself held in an opening that it does not create itself, as Lefort puts it (see Chapter 6, Section 2). It is this outside that Bentham sought to erase with his extirpation project. Considered from this extirpation perspective, utilitarian and economic thinking indeed shows a tendency to surrender to the positivistic fiction that the social is preceded by the social – *la fiction positiviste [qui met] la société avant la société*[24] – and the economic by the economic. In the case of exclusively or predominantly market-oriented assessments of social integration, one can indeed amend Lefort's observation for purposes of pointing out a positivist fiction that places the market before the market – *la fiction positiviste [qui met] le marché avant le marché*. This is another way of making the point that economic and utilitarian thinking invariably risk turning the totality of existence into *a total market* – *un marché total*, to resort to Alain Supiot's description of current developments in the EU.[25] Lefort's insight into the fundamental tautological gesture at work in any attempt – such as Bentham's extirpation project – to escape from the conundrum and dilemma of the theologico-political prompts one to understand Supiot's invocation of a total market as a dispensation in which the market itself becomes the only limit to the market.

The realisation that no "totality" can be held in place (can have a context) unless it secures itself in a bigger totality that relates it to an outside or an opening that it did not create – as ancient and medieval Christian political theology endeavoured to do with reference to God as the totality of all totalities – has at times bothered economic thinking. The thinking of the Freiburg School of economic thinking, also known as the Ordoliberal School, may well be a case in point. Ordoliberal economic thinking pivots on the idea that the state should not interfere with the market from the outside, but merely sustain it as it is. By stressing the essential self-regulation of the market, and by essentially reducing the political to a repair kit with which exceptional cases of market failure can be remedied, Ordoliberal thinking evidently ends up with a vision of the economy as a system with no significant

23 See Krastev 2017.
24 Lefort 1986a, p. 281.
25 See Supiot 2010.

outside.[26] This understanding of the relation between politics and economics disqualifies the former from contextualising the latter, that is, from relating the economy to an outside that it – the economy – cannot be for itself. It rather reverses this contextualisation by shackling the state to the economy in the way an emergency repair kit may adorn the interior of a boat. Hence, perhaps, Walter Eucken's express recourse to a theological contextualisation of free market economies. The task of Ordoliberal thinking, he claimed, was to restore the natural order willed by God.[27]

If one follows Lefort in saying that democracy is the only form of power that acknowledges the opening in which it is held, any attempt to reconcile Ordoliberalism (or any line of economic thinking in which the market becomes the only terrestrial limit to the market) with democracy is bound to run into insurmountable difficulties. By invoking God as the great guarantor of an economic order that essentially wills nothing but this economic order, Ordoliberal economic thinking bricks up its outside with bricks produced on its inside. It becomes its own outside. If democracy is indeed the form of politics that recognises its outside as an opening in which it is held and which it did not create itself, it is evidently irreconcilable with a totalising form of economic thinking that obliterates the very concept of an outside.

This theological self-totalisation of economics evidently also amounts to a total collapse of the distinction between potentiality and actuality. If potentiality distinguishes itself from actuality with the promise of a destiny that may or may not materialise, Ordoliberal economic thinking, turning as it does on the idea of a *pre*-destined economic order, consists of a total absorption of potentiality into an ancient actuality. Ordoliberal thinking invokes an economic order that had always been there *before* it was there, and will always be there in the way it always has been. It totalises an eternal presence. This self-totalisation already lurks in the pure utilitarian thinking that Bentham contemplated with his extirpation project. Bentham, we saw, pursued the self-totalisation of utility by ridding it of any reference to God. Such a self-totalisation can hardly avoid self-deification. His friend and protégé John Austin perhaps sensed this when he identified – like an Ordoliberal *avant le lettre* – the utility principle with the will of God. In the final analysis, his invocation of God for purposes of anchoring the utility principle would appear to be perfectly in tune, and not at odds with, Bentham's attempt to anchor the principle in itself.

## 2 The historico-spiritual and conceptual unity of the people – Kant, Hegel, Savigny

At more or less the same time that Bentham and Austin developed their respective utilitarian philosophies and positivist theories of law in London, something

---

26 The view that Freiburg School Ordoliberalism has indeed become the essential thinking that informs the interpretation of the EU treaties, if not the treaties themselves, is widespread in literature on this question. For further references to these views, see Van der Walt 2016.

27 Eucken 1952, p. 176: "Die Wirtschaftspolitik aber soll die freie natürliche gottgewollte Ordnung verwirklichen." For an incisive discussion of this theological foundation of ordo-liberal thinking, see Manow 2001.

somewhat more spiritual was happening in Berlin. During the first decades of the nineteenth century, both Georg Wilhelm Friedrich Hegel and Friedrich Carl von Savigny, the two famous Berlin professors of the early nineteenth century, developed philosophies and theories of law in which the notion of *spirit* or *Geist* figured as *the* pivotal concept. Hegel and Savigny would seem to have had much in common. Not only did they appear to share a common regard for the way in which law was rooted in a "historical spirit," they both also drew inspiration from Kant's philosophy of individual autonomy and freedom. But, as we shall see below, they both also betrayed this inspiration in their respective philosophies or theories of law.

In one respect, however, Savigny and Hegel very definitely did not see eye to eye. They took different sides with regard to the most important question that the development of German law was facing in the nineteenth century – the question of codification. The respective positions they took with regard to this question of codification reflected the deep political differences between them. These political differences ultimately drove a deep wedge between their respective concepts of "spirit," but this did not shake the confident epistemological pretensions of either. In their own ways, their respective concepts of *Weltgeist* and *Volksgeist* both claimed rather triumphantly to have closed the gap between spirit and nature or mind and matter, and, for both of them, history was the vehicle of this closure. In the case of Hegel, however, this triumphant epistemology showed significant signs of ambivalence and this ambivalence will be highlighted in the engagement with his thought that follows.

Hegel developed a formidable philosophical system in which the historical development of essential aspects of European civilisation were presented as phases in the development of the *Weltgeist* ("spirit of the world" or "World-Spirit"). *Weltgeist* is a term that Hegel took over from the philosopher Schelling and used especially in his earlier works. In his later works he mostly just referred to this World-Spirit as *Geist*, that is, as *Spirit*. Hegel's *Geist* was basically modelled on the historical development of European political, social, cultural and religious consciousness. Hegel very evidently considered the spiritual and intellectual development of Europe the spiritual and intellectual development of the whole world. In this regard his thinking was deeply embedded in the time in which Europe still considered itself the "sacred centre of the world," as Schmitt puts it in *Der Nomos der Erde* (see Chapter 2). Hegel recorded the millennial diary of this European *Spirit* – the narrative of its sweeping dialectic progression and progress through the world from ancient Greece to the French Revolution and the rise of the modern constitutional state – in his posthumously published *Vorlesungen über die Philosophie der Geschichte* (Lectures on the Philosophy of History).[28]

The *Vorlesungen* tell the story of the long history through which the rudimentary idea of the freedom of citizens in ancient Greece expanded and became – especially under the influence of the Christian religion – the fully-fledged recognition of the moral autonomy of every individual reflected in the ideals of the French Revolution

---

28 Hegel 1970, vol. 20.

and the moral philosophy of Kant. Hegel's philosophy of law added the last "brush strokes" to this philosophical explanation of the history of the world as a history of freedom and moral autonomy. His *Grundlinien der Philosophie des Rechts* (*Foundations of the Philosophy of Law*) portrays the law of the modern constitutional state as the institutional realisation of the ideals of the French Revolution and the Kantian principle of moral autonomy. The *Grundlinien* thus completes Hegel's breath-taking *tableau* of the *Weltgeist*'s march through history. The rise of the modern constitutional state, averred Hegel, constitutes the full realisation of the idea of freedom in history – *der Staat . . . ist . . . die Verwirklichung der Freiheit.*[29]

Hegel considered the modern state the institutional guarantee of the *idea* of freedom as contemplated by reason (*Vernunft*). In this regard, his conception of the state as the realisation of freedom appears to echo Rousseau's contemplation of the *volonté générale* as a principle that has nothing to do with the empirical "freedom" of any concrete individual or majority of such individuals. As such, it also does not seem to be at odds with Kant's understanding of freedom as an on-going moral imperative. A closer look at this apparent proximity between Rousseau, Kant and Hegel nevertheless reveals a more complex reality. Notwithstanding the deep resonances between them, a considerable gap ultimately opens up between Rousseau and Kant, on the one hand, and Hegel, on the other. This gap results from their respective understandings of the relation between the idea of law, and the reality of its application and enforcement.

The works of Rousseau and Kant offer the concept of liberal democratic law the crucial insight that freedom is an ideal that cannot be *realised* under finite circumstances. In this regard, they both sustained a non-traversable gap between the potentiality and actuality of freedom. Hegel, at least sometimes, considered the modern state and modern law the *realisation* – *Verwirklichung* – of freedom. This seems abundantly clear from the sentence quoted above. In this regard, he seems to have considered the modern state an actualisation of the potentiality of freedom. If this is correct, his thought would have to be considered another chapter in the long history of metaphysics that failed to articulate a stable distinction between potentiality and actuality. The matter is nevertheless not so simple. At times, Hegel would seem to have come very close to articulating the relation between freedom and law, and life and law, in a way that confirms Rousseau's and Kant's insight into the non-actualisable potentiality of freedom on which liberal democracy turns. It is important to note just how close he came to this conception of freedom, and where exactly he began to move away from it again, for it is indeed from very "near misses" that any pursued target becomes clearer.

One may be tempted to observe, at first glance, that Hegel did not even come close to leaving the history of metaphysics behind him. No "near miss" would seem to be at stake here. His philosophy of freedom is, after all, still embedded in a stellar metaphysical vision, a vision in terms of which history figures as the grand

---

29 Ibid, vol. 7, p. 403 (§ 258 Zusatz).

metaphysical progress through which Spirit becomes matter and nature so that matter and nature can become Spirit. The process comprises three phases – Subjective Spirit, Objective Spirit and Absolute Spirit. Spirit at first exists as pure and immediate subjectivity. In the beginning, it exists *in itself* (*an sich*) in the way "God" can be imagined to have existed "before he created the universe." It then objectifies itself in matter and nature through a dialectic process of simultaneous self-alienation and self-reconciliation, simultaneous alienation from and reconciliation with itself. It finally emerges from this dialectic in a state of complete reconciliation and then continues to exist in the full glory of being both in itself (*an sich*) and for itself (*für sich*). The "for itself" gained in addition to the initial "in itself" concerns the full consciousness of itself that it attains in the process of objectifying itself and retrieving itself again from this (alienating) objectification.[30] Hegel expressly explained this whole process in theological or theologico-historical terms. He described history as the execution of God's government and plan – *Gott regiert die Welt, der Inhalt seiner Regierung, die Vollführung seines Plans is die Weltgeschichte*[31] – and the state as the march of God through the world – *es ist der Gang Gottes in der Welt, daß der Staat ist.*[32]

Now, if the aim of this book is to distil and extract the concept of liberal democratic law from its long history of metaphysics, it would appear that we have quite a bit of distilling to do in the case of Hegel. Is his whole philosophy not just a restatement of Aristotle's teleological metaphysics of nature by a modern philosopher who has evidently fallen very much in love with history, as the educated of nineteenth century Germany invariably did? No doubt, liberal democracy, as thus far explained in terms of a strict separation of the symbolic and the real, the ideal and the real and so forth, can hardly be imagined to have anything in common with the heavy metaphysics that Hegel put to work in order to explain the progress of the idea of freedom in the course of history. One can boil off all the fluids, but the vapours will yield nothing or little that is salvageable here, one might say. One must nevertheless avoid this all too rapid response, for one also finds in Hegel's works pertinent resonances with the concept of liberal democratic law that we are pursuing.

Let us therefore take a closer look at the *Grundlinien der Philosophie des Rechts*, the work that we described above as the last "brush stroke" in Hegel's grand *tableau* of the *Weltgeist*'s march through history. This last brush stroke adds another shade of grey to a canvas that is already grey, the melancholic preface to the *Grundlinien* tells us. It completes the grey picture of a life that has grown old enough to come to know itself. Here is the complete statement:

> Philosophy paints its grey in grey when a form of life has grown old. And with this grey in grey this form of life will not be rejuvenated, it will only

---

30 The metaphysical historical process is fully described in ibid, vol. 3 and vols. 8–10.
31 Ibid, vol. 12, p. 53.
32 Ibid, vol. 7, p. 403 (§ 258).

become known to itself. Only when dusk falls does the owl of Minerva begin her flight.[33]

We do not pause at this famous statement because of its singular beauty. We pause at it because of its singular insight into the waning of life that conditions modern law; its singular insight into the difference between law and life, and into the irreducible tension or conflict between law and life. We pause here to reflect on its rueful recognition that law, at least as the modern age has come to contemplate it, is not rooted in life but extracted from life, uprooted from life, and only survives this extraction when life itself has become too weak to resist it. This is indeed the Nietzschean insight – before Nietzsche – that adorns the preface to Hegel's *Grundlinien*, as we have already observed elsewhere.[34] This is Hegel's *negative-Nietzschean* insight, to be more precise. Hegel does not articulate a vitalistic protest against modern law in this passage, as one can imagine Nietzsche might have done in his place. He articulates a non-vitalistic and resigned acceptance that law will always only be strong enough when life is weak enough, or when life has channelled its force into a realm where it no longer competes with law (something that is probably only likely when this force has become weak enough to be channelled thus).

This insight is absolutely pivotal for the distillation of liberal democratic law from the long history of metaphysical legal thought that we are pursuing. It will become clearer towards the end of this book, but we may as well already observe now that liberal democratic law only becomes possible when life has grown old, when philosophy has painted its grey in grey and when the owl of Minerva starts her flight into the evening dusk. Life that is youthful and strong is seemingly irresistibly inclined to seek the actualisation of its potential. This may well be the core of the ageless inability of Western metaphysics to contemplate something akin to liberal democracy. Western metaphysics has all along been rooted in life – or a conception of life – that is far too forceful to contemplate something as "lifeless" as liberal democracy. "Lifeless liberal democracy!" If it is fair to imagine Nietzsche pronouncing this phrase with derision, it is because he too belonged to the metaphysics of life. His ruthless critique of Western metaphysics was one of its most excellent chapters, not its discontinuation.

When Aristotle endeavoured to extract law from the sheer force of life, from *physis*, and to subject this force of life to *nomos* or law, he did so by replanting the roots of law in another conception of life – life understood as an expression of *kosmos*. He uprooted law from *zoē* and replanted it in *bios*, as Agamben may want to put it. Of concern here is the whole *nomos* as *physis* and *nomos* as *kosmos* narrative developed in Chapters 1–4. That narrative was all along designed to lead us to

---

33 Translated from ibid, vol. 7, p. 28: Wenn die Philosophie ihr Grau in Grau malt, dann ist eine Gestalt des Lebens alt geworden, und mit Grau in Grau läßt sie sich nicht verjüngen, sondern nur erkennen; die Eule der Minerva beginnt erst met der einbrechenden Dämmerung ihren Flug.

34 Van der Walt 2014b, p. 279.

the constellation of *nomos* <u>and</u> *physis* articulated towards the end of Chapter 5, a constellation that allows for the contemplation of law as a normative order that is not rooted in life, but accompanied and threatened by it. At stake here is an understanding of law and order that is charged with the task of fending-off the threat of life, and fending-off the threat that life always poses to itself. It is this constellation of *nomos* <u>and</u> *physis* – this constellation of law *and* life – to which Hegel's elegiac preface to the *Grundlinien* appears to be alluding. At stake in the *Grundlinien*, it seems, is a concept of law that is fully informed by the understanding of law as an *idea* – *die Idee des Rechts* – and not as *life*. At stake for Hegel would appear to be something very different from the concept of *Lebensrecht* that Schmitt would use in 1934 (see Chapter 5, p. 100). In complete contrast to Schmitt's vitalistic anti-liberalism, Hegel would indeed seem to be contemplating a very "lifeless liberalism."

All of this seems to be underlined by the passage in the *Grundlinien* that refers to the absence of heroes in the modern state. The state is not a place of heroes or heroism. It is no longer in need of great founding acts – *historische Grundvorgänge* and *grosse Politik* – as Schmitt puts it in *Der Nomos der Erde* (see Chapter 2). The history of Spirit that ultimately leads to the modern state is the stage of heroes, but the state comes at the end of this history and in a significant sense no longer takes part in it. History is the grand stage on which the personal passions of colourful heroes – Alexander, Caesar, Napoleon – promoted the universal aims of Spirit without even knowing that they were doing so, contends a powerful passage from Hegel's *Philosophie der Geschichte* with palpable disdain for the small mindedness of bourgeois culture.[35] But there is no work left for heroes and therefore no longer a place for them in the state, contends the *Grundlinien* – *[i]m Staat kann es keine Heroen mere geben.*[36] The heroes who once grounded states and introduced marriage and land cultivation – the heroes who performed the *nomos*-founding acts that Schmitt describes in *Der Nomos der Erde*, might one say – still did so under uncivilised and uneducated conditions – *ungebildete Zustande* – and without any recognised right to do so – *[sie] haben dieses . . . nicht als anerkanntes Recht getan.*[37] The colourfulness of these grand historical acts pertains exactly to the fact that they were not underpinned by recognised legal rights. This situation changes fundamentally once a state is properly founded. Then everything that is done must be done within a stable framework of law and recognised rights. That is why the state must be considered the grey end of history, the end of history where a retrospective philosophy finally paints away the colourful life and lives of earlier times under so many shades of grey.

It is important to look briefly at an important passage from the *Phenomenologie des Geistes* for purposes of gaining more insight into the unheroic and grey portrait of the modern state painted in the preface to the *Grundlinien*. The *Phenomenologie*, the major work that Hegel published in 1807 (fourteen years before the *Grundlinien*), tells the story of the different stages of consciousness that Spirit traverses in the

---

35  Hegel 1970, vol 12, pp. 45–50.
36  Ibid, vol. 7, p. 180 (§ 93 Zusatz).
37  Ibid.

grand historical process through which Subjective Spirit first becomes Objective Spirit and ends as Absolute Spirit. One of the key episodes in this history is the dialectic between the master and the slave from which self-consciousness emerges from mere consciousness. In terms of the three phases of the grand metaphysical process at stake in Hegel's work, this is the moment when Spirit takes one of its most crucial steps in the retrieval of its subjectivity (which it still possessed as Subjective Spirit) from the objectification and alienation through which it has to go by becoming matter, nature and life (*Objective Spirit*), before it can become reconciled with itself (as Absolute Spirit – which contains both Subjective and Objective Spirit in a reconciled state). The dialectic between the master and the slave explains how self-consciousness emerges from bare-consciousness or the bare-consciousness of life, to put it purposefully in terms that readers of Agamben will recognise as "quasi-Agambean." How does this happen? How does the angel finally emerge from its immersion in stone? It begins with one who sees the foundations of life shaken, and who holds on to life for dear life, only to discover something else, something that exceeds and transcends life. This is the story of the struggle between the master and the slave.

The slave yields to the master and becomes a slave in order to save his own life. What must count as one of the most magnificent passages of the *Phenomenologie* describes how consciousness becomes self-consciousness at the moment when the slave sees the world – the material world – trembling around him, the moment in which everything starts to move:

> The consciousness of the slave did not just fear for this or that, this or that moment, but for its whole existence. For it had faced the fear of death, fear of the absolute master. This fear completely resolved its inner existence. Everything inside it started shivering. Everything fixed started trembling. This pure and general movement, this moment in which the whole of existence becomes absolutely liquid, is the simple existence of self-consciousness. It is the moment of absolute negativity, the moment in which consciousness becomes pure consciousness in and for itself.[38]

This moment is, for Hegel, the inception of history as the history of Spirit. It is the moment at which Spirit, in the first experience of self-consciousness, separates itself from bare life and regains the subjectivity that it possessed before its immersion in matter. It is also the moment that conditions the history of objectivity – or of objects – that starts now. The history of the object – which can only begin once the

---

38 Translated from ibid, vol. 3, p. 153: [Das Bewusstsein des Knechts] hat nämlich nicht um dieses order jenes, noch für diesen order jenen Augenblick Angst gehabt, sondern um sein ganzes Wesen; denn es hat die Furcht des Todes, des absoluten Herrn empfunden. Es ist darin innerlich aufgelöst worden, hat durchaus in sich selbst erzittert und alles Fixe hat in ihm gebebt. Diese reine allgemeine Bewegung, das absolute Flüssigwerden alles Bestehens, ist aber das einfache Wesen des Selbstbewusstseins, die absolute Negativität, das reine Fürsichsein, das hiermit *an* diesem Bewusstsein ist.

history of the subject begins – starts when the slave begins to produce goods for the master. By producing goods for consumption by the master and by himself, the slave develops an awareness of the independent existence of things, an awareness that is not possible as long as life remains a process of ceaseless consumption. The slave thus develops a record or register of the enduring effect of work on the environment. He starts to recognise himself in his environment and accedes to the stable self-consciousness that results from seeing himself mirrored by his environment. Thus, then, begins the long history through which Spirit becomes reconciled with itself by recognising matter and nature as an embodiment of itself. It is important to note that Hegel disqualifies the master from playing this crucial role in the history of Spirit. The master does arrive at some level of reflective self-consciousness because of the recognition he receives from the slave. But this recognition is too dependent on the slave, contends Hegel, to effect the enduring and stable self-consciousness that the slave receives from seeing himself reflected in his environment.[39]

The slave retreats from the juvenile consumption and destruction of his environment – and of others – in a way the master never does. By doing so, the slave also initiates the millennial aging of life that culminates in the establishment of the unheroic but stable legal system invoked in the elegiac preface to the *Grundlinien*. The slave accordingly figures in the *Phenomenologie* as the very stabilisation of life that conditions the endorsement of the grey bourgeois existence that the *Grundlinien* present as an adequately objective instantiation of freedom. It figures, Nietzschean readers of the *Grundlinien* will observe. The bourgeois system of law that Hegel articulates in the *Grundlinien* will strike them as the end result of a long history of slave morality.[40] It is the end result of a long history in which the laborious camel displaced the ferocious lion and the playing child, Zarathustra can be heard scoffing.[41]

The *Grundlinien* surely appears to embrace this grey end of a "servile" history, if one insists to call it that. There is nevertheless much more to the *Grundlinien* than a bleak endorsement of a bourgeois century. Notwithstanding its reliance on many aspects of Aristotle's ethics and politics, the *Grundlinien* also constitute the most comprehensive statement of modernity's break with the ancient world – and with the persistent connection that the ancient world forged between law and life – that any philosopher who admired that world – as Hegel did – ever managed to articulate before him. Perhaps Hegel's admiration for the ancient world was also just too strong in the end, as the *Grundlininen*'s conspicuous equivocation – the rift caused by its allegiance to both Kant and Aristotle – ultimately underlines. We shall turn to this equivocation presently. Let us first take a closer look at Hegel's firm endeavour to break with the ancient world.

---

39  Ibid, vol. 3, p. 152. The interpretation of these passages of the *Phenomenologie des Geistes* corresponds largely to the seminal interpretation of Hegel by Kojève 1947 (Kojève 1947). This interpretation is dismissed by Rose 2009, pp. 138, 256 n. 35 for reasons that are not convincing.

40  See Nietzsche 1999, vol. 5, pp. 270–274.

41  See Nietzsche 1999, vol 4, p. 29. The *Genealogie* also refers to the *Lastthier moral* – see 1999, vol. 5, p. 272.

The significance of Hegel's break with antiquity becomes clear when one takes a look at the two key texts that he wrote during his Jena years (1801–1806), the *Differenz des Fichteschen und Schellingschen Systems der Philosophie*, and the gigantic *Phenomenologie* in which the dialectic between the master and the slave figures as a pivotal moment. In both these works, Hegel took leave of the Aristotelian and Spinozean pantheism that marked the early years of his friendship with Schelling and Hölderlin in Tübingen (1788–1793) and Frankfurt (1797–1801).[42] Schelling was instrumental in getting Hegel employed as a *Privatdozent* in Jena, but during his time in Jena, Hegel moved very definitely away from the pantheistic orientation of Schelling's philosophy. In the process, he also broke with the veritable circle of antiquity-adoration in which he partook during the Tübingen and Frankfurt years.

The key thought that came to the fore in the *Differenz* essay and the *Phenomenologie* concerns the need for philosophy to accept and comprehend the split and torn condition – the *Entzweiung* and *Zerissenheit* – of modern society. The *Differenz* essay stresses the *Zerissenheit* of modernity that conditions its constant nervousness and stress (*Zerrüttung*). It is against this background that its famous statement regarding the need for philosophy must be understood: The need for philosophy arises when life loses its power of integration or unification – *[w]enn die Macht der Vereinigung . . . aus dem Leben der Menschen verschwindet . . . entsteht das Bedürfnis der Philosophie.*[43] Much more than philosophy is needed to overcome the class divisions and alienation of bourgeois existence, Marx insisted later,[44] but he could make this claim so confidently because he believed the divisions and alienation of modernity could be overcome. Hegel did not believe this. In this respect, his grand metaphysical vision of the historical reconciliation of Spirit with itself would seem to be everything but redemptive. The reference to the grey old age of a form of life that cannot be rejuvenated in the *Grundlinien* underlines this.

There is a palpable resonance between the *Grundlinien*'s reference to the feeble and grey end of an age in 1821, and the 1801 reference in the *Differenz* essay to life that loses its powers of integration and unification. There is a palpable resonance, in other words, between the first and last works that Hegel published during his life. Again, the recourse to philosophy that the *Differenz* essay proposes in the face of the torn state of modern existence is surely far from redemptive. It concerns an insight into division, separation (*Trennung*) and non-identity (*Nichtidentität*) as the essential condition of existence. It is the condition of the Absolute, not a phase that the Absolute can overcome.[45] This ultimate philosophical insight would seem to stem from a sober Stoicism. The *Phenomenologie* indeed portrays the first phase of consciousness that emerges from the dialectic between the master and the slave as

---

42  See Taylor 1975, pp. 51–75, Ritter 1975, pp. 197–219 and Riedel 1975, pp. 249–263.
43  Hegel 1970, vol. 2, p. 22.
44  See Marx 1978, p. 7.
45  See Hegel, vol. 2, p. 96: "Das Absolute selbst aber ist darum die Identität der Identität und Nichtidentität."

Stoicism.[46] This Stoicism subsequently gets dialectically suspended by scepticism, and then by a deeply unhappy phase of consciousness – *das unglückliche Bewusstsein*. Thus begins a long dialectic journey that finally makes its way, through education or *Bildung*, to objective "ethical life," the "spirit of Enlightenment," "moral consciousness," "conscience," "religion," "art" and "absolute knowledge." The marks left by Aristotle's *paideia* and substantive ethics (the virtues) on the historical itinerary of Spirit are conspicuous where the milestones of *Bildung* and objective "ethical life" (*Sittlichkeit*) come into view, but also with the exultation of "absolute knowledge" at the end of this spiritual journey. Before the journey arrives at religion, art and absolute knowledge, the phases of moral consciousness and conscience indicate the crucial turn to Kant close to the end of the *Phenomenologie*.

Thus does Hegel's fantastic portrait of the Spirit's journey through the world endeavour to reconcile the very different worlds of Aristotle and Kant.[47] The journey, we saw, commences with a foundational Stoicism. It should be noted that this Stoicism with which the journey begins is in principle inerasable. It is a fundamental feature of Hegel's dialectic that the antithetical suspension (*Aufhebung*) of earlier phases of the Spirit's journey through history does not simply cancel out those earlier phases. It negates them but simultaneously lifts them up (*hebt sie auf*) into the next phase of consciousness or Spirit, and thus also conserves or salvages them.[48] In principle, then, the Stoicism and scepticism with which the Spirit's journey begins must remain essential aspects of the Spirit throughout its arduous journey – through matter and nature – to full reconciliation with itself. Absolute knowledge must therefore be understood to pivot on the fundamental Stoicism with which it begins. The *Differenz* essay communicated this insight. It described philosophical knowledge as the comprehension of the torn and divided condition of existence, that is, of *Trennung* and *Zerissenheit* as part and parcel of the Absolute. Another magisterial passage from the *Phenomenologie* highlights this insight in the most vivid of terms. Hegel writes:

> The life of Spirit does not shy away from death and does not shield itself perfectly from destruction. It endures death and sustains itself in the midst of it. It gains its truth only through finding itself in the absolutely torn state of its existence.[49]

The melancholic description of the Hesperian flight of the owl of Minerva in the preface of the *Grundlinien* would seem to be a further reflection of the Stoic regard for the unreconciled state of existence that Hegel had already articulated

46 Ibid, vol. 3, pp. 155–163.
47 See Ritter 2003, pp. 281–309, 1975, pp. 217–246.
48 See Hegel 1970, vol. 3, p. 94: "Das Aufheben . . . ist ein *Negieren* und *Aufbewahren* zugleich."
49 Translated from ibid, p. 36. "Aber nicht das Leben, das sich vor dem Tode scheut und von der Verwüstung rein bewahrt, sondern das ihn erträgt und in ihm erhält, is das Leben des Geistes. Er gewinnt seine Wahrheit nur, in dem er in der absoluten Zerissenheit sich selber findet."

in the *Phenomenologie* and in the *Differenz* essay. It would seem to introduce this regard *into* the philosophical conception of modern law articulated in the *Grundlinien*. If this is correct, the "reasonableness of the real" and the "reality of reason" – *[w]as vernünftig ist, das ist wirklich; und was wirklich ist, das ist vernünftig,*[50] which the preface of the *Grundlinien* also announces should be approached with due caution. Read against the background of Hegel's insistence on the torn state of existence from which Spirit – and therefore *reason (Vernunft)* – never escapes, this statement can hardly be considered a euphoric affirmation of law and the state as the comprehensive realisation of reason and freedom on Earth. On the contrary, the torn or divided state of existence is written all over Hegel's explication of the relation between the state and civil society (*Staat* and *bürgerliche Gesellschaft*) in the last part of the *Grundlinien*.[51] The origin of this concern with the irreducible tension between the private or particular interests that inform civil society and the universal or public concerns of the state can be traced to the same crucial insights that prompted Hegel's emphasis on division and splitting – *Trennung* and *Entzweiung* – in the *Differenz* essay. The insights of concern here relate to the hard facts of modern political economy that Hegel came to know in Bern and Frankfurt through reading the works of James Steuart, David Ricardo and Adam Smith. The *Grundlinien* also refers to the latter two, along with Jean-Baptiste Say.[52]

It is through the encounter with the "iron realities" of modern society – labour and division of labour, mechanisation, money, stock, wealth and poverty – that Hegel came to grasp the non-traversable gap between the ancient and modern world. It is through this encounter that he learnt that the yearning admiration for antiquity as an alternative to the soullessness of modernity – in which he himself still partook in Tübingen and Frankfurt, and in which the Romantic and Restoration movements of the time continued to indulge – cannot lead anywhere.[53] On the contrary, he came to understand that this romanticist yearning for the past only contributes further to the soullessness of the present, a soullessness to which the *Grundlinien* refers as the *Atheismus der sittlichen Welt* – the atheism of ethical life. Hegel's statement regarding the "reality of the reason" and the "reasonableness of the real" must therefore be understood as a critical response to the romanticism of the time that turned its backs on the present for purposes of living in a glorified past. This becomes even clearer when one considers the equivalent pronouncement that comes up two pages later: *Hic Rhodus, hic saltus. Hier ist die Rose, hier tanze* – *here is the rose, here is where one must dance.*[54] Against the background explained here, this statement can hardly be considered a euphoric proclamation of a reconciled world. It much rather comes across as a sober observation of the fact that there is no escape from the world as it is. Whatever reason and reconciliation one is searching

50  Ibid, vol. 7, p. 24.
51  Ibid, pp. 339–398 (§§ 182–256).
52  Ibid, p. 347 (§ 189). See also Riedel 1975, pp. 260–261, Ritter 2003, p. 218.
53  See Riedel 1975, p. 260.
54  Hegel 1970, vol. 7, p. 26.

or hoping for would have to be found here and nowhere else. And this is precisely where the ways of Hegel and Savigny parted. Savigny, to whom we turn now, was deeply immersed in the Romantic and Restoration movements of his time, and so was his theory of the *Volksgeist* as the historical source of all law.

It is important to grasp what Savigny meant by this *historical* source of law. Of concern for him was not history conceived as an on-going and open process that can lead anywhere and requires from all humans, but especially from politicians and jurists, an open-minded responsibility that responds to the exigencies of new times as fittingly as they deem possible. For Savigny, the concern with history was a concern with a grand and authoritative past – a distant past, at that – that had to be honoured. The authoritative past, with which he was concerned unfalteringly from his student years until the end of his life, was Roman law. This deference to Roman law was not unusual among lawyers at the time. As Franz Wieacker puts the matter with his inimitable clarity and grasp: "Over centuries, the early culture of antiquity developed into a timeless guideline for life. It turned into a kind of natural law because of its historical dignity and metaphysical authority."[55]

This deferential and conservative frame of mind was not unique to the nineteenth century. The work of Michel Villey with which we engaged in Chapter 1 is surely clear evidence of its survival deep into the twentieth century, and current strands of this frame of mind still enjoy considerable prominence in European law scholarship particularly.[56] For Savigny, the timeless authority of Roman law became the moral and normative source with which the historical developments of his time could be resisted. In this regard, the "historical school" in nineteenth century German legal science, of which Savigny was the founding and principal exponent, was a very "unhistorical" school.[57] Instead of a concern with *historicity*, that is with the open-ended eventfulness of history that constantly poses new challenges to human responsibility, it was evidently a deeply conservative *historicist* concern with a cultural heritage that demanded deference and reverence. It is this conservative and historicist frame of mind that made Savigny an opponent of legislative statements and restatements of the law aimed at adjusting it to the exigencies of present times and at making it easily accessible and assessable to all citizens as the principles of the Enlightenment demanded. This resistance had already made Savigny a bitter critic of the Prussian *Allgemeines Landrecht* of 1794. And it would make him the principal spokesman of the conservative opposition to the call for the codification of German civil law that came to a head in 1814.[58]

In 1814, the Heidelberg law professor Anton Friedrich Justus Thibaut published a call for a general civil law code for Germany under the title *Ueber die Nothwendigkeit*

55 Translated from Wieacker 1996, p. 51, also quoted by Lahusen 2013, p. 65.
56 See for instance Zimmermann 2001, pp. 107–189 and 2015, pp. 452–480, especially at 470 for the claim that Roman law could and should again be considered the guiding spirit of transnational legal development in the EU as well as in other spheres of transnational law.
57 Lahusen 2013, p. 76, Schmitt 1958, p. 417 fn. 37, Böckenförde 2016, p. 13.
58 See Lahusen 2013, p. 36–44, Rückert 1984, pp. 160–193.

*eines allgemeinen bürgerlichen Rechts für Deutschland.*[59] The call came against the background of a nationalist surge in Germany in the wake of the *Leipziger Völkerschlacht* of 1813, the decisive battle that terminated Napoleon's occupation of Germany. It should be noted here that the inception of this occupation with the Battle of Jena in 1806 was greeted by Hegel with an acclamation of the World-Spirit's arrival in Germany on a white horse – *der Weltgeist zu Pferde.* Napoleon brought with him the *Code Civil*, the French civil code that also turned subjects of the German kings and princes into free citizens. After his defeat in 1813, the *Code Civil* was thrown out of many German courts with little delay so as to restore the old law that was often little more than a confusing mix of Roman law and uncertain customary practices – *das krause Gemisch des alten Wirrwarrs*, as Benjamin Lahusen calls it.[60] Thibaut's call for codification complained specifically about the constant recourse to Roman law in the courts: For every hundred legal questions, he said, at least ninety must be resolved with recourse to Roman law books.[61]

Savigny considered Thibaut's call for codification scandalous – a *Schandschrift.* He responded to it in the same year with his famous essay *Vom Beruf unserer Zeit für Gesetzgebung und Rechtswissenschaft* (The Need of Our Time for Legislation and Legal Science). It is in this essay that he articulated the first coherent expression of the notion that the law is derived from the spirit of the people – *das gemeinsame Bewusstseyn des Volkes* – and not from kings or parliaments. The work of legislators always interrupts and distorts the evolutionary development of the law in the mind or spirit of a people, claimed Savigny.[62] A year later, Savigny, together with his colleagues Karl Friedrich Eichhorn und Johann Friedrich Ludwig Göschen, founded the *Journal for Historical Legal Science* – the *Zeitschrift für geschichtliche Rechtswissenschaft.* This was eight years after the publication of Hegel's *Phenomenologie* and seven years before the publication of the *Grundlinien.* Savigny articulated the aim of the journal in an introductory essay. The essay drew a distinction between historical and unhistorical legal science. The latter included all jurists and legal scientists who believed the law could be reformed at any time and at will by people who happened to be clad with legislative power – *in jedem Augenblick durch die mit der gesetzgebenden Gewalt versehenen Personen mit Willkühr hervorgebracht.*[63] Historical legal science, on the other hand, the science to which the founders of the journal committed themselves, pivoted on the principled denial and rejection of this arrogant creativity. Historical legal science, insisted Savigny, considered every epoch part of a bigger whole – *ein Glied eines höheren Ganzen* – and a continuation of earlier times. The law of this historical unity of all times had been fixed long ago and could not be altered. All that is required is to study the ancient documentation and to refresh and rejuvenate it so as to keep it alive – *[durch zu schauen], zu verjüngen, und frisch zu*

---

59  Thibaut 1814.
60  Lahusen 2013, p. 67.
61  As quoted by Lahusen 2013, p. 67.
62  See Savigny 1840b, pp. 9, 11, 12, 14.
63  See Savigny 1815, p. 6.

*erhalten.* And this task is to be accomplished by jurists, not legislators.[64] These were the essential characteristics of the aims of the Historical School which Hegel would later describe as an insult to an educated nation:

> To deny an educated nation and its jurists the capacity to enact a code of law – given that it is not necessary or possible to make new law with new contents, but only to study the existing content of the law so as to thoughtfully determine its already specified universality and to apply it to the particular case – would be one of the biggest insults that one can inflict on that nation and its jurists.[65]

It is here – with regard to their respective assessments of the need for legislation – that we clearly see parting of the ways of the two Berlin professors. Here also lies the clue to the difference between their respective conceptions of *Volksgeist* and *Weltgeist* – the spirit of the people and the World-Spirit. Hegel clearly embraced the open historicity of a future that demands new laws with "new contents" made by a people with autonomous law-making capacity. Savigny believed the law required for present times can and must be extracted from the ancient principles of Roman law. According to him, the legislative process conducted by non-jurists with no understanding of Roman law would only distort its ancient wisdom. It is here that we also see surfacing again the opposition between *nomos* and legislation – *thesmoi* – that Schmitt stresses in *Der Nomos der Erde*. *Der Nomos der Erde* expressly and predictably endorses Savigny's "warning" against legislation.[66] However, Schmitt's position with regard to Savigny and Hegel is surely not unambiguously in favour of the former and against the latter. His 1943/1944 essay on the state of European legal science evidently struggles to reconcile his admiration for both.[67]

One may be tempted to simply attribute Schmitt's inability to choose unambiguously between the two spiritual Berlin professors to his own ambivalent position regarding ancient legal orders and new legislation, that is, to the continuing tension in his own thinking between *Ortungsdenken* and *Dezisionismus* that his former doctoral student Rudolf Ernst Huber recognised so clearly.[68] This, however, would be an oversimplification of the matter that passes all too quickly over significant ambiguities regarding elements of "*Ortung, Ordnung* and *Dezisionismus*" in Hegel's thinking, to which we pay closer attention below. Let us nevertheless first continue to unpack the basic differences between Hegel and Savigny.

That Hegel and Savigny represented two very different positions regarding the politics of law and law-making should be abundantly clear by now. Savigny was an exponent of a very conservative juridical tradition that insisted on the eternal

---

64  Lahusen 2013, p. 70
65  Translated from Hegel 1970, vol. 7, p. 363 (§ 211).
66  See Schmitt 1997, p. 45.
67  Schmitt 1958, pp. 386–429.
68  See Chapter 5, fn. 55.

legacy that ancient law bequeathed to the present. According to him, the task of the lawyer was restricted to the application of ancient principles of law to new cases. This task was to be entrusted to well-educated jurists who knew how to extract the fitting legal rule for every new case from the mass of inherited legal materials and centuries of case law. Savigny evidently showed no regard for the fact that the dramatic transformation of the world that occurred in his lifetime rendered all law inherited from the past in need of fundamental revision. He also appeared completely out of touch with the rising demands for democratic self-government that rendered the practice of law reform by a handful of jurists – commissioned by a king or emperor without parliamentary endorsement – highly questionable. Hegel, on the other hand, was very aware how fast the old world was changing and how the pace and drastic nature of this change demanded an unprecedented tempo of incisive law reform that could hardly be achieved by jurists who painstakingly extracted new applications from the archaic language of ancient juridical texts.

It is with regard to these two vastly different understandings of law reform that Franz Wieacker assessed nineteenth century German legal science as follows:

> Hegel was the first thinker who reconciled the possibility of a closed system of legal theory with the dimension of history and who therefore could have clad the discovery of historicity with the same normative meaning for legal science that anthropological conceptions of natural law had for the unhistorical systems of law of the Enlightenment. That his philosophy had no influence on the science of civil law of the time is one of the many paradoxes of the spirit. The civil law science of the nineteenth century was duly aware of the lack of historicity of the modern systems of natural law, and resorted to the historicity of culture and of the spirit of the people [to overcome this lack of historicity]. In the process, they ended up serving the [historicist] ideals of the restoration movement of the time.[69]

The difference between Savigny and Hegel was in the final analysis not just a legal philosophical or legal theoretical difference. It did not only concern two very different views of law and law reform. It concerned the fundamental political difference pervasive at the time, the difference between those who embraced the Enlightenment, and the French Revolution as the political embodiment of the Enlightenment, and those who wanted to turn the clock back to the feudal order of old Europe. Savigny belonged to the latter group, Hegel to the former. To the extent that they both were influenced by Kantian philosophy, Hegel fully embraced the spirit of Kant's philosophy of individual freedom, Savigny reduced it to a concept of legal autonomy.[70]

---

69 Loosely translated from Wieacker 1996, pp. 414–415.
70 My reading of Savigny that follows basically reduces Kant's influence on him to the impact of Kant's definition of law on Savigny's definition of subjective rights. It should nevertheless be noted that Wieacker finds more Kant in Savigny than I do when he observes that Savigny held on not only

The civil law science founded and developed by Savigny and the "Pandectists,"
as they soon came to be called, turned on the modern reconstructions of Roman
law – the *usus modernus Pandectarum* – which they forged out of Justinian's *Digest*
(widely known at the time as the *Pandects*). However, there was much more to this
programmatic return to Roman law than a merely methodological re-foundation
of legal science. The whole movement testified to a political conservatism that
distanced itself from the modern world and resisted it. This was already clear from
Savigny's essay *Vom Beruf unser Zeit*. The essay referred expressly to the "scourge of
this revolution" (*der Fluch dieser Revolution*) and to the need to get the *Code Civil*
("which was eating into German law like a cancer") out of Germany again.[71] In
letters written to Karl Friedrich Eichhorn and Jacob Grimm in 1830 and 1832
(in the wake of the July Revolution in Paris in 1830 and amidst escalating unrest
in Germany) Savigny expressed his commitment to the Restoration movement in
even stronger terms.[72] The "historical spirit of the people" – *historisches Bewusstsein*
or *Volksgeist* – that he considered the source of law, evidently had nothing to do
with the popular movements afoot in Germany at the time. It entailed a mythical
and mystifying construction of a "people" whose definitive characteristics were
derived from the old concepts of Roman law. The people of Germany and the
actual history that they were making at the time that Savigny founded his historical
school were realities from which he distanced himself as far as possible, and probably feared more than anything else.[73] The historical school evidently had little to
do with the history of its time.

We will come back once more below to Savigny's endeavour to turn the German people into a set of Roman law concepts for purposes of chaining them to
the feudal order from which they were purposefully seeking to liberate themselves.
It should nevertheless already be very clear that the theory of liberal democratic
law does not stand to gain much from Savigny and the Pandectist movement. At
least not in positive terms. It can, however, take the whole nineteenth century

to Kant's theory of law, but also his ethics of liberty (*Freiheitsethik*) from the first moments of intellectual maturity right up to his late works. Wieacker (1996, p. 385) notes the contradiction between
this Kantian Savigny and the Savigny that endorsed the conservative restoration politics of his time,
but believes that it was to his credit that he held out and managed this tension throughout his life –
*es ist mehr Ruhm als Vorwurf für Savigny, daß er diese Spannungen ausgehalten hat*. Rückert's extensive
discussion of Savigny's politics – see Rückert 1984, pp. 376–415 – leads him to conclude that he
was both against real revolution and real restoration but in favour of a "natural liberty"– *gegen echte
Revolution und gegen echte Restauration, für "natürliche" Freiheit* (at 415). However, many private letters
of Savigny make it rather difficult not to think of him as a very committed anti-revolutionary and
very pro-restauration. See fn. 72.
71  See Savigny 1840b, pp. 2, 57–58.
72  Lahusen 2013, pp. 78–79 cites multiple statements from these letters, and from one to a cousin in
1849 that leaves one in no doubt about Savigny's arch-conservatism and arch-restoratative mentality.
Lahusen therefore also concludes that Savigny and the Historical School essentially belonged to the
Restoration movement – *Das viel berufene geschichtliche Denken Savignys und seiner historischen Schule
ist in seinem Kern also ein restauratives Denken* (at 79).
73  Ibid, p. 79.

development of civil law science in Germany, and elsewhere in Europe,[74] as evidence of the way in which a certain kind of civil law thinking tends to form allegiances with forms of feudalism or neo-feudalism, and still does so today, as Alain Supiot points out.[75] In doing so, it still endeavours to wrest the law from the procedures of liberal democratic law-making envisaged by parliamentary legislation, as the Pandectists once did.

Should we infer from all of the above that Hegel is the undisputed nineteenth century champion of liberal democratic law to whom the theory of liberal democratic law can and should turn for unequivocal inspiration? Liberal democracy can indeed take much inspiration from a great philosopher who raised a glass to Bastille Day every year of his life until he died,[76] but that does not necessarily mean that it can also learn much from his concept of law. There was certainly a vast difference between Hegel's revolutionary and Savigny's restorative concepts of law, but there is one respect in which they were still too close to one another for any liberal democrat to become very comfortable with Hegel's philosophy of law. Both Savigny and Hegel turned Kant's definition of law into an essentialist construction that Kant never intended it to be.

Kant defined law as "the sum of conditions under which the arbitrary will of one person can be reconciled with the arbitrary will of another under a general law of freedom" – *[d]as Recht ist also der Inbegriff der Bedingungen, unter denen die Willkür des einen mit der Willkür des andern nach einem allgemeinen Gesetze der Freiheit zusammen vereinigt werden kann.*[77] Savigny fully endorsed this definition of law, only to turn it into something that Kant certainly never contemplated.[78] Hegel rejected it outright, as we shall see below. He brought his whole philosophy of Spirit to bear upon it for purposes of developing a concept of law that Kant also never contemplated. Savigny's and Hegel's respective retreats from Kant's definition of law evidently proceeded very differently, but, in the process, at least one significant point of convergence between their respective concepts of law became apparent. It is at this convergence that we will take a closer look now.

Savigny did not rely on the wording of Kant's definition as cited above, but on Kant's further explication of the definition in the paragraph that followed immediately after it. In this further explication, Kant stressed that the reconciliation

---

74 The method of the Pandectists ultimately came to dominate the German Civil Code or *Bürgerliches Gesetzbuch* (BGB) that Savigny resisted for so long but could not avoid in the end. In other words, the *BGB* was a veritable product of Pandectism and a highly successful one at that. It became an example of civil law reform in many European countries, including France. See Lahusen 2013, p. 105.

75 See Supiot 2007, pp. 100–110, 2010, pp. 103–108; 2013, pp. 129–145. For an extensive discussion of this re-feudalisation and the endeavour to run contemporary societies by private law, see Van der Walt 2014b, pp. 252–260, 284.

76 See Ritter 2003, 196.

77 Kant 1983, vol. 7, p. 337.

78 Not only Savigny, but almost all the scholars associated with Savigny's Historical School took Kant's definition of law as the key point of departure for the *Pandektenrecht* systems that they developed. See Kiefner 1969.

contemplated in the definition concerned the reconciliation of the *external* or *outward* (*äusserliche*) conduct of one person with the freedom of others: *Also ist das allgemeine Rechtsgesetz: handle äusserlich so, daß der freie Gebrauch deiner Willkür mit der Freiheit von jedermann nach einem allgemeinen Gesetze zusammen bestehen könne. . . .*[79] This explication of the fundamental principle of law became the point of departure of Savigny's whole *System des heutigen römischen Rechts* (System of Contemporary Roman Law), and of the Pandectist systems of law of the other major scholars associated with Savigny's historical school.[80]

The first thing that should strike one with regard to this reliance of Savigny and the Pandectists on Kant's definition of law is its historical incongruity. One can accept that the Villey thesis expounded in Chapter 1 holds enough water to warrant an endorsement of his insistence that the rise of the principle of subjective or individual freedom as the new foundation of law towards the end of the Middle Ages constituted a fundamental rupture with the Aristotelian cosmology that informed Roman law. One can further accept that Kant's foundation of morality and law on the principle of subjective freedom and autonomy constituted a clear consolidation of this break with the Aristotelian worldview that informed Roman law. Considering that both these theses are warranted, it should be clear that there is something fundamentally odd and incongruous about founding "contemporary" or "modern" systems of "Roman law" on Kant's definition of law. Anyone who does this transforms either Roman law, or Kant, or both, into something it never was or they never were. Of these three options, the last one appears the most compelling: The Historical School's re-foundation of Roman law on Kant's definition of law turned both Roman law and Kant's definition of law into something they were not.

One need not agree with every aspect of Villey's overstated thesis that the Romans did not recognise subjective or individual rights in the way modern law does. But one should concede that it becomes too much of a stretch to consider Roman law founded on an idea of subjective autonomy and indeed subjective power (see Chapter 1, Section 5). This would mean simply projecting too much of the expansionist and entrepreneurial spirit of nineteenth century capitalism onto an economy and society that was still largely based on agriculture and basic bartering. In this society, the regard for long established and enduring "ways of doing" conditioned by centuries of slow or no technological progress surely outweighed and incisively constrained any sense of entrepreneurial freedom that may have existed at the time. The ancient world was not the world of the free wheeling and dealing entrepreneurial subject that the nineteenth century concept of subjective rights (considered by the Pandectists to be in principle unconstrained) came to underpin.

Let us take a closer look at the Kantian definition of law that came to underpin the Pandectist conception of subjective rights. Why did Kant stress the imperative

---

79  Kant 1983, vol. 7, p. 338.
80  See Savigny 1840a, Vol. I par 59 (410): "[D]as Recht [gehört] seinem Wesen nach dem Gebiet des äusseren Zusammenlebens." See also Vol. I par 8 (18): Es liegt nun sehr nah . . . das Recht al eine Erfindung derselben zu denken, ohne welche die äusseren Freyheit keines Einzelnen bestehen könnte."

to act *outwardly* in a way that renders the free use of one's arbitrary will reconcilable with the arbitrary will of others? He did so to make clear that legal obligation should not be confused with moral obligation. He explained this "outwardly" by emphasising that the point of law is not moral education – *die Absicht [ist nicht] Tugend zu lernen*.[81] Reconciling your conduct with the freedom of others concerns an external constraint, it need and must not be the inner motivation or your conduct – *so darf und soll man selbst nicht jenes Rechtsgesetz als Triebfeder der Handlung vorstellig machen*.[82] Kant's insistence in this regard is fully consistent with the clear distinction between legality and morality – *Legalität* and *Moralität* – that he draws in the Introduction to the *Metaphysik der Sitten*.[83]

By insisting on these distinctions between inner motivation and outward conduct, and between morality and legality, Kant sustained the overarching framework of a practical philosophy that rigorously avoided any confusion between morality and any particular course of action. It is with regard to this avoidance that Savigny's adoption of Kant's definition of law turned it into something that it was not. By making it the cornerstone of a legal system that is the expression of the spirit of a people, Savigny gave Kant's definition of law a spiritual status – a status of spiritual agreement – that Kant expressly refused to give it. Borrowing two key terms from a later engagement with the same problematic, one can say Kant's definition of law evidently tries to sustain a distinction akin to Rawls' distinction between an "overlapping consensus" and a "modus vivendi."[84] But quite unlike Rawls, Kant firmly dismisses the idea that the law should be an expression of an overlapping consensus that signals moral agreement. The law is for Kant the idea of how individuals can reconcile their external conduct with one another without imposing on one another moral convictions that they may or may not share.

By turning Kant's definition of law into the cornerstone of the spiritual life of a people, that is, by turning it into a veritable overlapping consensus, Savigny essentialises this definition of law in a way that Kant never did or intended to do. Kant's definition of law conforms to his separation of law and morality, and this separation, in turn, conforms to the whole critique of knowledge and metaphysics that he developed in his critiques of theoretical and practical reason. These critiques separated the realm of concrete phenomena categorically from the realm of morality. Savigny, quite on the contrary, turned Kant's definition of law into a reflection of a historical reality on the basis of which the whole legal system could be considered a framework of neatly cohering historical essences.

The essentialisation of Kant's definition of law that occurred in the work of the Historical School was the result of two essentialising procedures, as Benjamin Lahusen points out. Roman law itself pivoted on a first formidable process of essentialisation, to which the Pandectists added a second. The process of conceptual

---

81  Kant 1983, vol. 7, p. 338.
82  Ibid.
83  Ibid, p. 318.
84  See Rawls 1996, pp. 144–150.

essentialising among the Roman jurists consisted of the differentiation of the concepts they received from their predecessors so as to adjust them to the exigencies of current circumstances. In doing so, they "preserved" the procedure of essentialisation that had already characterised the work of the Roman priests before them. They abstracted simple elements from concrete cases and built maxims on the smallest of details which eventually became understood as elements of life itself.[85]

Lahusen's description of the essentialising methods of ancient Roman law reminds one of the distinction between legislation and *nomos* (the unity of place and order, *Ortung* and *Ordnung*) that Schmitt draws with such conviction in *Der Nomos der Erde* (see Chapter 2). What Lahusen is portraying here reflects the way in which jurists participated in, and completed, the historical ground work – *historischer Grundvorgang* – of land taking and land sharing that founds *nomos*. Considered from the perspective that Schmitt puts forward in *Der Nomos der Erde,* the ancient jurists can be said to have participated in the fundamental act of *nemein* – taking and sharing – that made it possible for *nomos* to become the veritable *law of the land.* It is this painstaking juridical grafting of links between legal concepts and the way things are that distinguished *nomos* from arbitrary legislation. This, in any case, is how the members of the Historical School understood their work, which Lahusen describes as follows:

> Kantian philosophy . . . and the historical materials of law were fused together under the rubric of "legal science" and duly endowed with the status of "truth." Starting on this foundation, Savigny's legal science could now proceed to dedicate itself to the forging of timelessly valid juridical truths. It would search behind the hazardous appearances of law in positive legal materials the "inner and enduring essence of legal concepts." . . . Rome again proved to be truth and fate. Recourse to the immortal examples of the Roman jurists inspired Savigny and his colleagues to rekindle their ancient artistry in their own work. The ground rules of this artistry were devoid of arbitrariness. The concepts it produced were essential realities, the existence and genealogy of which became known through long-standing familiarity. Their method was as certain as the method of mathematics. They produced a super-historical and super-human truth and continued to do so also in later times without distortion and disruption. Thus did the ancient jurists produce a living system of law that continued to develop further through the ages, and it is this further development to which their modern successors considered themselves called to contribute further in their own time.[86]

From the perspective of a concern with *nomos* and the unity of *Ortung* and *Ordnung*, Schmitt's admiration for Savigny is not without substance, notwithstanding the latter's reliance on Kant's definition of law. Kant is probably the most definitive opponent of *Ortungsdenken* conceivable and one of the great pioneers of the

85  See Lahusen 2013, pp. 60–61
86  Translated freely from Lahusen 2013, pp. 96–97.

normative thinking that Schmitt would abhor and malign throughout his life. However, Schmitt need not have been worried by the Kantian elements in Savigny's work, had he noticed them. There is hardly anything left of Kant in Savigny's recourse to him, hardly anything of the Kant who articulated a critical epistemology that prohibits scientific invocations of the real essences of things, hardly anything of the Kant who insisted that all such invocations belong to the domain of metaphysics, hardly anything of the Kant who considered law founded on the *idea* – not the reality – of reconciling the external conduct of multiple human beings without appealing to any morality.

Nor does this Kant ultimately survive in the work of Hegel. Hence perhaps, Schmitt's evident admiration of Hegel. This admiration for Hegel, we suggested above, should not be attributed purely to Schmitt's own ambivalence, his own inability to choose between *Ortungsdenken* and *Dezisionismus*. It should also be attributed, to some extent, to Hegel's own deep ambivalence with regard to Kant. Hegel took Kant's affirmation of the principle of freedom and individual autonomy as the cornerstone of his gigantic metaphysical and legal philosophical framework. But he considered this idea of freedom and individual autonomy still very weakly articulated in Kant's work. Hegel's formidable critique of Kant's theory of law – to which we turn now – is part of his global critique of Kant's critical philosophical project, a global critique under the umbrella of which his specific critiques of Kant's critical epistemology and practical philosophy dovetail perfectly.

According to Hegel, Kant's epistemological insistence that humans only know reality as it appears to us, and not how it is in itself (*das Ding an Sich*), concerns a self-inhibition or constraint of knowledge that is foreign to Spirit or Reason (*Vernunft*). In its sweeping dialectical march through history, the Spirit overcomes all binary oppositions conceivable. Spirit does not perceive matter and nature as its "opposites," but recognises them as different manifestations of itself. Through this recognition, Spirit becomes reconciled with itself again. This reconciliation bridges or erases the gap between subject and object which, according to Hegel, underpins Kant's distinction between phenomenal reality (reality as it appears to the subject) and noumenal reality (reality in itself). Phenomenological history – also considered the march of God through the world, we saw above – finally leads to Absolute Spirit and absolute knowledge. The essence of this absolute knowledge is the recognition that nature is not the opposite of Spirit, but a mirror in which it comes to see itself, the necessary mirror in which it comes to see itself *for* itself.

Once this overarching opposition between Spirit and matter collapses, all other oppositions also topple over like dominoes. The opposition between Kant's phenomenal sphere of knowable appearances and the noumenal sphere of *das Ding an Sich* comes tumbling down and allows for the attainment of real knowledge of the essence of things.[87] The opposition between essence and appearance comes tumbling down.[88] The opposition between moral duty and natural inclination, which is

---

87  Hegel 1970, vol. 6, p. 135 (stating that *das Ding an Sich* is nothing but an empty abstraction devoid of determination).

88  See ibid, p. 124: "Das Wesen muss erscheinen" (Essence must appear).

central to Kant's understanding of moral duty, comes tumbling down and allows for an objective morality – *Sittlichkeit* – that is substantive and real.[89] And Kant's opposition between law and morality also collapses and allows for an understanding of law as an effective reconciliation between the *outer and inner* freedom of every person with everyone else. It is instructive to quote Hegel extensively on the collapse of this last distinction:

> The Kantian definition, according to which the restriction of my liberty or arbitrary will so that it can be reconciled with everyone's arbitrary will under a general system of law is the main element, contains partly only a negative determination, namely, a limitation, and partly points to a positive determination, that appeals to a general law or a so-called law of reason, that postulates the correspondence of the arbitrary will of the one with the arbitrary will of others and culminates in the well-known formal identity and principle of contradiction. This proposed definition of law contains the since Rousseau especially widely spread insight, according to which the will is in the first place and essentially not the in- and for-itself existing reasonable will, the spirit not the true spirit, but the will of the particular individual will, the will of the singular person in his own arbitrary will. Once this principle is adopted, the reasonable can only figure as a limitation of individual freedom, given that it is considered, not something immanently reasonable, but only an external, formal universal. That view is as devoid of proper speculative thinking and philosophical conceptualisation, as it is responsible for putting into our heads, and into reality, appearances of which the horrifying nature is only paralleled by the shallowness of the thoughts that produced it.[90]

With this energetic and vociferous critique of Kant's strict distinction between morality and legality also comes crashing down any attempt to contemplate Hegel as a significant pioneer of liberal democratic law. Two aspects of this passage are crucial to note in this regard. The first concerns the way in which this fervent critique of Kant's definition of law leads directly – in the ensuing paragraphs of the *Grundlinien* – to a general conception of law that echoes the conceptual realism of the Historical School in significant respects. The second concerns the rejuvenation of life that suddenly returns to the *Grundlinien* in this paragraph.

Let us turn to the first aspect, the conceptual realism. The passage quoted above takes issue with a distinction between the idea of law and its empirical reality. The passage attributes this distinction to both Rousseau and Kant. We have already engaged with this distinction above in the case of Rousseau. Of concern here is the distinction between the *volonté générale*, on the one hand, and the actual will of the people that may become manifest in the will of an actual majority (see Chapter 6,

89 Hegel 1970, vol. 3, pp. 192–193; vol. 5, pp. 142–148, especially 147–148.
90 Translated from Hegel 1970, vol. 7, pp. 80–81 (§ 29).

Section 3). It is this distinction that Hegel saw resurfacing in Kant's definition of law. Kant's definition of law, stressing as it does the reconciliation of the *external liberty* of persons, refuses to extend this reconciliation to their inner freedom or moral autonomy. It rests content with a legal system that compels the external conduct of persons to comply with the idea of universal freedom. This understanding of the law presupposes or accepts the moral imperfection of all actual instances of conduct. It rests content with this moral imperfection as long as it does not express itself outwardly.

The same constellation of "outer and inner will" is evident in Rousseau's notion of the *volonté générale*. Rousseau's insistence that any individual who refuses to abide by the general will be forced to be free (*on le forcera d'être libre* – see Chapter 6, Section 3 again) evidently recognises the possibility of a clash between the empirical reality of individual freedom and the universal demands of freedom associated with the *volonté générale*. Coerced compliance would not have been necessary if the empirical exercise of freedom always conformed to the universal demands of freedom. The essence of the Hegelian critique of Kant and Rousseau of concern here, relates to the way in which it seeks to negate or soften the reality of coercive law enforcement. Hegel's whole metaphysical system – in terms of which all oppositions collapse and everything ends up well reconciled with everything else – commits him to an understanding of law that renders coercive law enforcement, not only unnecessary, but also philosophically spurious (*ohne allen spekulativen Gedanken und von dem philosophischen Begriffe verworfen*), horrifying (*Fürchterlich*) and shallow (*Seichtig*).[91]

In Hegel's system, enforcement of penal law through punishment does not disappear, but it no longer figures as an external imposition of coercive measures. It becomes the vehicle through which the criminal becomes reconciled with a morality that is also his or her own inner morality. And this reconciliation contains a gain. Through punishment the criminal becomes conscious of his or her own morality in a way he or she never was before. The criminal act, along with subsequent reconciliation through punishment, accordingly facilitates the development of the higher level of consciousness that allows for morality. The theodicy that underpins Hegel's whole metaphysical scheme theologically becomes evident in this theory of punishment. The criminal act itself becomes a necessary phase, not only in the self's ascent to moral consciousness, but also in the Spirit's ascent to a higher level of self-reconciliation. Evil – and the overcoming of evil – thus becomes a necessary element or phase of God's plan with the universe.[92] That is why Hegel confidently considered the coercive imposition of punishment unnecessary. Coercion is not necessary – and is in fact conceptually impossible – because the criminal receives his punishment willingly. From this follows that a criminal convicted of a capital

---

91 These are the strong terms that Hegel employs in the original German text of the passage quoted above. See Hegel 1970, vol. 7, pp. 80–81 (§ 29).

92 See Hegel 1970, vol. 20, p. 455: "Die Philosophie ist die wahrhafte Theodizee." See also Marquard 1982, pp. 52–65 and Geyer 1982, pp. 393–405.

crime does not get executed against his or her will, but actually commits suicide willingly and autonomously.[93] There is no heteronomy left in this best of all possible worlds.[94]

Hegel's critique of Kant and Rousseau's distinction between the "inner and outer will" of the legal subject erases the separation between law and morality along with the separation between morality and historical reality. As a result of these erasures, his theory of law becomes a conceptualism or conceptual realism in terms of which the concept grasps and assimilates the real. In this regard, Hegel's theory of law is ultimately hardly distinguishable from Savigny's conceptual realism, and barely distinguishable from Schmitt's conception of *nomos* as the unity of *Ortung* and *Ordnung*. The paragraphs that follow the passage quoted above make this clear. They expound the idea that law is not something separate from reality that requires *application to* reality. The dialectic development of law accordingly concerns *no application* in the sense of an external act through which a subject imposes itself or its "rule" on the object so as to realise itself or give effect to itself in the object. It entails an "organic development" of the "soul" of the object itself – *[d]iese Dialektik ist dann nicht äußeres Tun eines subjektiven Denkens, sondern die eigene Seele des Inhalts, die organisch ihre Zweige und Früchte hervortreibt.* It is no wonder that Schmitt had such difficulty in choosing between Savigny and Hegel. Notwithstanding their very different political orientations and their conflicting positions on legislation, both of them ultimately come across as very Aristotelian contemplators of *nomos* who consider law rooted in nature and nature rooted in law.

Hegel's *Grundlinien* are generally understood as a dialectic synthesis of Kant's morality and Aristotle's substantive ethics, but this synthesis ultimately tilts the balance heavily towards Aristotle. It is therefore also not surprising that Hegel relied on education or *Bildung* to effect the essential link between life and law and subject and object,[95] just as Aristotle relied on *paideia* to effect the essential mechanism that turns *physis* into *nomos* and *kosmos*. It is no wonder then that he referred to the insult of depriving "an *educated* nation" of the capacity to produce their own law through legislation, in his response to Savigny. This express reference to the legislative competence of an "educated" people makes it clear that Aristotle would have had no need to fear the legislation Hegel contemplated in the way he generally feared majority decisions (see Chapters 1 and 4). The legislation that Hegel contemplated would not and could not have been at odds with *nomos*. It would have been its embodiment. In Schmitt's terms, it would have been part of the historical

---

93 See Hegel 1970, vol. 7, pp 190–192 (§ 100). Hegel sensed the extreme consequences of this conception of law – the fact that the construal of punishment as self-punishment must lead to a postulation that the execution of the criminal is a matter of willing self-execution. Having made this point, he immediately commends Beccaria's efforts to get capital punishment proscribed for having at least reduced the scope of capital punishment to cases where it is really merited by the gravity of the crime.

94 It should be noted that Hegel does not deny the empirically observable fact of coercion that accompanies law enforcement, but considers it a psychological reality that has nothing to do with the moral essence of the person and of law, and this is all that ultimately counts for him. See ibid, pp. 178–190 (§ 90–99).

95 Ibid, pp 71–74 (§§ 20, 21).

intervention – *historischer Grundvorgang* – that secures the link between *Ortung* and *Ordnung*.

Assuming that it would not have been vulnerable to the critique of Rousseau and Kant that he articulated in the passage quoted above (at note 90), Hegel's legislation would have closed the gap between law and life that his *Differenzschrift* perceived with such force. It would have rejuvenated the life that the preface to the *Grundlinien* considered beyond the reach of philosophical rejuvenation. We shall see towards the end of this book that the theory of liberal democratic law must commend Hegel for recognising legislation as the principal source of modern law. But the redemptive legislation that Hegel contemplated, was surely not liberal democratic legislation. Liberal democratic legislation, as we shall see, is premised on the unbridgeable gap between life and law.

In the final analysis, the proclamation in the preface of the *Grundlinien* that "the real is reasonable and the reasonable real" may not have been the Stoic recognition that reason should not be looked for somewhere else, in some perfect past or future, but amidst the imperfection of the present. The phrase *hic Rhodus, hic saltus* may not have been an articulation of the resigned insight that we have nowhere else to dance. The Stoicism and scepticism with which the terrestrial journey of Spirit begins in the *Phenomenologie* may not have survived the dialectic *Aufhebung* – the suspension and upliftment – that leads from the embryonic self-consciousness of Subjective Spirit to the absolute knowledge of Absolute Spirit. This Stoicism and scepticism may ultimately have fallen prey to a triumphant vision of law that is fully reconciled with – and rooted in – life.

We shall never know where Hegel really stood in the end. Against the background of the time in which they were living, Hegel was undoubtedly a liberal and progressive mind, Savigny a conservative and reactionary. Hegel endorsed the ideals of freedom and equality of the French Revolution and the principle of intellectual moral autonomy central to Kant's philosophy, Savigny was an opponent of the Revolution who wanted to turn the clock back to a hierarchical past. However, if it is the case that Hegel considered the principles and ideals of liberalism historically realisable in the form of a substantive ethics that unites every member of society into a deep moral consensus, he must be considered to have turned his liberalism against itself.

Suffice it to conclude that it is from the less triumphant, Stoic and sceptical Hegel, if there ever was one, from whom the theory of liberal democracy stands to learn much about the fundamental torn and divided status of life, not from the triumphant Hegel who appeared to contemplate the reconciliation of life with itself and the erasure of the gap between law and life.

## 3 The social unity of the people: living law, *Freirechtsbewegung* and American realism

One must give it to Spirit, once it got going, it had a way of travelling the world, crossing the high seas and erasing ancient "amity" lines. Towards the end of the nineteenth century, the New World, more specifically the United States, became an important partner in the spiritual project launched by nineteenth century German legal science. It is somewhat ironic that it would be Savigny's *Volksgeist* and not Hegel's *Weltgeist* that founded this international partnership, but the partnership was legal, not philosophical, and, as we learned from Wieacker above (see the previous section), Hegel did not even make it into the German law firm. But the *Volksgeist* that travelled to the United States took almost everything along that Hegel may have wanted it to. As we saw above, the *Volksgeist* was as good as the *Weltgeist* in crossing the abyssal gap between subject and object, between spirit and matter or nature, between concept or idea and reality, between essence and appearance and between law and life. Notwithstanding their very different methods and visions, the *Volksgeist* was as adept as the *Weltgeist* in forging the conceptual essences required for turning legal concepts into social realities. The only thing that the *Volksgeist* did not share with the *Weltgeist* was the latter's *progressive* essentialism. This is the one thing that Hegel would have wanted to see the *Weltgeist* take to America, but the *Volksgeist*, unsurprisingly, took its hallmark restorative spirit to America.

Of concern in this little narrative of the *Weltgeist* that stayed at home and the *Volksgeist* that went travelling is the influence of nineteenth century German *Begriffsjurisprudenz* on American legal formalism or conceptualism. The influence of nineteenth century German legal science – generally known as "Pandectism" for the reasons explained above – in Europe is well-documented.[96] Its influence further abroad less so. To be sure, Savigny's influence on his American counterparts is not completely undocumented, but it largely remains a history "that has yet to be written," as Stefan Riesenfeld puts it in his 1989 exploration of the influence of German legal science on American jurisprudence.[97] Not much progress has been made since then as far as writing this history is concerned. One can therefore not conclude here that the German Pandectism had a decisive and direct influence on American legal formalism. The following observation of Roscoe Pound nevertheless speaks volumes:

> In America, distrust of legislation bred by our system of judicial tradition brought about a ready acceptance of Savigny's doctrines, with their incidental limitations, and a learned tradition arose which confined the jurist to the classical common law.[98]

The method that Savigny and his followers made famous towards the end of the nineteenth century was generally known as *Begriffsjurisprudenz* – *the jurisprudence of concepts*. A very similar jurisprudential method took root in the United States at the same time. It became known as "conceptualism" or "formalism." Irrespective of how it actually happened, a conservative conceptualism with all the trappings of essentialising links between law and life – the hallmarks of the Historical School in

96 See Wieacker 1996, pp. 483–485.
97 See Riesenfeld 1989, p. 7.
98 Pound 1911, p. 148.

Germany – also came to flourish on the other side of the Atlantic, and it is to this flourishing of conceptualism on both sides of the Atlantic that the European Free Law and the American Realist movements responded and rebelled.

Notwithstanding their initial resistance to codification, the conceptualist legal science of Savigny and his collaborators contributed substantially to the codification of German civil law that took place towards the end of the nineteenth century – the German *Bürgerliches Gesetzbuch* (*BGB*) which was promulgated in 1896 and entered into force in 1901.[99] The *BGB* was hugely successful and became a model for other civil codes in Europe,[100] and even influenced the interpretation of the French *Code Civil*.[101] However, the new civil codes soon became widely criticised for being compilations of abstract legal concepts that had little to do with the social realities of their time.[102] No codification of civil law took place in the United States, but the work of the famous American Formalists – among whom especially Christopher Langdell and Joseph Storey were leading figures – found expression in grand legal treatises. These treatises purported to make scientific sense of massive records of case law that no longer allowed for a systematic overview from which a clear set of precedents could be drawn and with reference to which new cases could be decided with clarity and conviction. The first treatises were soon followed by the Restatements of the law commissioned by the American Bar Association. These Restatements were invariably written by a select team of authors chosen from the most renowned treatise authors and they soon attained the reputation of "super treatises." In practical terms they enjoyed the status of official statements of the law and in this respect became the American version of the codifications of continental Europe.[103]

Both the civil codes of Europe and the major treatises and Restatements of American law pivoted on the idea of law as a *numerus clausus* of legal concepts, the essential logical properties of which could be extrapolated to find precisely the correct legal rule for all conceivable cases. They all turned on the idea that one could "calculate" the correct rule for each case with mathematical certainty, as Savigny's expression "*rechnen mit Begriffe*" suggested.[104] Moreover, they all also turned on the essentialist idea that these conceptual calculations of legal rules were accurate calculations of the concerns of life itself. It is against this conceptualist reduction of life to legal concepts to which the Legal Realists, Sociological School and *Freirechtsbewegung* rebelled. It is difficult to pinpoint the precise inception of their rebellion. Montesquieu is often invoked as an early ancestor of the movement.[105] This implies that an anti-formalist spirit actually preceded the rise of late nineteenth century formalism.

---

99 Windscheid, one of the renowned Pandectists at the time, also became one of the principal authors of the *BGB* –see Wieacker 1996, p. 473, Lahusen 2013, p. 103 and Herget and Wallace 1987, p. 406 n. 31.
100 See Lahusen 2013, p. 105, Wieacker 1996, pp. 483–485.
101 See Herget and Wallace 1987, pp. 399–455.
102 Lahusen 2013, pp. 132–135, Wieacker 1996, pp. 474–479.
103 See Herget and Wallace 1987, pp. 428–430. Ehrlich 1916, pp. 582–600.
104 Rückert 1984, p. 374.
105 See Ehrlich 1916, pp. 582–600.

Among the more direct influences, the work of Eugen Ehrlich and the late work of Rudolph von Jhering must surely count as crucial. Von Jhering, himself a conceptualist and among Savigny's close collaborators in his early work, published an essay in 1894 which derided the "heaven of concepts" in which the jurisprudence of the time wallowed.[106] This essay very definitely crossed the Atlantic, as its 1935 citation by Felix Cohen confirms.[107] The article in which Cohen cited Von Jhering became a seminal statement of the "functionalist" rebellion of the American Realists against the "transcendental nonsense" cultivated by conceptualist jurisprudence. Be that as it may, Von Jhering had already published major statements in 1877 and 1883 on the social purpose (*Zweck*) of law and jurisprudence that highlighted the ways in which jurists and judges manipulated legal concepts in the pursuit of desired policy outcomes.[108]

In 1888 Joseph Kohler published an article that proposed problems in statutory interpretation could be resolved by considering the economic and social purposes that informed them.[109] In the same year Eugen Ehrlich published an article titled "Ueber Lücken im Recht" ("About Gaps in the Law") and followed it up in 1903 with an article titled *Freie Rechtsfindung und freie Rechtswissenschaft* (Free Finding of Law and Free Legal Science).[110] In 1906, Hermann Kantorowicz published an essay under the pseudonym Gnaeus Flavius that called for resistance against the "scholasticism" of the conceptualist jurisprudence.[111] Most of these publications were cited by François Gény in his *Méthode d'interprétation et sources en droit privé positif* of 1899 and its second edition of 1919. This work was pivotal for the consolidation of the *Freirechtbewegung* (Free Law movement) and Sociological School in Europe. Ehrlich became widely known as the leader or founder of these movements, but Gény was actually the first to coin the term *libre recherche scientifique* from which the German movement got its name. Gény used this term to describe the practice in which the judiciary must engage when faced with cases where the law is not clear. James Herget and Stephen Wallace – whose impressive chronological construction and assessment of these developments underpins the brief historical outline presented here – refer most instructively to "the gap problem" that came to preoccupy the scholars associated with this movement. Of concern for them were the "gaps" in the law that become manifest every time a judge was faced with a situation for which the law did not provide a clear rule.[112]

The "gap problem" was of course exactly what the conceptualists and formalists of the time had been dismissing as non-existent. Proper mastery of the logic of the legal concepts will always produce a clearly applicable rule, they claimed. All the scholars

---

106 Jhering 1924, pp. 246–316.
107 Cohen 1935.
108 Jhering 1916, 1883.
109 Kohler 1886.
110 Ehrlich 1888, 1903.
111 Kantorowizc 1906.
112 See Gény 1932, vol. 1, pp. 193–204, especially at p. 195, Herget and Wallace 1987, pp. 410, 413.

mentioned above – Von Jhering, Kohler, Ehrlich, Kantorowizc and Gény – rejected this claim. They brought the problem of "the gap" to the attention of European jurisprudence and legal theory. The exponents of the Sociological School and Realist movement in the United States – most prominent among them Roscoe Pound, Oliver Wendell Holmes, Karl Llewellyn, Felix Cohen and Jerome Frank – must be credited for putting the "gap problem" under the magnifying glass in the United States. In the process, they gave it a pertinence in American jurisprudence that was never quite matched in Europe. Legal conceptualism and formalism survived on both sides of the Atlantic in the course of the twentieth century, but European jurisprudence remained by and large significantly more formalist and conceptualist than its American counterpart. Nevertheless, the gap-problem persisted on both sides of the Atlantic and would not go away. All the legal theorists with whom the last chapters of this book engage – Hart, Dworkin, Kennedy, Schmitt, Smend and Kelsen – were essentially still entangled in the "gap." The concept of liberal democratic law that will be put forward towards the end of this book will essentially also be concerned with the way in which the "gap problem" should be understood and addressed in liberal democracies.

How did the Free Law movement, the Sociological School and the American Realists propose to deal with the "gap problem"? We shall assume in what follows that the American Realists were not Hegelians. They probably were not.[113] They were pragmatists and sociologists and in this respect one would not be too far off the mark if one were to attribute to them a "contra-Hegelian" concern with empirical social facts.[114] From this it would follow that the Realists did not entertain idealistic visions of closing the gap between law and society and law and life. But the idea of closing this gap remained an important part of their thinking. In the early years of the Free Law movement and the Sociological School, the idea of finding or developing law that would be closer to society and closer to life was clearly key to their agenda. In a nutshell, they tried to plug or close the gap between law and *life* that they had just discovered themselves. In this respect they would appear not to have been all that different from the Hegel who discovered the gap

---

113 There is some evidence that Holmes read Hegel. See Grey 1989, p. 849. Pound referred to Hegel several times, but basically associated him with the Pandectist version of the historical school in Germany. See Pound 1911, p. 600. It is nevertheless safe to say that it is only much later that he received serious attention in American legal scholarship. For this later reception, see the essays in Cornell et al., 1991 of which four are authored by American and two by Canadian legal theorists. The editors assert confidently (at p. vii) that "the birth of Hegelian studies within American legal scholarship can be traced to a conference held on March 27–29, 1988, at the Benjamin N. Cardozo School of Law. . . ."

114 This reference to "contra-Hegelian" sociology inverts Gillian Rose's thoughtful phrase "Hegel contra Sociology." See Rose 2009. Rose's "Hegel contra sociology" actually concerns a defence of Hegel against the scientific sociology that emerged from the Marburg and Heidelberg schools of neo-Kantianism. See Rose 2009, p. 6. The invocation of the inverted "sociology contra Hegel" should be read as a broader reference that includes the field of empirical sociology that can be traced to Jeremy Bentham and Auguste Comte (notwithstanding the significant element of quite "Hegelian" historical speculation in the latter's work). See Marvin 1965, pp. 162–186.

between law and life (in the *Differenzschrift*), only to consider it closed again in his later works. It is this essential dialectic or "Hegelian" trajectory in the work of the Free Law movement, the Sociological School and the American Realists that will be highlighted in what follows.

Eugen Ehrlich coined the term "living law" or *lebendes Recht* in a 1911 essay titled "*Erforschung des lebenden Rechts.*" The essay described the work he was doing in a seminar at the University of Czernowitz. The concept of "living law" was developed further in his book *Grundlegung der Soziologie des Rechts* that appeared in 1913 of which the English translation – *Fundamental Principles of the Sociology of Law* – appeared in 1936. The book had a dual aim. On the one hand, it pointed out an array of cultural institutions and customs that constitute a sphere of informal law. According to Ehrlich, this sphere of informal law exists independently of state or formal law, and is much more in touch with the daily lives of people. This aspect of the book made it one of the key texts in the literature that would later be associated with the Legal Pluralism movement of which Gunther Teubner became a prominent exponent.[115] On the other hand, the book also tried to show that the state legal system is itself a living entity that adjusts itself to the exigencies of new times and regularly does so without the aid of formal legislation. Ehrlich emphasised the creative work of jurists and judges that the formalist and conceptualist conceptions of law in mainstream jurisprudence mostly ignored.[116]

Ehrlich's book was received enthusiastically by many members of the American Sociological School and Realist movement. However, they did not have to look towards him for purposes of introducing the concept of "living law" into their own writings, as Louis Brandeis' 1916 article "The Living Law" made clear. Brandeis' article advocated the need for a new jurisprudential consciousness that would be rooted in the life experiences of the people it served and bemoaned the fact that legal science was still largely deaf to this need.[117] Brandeis did not refer to Ehrlich, as Brian Tamanaha points out, and did not need to. The concept of "living law" and the concomitant freedom of judges to creatively sustain this "living law" was well established in the common law tradition and received many endorsements from jurists and judges alike in the course of earlier common law history.[118] Much of the Realist rebellion against formalism can therefore be regarded as a concern with rehabilitating and enhancing a socially sensitive and informed jurisprudence for which there were ample examples in common law scholarship and case law, but which had been marginalised because of the way in which the formalists opted for a "mechanical jurisprudence," as Roscoe Pound put it in a seminal essay.[119]

Pound himself articulated a very forceful call for a turn or return to "living law," and he certainly did not shy away from the most vitalistic rhetoric imaginable. In a

115  See Singh 2010.
116  See Tamanaha 2011, pp. 297–318.
117  Brandeis 1916, pp. 461–471.
118  Tamanaha 2011, pp. 299–301.
119  Pound 1908, pp. 605–623.

1907 article, "The Need for a Sociological Jurisprudence," he penned the following classic statement:

> The modern teacher of the law should be a student of sociology, economics, and politics as well. You should know not only what the courts decide and the principles by which they decide, but quite as much the circumstances and conditions, social and economic, to which these principles are to be applied; he should know this state of popular thought and feeling which makes the environment in which the principles must operate in practice. Legal monks who passed their lives in an atmosphere of pure law, from which every worldly and human element is excluded, cannot shape practical principles to be applied to a restless world of flesh, and blood.[120]

The word "application" still features firmly in this passage. It points to the remainder of a gap between life and law, notwithstanding the close link between life and law for which the passage pleads. It marks the transition from "practical principles" to the "restless world of flesh and blood" to which these principles should be applied. The gap between concept and reality and subject and the object is not quite closed. To put it in terms developed in the previous section, the moment is still Kantian, not Hegelian. But a sentence from "The Scope and Purpose of Sociological Jurisprudence," published in three parts four years later, would finally cover this last stretch. Here Pound "insisted," quoting Kantorowicz: "But the life of the law is in its enforcement."[121] One would not be exaggerating if one construed this sentence as a suggestion that Pound considered the law itself to be "coming alive" in the moment of transition from "practical principles" to "a restless world of flesh and blood" that he invoked in the passage quoted above. One should also not burden one sentence with the task of summarizing the position of any author comprehensively, not to mention the era and movement to which his or her thought belonged. However, one cannot imagine any one of the authors mentioned above – from Von Jhering, Kantorowizc, Kohler, Gény and Ehrlich, to Brandeis, Cohen, Holmes and Llewellyn, and of many others not mentioned – rejecting it as a misstatement of what they stood for.[122]

The theory of liberal democratic law developed in this book appreciates the historical significance of the *Freirecht*, Sociological and Realist movements in early twentieth century jurisprudence and the sobering impact they had on the intoxicated legal formalism of the time. It nevertheless remains wary of the approximation of life and law that takes place in the jurisprudential imagination common to all these movements. It finds itself unable to shake off the even more sobering thought that National Socialist judges and law professors turned out the most ardent endorsers of the *Freirechtsbewegung* in Germany and of the "living law" that it stood

---

120 Pound 1907, p. 612.
121 Pound 1911/1912, p. 514.
122 See Pound 1940/1941 for another firm sign of the "vitalism" that informed his thinking.

for.[123] Schmitt's coinage of the term *"Lebensrecht"* in 1934 (see Chapter 5, pp. 00–00) is a chilling testament of this approximation of life and law in Nazi Germany. This testament must render any theory of liberal democratic law deeply apprehensive of any jurisprudential conception that entertains visions of an approximation of law and life. That is why the *Freirecht*, Sociological and Realist movements discussed above should not be considered representative of the liberal democracy contemplated in this book, notwithstanding the fact that this contemplation endorses many if not all of the practical concerns with socially relevant law that these movements endorsed.

By stressing the Realist *moment* – the moment that *the law itself comes alive* and becomes *part of life* through the *application of practical principles to a restless world of flesh and blood* – the Realists and the Legal Sociologists effectively moved from Kant to Hegel, so to speak, notwithstanding any contra-Hegelian sentiments they may have shared. Pound's invocation of the application of practical principles to "a restless world of flesh and blood" and of "law [that comes alive] in its enforcement" reminds one of Hegel's statement in the *Phenomenologie* regarding the "life of Spirit" that does not shy away from, but finds its truth in "the absolutely torn state of its existence."[124] However, we know that Hegel did not consider "the absolutely torn state of [Spirit's] existence" torn for long. The wounds of Spirit heal soon enough, and do so without leaving scars – *die Wunden des Geistes heilen, ohne daß Narben bleiben* – he proclaimed towards the end of the *Phenomenologie*, the same work that affirms the torn state of Spirit's existence in its preface.[125]

When the wounds heal and the scars disappear, life and history become the full actualisation of the potentiality that Spirit already carried in its breast when time began. This was Hegel's noble vision. And for him too, the moment of actualisation was the moment of law. His *Grundlinien* ultimately became its monumental and triumphant statement, notwithstanding its melancholic moments. It is this actualisation of the potentiality of law that Western legal thought has been contemplating – not just since Hegel, but since Aristotle – that again haunts the moment that law comes alive for Pound, the moment indeed in which it passes from books to action.[126]

Hegel restored the link between law and life on the back of a confident speculative philosophy, part of which was an epistemology that restored the relation between subject and object, knowledge and reality. The *Freirecht*, Sociological and Realist movements did it likewise on the back of the confident epistemological realism that was typical of the empirical social sciences of the time,[127] as it still is all

---

123 See Van der Walt 2014b, pp. 308–309, Mauss 1989, pp. 81–103; Behrends 1989, pp. 34–79; Walther 1989, pp. 323–354; Herget and Wallace 1987, pp. 418–419.

124 See fn. 49 above.

125 Hegel 1970, vol. 3, p. 492.

126 See also Pound 1910, pp. 12–36.

127 This point is made by Williams 1987, pp. 429–496. Williams argues that the Realists simply replaced the rationalist objectivism (what I refer to as essentialism above) with an empirical objectivism rooted in the confidence of the new social sciences.

too often today.[128] Could they have averted this social scientific erasure of the gap between subject and object, and knowledge and reality, with which they sought to address "the gap problem" in law? Could they have averted this contra-Hegelian Hegelianism?

They could indeed have done so by realising, as Hans Kelsen already did in 1920, that the "gap problem" concerns much more than the occasional "gaps in law" that become manifest when the available rules of a legal system do not seem to cover a particular case . Kelsen saw that the "gap problem" concerned something much bigger. He understood that the law is itself a reflection of a gap that neither life nor any life science can close. He knew that the law is nothing but the gap that life always is for itself. Herbert Hart arrived at the same insight some forty years later. Between the two of them, Kelsen and Hart took the first significant steps away from the metaphysics of life in which Western legal thought had been entangled for two and a half millennia, and the first definitive steps towards the threshold of liberal democratic law. This is the story that Chapters 8 and 9 will now tell.

128  See Kaupa 2013, pp. 56–75.

# 8

# RULES, PRINCIPLES AND POLITICAL MORALITY

## 1 Law as primary and secondary rules – Hart

In the course of the almost six decades that have passed since the publication of H. L. A. Hart's *The Concept of Law* in 1961, lecturers in legal theory and jurisprudence have generally come to take it for granted that Hart's rule theory of law can be taught to students by focusing on the following key points:

1) the critique of Austin's command theory of law with special emphasis on Austin's failure to pay attention to the "internal aspect" of rules;
2) the replacement of Austin's command theory with a rule theory of law that defines law in terms of a combination of primary and secondary rules;
3) the analysis of the structure of a rule in terms of its unambiguous and certain core and the penumbra of uncertainty that pertains to its periphery, and the need for judicial discretion to settle the meaning of the rule in the case of the latter;
4) the distinction between law and morality and the positivist insistence that the former is generally unconcerned with the enforcement of the latter;
5) the concession that a minimal natural law content is necessary for sustaining even positivist systems of law.

Over the years, these five points have become less and less complicated and more and more teachable, with dire consequences for Hart's legacy. The ground-breaking force and full complexity of the rule theory of law has, as a result, fallen prey to widespread oblivion.

It is, however, not only the teaching of Hart to students that has become more and more stale over the years because of the repetitive reduction of his rule of theory of law to the five key points above. Scholarly engagement with Hart's work

has likewise become increasingly bland in the wake of the first wave of probing responses to Hart by Ronald Dworkin (see Section 2 of this chapter), Joseph
Raz, Lon Fuller, Neil MacCormick and Wil Waluchow.[1] Brian Tamanaha recently
observed: "Of late, the discussion within legal theory regarding legal positivism
appears, at least to an outsider, to involve an increasingly narrow and arcane debate,
with less and less at stake."[2] This is "not the fault of current legal theorists," he
added, suggesting that the old mine has had a good run, but cannot yield any more
gold: "Hart got a lot right [but s]tagnation in the discussion might also be a sign
that the prevailing theoretical paradigm has reached the limits of the insights it can
provide." In an attempt to break out of what appears to have become a constraining
mould, Tamanaha strikes out to offer a new approach which he refers to as "socio-
legal positivism." We shall briefly consider aspects of his venture below. Suffice it
to observe now that we return very definitely in what follows to the main theses
of Hart's rule theory, outlined above. This old mine is not overmined as Tamanaha
suggests. Quite to the contrary of what he believes, the problem that he perceives –
regarding a debate about positivism that has become too narrow and arcane – may
well be "the fault of current legal theorists" who only dig around in the already
exploited and perhaps indeed overexploited shallower parts of the mine and fail to
observe that it has profounder chambers that merit deeper exploration.

The suggestion here – that Hart's rule theory of law is profounder than many
legal theorists who engage with his work realise – may be surprising to anyone with
some knowledge of the context in which his theory developed. Of concern here
is the "philosophy of ordinary language" movement that dominated Oxford at the
time Hart was making his way from the Philosophy Department to the Faculty of
Law. This movement showed itself rather openly disdainful of the "deeper" questions
that traditionally characterised philosophical inquiry. It also showed no particular
interest in history and the history of philosophy. On the contrary, it consciously and
confidently dismissed vast areas of traditional philosophical inquiry for purposes of a
straightforward inquiry into the meaning of words. This was the spirit of philosophy
to which Hart was exposed in the years before his appointment to the chair in jurisprudence in the Faculty of Law. A remarkable passage from Nicola Lacey's probing
and instructive biography of Hart paints the picture in no uncertain terms:

> Yet there was a strong sense of the opportunity to make a fresh start on the
> English side of the channel, casting off the historical, political, and metaphysi-
> cal baggage of continental traditions (the French and Italians being lumped,
> for these purposes, with the German traditions whose political contribu-
> tion to fascism was perhaps more plausible) and constructing an indigenous,
> English, no-nonsense, post-war philosophy. As one philosopher, a graduate
> student in the early 1950s, put it, there was a feeling that much of what had

---

1  See Raz 1980, Fuller 1958, MacCormick 1979, 1981, Waluchow 1994.
2  Tamanaha 2001, p. 32.

gone before in philosophy was 'nonsense': 'they had won the war, got rid of the evil people, and didn't need to learn anything from earlier traditions.' Inevitably, Kant and Descartes sat alongside Aristotle and Plato in the Oxford undergraduate syllabus. But Nietzsche, Marx, Kierkegaard, and Hegel were notably absent. Only the so-called English empiricists – Locke, Berkeley, Hobbes, Hume, and Mill (as well as, to some extent, Kant) – appear to have engaged the enthusiasm of the linguistic philosophers.[3]

Lacey's principal concern is with Hart's personal history and not with the history of Oxford or English philosophy. It would therefore be irresponsible to draw overly broad inferences from this assessment of the philosophical climate at Oxford at the time. However, no one who has spent some time studying the respective developments of English "analytical" and European "continental" philosophy in the course of the twentieth century would consider this passage an inaccurate description of Oxford and English philosophy during the years that Hart was associated with the Oxford Philosophy Department. It is therefore fair to rely on it as an adequately accurate description of the broad context from which Hart's rule theory emerged. And it also seems fair to wonder for a moment whether anything profound can ever come out of a context that so deliberately insulates itself from its own past and the past of its neighbours, and purposefully reduces itself to a "no-nonsense philosophy" that considers everything beyond its own focus "nonsense." Any hypothesis or theory that emerges from a context as historically and intellectually narrow as the one described in this passage must run a risk of superficiality. However, nothing prevents one from taking such a theory out of these adverse conditions and resituating it in a broader context in which the concerns of ingenious and perceptive predecessors (however ancient) and neighbours (however "evil") are duly acknowledged; and nothing prevents one from reading it as a response to a vast historical record of trauma and perplexity. This is what this chapter does in this first section. It resituates Hart's rule theory of law in a context of a long history of philosophy and politics that allows one to dig deeper into this theory than has been the practice in recent years.

Hence the pertinence of the broad historical and philosophical background developed in this book. This background is duly needed to rediscover the real depth of Hart's rule theory of law, as well as the depth of the questions that several generations of analytical jurisprudence have been excluding from its job description.[4] We shall resituate Hart's rule theory of law against this background. We shall make it part of it. We shall do so, however, for purposes of showing how incisively Hart managed to extract his rule theory from the metaphysical bedrock of this background. In other words, we shall consider his theory the outcome of a long process of historical distillation from which a pure concept of liberal democratic law began to emerge from the

---

3 Lacey 2006, pp. 141–142.
4 See Horwitz 1997.

heavy materials of Western metaphysics. However, by extracting Hart's rule theory from the metaphysical context from which it emerged, we shall not be returning it to whatever shallowness may be imputable to its initial context. The vast and heavy depths of history and metaphysics from which it will be extracted will leave innumerable and unnameable traces on it, traces that will demand that we do not speak of its "shallowness," but of its *negative-depth*.[5]

Perhaps we "owe" it to Hart to restore the trajectory of the rule theory's emergence from the political, philosophical and metaphysical history in which all European and Western political and legal thought remains rooted, irrespective of the extent to which it has become uprooted, and irrespective of the extent that we need to uproot it even further. We "owe" it to him because of the way the quirks of his personal trajectory happened to deprive him of considering this broader philosophical and political history himself. He gave legal theory a lot. Perhaps legal theory can give him something back by reconstructing the philosophical and historical background that he did not and perhaps could not construct himself. Another passage from Lacey's biography gives us the essential personal background that is worth considering here:

> First – and not unconnected with his need for belonging and status – the coterie around Austin and Ryle was, to put it crudely, the main show in town within the discipline in which Herbert wished to make his mark. Notwithstanding the diversity within Oxford philosophy, it was acceptance and regard among the group around Ryle, Austin, Hampshire, and Strawson which – as the cause of Herbert's career over the next seven years would prove – was the ultimate mark of reputation and guarantee of success.
>
> Secondly, common-sense, linguistic philosophy must have held some discrete attractions for a late returner to philosophy who had doubts – as his 1940s notebooks show – about his capacity to get to the bottom of the deepest questions of epistemology and logic. The flight from metaphysics, in other words, offered the seductive prospect of escape from a painful further period of apprenticeship in the arcane aircraft of traditional philosophy – an apprenticeship which some of Herbert's colleagues felt that he had left too soon. This was a judgement which he himself endorsed in his later work – notably in his *Essays on Bentham*.[6]

It is with these considerations and this personal and scholarly background in mind that we now take a closer look at the five aspects of Hart's rule theory of law outlined above. To begin with, Hart criticises Austin's definition of law as a sovereign command for ignoring important characteristics of a legal system that cannot be explained in terms of sovereign commands that are habitually obeyed. The first

---

5  Cf. Van der Walt 2012, p. 82.
6  Lacey 2006, pp. 142–143.

characteristic concerns the reality of customary law. Legal systems invariably comprise, alongside legislation and judicial orders (the two elements of the legal system that can plausibly be construed as commands), customary rules that clearly do not issue from commands. The second characteristic concerns the continuing endurance of the law when the reign of one sovereign (Rex I) ends and that of another (Rex II) begins. The third feature of a legal system that does not seem to fit into the command theory concerns the fact that, in systems characterised by the general rule of law, law invariably also binds the sovereign or law-maker, whereas "commands" are generally orders that a person gives to others to follow, and not to one self.

Arguments that seek to construe these features of a legal system in terms of sovereign commands do not convince Hart. Customary law can, for instance, be considered tacit commands of the sovereign, but this construal does not convince Hart because it ultimately attributes knowledge of the custom to the sovereign, and this is often not the case.[7] The enduring force of the law of an earlier sovereign in the reign of a later sovereign can likewise be construed as a tacit demand of new sovereigns that the law of former sovereigns remains valid, but this construal is even less convincing to Hart than it is in the case of customary law, considering the way it attributes to the new sovereign detailed knowledge of a mass of repealed and unrepealed statutes, of which he tacitly accepts the continued validity of the latter but not of the former.[8]

The third feature of a legal system invoked above – the fact that law also applies to the law-makers when the general rule of law prevails in a legal system and does therefore not only consist of commands given for others to obey – can be accommodated under the command theory by distinguishing between the official and private statuses of law-makers. This allows one to view law as commands that the law-maker passes in his official capacity and obeys in his private capacity. Hart accepts the plausibility of this view, but insists that it does not save the command theory, because it does not account for pre-existing rules of law that define and create the capacity for official law-making and thus also bind the sovereign in his official capacity.[9]

The difficulties of the command theory highlighted above can easily be resolved, contends Hart, by accepting that the origin of all legal rules is conditioned by other legal rules that predate them. From this basic insight follows the centrepiece of Hart's rule theory of law: In relatively developed legal systems, law always consists of a combination of primary and secondary rules. Primary rules are rules that regulate conduct. Secondary rules are rules that determine how primary rules come into existence (rules of recognition), develop over time (rules of change) and must be applied (rules of adjudication).[10]

---

7  Hart 1961, pp. 43–48. The exposition above skips some steps of these three arguments for the sake of conciseness.
8  Ibid, pp. 60–64.
9  Ibid, pp. 74–75.
10  Ibid, pp. 89–96.

Considering the way this book highlights the separation of law from life as the
key element of the distillation process through which it seeks to extract the concept
of liberal democratic law from the history of metaphysics, one may well be tempted
to move quickly now by simply attributing the significance of the rule theory of
law to the way its reliance on a structure of primary and secondary rules appears to
sever law from life. Hart indeed does not go to much  trouble of linking this basic
constellation of rules to the life of any person or group of persons. One would,
however, move much too quickly by jumping to this conclusion. It is necessary to
scrutinise the status of the rules invoked in Hart's rule theory of law more closely to
determine whether they actually meet the demand for a separation of law from life
that is central to the concept of liberal democratic law. And one would also need to
inquire whether the rest of the rule theory of law confirms this separation.

Let us begin with the first of these two questions: Can an adequate separation of
law from life be inferred from Hart's rule theory of law? For purposes of responding
to this question one needs to pose a further question about the origin of the secondary rules that allow persons to recognise, change and consistently apply primary
rules. Where do these secondary rules come from? Hart does not really answer this
question. He simply presents his rule theory of law as a product of "descriptive
sociology."[11] Secondary rules are, in other words, social facts that one observes, and
which one observes especially well when one maintains a "sharpened awareness
of words" that "sharpen our perception of the phenomena," as the preface of *The
Concept of Law* tells us with reference to J. L. Austin.[12]

The link between "words" and "phenomena" that appears so early in *The Concept of Law* (on the first page of the preface!) raises troubling questions about any
separation of law from life that one may wish to impute to the rule theory of law.
The last time the word "phenomena" came to the fore in this book (see Chapter 4, Section 1), it concerned Paul Shorey's invocation of the "ingenious scheme"
with which Aristotle "save[d] the phenomena."[13] There is something surprising and
intriguing about Hart's highly conspicuous recourse to a word that one is more
likely to associate with Aristotelian metaphysics or Husserlian phenomenology than
with a "descriptive sociology" based on the "awareness of words" contemplated by
J. L. Austin.[14] What are these "phenomena," where do they come from and what is
the relation between them and the "subjects" of law that are of concern in Hart's
rule theory of law? For Aristotle, the word "phenomena" triggered a comprehensive theory about the totality of existence. What did it trigger for Hart?

When one follows the instruction of ordinary language philosophy rigorously,
one should consider oneself constrained to only pose questions about the normal
use of words. That is to say, we should remain *inside* our linguistic practices and
refrain from questions that invoke the origin, functional boundaries and general

11  Ibid, p. v.
12  Ibid.
13  See Chapter 4, fn. 8.
14  This is so notwithstanding the fact that some parallels have been pointed out between Austin's lan-
    guage analysis and phenomenology. See, for instance, Durfee 1976.

operation of these linguistic practices themselves. As Lacey observes, even Wittgen-steinian questions about the conventional conditions of linguistic utterances threaten to leave the practice of ordinary language analysis and stray too far off course.[15] At first glance, this methodological constraint seems to promise a rigorous separation of law from life. And it seems to comply with the proscription of metaphysical specu-lations that any "contra-Hegelian" sociology may require from it. But it inevitably causes considerable perplexity. One can hardly avoid wondering about this elemen-tary encounter with "phenomena" of which language is considered to be an adequate record. The proscription of any questions about the experience of the world itself reduces the "phenomena" to spectral entities that just happen to be amenable to an ordinary linguistic register. What about the agency that employs this register? In other words, what about those other phenomena that appear to have a "capacity to per-ceive" phenomena, those phenomena to which the linguistic register refers as "selves" or "subjects?" The methodological constraints imposed by ordinary language analysis seem to prevent any further fundamental questions about this "subjectivity" and the "world out there" in which the act or fact of perception appears to take place.

In other words, the "phenomena" somehow just drift into words such as "rules," "law," "primary rules," "secondary rules," etc., among or alongside other similarly ghost-like entities that somehow get stuck on the words such as "sub-jects of law," "citizens," "law-makers," etc. Beyond this observation, J. L. Austin and Hart cannot tell us what is going on here, because "ordinary language phi-losophy" absolved them from the trouble of addressing "the deepe[r] questions of epistemology and logic," as Lacey puts it.[16] "To each philosopher his own," one may observe with a shrug of the shoulders, but, against this background of spooky things – or sheer spookiness – that somehow mutate into words, one does begin to sense the point of the metaphysical imaginations that Aristotle and Hegel employed to situate the appearance of phenomena in a cosmological setting of "stable phenomena" and "meaningful history." Against the background of the ordinary language philosopher's unmapped invocation of phenomena that some-how become amenable to accurate description, even Hegel's fantastic invocation of a *Weltgeist* that travels through history begins to attain the status of a common sense awareness of the need to tell a story that may alleviate the abyssal burden of ignorance and incomprehension that weighs down upon the human mind's encounter with its environment.

The whole point of this book is to extract the concept of liberal democratic law from Western philosophy's metaphysical invocations of "Nature" and "Spirit." However, one only avoids the Spirit by exposing oneself to ghosts, it seems. Or one big ghost, the ghost of our existence. Some *Poltergeist* takes the stage as soon as one removes the *Weltgeist* from it. This is the dilemma that confronts every attempt to make sense of life without recourse to the ancient imagination of Western

15 Lacey 2006, p. 146.
16 Cf. Lacey 2006, p. 143.

metaphysics, and it also burdens the task of severing our understanding of law from the metaphysics of life that we have undertaken in this book. Be that as it may, the ordinary language philosopher will surely not indulge in Hegel's fantastic game of "make-believe" for purposes of resituating "the phenomena" in a stable narrative of meaning (especially not after what appears to have been a bad scrap with J. M. Findlay[17]), but how long and how consistently can he sustain the game of "not making-believe"? How long can this separation of "law" from "life" last?

This is where we turn to our second question posed above: Does the rest of Hart's rule theory of law testify to a consistent separation of law from the metaphysics of life? Significant separation of law from life seems to have been achieved with the insistence that "secondary rules" are just products of a "descriptive sociology [with] a sharpened awareness of words." But how long can the ordinary language philosopher consistently insist that he is solely concerned with phenomena that happen to hook onto words, and not with any significantly deeper link between them that threatens to link "law" to "life"? Not long, one would expect, when he moves over to the law faculty and becomes one of the most prominent legal theorists of his time, for the legal theorist deals with "experiences" that weigh particularly hard upon capacities of perception, whoever or whatever it is that is actually endowed with these remarkable capacities. The plot of this phenomenal or spectral "ghost story" therefore thickens considerably and quite understandably when Hart turns to the core of his argument against Austin's command theory of law. Legal rules are not experienced like the extortion that one faces when confronted by a gunman who demands one's money. They come across as "reasonable" and "sensible." They therefore need not extort compliance, because compliance is generally freely given long before extortion becomes an issue. Hart calls this the "internal aspect" of legal rules and it is this "internal aspect" of rules that, above all, distinguishes legal rules from mere commands, he claims.[18]

It would appear that there are at least some "benign" or "benevolent" phenomena out there − or wherever − called "legal rules with an internal aspect." These phenomena solicit voluntary compliance from other phenomena ("legal subjects") without requiring recourse to extortion. The ordinary language legal theorist will not tell us much more about this "internal aspect of rules," but there is a "thickening in the air" with the arrival of this new phenomenon. The merely spectral or ghostly status of phenomena with which the ordinary language, sociological and positivist legal theorist appears to rest content methodologically in the preface of his epochal book now begins to attain quite a spiritual quality, a quality that a more idealist or metaphysical philosopher or legal theorist may well be inclined to recognise as some kind of reasonable and/or rational correspondence between "subject" and "object," "inside" and "outside," "mind" and "matter" or even "Spirit" and "Nature" (note the capital letters that elevate the last pair to cosmological status).

17  See Lacey, 2006, p. 147. On Hart's dismissal of Hegel's metaphysical narrative of crime and punishment, see Hart 1968, p. 235, MacCormick 1981, p. 142

18  Hart, 1961, pp. 79–88.

The *Poltergeist* does appear to retreat at least somewhat here. It seems to allow some element of *Weltgeist* to return to the scene of analytical legal theory. And the question is whether and how Hart's legal theory manages to avoid turning this pneumatic thickening in the air – that occurs as soon as he invokes the internal aspect of rules – into a metaphysical trip switch that sets off the whole chain of Spiritual opposition-erasures, which finally leads to the "thick internal aspect" that Hegel describes when he tells us that capital punishment does not execute the criminal, but merely grants his wish to commit suicide (see Chapter 7, Section 2). What is it, then, that ultimately safeguards the ordinary language legal theorist from recognising the "internal aspect of rules" as the tell-tale sign of the "rationality of the real" that underpins Hegel's philosophy of law and renders all legal subjects fully reconciled to the legal rules under which they live?

If Hart manages to avoid the metaphysical trip switch invoked here, he duly becomes the pioneering champion of the concept of liberal democratic law that he has been made out to be since the first page of this book. If he does not, he must be considered just another metaphysician of the link between life and law, however much his descriptive sociology and common language legal theory claims to avoid this metaphysics. Does he manage to avoid the trip switch? He does indeed. It helps to return to Tamanaha's critique of Hart's internal aspect to explain how he manages to do so. According to Tamanaha, one can only avoid the metaphysical trip switch invoked here by avoiding the notion of the internal aspect of legal rules completely. Legal rules can exist without them, he claims, and do so regularly. He invokes the case of the people of the island state Yap in the Federated States of Micronesia. There is an official or "state" legal system in Yap, but the people basically could not care less about this system. They organise themselves with recourse to their own cultural practices. "For Yapese," writes Tamanaha, "when confronted with the law, it was like being confronted with the command of an alien sovereign ... despite the fact that ... this was their own legal system." This situation is not unique, he claims, but is paralleled in many parts of the world where an array of different normative practices exist alongside official or state legal systems that actually have little effect on the daily lives of people, "especially in many formerly colonized countries where the language of the law is often not the same as the spoken language(s)."

Tamanaha makes these observations for purposes of an argument in favour of a legal pluralism that recognises the possibility of many "legal systems" within one territorial space, and to dismiss the positivist conception of Hart – and other positivists such as Kelsen and Raz – that the state legal system must be an effective one that is generally obeyed. In this regard he even rejects Raz's insistence that the most important normative code in a country should be considered the official legal system.[19] The argument is badly miscued, considering that no official legal system in a non-totalitarian state ever aims to govern all aspects of existence. It is standard that they allow for other normative codes to exist alongside them. The question

---

19 Tamanaha 2001, p. 6, referring to Raz 1979, p. 116.

nevertheless remains which of these normative codes will prevail in cases of serious conflict between them, and the answer will always point one to the most important normative system that Raz correctly singles out as the legal system. More important to note here, however, is Tamanaha's imputation of a "metaphysical" status to the positivist insistence on the effectiveness of law. This insistence, he contends, is as unfounded as the metaphysical claim of natural lawyers that natural law must prevail over positive law.[20]

At stake in Tamanaha's argument, in other words, is a general jurisprudence – called "social-legal positivism" – that breaks away from the metaphysical privileging of official state legal systems in positivist theories of law. Evident here is a far-reaching endeavour to separate "law" from the "life" of people, an endeavour that seems aimed at decolonising this life from intrusions of law that is foreign to it. But this endeavour comes at a cost. It comes at the cost of ignoring the fact that some sovereign will still be exercising an ultimate right of "life and death" over this "de-colonised" life when, for instance, the enforcement of penal law becomes an issue (to make Raz's point somewhat more concretely). And it also comes at the cost of ignoring essential elements of the "general rule of law" that Hart actually describes much more accurately than Tamanaha recognises.

An accurate understanding of Hart's position requires that we take a much closer look at the "internal aspect" of law that he invokes to distinguish legal rules from the extortion of the gunman. It is especially important to zoom in, in this regard, on a sentence that has received much less attention in scholarly engagements with Hart's work than one might have expected. Hart writes:

> At any given moment the life of any society which lives by rules, legal or not, is likely to consist in a tension between those who, on the one hand, accept and voluntarily co-operate in maintaining the rules, and so see their own and other persons' behaviour in terms of the rules, and those who, on the other hand, reject the rules and attend to them only from the external point of view as a sign of possible punishment. One of the difficulties facing any legal theory anxious to do justice to the complexity of the facts is to remember the presence of both these points of view and not to define one of them out of existence.[21]

Hart's critique of Austin's command theory of law is basically that it "defined [the *internal aspect* of obligatory rules] out of existence."[22] In other words, Austin ignored the significance of the fact that people regularly live by rules that they consider good, reasonable or justifiable, and do not experience these rules as "external" commands that they only obey out of fear of punishment. Hart, however, remarkably does not replace Austin's theory with a theory that reduces all rules to their

20 Ibid, p. 11.
21 Hart 1961, p. 88.
22 Ibid.

*internal aspect.* The passage recognises clearly that many members of a society indeed experience some rules from the "external point of view." They do not experience these rules as good and reasonable, or even remotely justifiable, but they comply with them in order to avoid the negative consequences attendant upon non-compliance. Hart clearly states that any legal theory that seeks to do justice to "the complexity of facts" must recognise both the internal and external aspects of legal rules. The "complexity of facts" that he has in mind here concerns the fact that societies are not homogenous, but consists of different groups and individuals with very different attitudes to the law that governs them.

The passage quoted above underlines Hart's recognition that law and law enforcement never constitute the accomplishment of any global social ideal or vision. The effectiveness of law does also not depend on such an accomplishment, according to Hart. On the page that follows this passage, he observes that the stability of a legal system indeed depends on conditions where those who only experience the law from an external point of view remain a relatively powerless minority.[23] In other words, the effectiveness of a legal system can only be maintained under circumstances where the majority of individuals who live under the law generally consider the law reasonable and sound. Of concern here is the realistic concession to the elementary reality that any legal system that contradicts the convictions of wrong and right of the majority of the people it serves, can hardly be expected to last for long as a stable and regular system of law. It will hardly survive as a *regular* system of law that is not regularly susceptible to states of exception or emergency measures. By making this concession, Hart underlines the fact that the legal system he contemplated does not envisage the full realisation of any complete worldview. It envisages, instead, the sustenance of a situation where the world view of a majority exists alongside the world views of minorities, and vice versa.

Lacey observes that Hart can be considered to have pioneered the liberal conception of law that especially John Rawls would articulate comprehensively later, as his epochal debate with Patrick Devlin shows.[24] The regard that the passage quoted above shows for the reality that "at any moment in time" legal systems are marked by tensions between individuals and groups who have an internal perspective on law, and others who have an external perspective, confirms this observation. It makes social division a central concern of the theory of law in a way that Rawls would later make it a central concern of political theory. In this regard it also moves decisively in the direction of the concept of liberal democracy that Hans Kelsen already articulated meticulously in 1920, as we shall see in Chapter Nine. It is indeed because of the way *The Concept of Law* introduces the reality of social division into the heart of the theory of law that he has been championed from the first page of this book as a pioneer of liberal democratic law. It should nevertheless be stressed that Hart does not put forward a theory of liberal democratic law. He

23  Ibid, p. 89.
24  Lacey, 2004, p. 6. See also Hart 1958.

purposefully articulates a broader concept of law that includes systems of law that do not at all comply with the morality of liberalism, as the later chapters of *The Concept of Law* make abundantly clear.

In other words, Hart counts all coercive systems of government that consist in a combination of primary and secondary rules as duly formed systems of law, even if they do not accommodate individuals or groups with an external perspective to their coercion respectfully, but exploitatively and oppressively. Not even his recognition of a minimum content of natural law (that serves essential concerns with survival) as a necessary condition of any legal system that endures for any significant length of time persuades him that that oppressive, exploitative or even murderous legal systems are not systems of law. According to him, such systems evidently also contain a minimum content of natural law, but reserve its benefits for one social group at the expense of others.[25]

Hart has his reasons for not restricting his concept of law to legal systems with a duly liberal conception of law, and he articulates them well.[26] The fundamental insight into irreducible social division articulated in the passage above – an insight sustained throughout the later chapters of *The Concept of Law* – must nevertheless be highlighted as a crucial moment in the historical distillation of the concept of liberal democratic law in the history of Anglo-American jurisprudence. It is exactly this moment or turn that was still lacking in the jurisprudential revolution that the American Realists brought about, and this lack was exactly what prevented them from separating law from life (see again the end of Chapter Seven). The insight that Hart articulates regarding the tension between the internal and external perspectives of law that conditions all legal systems, underlines the reality that law can only be rooted in life if it becomes completely reduced to an internal perspective sustained by one social group (usually a majority) at the complete cost of an external perspective held by another social group (usually a minority). In other words, to be or become rooted in life, law has to give up all liberal democratic pretensions that purport to respect the equal worth of the external and internal perspectives to law that inform divisive social pluralities.

If, to the contrary, a system of law aspires to honour its liberal democratic pretensions, that is, if it refuses to become reduced to a system of coercive rules to which some citizens happen to hold internal perspectives, but aspires instead to remain a normative framework that sustains a reasonable and respectful compromise between those who hold external and those who hold internal perspectives on its coercion, it can obviously not be rooted in the life of any of these citizens.

25 Ibid, p. 196.
26 The essence of his argument is this: It is better to duly consider law all legal systems that comply with the criteria of law as a combination of primary and secondary rules, irrespective of how unjust or immoral they may be, and to keep the moral questions that such unjust systems of law raise – whether, for instance, they should be obeyed or not – a separate concern. Raising the moral questions that surface here in the form of the question whether unjust law is really law only clouds the issue. See Hart 1961, pp. 195–207.

Not only will the minority certainly not find the law rooted in their lives under these conditions. The majority will also experience the law as significantly removed from their lives as a result of the compromises it sustains with the minority. For the majority too, the law will not be rooted in life. Moreover, anticipation of changing vicissitudes of democratic outcomes – the fact that internal perspectives can change into external perspectives with changes of government – will surely inculcate the sense that the law is not rooted in the lives of those who currently constitute a majority. Individuals or groups of individuals who would like to experience the law as firmly rooted in their own lives will first have to annihilate, enslave or significantly oppress all political dissidents, and then prevent the changes of government that democracies sustain as a constant likelihood.

The suggestion here, of course, is not that external and internal perspectives to law switch with regard to every aspect of law and every legal rule with every change of government. However, a significant change of government can bring about significant changes of perspective with regard to politically or existentially charged areas of law. Social security law is a pertinent example. Law that regulates procreation freedom is another. Any change in these areas of law will always underline the reality that liberal democratic law will and can never be rooted in the life of a divided society or of any one of the minority or majority groups in such a society. As will failures to change these areas of law. The sociological turn advocated by the American Realists never led them to a clear and firm articulation of this insight. Perhaps it was just too early. The problem of social division and minority and majority relations – that resurfaced even more apocalyptically and murderously in twentieth century political history than it did during the religious wars of the sixteenth and seventeenth centuries – was just raising its head again at the time of the Realists' revolt against formalism. This means that Hart was really the first to articulate this concern pertinently in twentieth century Anglo-American jurisprudence. And after him, as we shall see in the next section of this chapter, Ronald Dworkin staged a Herculean effort to erase it again. As we shall see, however, Dworkin's endeavour to erase Hart's insight into the irreducible tensions between external and internal perspectives to law did not take issue with the passage from *The Concept of Law* cited above. His response to Hart largely took issue with the last element of Hart's rule theory of law that must still be highlighted here, namely, his conception of the role that judicial discretion plays in the enforcement of any legal system.

Hart considers all legal rules to have a core and a penumbra. The meaning, scope and reach of rules are clear at the core, but become unclear the more the penumbra of the rule comes into view. The textbook example that Hart uses is a legal rule that proscribes the use of vehicles in a park. It is clear, he argues, that the rule prohibits entry of normal vans, motor cars and motorbikes. Should a legal dispute arise regarding any one of these vehicles, judges would hardly have to think twice to ascertain whether it was covered by the proscription or not. But the same would not be the case if some complaint was raised about the use of toy motor cars or motorbikes in the park. The judge who needs to determine whether the proscription applies to toy vehicles would not be able to decide the matter with the certainty available to her in the case of normal motor cars, etc. In these cases, contends Hart, the judge would need to rely on good discretion to make a good decision.

If this were to happen in legal systems where judicial decisions become precedents for similar cases that arise later, the discretionary interpretation of a rule to which judges resort when the applicable rule is unclear does not become a precedent without further ado. Only time will tell whether the decision will be acknowledged as a good rule to which courts can take recourse with the certainty they generally have with regard to the core of long standing rules.[27] Hart nevertheless does not consider this interim uncertainty of the law a cause of consternation. Disputes can generally be resolved with recourse to clear rules of law. The rare cases in which judges have to resort to discretion are exceptional enough not to threaten the stable and proper functioning of a legal system properly constructed on the basis of a solid combination of primary and secondary rules. In this way Hart claims to avoid the two extreme positions that preoccupied the jurisprudence of his time, legal formalism and legal realism. Law is not the heaven of concepts that allows for a mechanical jurisprudence, but neither does it warrant the complete rule scepticism of the American Realists. It is neither the sweet dream that there is always a precise rule for every legal dispute, nor the nightmare that we have no clear rules at all. The reality of a good legal system − for which Hart invokes the metaphor of "a good night's sleep" − lies somewhere between this dream and nightmare.[28]

It is important to point out an inaccuracy that burdens Hart's conception of the core and penumbra of legal rules. He appears to regard the core and penumbra constant features of all legal rules and does not consider the possibility that the core and penumbra of the rule are much rather functions of the tension between external and internal perspectives of law recognised in the passage quoted above. The whole idea that the scope of the word "vehicle" can suddenly lose the clear meaning that it usually has, just because one is confronted with a dispute regarding a toy vehicle, seems odd. It would seem much more accurate to describe disputes that arise regarding the meaning of words in terms of social conflicts that move persons or groups of persons to strategically abandon, enlarge or shrink the spectrum of meaning usually associated with a word or phrase. The kind of conflict that typically informs legal disputes can − and should for the sake of more accuracy − be explained with reference to a social tension that arises between two or more persons. The dispute regarding the meaning of the rule results from the conflict between them, and not vice versa. It is the conflict between the parties to the dispute that suddenly moves one of them to take an external perspective to a rule by attributing a meaning to it that deviates from the meaning it usually had before the dispute erupted. In Hart's example: Because of an eruption of discontent with a factual situation that ends in a dispute, someone starts to attribute a meaning to the world "vehicle" that it clearly − not just vaguely − did not have until the dispute erupted.

---

27 See Hart, 1961, pp. 149–150.
28 Hart 1983, pp. 123–144.

The reason for stressing this explanation of disputes regarding the meaning of a word or a legal rule concerns the need to highlight the status of language in general, and language in particular, that is at stake here. Linguistic reference is not real in the sense that it is logically or semantically linked to the "reality" it invokes. The "reality" that language invokes is a contingent function of relatively stable and enduring linguistic conventions and practices. The gap between language and the world, which relatively stable linguistic usage renders forgotten, suddenly becomes manifest again when an incident – and the harm or discontent it causes – renders a word or the hitherto standard usage of a word unacceptable to someone. This is how the "clear" meaning of words suddenly become "unclear" and this is what calls for a new or changed use of the word, or recourse to new words. The new use of the word will certainly not have the credentials of "rightness" until such time as a stable practice ensues from the new usage. The ordinary language analysis background from which Hart's rule theory of law emerged did not encourage him to explain this historical process of linguistic change and development better, as Lacey observes.[29] One must indeed look towards Wittgenstein for an accurate understanding of this process, or even better, to the ground-breaking work about disputes – *Le différend* – that Jean-François Lyotard wrote in response to Wittgenstein.

Hart's conception of the judicial discretion that becomes necessary when a rule suddenly becomes "unclear" and contentious is nevertheless largely in line with this Wittgensteinian or Lyotardian understanding of the radical historicity of language and the sheer eventfulness of human existence in which language is never rooted, but to which it is irreducibly and relentlessly exposed. According to Lyotard's reading of Wittgenstein, language can never be rooted in its own history or historicity. It remains exposed to its historicity but cannot put down roots in it. In fact, it can only respond to its own historicity by insulating itself from it. Language is nothing but an insulating device, an artifice that suspends the infinite potentiality of history in order to render its infinity inhabitable under finite conditions.[30]

It is on the basis of this insight that one can ex post facto commend Hart for not taking the route that the judicial craft movement once offered him and which he explored in a paper that remained unpublished and even lost until recently. In the wake of the American Realist Revolution – and the rule scepticism it advocated – the judicial craft movement pioneered by Henry Hart and Albert Sacks sought to re-establish legal certainty by stressing that judicial practices can be stabilised by incisive inculcation of the professional craft that judges employ when they decide

29  See Lacey 2006, p. 146.
30  The Wittgensteinian thought that Lyotard explores in *Le différend* concerns the way in which linguistic conventions not only render linguistic responses possible, but also insulate all such responses (through a network of names) from the historical exigency (the event) that calls for a response. Hence the liberating incapacity of language to link "reference" to "reality." See Lyotard 1983, especially pp. 57–92. For a more extensive discussion of this conventional conditioning (or enabling) of language that separates and insulates it from the historical exigency to speak (this enabling insulation of language), see Van der Walt 2018.

cases.[31] Hart did not take this route. The reason for not doing so may well be, as Lacey suggests, that his commitment to legal positivism simply prevented him from introducing into his rule theory of law a consideration of multi-faceted judicial crafts that could not be accommodated under a clearly definable secondary rule.[32] There is nevertheless nothing that prevents one from sensing a profounder insight behind Hart's decision not to take this route. His recognition of the inevitability of a significantly free judicial discretion – however mediated by craft consciousness, etc. – testifies to an acute understanding of the way in which humanity always exists outside its own history and therefore outside or "before" the law, notwithstanding the tendency of relatively stable linguistic and juridical practices to effectively produce persuasive "internal perspectives" to law that create the impression of close links between law, life and history, or language, life and history.[33]

Hart's rule theory of law and the conception of judicial discretion that completes it can accordingly be said to sustain an acute regard for the "eternal external perspective" that always haunts the law, always threatens to disrupt its apparently settled and peaceful constellations of (temporarily dominant) "internal perspectives." If this is correct, the rule theory can also be said to understand law as a placeholder that organises the extrinsic relation between law and life. The interpretation and application of a rule of law to life, that is, to a concrete case, should accordingly not be understood as the actualisation of law or the actualisation of the link between law and life. Application of a legal rule does not concern the realisation of the hitherto unrealised potential or potentiality of the law. It is nothing but a place holder that sustains the separation of law and life, a place holder that keeps life "at bay" so as to postpone, for as long as possible, the anarchic force with which it invariably threatens to destroy law.

Did Hart indeed sense that the key tenets of the "judicial craft" movement ran the risk of connecting law and judicial language too confidently to life again? Was his insistence on instances of free judicial discretion, which may or may not normalise in the course of time, indeed the *nominalist* testimony (see the discussion of the Nominalist revolt against Aristotle in Chapter 1) to the irreducible gap between law and life, and between language and life, which we are attributing to it here? Of course, we do not know, in any case not as far as his personal biography is concerned. The textual evidence available nevertheless makes such an interpretation of his legacy plausible enough. It also renders it plausible to consider him the pioneer, not only of the broad concept of law that he contemplated, but also of the narrow concept of liberal democratic law that we are contemplating in this book. This is also the legacy, we shall see now, of which Ronald Dworkin most decidedly took leave when he dismissed Hart's conception of judicial discretion for purposes of an "imperial" rehabilitation of the close link between law and the historical life

---

31  Hart and Sacks 1994.
32  Lacey 2013, p. 639.
33  See Kafka 2012, pp. 154–155. For other interpretations of the parable, see Teubner 2013 and Derrida 1985.

of a people that the common law used to claim before the rise and demise of legal formalism.

## 2  Law as rules, principles and political morality – Dworkin

If judges have some discretion when they decide cases, it is only a weak discretion, argued Dworkin in response to Hart. Weak discretion, he explained, concerns the last step of a selection process that follows *after* the selection criteria have been defined. His example is the selection of ten good marksmen that is entrusted to an officer of lower rank after the decision to employ ten marksmen has already been made by officers of higher rank. The officer of lower rank only judges the factual situation to determine which facts fit the criteria stipulated.[34] The judge finds himself in a similar situation, claims Dworkin. He judges whether relevant facts meet or do not meet the criteria stipulated by a legal rule. And if a legal rule appears to confront the judge with the possibility of judging the facts in different ways (for instance, the proscription of vehicles in the park does not apply because the alleged motorbike that causes the trouble is only a toy; or the proscription applies because the alleged toy is really powerful enough to be considered a vehicle), the legal principles underlying the rule will determine whether the proscription applies or not.

In other words, legal principles already contain the selection of criteria that must be applied when all applicable legal rules fail to provide a conclusive assessment of the facts under scrutiny. The judge does not invent the criteria of assessment that are applicable when a case is not conclusively resolvable with recourse to rules. He or she does not have this kind of discretion, a discretion that Dworkin called "strong discretion." He or she only has the weak discretion that comes into play when a final selection of facts must be made on the basis of a clear rule. When no clear rule appears to apply to the facts, the broad legal principles will nevertheless guide the judge to a decision that is not based on personal discretion, but on criteria that are predetermined by duly applicable legal principles. The decision whether or not the proscription of vehicles in the park applies to toy motorbikes will then come to turn, for instance, on the principle embodied in the right (supposing there is one) to safe and calm public places where people can relax without fear of injury to themselves or their children. If it now turns out that the facts point to a toy that is actually dangerous to other children, the judge will be obliged to proscribe the presence of toy motorbikes, now not with reference to the "vehicle rule," but with due reference to the principle stated.[35]

It can of course also happen that more than one principle applies to a case in a way that appears to demand different responses from a judge. Suppose it turns out the toy motorbike in our example is indeed strong enough to cause some harm to other people in the park, but not very likely to do so. Another principle may then

34  Dworkin 1978, pp. 31–39.
35  Ibid, pp. 22–31.

also begin to demand compliance from the judge, say, the principle that people using public spaces should consider it a shared space that requires tolerance with regard to uses of the space that they do not like and approve of. After all, the park is the only place where a child growing up in a city can try out a toy motorbike that is, one can assume, perfectly legal to buy in that city. That child may well have a "right" to ride his or her largely undangerous toy motorbike in the park. What should the judge do now, according to Dworkin? He or she again has no discretion, Dworkin insists. Confronted with two principles that demand consideration in a legal dispute, he or she must decide which of the two principles ultimately outweighs the other under the circumstances. One must note here also a difference between rules and principles that Dworkin stresses. When the facts do not fit into the scope of a rule, the rule does not apply. However, when a principle is outweighed by another principle, it remains fully applicable. It just does not exercise a strong enough "pull" on the present case to compel the judge to select it, instead of another principle that competes with it.[36]

How can one convincingly maintain that the judge exercises no discretion when he weighs up two or more principles that compete for application in a particular case? According to Dworkin, it is perfectly coherent to do so because the principles themselves are rooted in a community morality of which the essential character can be determined accurately by a competent judge. Reverting to our "vehicle in the park" example, one can imagine the judge asking him or herself: What kind of people live in this city? Would they seek to avoid all possible harm done by a toy motorbike in a park, even relatively unlikely harm, at the complete cost of reasonable tolerance that one generally expects from urban communities? Or would they rather remain tolerant, even though this would require them to run slight risks of injury and endure some annoyance? Whatever decision the judge comes up with, contends Dworkin, will not result from personal discretion, but from an accurate assessment of the general moral character of the legal community whose law must be applied. Dworkin is not modest with the claim he makes in this regard. A good judge – especially his exemplary judge whom he sometimes calls Hercules – will assess the situation and the character of the legal community correctly and come up with the right answer. There is only one correct answer and Hercules will arrive at it, says Dworkin, when he does his work well.[37]

The outline of Dworkin's arguments developed above takes into consideration the main themes and arguments that he develops in an early collection of essays published in *Taking Rights Seriously*. Of concern here is a three level "tree-model" of the law that includes rules (first branch), principles (second thicker branch) and political morality (trunk). Dworkin uses the expression "tree-model" expressly in his last book, in which he also adds two more layers. In *Justice for Hedgehogs*, political morality itself is a branch of the whole tree of morality of which our basic *idea of*

36 Ibid, pp. 26, 115–116.
37 Ibid, pp. 279–290.

*what it means to live well* is the trunk. Here, *personal morality* becomes the first major branch that grows out of the trunk, followed by *political morality* and *law*. Law then branches out further into principles and rules.[38]

The essential claim that the essays in *Taking Rights Seriously* make – a claim that is not manifestly amended by any of the later works – concerns Dworkin's insistence that rights always exist in advance of any legal dispute that may come to the fore. They are real. They are not just the product of a judicial decision, as the American Realists claimed. They are also never simply the product of legislation. If the institutional and moral character of a legal community confers a right on someone, not even a legislator can terminate that right without falling foul of the fundamental law of that community which is usually duly registered in a written constitution. Such a written constitution should therefore also be duly considered the principal indicator of the moral character of a people, according to Dworkin. No legislator can introduce legislation that promotes governmental policy considerations that are in conflict with this moral character of the people and the rights that derive from it (hence also Dworkin's strict distinction between principle and policy).

In his work *Law's Empire*, Dworkin also contends that judges who do their work properly are able to assess the changing character of a people or legal community over time. The character of the people does not change abruptly but gradually. Good judges know how to assess new elements of a people's character over time and skilfully weave them in like new strands in an old rope, without weakening the rope or changing it into a different one.[39] Dworkin also uses the metaphor of a chain novel to describe this process. Different generations of judges all work on a chain novel to which they have to add new chapters without changing the plot that has already been developed in earlier chapters of the book. All judges work on this chain novel under obligation to maintain the essential plot and characters of the novel that are already established, but also to make the plot as good as it can possibly be without ignoring or changing essential aspects of the story that are already given.[40] Dworkin refers to this process as "constructive interpretation." The two key elements of constructive interpretation are the pursuit of justice and the concern with integrity or "fit." Good decisions must fit into the institutional history of the whole legal system. A decision can come to be considered a mistake that must be worked out of the system when later judges begin to find that it just does not fit into the character of the law as it has developed thus far. But as long as they fit, legal decisions must also constantly pursue justice. They must make the law the best it can be. All these elements of constructive interpretation pivot on the idea of the fundamental integrity of the legal system. Just as a person of integrity can be expected to act in a principled way that would be consistently true to his or her character, the law can be considered an institutional reality with a principled

---

38 Dworkin 2011, pp. 5, 405–407.
39 Dworkin 1986, pp. 69–70.
40 Ibid, pp. 228–232.

integrity.[41] The law does not chop and change. It is not a collection of "checker-board" decisions.[42]

The exposition of the key elements of the legal theory that Dworkin developed in *Taking Rights Seriously* and *Law's Empire* developed here is undoubtedly rudimentary and unoriginal. But neither is it distortive. None of Dworkin's readers should find this reading of his work objectionable. Assuming then that it is completely fair to Dworkin, one can begin to highlight the feature of his theory that appears most questionable from the perspective of the liberal democratic conception of law thus far developed in this book: Dworkin's theory does not seem to consider social division a significant concern in its conception of justice. It starts with the notion that judges can assess the key characteristics of a people for purposes of selecting the uniquely correct resolution of any legal dispute. The basic social unity assumed by this theory is further underlined by the metaphors of the one rope into which all the different strands of a legal community's existence can be woven without fear of fraying, and the single narrative to which new generations of judges add new chapters without changing its timeless plot. Pivoting as it does on these two key metaphors, unity and absence of division appears to be written all over Dworkin's theory of law. There would seem to be no place for an external perspective to the law in his theory of constructive interpretation. Dworkin's theory of law reduces the legal system to an object of consensus sustained by one ove-arching internal perspective.

If this is correct, this theory would have little or no role to play in the concept of liberal democratic law that has been pursued from the first chapter of this book. The pursuit of the concept of liberal democratic law that has been launched here has throughout been premised on the need to take leave of the long history of metaphysics that continued for two and a millennia to consider the law rooted in either the natural or historical existence of a people. If this history of metaphysics is to be put on the boiler in order to distil from it a pure concept liberal democratic law, Dworkin's theory of law would seem to end up in the bubbling cauldron, along with those of Aristotle, Aquinas, Hegel and Savigny. Of the theories or philosophies of law considered thus far, only those of Saint Paul, Saint Augustine, Ockham, Rousseau, Kant and Hart will send notable vapours into the distillation process from which a pure theory of democratic law may condensate. Dworkin's theory of law all too evidently harks back to the former group of theorists, not the latter. If there is one single passage in his work that seems to make this abundantly clear, it is this one from *Taking Rights Seriously*:

> [Hercules] will begin within, rather than outside, the scheme of values that approves the concept, and he will be able to put to himself, rather than to some hypothetical self, questions about the deep morality that gives the concept value. The sharp distinction between background and institutional

41  Ibid, p. 167.
42  Ibid, pp. 179–184, 187, 217.

morality will fade, not because institutional morality is displaced by personal convictions, but because personal convictions have become the most reliable guide he has to institutional morality. It does not follow, of course, that Hercules will even then reach exactly the same conclusions that any other judge would reach about disputed cases of the concept in question. On the contrary, he will then become like any reflective member of the community willing to debate about what fairness or equality or liberty requires on some occasion. But we now see that it is wrong to suppose that reflective citizens, in such debates, are simply setting their personal convictions against the convictions of others. They too are contesting different conceptions of a concept they suppose they hold in common.[43]

What exactly is Dworkin contending in this passage? Is he contending that we have different conceptions of a concept of law and justice that we all have in common, and that we usually resort to debate to strip our conceptions of elements that do not fit into "our common concept"? If this is what he is arguing, he is evidently retreating very decisively from Hart's recognition that some of us have an external perspective to law that cannot be wished away or reduced to the internal perspective of those who happen to belong to the most numerous and/or most powerful group. And if he is indeed doing so, he is also turning Hart's "internal perspective" into the thick internal perspective we saw at work in Hegel's view of the criminal who voluntarily assents to punishment, given that punishment is a reflection of the objective reason embodied in the law in which he himself also partakes, not as an outsider, but an insider (see the discussion in Chapter 7, Section 2).[44]

But, Dworkin tells us expressly in *Law's Empire* – as if he is anticipating that his readers could easily suspect him of this – that he is not engaging in a Hegelian spiritualism. In a passage that appears in the section of *Law's Empire* where he explains the need to think of the legal community as a person, he writes:

> I must make clearer what kind of personification [of community] this is. I do not intend now to resurrect [a] metaphysical theory . . . that we do not need. I do not suppose that the ultimate mental component of the universe is some spooky, all-embracing mind that is more real than flesh-and-blood people, nor that we should treat the state or community as a real person with a distinct interest or point of view. . . .[45]

---

43  Dworkin 1978, p. 128.

44  This point must not be confused with Dworkin's methodological distinction between the "external point of view of the sociologist or historian," on the one hand, and the "internal point of view" of people "who make and defend claims" about law. See Dworkin 1986, p. 13. Hart's external and internal perspectives are categories that would typically be contemplated from the perspective of Dworkin's "external point of view" but could also have a real impact on the "internal point of view" that seeks to determine what the law is in a particular case.

45  Dworkin 1986, p. 168.

So, considering that there is no textual evidence of a significant retreat in *Law's Empire* from the positions taken in *Taking Rights Seriously*,[46] we must assume that the "supposition" of a "concept that all citizens "hold in common" in the latter text entails neither the real metaphysical personification of community disavowed in the former, nor the thick or all-embracing internal perspective to law that would be attendant upon such a metaphysical personification of community. So what is Dworkin getting at in the passage from *Taking Rights Seriously* quoted above? Let us consider for argument's sake that the passage articulates a constructivist conception of legal and moral consensus. It should be noted at the outset that Dworkin states expressly in *Justice for Hedgehogs* that he is not offering a constructivist theory of law and morality.[47] Let us nevertheless read the passage as a constructivist statement for purposes of seeing whether we can take it out of the unliberal corner into which it seems to be painting its author. It is not impossible to do so. The key to such a constructivist reading of the passage would lie in the word "suppose" in the last line. The sentence of concern could have read: "They too are contesting different conceptions of a concept they hold in common." But as it stands, it reads: "They too are contesting different conceptions of a concept they *suppose* they hold in common." The word "suppose" is often used as a synonym for "believe" or "assume." However, one can also increase the work it does – increase its performativity as linguists would say – so that it takes on the quality of a *presupposition*. This is what one needs to do in order to read the passage above as a constructivist statement. When one does this, the following reading becomes plausible: "They too are contesting different conceptions of a concept that *they do not really hold in common, but suppose they do.*"

If this can be accepted as a fair reconstruction of Dworkin's sentence in the passage from *Taking Rights Seriously* quoted above, the passage would indeed seem to be fully reconcilable with his arguments in *Law's Empire*, for the latter text very expressly recognises real disagreements about law among lawyers and judges. Dworkin states expressly at the beginning that *Law's Empire* is a book about "theoretical disagreements in law," and by "theoretical disagreements" he means any serious disagreement about what the law essentially is and should be, as opposed to mere "factual disagreements" such as a disagreement about the answer to the question whether or not some statute exists.[48] And he stresses that these disagreements are fundamental. They do not only pertain to the penumbra or margins of legal rules, but to their very core.[49]

In other words, *Law's Empire* appears to raise the stakes vis-à-vis Hart as far as law and disagreement are concerned. If this is correct, we should conclude that Dworkin does after all not deny the external perspective to law that Hart recognises

---

46  Dworkin's reflections on the relation between the two works suggests no such fundamental break. See Dworkin 1986, pp. viii.

47  Dworkin 2011, p. 63–66.

48  Ibid, pp. 3–12.

49  Ibid, pp. 42–43.

as an irreducible element of a complex reality that legal theory should not ignore. He thus appears to also avoid the thick idealisation or spiritualisation that would lead him back to Hegel's "thick internal perspective." If there is an idealisation at work in Dworkin's theory, it would have to be considered a different kind of idealisation that one could call "Kantian" or "neo-Kantian," instead of "Hegelian." Or so it appears.

A "Kantian" or "neo-Kantian" idealisation entails the making of an assumption for the sake of contemplating the possibility of some kind of claim or concern coherently. Let us use two of Kant's examples: 1) To contemplate the possibility of morality, we must postulate the ideas of the eternal life of the soul, the existence of God and the highest good (*summum bonum*), without suggesting these ideas refer to any reality; 2) To contemplate the possibility of real knowledge that corresponds to "objective reality" (das *Ding an sich*), we must assume the regulative idea of infinite scientific investigation and progress, considering that science, at any given point *in* time, always concerns only phenomenal or empirically observable reality, and not reality as it exists in itself. We shall see in Chapter 9 that Hans Kelsen's pure theory of law pivots on a methodological move that is fundamentally Kantian or neo-Kantian in the sense explained here. In what respect can one argue that Dworkin's theory of law as "constructive interpretation" is typically "neo-Kantian"?

Well, Dworkin makes clear that the "personification of community," on which the idea of the "integrity" of the legal system pivots, depends on an attribution of responsibility akin to the attribution of corporate liability to a business or company. A business or company very clearly does not have "personality" in the usual sense of the word, but one attributes legal personality to it to deal with the legal interests that it pursues collectively and the collective responsibility that it holds towards anyone exposed to its pursuit of interests. Legal rights of individuals in a society, contends Dworkin, are conditioned by a similar attribution of a collective duty to respect and enforce these rights. This, then, is what he means by the "personification of society."[50] And, if this communal person is to be considered a person with integrity, the way it respects and guarantees the rights of persons over time will have to be consistent. The judges and legislators who allocate, identify and enforce rights on behalf of this communal person will have to do so consistently. They will have to stick to the same narrative and not change it into another. They will have to ensure that the same concept of law is sustained, notwithstanding the reality of different conceptions of this concept that will emerge over time, etc. And they will do all of this against the background of clear empirical evidence that societies very often do not respect and enforce the rights of their members consistently and with even-handed integrity.

Now, if this neo-Kantian construal of Dworkin's theory holds water, one would immediately have to observe that the whole Hart-Dworkin debate is a non-debate between two interlocutors who talk completely past one another. As we saw above,

50 Ibid, pp. 171–173.

Hart presents his rule theory of law as a "descriptive sociology." Hence his candid recognition of empirical evidence that many members of a society maintain an external perspective to the law of that society. Hence also his realistic recognition of the need for judges to resort to discretion in some cases. Dworkin, if indeed the neo-Kantian legal theorist that we have made him here, must be understood to be presenting his "constructive interpretation" theory of law as an idealist construction that acknowledges empirical or sociological evidence of legal disagreement (that is, of external perspectives on law), but ignores it for the sake of sustaining the idea of a common concept and narrative of law that consistently justifies the way a society allocates rights and imposes duties. If this reading of Dworkin is correct, he and Hart are simply talking past one another.

There is, however, an even more striking feature of the non-debate between Hart and Dworkin that would result from taking the former as the descriptive sociologist that he expressly claims to be, and construing the latter as a neo-Kantian idealist for which there seems to be some evidence in his texts. Construed as part of a non-debate between a descriptive sociologist and a neo-Kantian constructivist, the whole judicial discretion issue turns into a red herring. Hart's recognition of judicial discretion concerns an empirical observation of a descriptive sociologist. Dworkin's dismissal of judicial discretion results from a procedure of idealising or idealist constructivism. So once more at the risk of labouring the point: If our neo-Kantian construal of Dworkin's theory of constructive interpretation holds any water, we must conclude that the two theorists are also on this count not talking to, but completely past, one another.

Considered from the perspective of the complete collapse of the debate between Hart and Dworkin that would result if one were to take Dworkin as a neo-Kantian constructivist, it seems clear that we should not take him as one. Dworkin considers the debate between him and Hart real, pertinent and concerned with the same terms, and not a hapless exchange between two people talking about different things. Taking Dworkin seriously requires attributing the adequate level of social descriptivism to his theory of constructive interpretation that is necessary to consider the debate between him and Hart no less meaningful than he evidently considered it himself. And once one realises this, one should feel free and even obliged to duly register further evidence in *Law's Empire* that he was no neo-Kantian constructivist. *Law's Empire* adamantly claims that the theory it puts forward is "nonskeptical," for it considers rights real and takes them seriously. People really "have them."[51] This acclamation of rights is as un-Kantian as one could imagine. Kantian or neo-Kantian methodological procedures pivot on a very express disclaimer of knowledge. They are conditioned by a fundamental scepticism.[52] They don't take anything for real, but treat them "as if" real.[53] This "as if" methodological attitude, and the scepticism on which it turns, are precisely the characteristics that

---

51  Ibid, p. 152.
52  See Marquard 1958.
53  For the locus classicus of this Neo-Kantian "as if" construction, see Vaihinger 1911.

Dworkin attributes to his pragmatist opponents from which he distances himself in no uncertain terms.[54]

That Dworkin does not consider himself a neo-Kantian constructivist is also abundantly clear from *Justice for Hedgehogs*, which, to the contrary, expressly puts forward a comprehensively "realist" moral and legal theory that insists on the reality of the key values that inform law and morality.[55] As already mentioned above, he expressly does this in a thoroughly non-constructivist and fully constative mode of discourse. It should be clear from all of this that there is no point in trying to extract Dworkin from the history of metaphysics. He falls back into the bubbling cauldron where law and life bind into a primal sauce that gives nothing up for distillation. The paragraph quoted from *Taking Rights Seriously* must not be read in the way we have tried to read it. The "supposition" of concern in the phrase "a concept they suppose they hold in common" does not entail a presupposition of something that one knows does not exist, or does not know whether it exists. It is not the presupposition that is so central to Kelsen's theory of law, as we shall see in Chapter 9, but a postulation or predication that ultimately does not stop short of the "spooky" Hegelian metaphysics that he disclaims. The passage quoted from *Taking Rights Seriously* must therefore be taken as a veritable echo of the "thick internal perspective to law" that Hegel assumed when he attributed to criminals – those who, sociologically speaking, surely have an external perspective to the legal rules that condemn them – a voluntary acceptance of punishment, given that punishment is the recognition of the real reasonable person in them, and not pointless violence inflicted on someone who does not understand what he or she did wrong. A statement in *Taking Rights Seriously* comes within a hair's breadth of repeating this metaphysical or philosophical confidence. Considering that we attribute to the judicial resolution of a hard case the status of the "right answer," asks Dworkin, must we consider a person who loses a hard case that is properly decided "wrong" or "mistaken"? And he answers:

> Some readers will remain unconvinced. Surely it *cannot* be that in a genuinely hard case one side is simply right and the other simply wrong. But why not? It may be that the supposition that one side may be right and the other wrong is cemented into our habits of thought at a level so deep that we cannot coherently deny that supposition, no matter how skeptical or hardheaded we wish to be in such matters.[56]

Perhaps not even a hair's breadth separates this passage from the one in which Hegel appeals to the better self of the criminal to accept that his or her punishment

---

54 Dworkin 1986, pp. 154, 160.
55 Dworkin 2011, pp. 63–66. The invocation of realism in this context must not be confused with the "realism" invoked when one talks about the "American realist movement" of the early decades of the twentieth century (discussed in Chapter 7, Section 3).
56 Dworkin, 1978, p. 290.

is a recognition of his or her dignity as a reasonable person. The party who loses a hard case, Dworkin suggests here, is sufficiently party to the most profound "cementation" of our "habits of thought" to be able to arrive at the recognition that he or she is wrong. And vice versa: Being able to arrive at the recognition that one is wrong confirms that one shares in the common "cementation" of our "habits of thought." Whatever external perspective one may erroneously have held for a while can accordingly be discarded easily for purposes of returning to the "deeply cemented" internal perspective that recognises the soundness of the legal rule that condemns one's case.

We have already observed that *Law's Empire* neither announces nor evinces a significant break with the thoughts developed in *Taking Rights Seriously*. One must therefore also assume that it does not take leave of the metaphysical confidence displayed in *Taking Rights Seriously*. If this is correct, *Law's Empire* must be considered a betrayal of the two key programmatic contentions with which it commences, the contention that "this book is about theoretical disagreement," and the contention that it does not engage in a "spooky metaphysical theory." *Law's Empire* would, after all, not seem to be a book about theoretical disagreement, and it is highly metaphysical. The metaphors of the singular rope and single chain novel that it invokes to portray the life of a legal community attest to that. The way in which Dworkin juggles "theoretical disagreement," on the one hand, with an understanding of law as a singular, well-woven and adequately integrated tale or rope, on the other, ultimately pivots on the deep obfuscation that he perpetrates when he refers to the contestation of "different conceptions of a concept they suppose they hold in common."

This obfuscation begins in *Taking Rights Seriously* (see the passage quoted in footnote 42 above), continues and deepens in *Law's Empire*[57] and reappears in *Justice for Hedgehogs* where it is extensively discussed under the heading of conceptual interpretation.[58] The essence of this obfuscation in *Taking Rights Seriously* and *Law's Empire* concerns its pretension to duly consider the reality of moral conflict and division in modern societies with reference to competing "conceptions," only to forthwith render this conflict inoperative with reference to common "concepts." This obfuscating stratagem takes on a new dimension in *Justice for Hedgehogs* that is not only obfuscating, but mystifying. A large part of the position that Dworkin takes in *Justice for Hedgehogs* turns on the argument that we have real disagreements about morality and law that confirm that these disagreements are about something real. Our disagreements about morality are real, contends Dworkin, they are not mistaken misunderstandings such as the misunderstanding that occurs between two people who agree to meet at the bank, where one is thinking of the side of a river and the other of a financial institution.[59] We are talking about the same thing or things when we have moral disagreements, and that means those things must be

---

57  Dworkin 1986, 70–72.
58  Dworkin 2011, pp. 6–7, 157–188.
59  Dworkin 2011, pp. 158–159, 161.

real, he insists. They are not real in the sense of morality particles – "morons," as Dworkin calls them "teasingly" – that drift around in the universe.[60] They are real in the sense that they allow for meaningful inquiry and dialogue that can lead to real moral agreement.[61] Well, there is not a single philosopher in the history of Western metaphysics whose arguments did not pivot on this essential essentialising move. It is with this move that the obfuscation in *Taking Rights Seriously* and *Law's Empire* takes on a mystifying dimension. Not only does it pivot on a concept-conceptualisation constellation that hides from view the real political, social and existential tensions that inform the distinction between agreement and disagreement, it makes the latter the proof of the former. Through some remarkable alchemical procedure, it turns disagreement into a veritable sign of its own intrinsic resolvability.

It is important to stress again that one should not read a constructivist argument into the position that Dworkin is taking here. He is not arguing that we should presuppose that we are disagreeing about something real so that we can consider our disagreements meaningful (even though he sometimes takes recourse to phrases that lean in this direction[62]). His argument is unflinchingly constative. It is also important to note how he closes the net of this constative argument so as to also capture those who dismiss it. "Philosophical challenges to the truth of moral arguments are themselves substantive moral theories," he insists. And "[m]oral scepticism is itself a moral position."[63] Even more important to note, however, is the way in which this argument no longer renders moral disagreement immediately or forthwith inoperative, as it does in *Taking Rights Seriously* and *Law's Empire*. These two works are crucially dependent on the notion of an underlying consensus that renders the invocation of pre-existing "legal rights" cogent. They therefore move very fast to render disagreement invisible and devoid of substance. As we saw above, especially the former of these two works expressly attributes disagreement to a mere mistake that deprives any apparent disagreement of real substance. Something else happens in *Justice for Hedgehogs* on the shoulders of the same arguments developed in the earlier works. Here, full-blown disagreement is duly acknowledged, at first, for purposes of underlining the huge investments we make in our moral convictions. It is only after and through this acknowledgement that the objective reality of moral truth and its implications of necessary agreement among those with adequate knowledge can be confirmed. Dworkin writes:

> We fight campaigns, even wars, about justice, and it is obviously false that if we only reflected on what we mean by the term, we would see that we really had nothing to disagree about.[64]

60  Ibid, pp. 32, 43, 100, 117, 120.
61  Ibid, p. 60.
62  See ibid, p. 121: "I mean to describe method, not metaphysics: how you must proceed if truth is on your agenda." See also Dworkin 1978, p. 116. "The law may not be a seamless web, but the plaintiff is entitled to ask Hercules to treat it as if it is."
63  Ibid, pp. 34, 41. See also p. 67: "[T]he question whether moral judgements can be true or false is a substantive moral issue, not a distinct meta-ethical one."
64  Ibid, p. 162.

This, then, is Dworkin's view of the world and of history. It is a stage of a meaningful fight for the worthy prize of moral truth. The fact that the fight itself is the only proof that the prize exists strangely enough does not seem to bother this brave and bellicose world. It remains strangely convinced that the fight will sooner or later turn into gold.

There is more than a touch of Hegel's *Phenomenologie des Geistes* evident in this rather alchemical view of the world and vision of history. And there is much more than just a touch of the deep equivocation discernible in Hegel's formidable oeuvre in Dworkin's. Just like the former (see Chapter 7, Section 2), the latter too dismisses disagreement as unreal when it emphasises the deep rational consensus underpinning the law, only to highlight and stress the reality of disagreement, on another page, as the sign of humanity's ongoing moral commitment to a grand historical destiny. The former calls disagreement "dialectics." The latter calls it "interpretation." Which side of Dworkin should one consider the real Dworkin? As in the case of Hegel, one will probably never be able to answer this question conclusively, but it seems fair to assume that the point of gravity in his equivocation ultimately points in the direction of the suspension of disagreement at the expense of interpretation and the real need for it, just as the dialectic ultimately collapses into identity and conclusive reconciliation in Hegel's philosophy. In this respect, Hegel and Dworkin both appear to have insight into secret alchemical procedures that are unbeknown to a humanity that is regularly at wits' end with regard to its infinite potential for devastating disagreement, division and conflict.

Why does it seem fair to assume this ultimate point of gravity in Dworkin's work? It does so because of the way in which *Justice for Hedgehogs*, notwithstanding its stronger emphasis on real disagreements, ultimately pivots on the supposed point of possible agreement that animates real disagreement, and not on disagreement. This is what allows it to still invoke the concept-conception constellation coherently. This is also what betrays the fact that this work still turns on the personification argument put forward in *Law's Empire*. Why? Well, in the final analysis, the whole argument of the book concerns a moral philosophy that contemplates the way in which a single individual makes sense of his or her life, and ignores the insurmountable difficulties that arise when two or more individuals with significantly different life situations and experiences embark on a journey that requires them to make communal or common sense of both or all their different lives and life experiences, not to mention the insurmountable difficulties that are bound to arise when they do not even bother to embark on this journey *together*, but just happen to be in the same boat or bus.

Two telling examples that *Justice for Hedgehogs* puts forward unabashedly underline this overarching focus on personal moral responsibility that fails to account for the different register required to cope with the arduous and thorny encounters between different moral personalities. The first is the confident claim early in the book about Stalin: "Someone who lives as Stalin did has a bad life: his life is bad for him even if he does not recognise it."[65] One may totally agree with this statement,

---

65 Dworkin 2011, p. 51.

as most liberal democrats probably do, but would there be any point in communicating it to, say, local Stalinists in the neighbourhood, not to mention Stalinists in Russia, who, like it or not, have in some respects also become a "neighbourhood" of the global society that life on Earth has become? Does Dworkin really consider this statement amenable to a meaningful process of communal moral interpretation between, say, liberal democrats on the one hand, and Stalinists on the other?

The second example appears close to the end of the book: "Someone who spends his whole life in the trivial hobby [of] collecting matchbook covers . . . does not create a good life, even if his collection is of unmatched completeness and even if he acts always with great dignity."[66] When one comes from Dworkin's corner of the world, when one loves the fine things that a truly educated life brings, the thought of a life spent collecting matchbook covers is undoubtedly bound to send a chill down your spine. But, would any educated person with just reasonable "dignity" contemplate telling the matchbook collector to his or her face that he or she does not have a good life? One wonders whether anyone considering this a meaningful point of conversation has ever been in a neighbourhood where matchbook collecting may well offer some small but indeed dignified recreational escape from a life that has never been offered better opportunities. But let us replace this example with a similar one, varying the facts only so that an intelligent and educated person who has – it would seem – no real sense of what it may be like to live in a neighbourhood where matchbook collecting may come across as an appealing hobby, may begin to grasp the question: A young person spends a life learning every conceivable chess opening and memorising a thousand grand master chess games and becomes a very accomplished chess player. Chess continues to take up more or less all her time. Is our intelligent and educated person still going to conclude this life is not a good life? And if so, if really so, will she also consider it meaningful to tell our chess player that her life is not a good life?

The point of concern here takes one back to the programmatic statement of the liberal democratic ethic elaborated in the Introduction to this book. There we fully endorsed Dworkin's insistence that "those in power must believe that what they say is so."[67] Liberal democracy does not endorse or tolerate duplicity, we argued there with reference to Arendt's cogent reflections on this point. Duplicity, however, is one thing. The political skill of dealing with social complexity and division is another. Hence our programmatic statement:

> By all means believe that the principles and convictions by which you act are correct. You have to do so. Your game will all too soon be up and unmasked as shallow duplicity if you do not. *But, do not succumb to the temptation to insist that those who evidently and adamantly disagree with your principles and convictions ultimately have good reasons to agree with you, good reasons that somehow just remain*

---

66 Ibid, p. 420.
67 Ibid, p. 8.

*unbeknown to them and to which they should become enlightened. The moment you do this, you begin do betray liberalism. You then begin to descend into a dogmatic liberalism that ultimately risks becoming as illiberal as any adversary of liberal democracy imaginable.*

Dworkin gives us more than ample reason to believe that he is not worried by this illiberal liberalism, and by the politically unskilful and socially untactful liberalism to which it is likely to give rise. This lack of worry is underlined by his conception of society as one person that ultimately thinks the same, notwithstanding its apparent disagreements. It is underlined by his methodological insistence on the personification of community. This is the heart of Dworkin's apparent disregard for the truly profound and profoundly problematic differences between people. His intuition is sound when he supplements his elaboration of this methodological personification with an express disavowal of "spooky metaphysics." He evidently senses that there is something to disclaim here, it is just that the disclaimer does not stick. His methodological personification is the logical result of a personal and theoretical mentality that considers its own moral sensibilities effectively communicable to everyone else. Metaphysics begins with this mentality.

We have seen this methodological personification and the mentality behind it before. We have seen it expressly articulated in Ronald Coase's analysis of social cost (see Chapter 7, Section 1) and we will see it articulated again in Rudolf Smend's theory of political integration (Chapter 9, Section 2). But it is also the all too often inadequately articulated heart of the whole Western metaphysical tradition that begins with Aristotle and does not end with Hegel. This metaphysics is not spooky, though. It is thickly spiritual or Spiritual. "Spookiness" is a phrase that we must reserve for those – par excellence among them may well be Hart – who sustain a regard for the unexplained nature of the phenomena that words try to save, and for the interminable differences, conflicts and tensions to which this lack of explanation gives rise. It is with this regard that the ethics of liberal democracy begins.

# 9

# LEGAL NORMATIVITY AND SPIRITUAL CULTURE

## 1 The normative integration of society – Kelsen

The startling character of Hans Kelsen's theory of law and the state is perhaps best seen from the perspective of the ire that it elicited from several of his most notable contemporaries such as Carl Schmitt, Hermann Heller and Rudolf Smend. Kelsen dismayed the legal theorists of his time by insisting that law consists of nothing more than a hierarchical system of norms within the scope of which every single legal norm receives its validity from another norm higher up in the hierarchy. The controversy that this conception of law caused did not relate to the notion of a hierarchy of norms as such. Few if any serious legal theorist would contest the proposition that legal systems have hierarchical structures that allow higher norms, such as constitutional clauses, to determine the validity, scope and reach of lower norms, such as rules embodied in legislation, executive regulation or judicial decisions. The dismay that Smend, Heller and Schmitt voiced in response to Kelsen was directed at the latter's refusal to anchor the hierarchy of norms that his theory envisaged in some external ground or source of law. It is the apparent groundlessness of law in Kelsen's pure theory of law that they dismissed with disbelief. To them, Kelsen's system of norms appeared to simply hang in the air. It was not rooted in anything. We turn to Smend's, Heller's and Schmitt's responses to Kelsen below (see Smend's in the second section of this chapter, Heller's in Chapter 11, Section 7 and Schmitt's in Chapter 10, Section 1). For now, let us first take a closer look at Kelsen's conception of law as a "groundless" hierarchy of legal norms, for it is here that we find the clear extraction of law from life that we have been pursuing since the first chapter of this book.

In the preface to his *Hauptprobleme der Staatsrechtslehre* (1911) Kelsen makes it clear that the theory of the state that he contemplates pivots on a fundamental separation of the sphere of normative imperative (the sphere of ought or *Sollen*), on the one hand, and the sphere of natural and historical reality (the sphere of factual existence or *Sein*), on the other.[1] It should be evident that this announcement constitutes a decisive break with the positions of Aristotle, Saint Thomas, Hegel and Savigny that we have discussed at length in earlier chapters of this book.[2] In other words, Kelsen makes it abundantly clear in the first pages of his first major work on legal theory that he will be pursuing a theory of law that severs law from the metaphysics of both nature and history, and, of course, from the metaphysics of either natural or historical life that constitutes the core of the grand metaphysical tradition of ancient, medieval and modern Europe. What then, may one ask, is at stake in this "lifeless" theory of law which insists on a categorical separation of law from history and nature? This is the question that we will be addressing in what follows.

Any attempt to link the realm of normativity to the realms of either nature or history must take recourse to fiction, claims Kelsen. There is simply no non-fictional link between law and either nature or history. He accordingly also presents his *Hauptprobleme* as a fight against fiction.[3] One must for Kelsen's sake be a bit more precise in this regard. What Kelsen was combatting in his work was the presentation of fiction as statements of reality or fact. He himself put forward a theory of law and the state that was premised on the idea of fictionality. But the fictionality that he had in mind contained no illusions about its fictionality. In other words, what Kelsen was combatting was fictitiousness, not fictionality.

A closer look at Kelsen's concept of the state and the idea that the state cannot err or commit a wrong illustrates what is at stake here. According to Kelsen, the state is an ideal entity that derives from a conceptual construction of the essential normative properties of the state, that is, from a normative conception of what the state "is" and should be. This normative construction or conception of the state always takes place against a background of historical or factual representations of the state. There is, however, no intrinsic relation between the former and the latter. Historical or factual representations of the state are at best extrinsically related to normative constructions of the state. They may be guided or informed by the criterial demands embodied by some kind of normative conception of the state. However, the state envisaged by this normative conception has no historical or sociological existence. Being nothing but a normative construct, the state must also be considered incapable of doing wrong. Historical or sociological representations of the state can certainly do wrong, but to the extent that they do, they no longer represent the state or its interests. Wrongful action allegedly committed by the state is action undertaken by a non-state person or persons who abused the machinery of the state.[4]

The structural parallel between this conception of the state and the doctrine of the two bodies of the king studied by Ernst Kantorowicz is striking (see Chapter 5,

---

1 Kelsen 2008, pp. 54, 80–116; 1994, pp. 19–38; 2017, pp. 120–121.
2 Indeed, when Kelsen returns to the point later, he traces this conflation of "ought" and "is" all the way back to Aristotle. See Kelsen 2008, p. 101.
3 Ibid, p. 56.
4 Kelsen 2008, pp. 362–373, 581–591; 2010, pp. 440–453.

Section 2). Kelsen's discussion of the infallibility of the state refers expressly to the old English law adage that the king can do no wrong.[5] However, the significant difference between Kelsen's infallible state and the transcendental (second) body of the immortal king must not be missed. Kelsen's infallible state is not grounded in an external normative or religious substance. It is not anchored in God or any other imaginable onto-theological instance. Its foundation is derived from nothing but the concept that renders it comprehensible to itself. In Kelsen's case, this definition of the state pivots on an identification of the state with its law. The will of the state, he wrote, is embodied in the law. It has no other will beyond or outside the law. It therefore cannot do anything unlawful – *Der Staat kann nicht unrecht handeln, denn er kann nur das Recht wollen.*[6]

Kelsen's later work takes recourse to a similar construction of the ideal and the real for purposes of putting forward "a pure theory of law." The fifth chapter of his *Reine Rechtslehre* elaborates the hierarchical scheme of legal norms under which every specified legal norm receives its validity from a higher norm.[7] The apex of the hierarchy consists of a *Grundnorm* (foundational norm) that validates all other norms. The predicament that this hierarchical scheme of norms raises is evident. If every legal norm derives its validity from another legal norm, the *Grundnorm* itself has no validity, considering that it is the first norm – preceded by no other – in the hierarchical sequence of norms that constitutes the legal system. The gravity of the predicament becomes apparent when one considers that any lack of validity that attaches to the *Grundnorm* will be transmitted through the whole hierarchy of norms, given that the *Grundnorm* is the source of validity without which no validation lower down in the hierarchy can take place. Kelsen stresses that the *Grundnorm* has no relation to any positive or factual constitution of state or nation from which it might draw historical or sociological legitimacy. The *Grundnorm*, he contends, is the unique norm that derives its validity from within itself. It pulls itself up by its own normative bootstrings, so to speak, and thus also pulls up the rest of the norms in the legal system – *[d]as Recht regelt seine eigene Erzeugung.*[8]

It is important to note the precise terminology that Kelsen employs to describe this process of hetero-validation that begins with an instance of auto-validation. Since the *Grundnorm* should not be identified or related to any *positive* or historical constitution posited by some or other constitutional assembly, it only exists in as far as its existence is *presupposed*. Kelsen relies on the illuminating wordplay through which the German language allows him to make his point: *[Der Grundnorm] . . . ist nicht gesetzt, sondern . . . vorausgesetzt.*[9] The foundational norm is never posited, it is presupposed. The effect of this construction of the legal system is, of course, that the validity of every legal rule is ultimately never posited, but always only presupposed,

5 Kelsen 2008, p. 367.
6 Ibid, p. 363.
7 See Kelsen 1994, pp. 62–89.
8 Ibid, p. 74.
9 Ibid, pp. 66–67.

given its dependence on a presupposed foundational norm. In other words, the validity of every legal rule turns on nothing but the act of presupposition that endows the *Grundnorm* with validity. Kelsen basically tells his readers: If one wants to talk about law – that is, about pure law and not about the peculiarities of a legal system that result from the incidental power constellations that sustain the law – one has to define the foundational norm that grounds the law and credit the resulting definition with validity, without reference to its factual embodiment.

It is instructive to compare this construction of legal validity once more with Kantorowicz's portrayal of the second body of the king. Faith in the existence of the eternal body of the king does not depend on whether the empirical king is a good king that warrants this faith. Faith entails an *act* of faith that sustains the existence of the king's second body, notwithstanding the imperfections of the factual king. There is a limit to this argument or way of thinking and Kelsen knows this. He knows that the *Grundnorm* can become ineffective. Subjects of the law can cease to credit it with the validity that it ultimately only receives from them. Adverse historical conditions can cause popular willingness to invest the *Grundnorm* with validity to drop below a threshold where even the most formalist of jurists will no longer find it useful to talk about existing law as law. Sometimes, the king will not only be dethroned so that the kingship – and the principle of long live the king – can continue under the reign of another king. Sometimes, the king will also be decapitated in order to terminate kingship and introduce a new foundational principle. The French Revolution was a case in point.[10] As recent literature points out, Kelsen's recognition of this possibility undoubtedly renders his pure theory of law much more "political" than its critics have taken it to be.[11] One must also note here Kelsen's observation regarding the Gorgon head of power that becomes visible when the law's veneer of normativity gets scratched.[12] Kelsen realises that the hierarchy of norms that he contemplates is like a thin layer of veneer that covers the rough reality of law beneath it. Why is this veneer so important to him?

The normative "veneer" of the law, insists Kelsen, allows one to talk about law as *law – pure law –* in circumstances where the effective functioning of the law requires one to talk in this way. Suppose a government descends into a legitimacy crisis and gets ousted. One cannot then just deem invalid the legislation it passed with due validity. One can also not simply embark on an extraordinary programme of judicial interpretation to amend or ameliorate its laws incisively. Should one do that, these amended laws would no longer receive their validity from another valid norm already in place, but from an interpretive act that occurs outside the chain of normative validation intrinsic to the law. A society that begins to engage in practices such as these, effectively no longer has a noteworthy legal system that can persuasively be said to exist as a relatively independent framework of legal order. What it calls law in the course or wake of such extraordinary amending practices

10  See Lefort 1986a, pp. 318–319.
11  See Van Ooyen 2008, p. xix; Chiassoni 2013; and Navarro 2013.
12  See Kelsen 1927, p. 55; Dyzenhaus 2000, p. 20.

would no longer be an independent source of legal authority on the basis of which disputes can be resolved without taking part in them (or without being vulnerable to the accusation of such partiality). Independence and objectivity are key characteristics that societies associate with the notion of "objective" or "positive" law. Whatever amendment of bad laws may be needed in a society would have to be amended by the usual (again: independent and objective) amendment procedures. The same applies to the amendment of bad amendment procedures, and so on, until one reaches the question of whether the foundational norm itself requires a revolutionary replacement and the introduction of a new legal system.

This association of actual positive law – which often does not comply with strict criteria of impartiality – with independent, objective or transcendent *law* remains an active or *performative* association. It concerns a neo-Kantian condition or precondition of the kind that we tried but failed to read into Dworkin's theory of law in Chapter 8. It is important to recall once more Kelsen's wordplay between "*setzen*" and "*voraussetzen*" to explain this methodological procedure, and to understand that the objectivity, independence, neutrality and transcendence of the law invoked here is never a posited but always a presupposed reality. Actual positive laws – statutes, governmental regulations, etc. – are, of course, enacted and posited (*gesetzt*) by some form of historical parliament or government in circumstances of constraining power relations and trade-offs. They will carry the marks of these contingent power relations and trade-offs and will therefore not be neutral and independent, let alone transcendent. Their neutrality and independence must be presupposed as long as it remains feasible to do so. Positive laws (*Gesetze*) are all too evidently posited (*gesetzt*), but the validity of these laws as law must be *presupposed* (*vorausgesetzt werden*). It is this "veneer" of presupposition that allows a society to talk about law as law, and shields it from having to consider law a mere function of the power relations that undoubtedly always lurk underneath this veneer. Kelsen is as aware as any American Realist that actual judicial practices cannot be credited with the objectivity that distinguishes law from raw power relations. A whole chapter of his *Pure Theory of Law* engages with the "non-objective" or "subjective" reality of judicial practices. Judges too, must be supposed or presupposed to sustain the objectivity of law. They do not do so as a matter of fact.[13]

In the same way that Hart considers the rule theory of law to apply to any legal system that evinces a stable constellation of primary and secondary rules and not only to those that comply with liberal democratic criteria, Kelsen also considers his pure theory of law applicable to any society in which the gap between the factual reality of law and the ideal objectivity of law does not frustrate the meaningful presupposition of the latter. In other words, the pure theory of law would not be inapplicable to non-democratic societies where monarchical or dictatorial conditions prevail, as long as the frameworks of government and law-making in these countries remain stable and consistent enough to render the presupposition of an

13 See Kelsen 1994, p. 94–99.

independent legal system with intrinsic legal validity viable. The pure theory of law outlined here is therefore not as such a liberal democratic theory of law. To understand why Kelsen has been hailed as the principal pioneer of liberal democratic law in the chapters of this book, one must turn to a 1920 publication – *Vom Wesen und Wert der Demokratie* – in which he expressly engages with the essential characteristics and values of liberal democracy. It is in this work that the separation of law from life – and from the power relations embodied in life – attains an additional dimension that turns Kelsen's pure theory of law into the most rigorous theory of liberal democratic law articulated to date.

*Vom Wesen und Wert der Demokratie* stresses the principle that liberal democratic law is not founded in the life of a people. It puts forward, instead, an inverted constellation of people and law. "The people," contends Kelsen, is rooted in law, and not vice versa. Of concern for him, in this regard, is the simple reality that citizenship, to which one may add residency today, is defined and conditioned by the law.[14] The law that articulates the will of the state, to which we paid attention above, is also the law that constructs the identity of the people. This construction of "the people" by law evidently effects an incisive severance between the legal status of a people and its sociological, historical and biological life. The concept of a "democratic people" that comes to the fore in *Vom Wesen und Wert der Demokratie* evidently takes leave of the naturalistic and historicist conceptions of the people that persisted in the history of European metaphysics from Aristotle to Savigny. It also takes leave of Hegel, considering the rigorous Kantian distinction between "is" and "ought" on which it pivots. At work in Kelsen's concept of a democratic people is not an idealist or philosophical construction of the true dialectic unity of a people that transcends and remedies their historical divisions. On the contrary, *Vom Wesen und Wert der Demokratie* stresses the essential split condition of the people in a liberal democracy and takes it as a key element of its defining concept. Democracy concerns the principle of majoritarian government, but the phrase "majoritarian government" obfuscates the reality that liberal democracy is not premised on a simplistic understanding of majority rule. In liberal democracies, contends Kelsen, government concerns the effective sustenance of majority-minority relations. Strictly speaking, the majority principle is a majority-minority principle.[15]

Premised as this majority-minority principle is on compromises between different and diverging worldviews and convictions, truth claims can play no role in liberal democratic politics.[16] The law that results from liberal democratic legislation is therefore not the actualisation or teleological fulfilment of any truth claim or conviction. It is not the fulfilment of anyone's truth, but the compromise that constantly displaces, dislodges and uproots all comprehensive truth claims. The point that we've already articulated with reference to Hart is again of concern here. Liberal democratic law ultimately depends on the possibility of sustaining adequately

14  See Kelsen 1981, p. 64.
15  Ibid, pp. 53, 57, 58.
16  Ibid, p. 58, 98–104.

satisfactory relations between those subjects of law that have an internal perspective to law, and those that have an external perspective. Under these conditions the law can never aspire to actualise the potential of any individual or group of individuals, let alone the potential of a whole or united people. Under adequately liberal and democratic conditions, all individuals and all groups of individuals, and anything that anyone may be contemplating when reference is made to "the people," remain *outside* the law or *before* the law, as Kafka's parable tells us.[17]

The conception of liberal democratic law that comes to the fore in Kelsen's work is bound to be irksome and irritating to anyone who wants to see him or herself or him or her people embodied in the legal system to which he or she is subject, that is, to anyone who yearns for Hegel's – or Aristotle's – thick internal perspective to law. The "purely ethereal" concept of self-government and popular sovereignty offered by Kelsen's normative theory of law – belonging as it does to the *"reinen Äther der Idee,"* as Hugo Preuß once put it[18] – is bound to frustrate and irritate expectations of fuller and more substantive concepts of "democratic self-government" or "popular sovereignty." The irate reactions to Kelsen in the work of Rudolf Smend and Carl Schmitt, to which we turn in the next section of this chapter and the first section of Chapter 10, underline this.

Before we turn to Smend, suffice it to conclude the outline above of key aspects of Kelsen's concept of law by observing once more the precariousness of the liberal democracy that Kelsen contemplates. Kelsen himself refers to the dearth – *Dürftigkeit* – of the pure law that he has in mind.[19] A regard for this dearth and the precariousness to which it exposes the law impresses upon the theory of liberal democratic law the need to consider the conditions that might render law as stable as one might hope. The prevalence and endurance of liberal democratic law may well be conditioned by cultural practices that compensate for the lack of fullness and substance – its bloodlessness and lifelessness – that a rigorous concept of liberal democratic law demands from it. The concluding chapter of this book will return to this point.

## 2 The cultural integration of society – Smend

From the very spiritual point of view of Rudolf Smend's *integration theory* of law, replenished as this theory is with Hegelian and perhaps even Savignian concerns with *Geist*, and even a "quasi-Aristotelian" concern with life and nature, Kelsen's normative integration of society is bound to be viewed as an empty formalism

17 See Chapter 8, fn. 32.
18 See Preuß 1900, p. 359, referring deridingly in this regard to the Austrian flight into the pure ether of ideas to escape from a dismal political reality. See also the reference to Preuß in Schönberger 2008, p. 31, which is followed up by a reference to Kelsen's own observation that the cosmopolitan composition of the Austrian state (not a dismal reality according to Kelsen) consisted of nothing more than a legal unity – *Rechtseinheit* –that all too evidently rendered fictitious all invocations of the socio-psychological (*sozial-psychologische*) or socio-biological (*sozial-biologische*) unity of the state.
19 Kelsen 2008, p. 57.

and nominalism unworthy of the word "integration." Perhaps it would have been enough to just mention this late-Hegelian and neo-Aristotelian reaction to Kelsen's neo-Kantian legal theory and move on, considering the ample attention already dedicated to Hegelian and Aristotelian visions of law and society in previous chapters of this book. Smend, however, "quietly" became one of the most influential legal thinkers of the twentieth century. The European legal context of the late twentieth and early twenty-first century cannot be understood well without adequate awareness of how his "spiritual" or *geisteswissenschaftliche* conception of constitutional jurisprudence came to influence not only post-war German, but also broader European legal thought and jurisprudence.[20]

Smend became one of the most prominent legal theorists in post-war Germany. His work is considered a pivotal influence on the judicial method of the German Federal Constitutional Court in the 1950s.[21] Of concern here is a method of "balancing competing values" that also became widely employed elsewhere in Europe and the world. This method has also become one of the key tools with which the Court of Justice of the European Union has developed European law in recent years.[22] This method has allowed both the German and EU judiciaries to develop a mode of judicial review that assumes a proximity between life and law that is in many respects irreconcilable with the conception of liberal democratic law developed in this book. We will come back to this point in Chapter 11.[23] In what follows we take a closer look at key elements of the theoretical and scholarly position that became so influential in post-war German and European jurisprudence. This theoretical position, we shall see, pivoted on an almost obsessive articulation of yet another Aristotelian and Hegelian "law and life" constellation.

The concern with *Geist*, *Leben* and *Integration* (life, spirit and integration), and with the state as an ongoing process of socio-cultural integration, tirelessly peppers the pages of Smend's writings from 1923 onwards, not only those of his major work *Verfassung und Verfassungsrecht* which appeared in 1928. Towards the end of an essay of 1973 (one of his last) one still finds the telling phrase that any patient reader of Smend's work will recognise as one more variation of the almost mantric refrain which began to appear in his writing in 1923: "The doctrine of integration was a radical and exclusive concern with tracing every aspect of the state and legal

---

20 The words *Geisteswissenschaft* and *geisteswissenschaftlich* are usually translated by phrases such as "human sciences" or "humanities" that do not capture the incessant emphasis on spirit or "Geist" in Smend's texts.

21 Much has been written about the impact of Smend's thinking on the jurisprudence of the German Federal Constitutional Court and the assessments of the extent of the impact differ significantly. Some views consider Smend as the "Hausgott" of the Court in the 1950s and 60s, others consider his impact slight. The fact that the Court invited Smend to deliver the keynote address on the occasion of its tenth anniversary is nevertheless a clear sign of the esteem in which the Court held his work. See Ruppert 2005, p. 344.

22 See Van der Walt 2014b, pp. 352–360 for a discussion and further references.

23 In this respect, key aspects of German and European judicial review must be considered at odds with the unique demands of liberal democratic law as envisaged in the chapters of this book. See ibid, pp. 334–361.

order to an immanent development of life."[24] One finds this same thought already fully developed in a 1923 essay on the individuality of the state (*Entwicklung und Auswirkung der staatlichen Individualität*):

> The – in many respects dangerous – analogy of the life of human personality can show one the way here. The unity of personhood develops, on the one hand, out of the natural human being by virtue of isolated conduct and spiritual life that – consciously or unconsciously – continuously brings about this unity, deals with it, brings it to consciousness, and develops it further through acts that give form to the self and to reality as such; and on the other hand, through the way in which a singular personality finds and affirms its life call, its unique sense, and meaning of life in the engagement with its environment.[25]

On the basis of this analogy of the two sides of the formation of the human individual – the formation of consistent inner personhood, on the one hand, and the engagement of this consistent inner person with its external environment, on the other – Smend sets out to describe the two sides of the formation of the individual state, the internal or domestic action of the state and its conduct in the context of external or international relations.[26] The task of the law of the state (*Staatsrecht*), he contends further, is to effect this process of state integration:

> The first task of the law of the state is to integrate the unitary wholeness of the state, the objectless existence of the highest state law institutions, the monarchy, parliamentary dialectic and critique, as well as government formation.[27]

The rather enigmatic reference to the "objectless existence" of the state in this statement alerts one to the way in which Smend considers the state a purely "subjective" existence that consists of nothing but an integrative will. What becomes apparent here, in other words, is the way in which Smend begins to consider the state the bearer of the historical and spiritual subjectivity that Hegel attributed to the state a century before him. This Hegelian understanding of the state becomes all the more evident in *Verfassung und Verfassungsrecht*, his main work which appeared in 1928. It is in this work that one finds Smend's fully-fledged elaboration of the institutions and functions of the state in terms of an ongoing dialectic, historical and spiritual process of societal integration. *Verfassung und Verfassungsrecht* commences with an invocation of the crisis in which the theory of the state finds itself.[28] Smend

---

24 Translated from Smend 2010, p. 631.
25 Translated from ibid, p. 80–81.
26 Ibid, p. 81.
27 Ibid, p. 83:
28 Ibid, p. 121.

describes this crisis with reference to the fact that the leading and most prominent school of state law theory articulated in the German language insists that the state has no reality – *[daß] der Staat nicht als ein Stück der Realität betrachtet werden darf.*[29]

Smend has in mind here the epistemologically sceptical line of thinking leading from Georg Jellinek to Hans Kelsen, with which he also associates Max Weber's functional theory of the state. The crisis of the theory of the state, Smend adamantly avers, should not just be attributed to the war and the disruption of recent times. According to him, the crisis was nothing less than a spiritual event in the history of science (*ein geistes-, zunächst wissenschaftsgeschichtliche Ereignis*), the main elements of which are ethical scepticism and theoretical agnosticism (*ethische Skepsis* and *theoretischer Agnostizismus*).[30] It soon becomes clear that Kelsen's purely normative and juridical concept of the state (*rein normativer juristischen Staatsbegriff*) remains the main target of Smend's critique of the theories of the state prevalent in Germany and Austria at the beginning of the twentieth century. Kelsen in particular, and the Vienna School in general, were, according to him, methodologically blind to the fundamental reality of the state for which they claimed to offer a theory. They were stuck in an "outdated neo-Kantianism" that insisted on a scientistic distinction between the natural sciences, on the one hand, and cultural studies, on the other, and dismissed the scientific status of the latter.[31]

For Smend, the "two main frailties" of the German people of his time – their unpolitical withdrawal from the state (*unpolitische Staatsenthaltung*), on the one hand, and their unpolitical worshipping of power (*unpolitische Machtanbetung*), on the other – were related to this theoretical agnosticism and ethical scepticism.[32] The main culprits of this agnosticism and scepticism, however, were the Austrians, Smend observes with rather sarcastic fervour:

> Unless you are from Vienna" (*wenn man nicht von Wien ist*), everyone agrees that the theory of law is urgently in need of a material theory of the state (*eine materiale Staatstheorie*) that can claim in its own right to be the science of the spiritual and cultural reality and life of the state.[33]

It is the foundations of this material theory of the state – that is for him simultaneously a spiritual or *geisteswissenschaftliche* theory of the state – which Smend sets out to articulate in *Verfassung und Verfassungsrecht*.[34] It is this *geisteswissenschaftliche* orientation that later became one of the most influential schools of constitutional theory in Germany after World War II.[35] It is evident that a spirit-matter opposition

29  Ibid.
30  Ibid, pp. 122, 123.
31  Ibid, pp. 122, 135, 131.
32  Ibid, p. 123.
33  Translated from ibid, p. 124.
34  Ibid, p. 124.
35  See Günther 2005, pp. 307–312.

plays no significant role in the theoretical imagination at work here. It should there-fore also be clear just how deep we are back in Hegelian territory now.

What were the influences that marked Smend's thinking and what were the key ideas that developed out of them? The Hegelian influence on Smend's conception of the state has already been noted above. This influence plays a key role in *Verfas-sung und Verfassungsrecht*. This work contains numerous sonorous passages in which the state and the law are presented as the essential vehicles that bring about the his-torical and spiritual integration of society in the course of time. The fourth section of the text is presented under the heading *Integration als grundlegender Lebensvorgang des Staats* (Integration as the Foundational Life Process of the State). Two of the early passages of the section portray this integrating life process as follows:

> The state only exists while and as long as it continuously integrates itself, and builds itself up out of individuals. This process is the essence of its existence as a spiritual-social reality.[36]
>
> It lives and is only there as this process of consistent renewal and of con-tinuously experiencing itself anew; it lives, to use Renan's famous characteri-sation of nationhood, by virtue of a plebiscite that repeats itself every day.[37]

Neither of these passages are adorned with express references to Hegel, but a combined reference to Hegel and Schleiermacher later in the work makes it abun-dantly clear that Smend has all along been thinking in the shadow of Hegel here:

> One only needs to remind oneself of Schleiermacher's philosophy of polarity and oscillation, as well as Hegel's concept of the living totality and sustenance of the state – that is the ongoing creation of the state as such and of its consti-tution, and his view of the state as a process of organic life and living ethics.[38]

The influence of Hegel again comes to the fore when Smend describes the relation between the different powers of the state in terms of a living dialectic with direct reference to the *Grundlinien der Philosophie des Rechts*.[39] The influence of Theodor Litt's dialectic conception of social integration – itself also deeply influ-enced by Hegel[40] – must also be noted here. Central to the dialectic of social inte-gration that Smend takes from Litt is the idea of the social entwinement – *sozialen*

---

36  Smend 2010, p. 138.
37  Ibid, p. 136.
38  Ibid, p. 183.
39  Ibid, p. 206.
40  Notwithstanding his emphasis in 1948 on the need to take leave of Hegel's optimistic metaphysical logic (*logisch-metaphysischen Optimismus*), Litt stressed that this turn away from Hegel's metaphysics does not imply any need to take leave of the basic logic of his dialectic thinking (*Logik des dialek-tischen Denkens*). See Litt 1948, p. 336. Hence also his attempt at a critical revision of Hegel's philo-sophical legacy five years later. See Litt 1953.

*Verschränkung* – that mediates the polarity of individual and community – *polarität von Individuum und Gemeinschaft* – in any society.[41]

Smend tirelessly elaborates this vision of the living, spiritual and historical integration of society by the state,[42] by the constitution,[43] by the law,[44] by judges and administrative officials,[45] and by constitutional interpretation,[46] always with the same mantra of *Geist, geistliche Wirklichkeit, geschichtliche Wirklichkeit, Leben, Lebenstrom, Dialektik*, etc. The portrait should be clear enough by now. Smend conceives of the state as the overarching movement of living integration that turns all oppositions and all instances of tension and conflict into productive occasions for constructive historical self-renewal of the social totality.[47] There is no conflict or tension contemplated here that would seem to demand recourse to words such as "division" and "disintegration" to describe this process. One ultimately discerns in Smend's texts an obsessive concern with integration that ultimately affirms the thickest of the thick internal perspectives to law that we detected in the thought of Hegel and Dworkin above. This affirmation evidently also pivots on the same alchemical secret to which Hegel and Dworkin appeared party (see Chapter 8, Section 2). For Smend, too, any possible sign of social dissent, division and disintegration becomes a signal of the process of integration that overcomes dissent and division. Hence, perhaps, the mantric character of his texts. Access to alchemical secrets can be imagined to demand focused formulaic repetition.

Smend's Hegelian alchemy continued to influence German philosophical, political and legal thinking deep into the twentieth century. It continues to do so today among a new generation of German legal scholars who actually believe they are critically distancing themselves from Smend with a sophisticated Lyotardian regard for the depths of difference and dispute, only to once more end up hailing a linguistic reconciliation in which all social discontent and strife just so happen to come to an end.[48] Against this background of an irrepressible theoretical appetite for alchemy that has endured for two centuries and continues to do so today, it is perhaps no wonder that German judicial reasoning should so confidently bequeath to the world a judicial review procedure – known in Germany as the "*schonendste Ausgleich*" (best balancing) of competing values – that contains no register of the debris that it leaves in its wake. Apparently enough German philosophers and legal theorists have put their hearts and souls tirelessly into two centuries of scholarship to make the notion of "best balancing" stick without such a register being necessary.

---

41 Ibid, p. 128.
42 See fnn. 26, 35, 36 and 37 above.
43 See Smend 2010, pp. 188–198, 215–218, 260–268.
44 Ibid, p. 139.
45 Ibid, pp. 144, 146.
46 Ibid, pp. 233–242, 583–584, 588, 593.
47 Ibid, p. 151.
48 See Christensen and Fischer-Lescano 2007, p. 40. For a critical discussion that attributes to Christensen and Fischer-Lescano the same integrative vision that they attribute to Smend, see Van der Walt 2014b, pp. 260–274.

This dialectic underplaying of social division began with Hegel, as Marx noted well, and very definitely never stopped after him, neither in Germany, nor elsewhere in the world, as is clear from the work of Dworkin which we examined in Chapter 8. The resonances between Smend's and Dworkin's theories of law are tangibly visible. They are both concerned with interpretation as a mode of integration, or integrity, as Dworkin calls it. They both model their concepts of interpretive integration on a personification of society. They both assume that the way in which an individual sorts out his or her life by integrating different and divergent concerns into a coherent personality can be extrapolated to a whole society with vastly different cultural orientations and millions of vastly different life experiences. It is this reality of social division and cultural plurality that Kelsen endeavours to take seriously with his neo-Kantian constructivist conception of law and the state, and it is this constructivist endeavour that Smend dismisses with uncamouflaged disdain. He just cannot accept that the law and the state have no deep roots in life itself. He cannot accept that the law and the state always remain a problematic imposition on life, as must have been clear, even to him, in the turbulent times of the Weimar Republic (not to mention the cataclysmic years that followed it). That is why he has to return to the grand history of the metaphysics of life and law.

As we saw in earlier chapters of this book, the heart of this metaphysics of life and law consists of the conception of life as orderly enough to embody law. It turns on an Aristotelian concept of life as an embodiment of order and *kosmos*. Smend never commits himself to an express Aristotelianism. He generally considers Aristotelian thinking to belong to a pre-critical era still confident about its capacity to grasp the nature of things directly.[49] He is aware that the "nature" of things were only indirectly accessible to the modern mind, that is, indirectly accessible by way of a historical dialectic of spirit and nature. However, the Hegel from whom Smend takes this notion of a historical dialectic of spirit and nature did not take leave of Aristotle when he left Tübingen and Frankfurt for Jena. He just took him along on a journey through history. Hegel historicised Aristotle, but he never tore him out of his heart. From this historicisation of Aristotle resulted all the impenetrable conflations of nature and spirit that German Idealism would bequeath to nineteenth and twentieth century European philosophical, political and legal thought. It is this historicised Aristotle and this idealist conflation of spirit and nature that surface again in Smend's reference to the *Stufentheorie* of the Vienna School (Kelsen's conception of the law as a hierarchy of norms) as a "radical denaturalisation of the state that deprives it of its own proper nature" – *[eine] radikale Denaturierung des Staats von aller Eigennatur.*[50]

That Smend's spiritual theory of the state and law is still deeply embedded in the metaphysics of life and nature that Aristotle bequeathed to two and a half millennia of European philosophy is especially clear from his invocation of life itself as an

49 Smend 2010, pp. 131 (here even with a conditional endorsement of Kelsen's critique of naturalistic theories of the state), 134, 196, 218.
50 Ibid, p. 215.

embodiment of normativity. In a restatement of his theory of integration in 1956, Smend articulates this intrinsic entwinement of life and normativity as follows:

> The theory of integration dismisses all conceptions of the norm that separates it from life. The norm derives the ground, quality and content of its validity from life and the meaning of life, just like life itself can, inversely, only be understood in relation to its normative meaning.[51]

This metaphysics of life also underpins Smend's metaphysics of the political. In another text of 1956 Smend elaborated his view of the intrinsic entwinement of life and normativity with these words:

> [The state] is not an instrument that can be used in pursuit of ends. . . . It is essentially identical with the realisation of its own meaning. It gives reality and form to itself and to everyone who belongs to it through its conduct, not only in the express self-formation of some or other instance of constitutional politics or politics of power, but through its very life. . . . This life can only be understood as the totality of life in which the setting and pursuit of all individual goals hang together dialectically and orderly and thus become one with the grand dialectic process of political life. . . . It is from the perspective of this totality of life that the orderly insertion of the individual into the whole also becomes understandable. The individual is not something that stands in a spatial relation to this dialectic and therefore becomes subject to its power. . . . He is himself intrinsically part of the social and political normativity and law of life, into the dialectic ordering of which he inserts himself freely, but also with necessity.[52]

How can this thick political metaphysics not also culminate in a full-blown political theology? Smend unsurprisingly does not neglect to complete his baroque vision of social totality with the theological keystone that holds it together. The political integration and dialectic self-insertion of the individual into the totality of life, he observes in 1956, concerns his commitment to fulfil the will of God – *[der] Wille Gottes zu erfüllen*.[53] This is how Smend consolidates his onto-theological vision of law and the state. This metaphysical vision underpins his conception of social integration as a process that is rooted in life, life that is intrinsically normative; life that is correct and healthy life – *rechtes, gesundes Leben*.[54]

There can be little doubt that Schmitt also contemplated something like *rechtes, gesundes Leben* when he invoked the *Lebensrecht* of the Germans in 1934 (see Chapter 5, p. 100). Smend's concept of normative, healthy and correct life nevertheless

---

51 Translated from ibid, p. 478.
52 Translated from ibid, pp. 504–505.
53 Ibid, p. 486. See also 2010, pp. 515–516.
54 Ibid, p. 504.

moves him to distance himself expressly from Schmitt's "normatively indifferent" (*normatif indifferente*) concept of the sovereign decision.[55] Later, he would also refer to Schmitt's *völliger Amoralismus.*"[56] According to Smend, this understanding of sovereignty was grounded in a blind facticity (*maßstablose Faktizität*) that was bound to end in a sceptical, anarchic and sheer vitalistic decisionism (*anarchischen, skeptischen [und] allenfalls vitalistischen Dezisionismus*).[57] The normatively indifferent vitalism that Smend discerns in Schmitt's thought concerns, of course, the physicalist branch of the metaphysics of life and nature that we identified in ancient Greek thinking in Chapter 3. Smend's integration theory, we showed here, clearly belongs to the cosmological conception of *nomos* that can be traced back to Aristotle. As in the case of Hegel, it presents a historicised version of this cosmological *nomos*.

The work of Schmitt – which Smend respected greatly and admired in many respects in the course of four decades of friendship and/or friendly collegiality, but from which he completely distanced himself in 1961[58] – can indeed be traced all the way to the physicalist branch of Greek thinking, that is, the anarchical, physicalist and normatively indifferent conception of *nomos* that Thucydides identified in the discourse of the Athenian envoys to Melos. It is this physicalist side of Schmitt's thinking that Smend aptly calls *vitalistischen Dezisionismus* (vitalistic decisionism). Chapter 2 paid extensive attention to the other side of Schmitt's thinking, his so-called *Ortungsdenken*. The time has come now to take a closer look at his *vitalistischen Dezisionismus*.

---

55 Ibid.
56 Mehring 2012, p. 150.
57 Smend 2010, p. 514.
58 See Mehring 2012, pp. 149–152.

# 10

# POLITICAL ANTAGONISM AND NORMATIVE CONTRADICTION

## 1 Law as political antagonism – Schmitt

Carl Schmitt's response to Kelsen was similar to Smend's. With a sense of disbelief and dismay Schmitt wrote in his *Verfassungslehre*:

> The theory of the state that H. Kelsen repeats in many books presents the state as a system and unity of legal norms, without offering the slightest effort to explain the material and logical principle of this unity. It also fails to explain how it came about and why it was necessary that the many positive legal determinations of a state and the various constitutional norms on which they turn constitute such a system or unity. The political *existence* and *development* of this statal unity and order thus get transformed into a mere matter of *functioning*.[1]

According to Schmitt, Kelsen's political theory was one of the last outgrowths of the theory of the bourgeois constitutional state (*letzte Auslaüfer der . . . Theorie des bürgerlichen Rechtsstaates*) of the seventeenth and eighteenth centuries. This bourgeois theory of the state, he argues, turned on individualistic conceptions of natural law. During the sixteenth and seventeenth centuries, these conceptions of natural law endowed bourgeois constitutional conceptions with real meaning and a real sense of compelling normativity (*echtes Sollen*). But in Kelsen's system of law, this real and compelling normativity is replaced by an empty normativity. Kelsen's legal system turns on a bottomless positivism in terms of which a norm applies simply because and when it applies – *[E]twas gilt wenn es gilt und weil es gilt. Das ist Positivismus.*[2]

1 Translated from Schmitt 2003, p. 9.
2 Ibid.

For Schmitt, Kelsen's normative theory of law fails to explain why norms are compelling. It insulates itself conceptually against all facticity and all factual foundations of law. It therefore ends up completely isolated from any act of constituent power and the actual will of a people to give itself law. Such concrete law-giving accordingly gets dismissed as historical events that have no bearing on the real foundation of law.[3] Schmitt portrays Kelsen as the latest exponent of the Gerber-Laband school of positivism. This line of positivism, he claims, purposefully separated law from its political roots and from the principle of sovereignty.[4] The political and legal theory that Schmitt puts forward does exactly the opposite. It founds politics and the law on the principle of sovereignty and the corresponding principle of constituent power. Both these principles root Schmitt's thinking about law and politics firmly in the history of European metaphysics that we traced in the first four chapters of this book. That history, we showed in Chapter 3, had two branches, one that conceived of nature as *kosmos*, and one that considered nature a matter of *physis*. The first conceived of nature as a coherent order in which everything had its proper place. The second considered nature an anarchic sum of contingent forces that compete with one another, and constantly displace and replace one another.

Schmitt found the choice between these two metaphysics difficult, as his doctoral student, Rudolf Huber, observed accurately. One of his lines of thought – his so-called *Ortungsdenken* – definitely emphasises a link between order and space (*Ort* and *Ordnung*) that evinced undeniable affinity with the cosmological thinking with which especially Aristotle was associated, hence also his comfortable invocation of Aristotle's concept of law for purposes of distinguishing *nomos* from positive legislation (see Chapter 2). The other line of his thinking is evidently much more representative of the anarchic *physis* thinking with which the Sophist opponents of Plato and Aristotle were associated, and which Thucydides attributed to the envoys Athens sent to Melos in 416 BCE (discussed in Chapters 1–3). However, even the *nomos* line in Schmitt's thinking stresses the major historical intervention (*historischer Grundvorgang*) that founds a new order. In other words, even his *nomos* or *Ortungsdenken* is permeated with a vision of an anarchic constituent power or sovereignty that operates outside established orders and actually underpins and conditions them for as long as they last. His invocation of Spinoza's conception of *natura naturans* and *natura naturata* in his *Verfassungslehre* – which becomes *ordo ordinans* and *ordo ordinata* in *Der Nomos der Erde* – goes to the heart of this inseverable link between order and anarchy in Schmitt's thinking (see Chapter 5, Section 3). In the final analysis, however, Schmitt gives priority to the anarchy side of this order-anarchy constellation, as Huber also pointed out.

Sovereignty, proclaims Schmitt in his *Politische Theologie* of 1922, consists of the power to decide the exception – *Souverän ist, wer über den Ausnahmezustand entscheidet*.[5] This concern with the exception also becomes the key thought in his *Der Begriff des Politischen* of 1932. Politics, avers Schmitt in this work, concerns the

---

3 Ibid.
4 Schmitt 1996c, p. 21.
5 Schmitt 1996c, p. 13.

drawing of the line between the friend and the enemy. This "drawing of the line" relates to the exceptional moment and the serious case – *Ernstfall* – that calls for sovereign intervention. Politics does not have its own sphere of normality and normativity, explains Schmitt. It is the reality that becomes manifest when a normal and normative sphere – such as economics, religion or ethics – becomes burdened with tensions that require resolution. The political commences when such tensions develop an intensity that solicits the sovereign to draw the line between the friend and the enemy. This is also the moment at which the existential unity of the people becomes manifest.[6] The following lines from *Der Begriff des Politischen* describe this sovereign moment as follows:

> The political group is always the group that finds its orientation in the serious case. . . . It is therefore always the decisive human grouping, the political unity from which derives always, when it is present at all, the decisive unity and sovereignty in the sense that the decision of the decisive case, even when it is the exception, belongs to it as a logically necessity. . . . The word "sovereignty" makes good sense here, as does the word "unity."[7]

*Der Begriff des Politischen* appeared in 1932, but the emphasis on the essential unity of the political that comes to the fore in these lines is already prominently present in the *Verfassungslehre* of 1928, as the following statement on the opening page makes abundantly clear:

> The word "constitution" must be understood strictly with reference to the constitution of the *state*, that is, to the political unity of a people. . . . it then signifies the totality of political unity and order.[8]

Schmitt's emphasis on the political and constitutional unity of the people in 1928 and 1932 soon translated into a concept of judicial review that is likewise premised on the fundamental political unity of the legal system. His essay *Staat, Bewegung, Volk* of 1933 puts forward a concept of judicial review that commissions the judiciary to ensure that the fundamental principles of the National Socialist movement become effective in every area of German law. According to Schmitt, the judiciary had to take recourse to the general principles (*Generalklauseln*) of the German legal system for purposes of infusing every aspect of the law with the spirit of National Socialism.[9] This is Schmitt's version of the "radiation theory" of judicial review that the German Federal Constitutional Court articulated in its famous *Lüth* decision of 1958. This concept of judicial review was adopted in so many jurisdictions of the world that it can reasonably be said to have become the general jurisprudence of the global legal order during the second half of the twentieth century.

---

6 Schmitt 1996a, p. 39.
7 Translated from ibid.
8 Translated from Schmitt, 2003, p. 3.
9 Schmitt 1933, pp. 43–44.

Schmitt's work is of course not the source of inspiration of the German Federal Constitutional Court's new jurisprudence. To the extent that this honour goes to particular person, it goes to Smend, not to Schmitt (see Chapter 9, Section 2). Smend and Schmitt's jurisprudential positions differ in many respects, but they both subscribe to deeply substantive visions of social integration. However, the real differences between the modes of social integration that they contemplate cannot be overlooked. Smend contemplates a cultural, interpretive, spiritual and ultimately religious integration of society. Schmitt contemplates an amoral existential integration of society in an encounter with a political enemy. Smend acknowledges political differences and conflicts in society, but considers them part and parcel of the spiritual process through which society integrates itself and attains a coherent self-understanding. Schmitt, as we saw above, considers political conflict the moment at which a society comes to stand united against an external enemy. In the final analysis, however, they both entertain visions of a fundamentally united society, and of a legal system that is rooted in the life of a united people. It is this understanding of political community and of law that makes them such bitter opponents of Hans Kelsen. Kelsen, we saw, refuses to consider law rooted in a people. The people is for him a product of legal construction. Moreover, in liberal democracies, this legal construction of peoples endows them with an ineradicable duality that compels them to live a life – or lives – of constant compromises (see Chapter 9).

With this synopsis of the three positions of Schmitt, Smend and Kelsen we reach the end of our Weimar sojourn. Of the three Weimar theoretical positions discussed, only Kelsen makes a significant impact on the concept of liberal democratic law pursued in this book. In fact, with Kelsen's dualist construction of the people we arrive at a pure concept of liberal democratic law, that is, a concept of liberal democratic law that is adequately distilled from the heavy liquids of Western metaphysics. Schmitt and Smend evidently fall back into the bubbling cauldron. We leave them behind now. Or almost. A surprising reappearance of Schmittian thinking in the 1970s, in the New World of all places, demands one last encounter with Schmitt's vitalistic decisionism.

## 2 Law as fundamental contradiction – Duncan Kennedy

The rise of the Critical Legal Studies (CLS) movement in the United States in the 1970s was a veritable event. It was part of the broader resistance movement that rose up in the streets of many major cities and university campuses of the Western world in 1968. The broader resistance movement put forward many claims and battle cries in the name of an unalienated counter culture that could and would be innocent of the distortion, reification and general inauthenticity of human relations in the consumerist capitalist societies that emerged in the post-war era. Peter Gabel and Duncan Kennedy's 1984 dialogue-form article "Roll over Beethoven" was surely a clear signal that key exponents of the CLS movement participated in this resistance.[10] The movement as a whole can surely be considered an attempt to

---

10 See Gabel and Kennedy 1984.

re-root culture and society in "uncorrupted life." If this assessment is correct, the scholarly endeavours of the CLS movement may well have been another metaphysical attempt to re-root law in correct and healthy life, to revert to Smend's terminology again. If this is indeed the case, the whole resistance movement of these years in general, and the CLS movement in particular, should be considered deeply at odds with the ideal of liberal democratic law.

From the perspective of the concept of liberal democracy developed in this book, the 1968 movement appears to have been too steeped in a metaphysics of healthy life and true social relationships to be counted as a concern with liberal democracy. That it may have made, paradoxically, a significant contribution to the societal conditions under which the ideal of liberal democracy may remain sustainable, is highly likely, but this is a consideration that cannot be explored further on the remaining pages of this book. It is, however, a consideration that merits further exploration and the last chapter of this book will give some indication of how this might be done in future scholarly engagements. In the rest of this chapter, however, we shall only explore the relation between the mode of legal thinking that may be considered representative of the CLS movement, on the one hand, and the concept of liberal democratic law, on the other. For this purpose we shall take a closer look at the work of Duncan Kennedy. The reason for selecting Kennedy is not self-evident. Many other scholars associated with the movement produced important scholarship with many implications for the theme we have been pursuing in this book. The main reason for selecting Kennedy concerns his express assocation of his own position with Carl Schmitt's and this allows one to extend the narrative line developed in this book coherently to the CLS scholarship of the 1970s, given the prominence that this narrative has given to Schmitt.

Kennedy wrote glowingly about his discovery of Schmitt's decisionist understanding of politics in an article published in 2001.[11] For anyone familiar with the development of Kennedy's work, his positive appraisal of Schmitt's concept of the political will not come as a surprise. The Sartrean existentialism that characterised his thinking in the early years of his scholarship goes a long way towards explaining the fascination with Schmitt that he would develop many years later.[12] In what follows, we shall take a closer look at key moments in Kennedy's scholarship for purposes of explaining his receptivity towards Schmitt, and for purposes of assessing the significance of his concept of law and adjudication for the concept of liberal democratic law thus far developed in this book.

Kennedy made the following three essential claims in his seminal 1976 essay "Form and Substance in Private Law Adjudication"[13]:

1) Bourgeois law portrays an irreconcilable dual commitment to mechanically applicable rules, on the one hand, and the *ad hoc* situation sensitive consideration of general values and informal standards, on the other.

11 Kennedy 2001, pp. 1162–1167.
12 For an analysis of this Sartrean side of Kennedy's work, see Van der Walt 2005, pp. 154–159.
13 See Kennedy 1976, pp. 1685–1778.

2)  The contradictory commitment to both rules and standards is accompanied by
    a range of arguments that favour reliance on either rules or standards.
3)  The commitment to both rules and standards in legal reasoning is the result of
    an underlying commitment to the contradictory values of individualism and
    community in bourgeois culture. The commitment to rules is related to the
    deeper commitment to individualism and self-reliance. The commitment to
    standards reflects the deeper commitment to altruism and community.

The inescapable conflict between these two positions, argues Kennedy, gives rise
to an inevitable indeterminacy in legal reasoning. In the final analysis the decision
is inevitably subject to political preferences. Kennedy's own position favours the
altruist position invoked under point 3. He wants it to prevail over the individualist position that, according to him, enjoys priority in American courts. The altruist
end can be pursued in two ways, he argues. One can subscribe to the formalism of
the rule position in contract law in an aggressive fashion. This would, as it did in
the *Lochner* cases, "heighten the level of political and economic conflict within our
society," thereby opening the door for more fundamental social change.[14] But he
himself favours a more direct altruist approach that he describes as follows:

> Nonetheless, I believe that there is value as well as an element of real nobil-
> ity in the judicial decision to throw out, every time the opportunity arises,
> consumer contracts designed to perpetuate the exploitation of the poorest
> class of buyers on credit. Real people are involved, even if there are not very
> many whose lives the decision can affect. The altruist judge can view himself
> as a resource whose effectiveness in the cause of substantive justice is to be
> maximized, but to adopt this attitude is to abandon the crucial proposition
> that altruistic duty is owed by one individual to another, without the inter-
> position of the general category of humanity.[15]

Of interest in this passage is not only the preference that Kennedy expresses
for "altruism," but also the further statement regarding the casting of this altruistic
duty in terms of a general "maximization of substantive justice" or of a "general
category of humanity" that already betrays it. According to Kennedy, these general
terms reify the direct moral "altruistic duty . . . owed by one individual to another."
With his objection to these general terms, he is already invoking the experience
of a direct, living and intuitive relation between individuals that he would later call
"intersubjective zap." And already here – in the same breath – he is distancing himself from, or at least lamenting, the law's inability to reflect and embody "intersubjective zap" (and the direct "altruistic duty . . . owed by one individual to another)
without having to interpose "the general category of humanity."[16] The editors of
the *Stanford Law Review* explain "intersubjective zap" as follows:

---

14  Kennedy, 1976, p. 1777. The synopsis above is taken from Van der Walt, 2005, p. 152.
15  Ibid.
16  Gabel and Kennedy, 1984, p. 4.

'Intersubjective zap' is a sudden, intuitive moment of connectedness. It is a vitalizing moment of energy (hence 'zap') when the barriers between the self and the other are in some sense suddenly dissolved. Reflective understanding of another person is *not* what is meant by the phrase.[17]

However, Kennedy himself has not always been so convinced of this idea of intuitive connectedness between the self and the other. In "The Structure of Blackstone's Commentaries" – another major text of the early years – his main focus was still on the idea of the "fundamental contradiction," which can for all practical purposes be considered a restatement of the deep division in bourgeois culture between selfishness and altruism articulated in "Form and Substance." Kennedy articulated the fundamental contradiction as follows:

The fundamental contradiction – that our relations with others are both necessary to and incompatible with our freedom – is not only intense. It is also pervasive. First, it is an aspect of our experience of every form of social life. It arises in the relations of lovers, spouses, parents and children, neighbors, employers and employees, trading partners, colleagues, and so forth. Second, within law, as law is commonly defined, it is not only an aspect but also the very *essence* of every problem. There simply are no legal issues that do not involve directly the problem of the legitimate content of collective coercion, since there is by definition no legal problem until someone has at least imagined that he might invoke the force of the state. The more sophisticated a person's legal thinking, regardless of her political stance, the more likely she is to believe that all issues within a doctrinal field reduce to a single dilemma of the degree of collective as opposed to individual self-determination that is appropriate. And analyses of particular fields tend themselves to collapse into a single analysis as soon as the thinker attempts to understand together, say, free speech and economic due process, or contracts and torts.[18]

The "fundamental contradiction," as explained in this passage, is plainly irreconcilable with the notion of "zap" invoked and described above. The vision of social relations – ranging from the most intimate and private to the most formal or public – as incompatible with one's freedom renders the notion of intuitive connectedness quite unlikely if not downright impossible. Another passage from "Blackstone's Commentaries" makes this abundantly clear:

We sometimes experience fusion with others, in groups of two or even two million, and it is a good rather than a bad experience. But at the same time that it forms and protects us, the universe of others (family, friendship, bureaucracy, culture, the state) threatens us with annihilation and urges upon us forms of fusion that are quite plainly bad rather than good. A friend can

17  Ibid.
18  Kennedy, 1979, p. 213.

reduce me to misery with a single look. Numberless conformities, large and small abandonments of self to others, are the price of what freedom we experience in society. And the price is a high one. Through our existence as members of collectives, we impose on others and have imposed on us hierarchical structures of power, welfare, and access to enlightenment that are illegitimate, whether based on birth into a particular social class or on the accident of genetic endowment.[19]

It is therefore only consistent that Kennedy would renounce the fundamental contradiction in a text that is concerned with the possibility of "zap." One of his proclamations in "Roll over Beethoven" does this unflinchingly:

> I renounce the fundamental contradiction. I recant it and I also recant the whole idea of individualism and altruism, and the idea of legal consciousness. . . . I mean these things are absolutely classic examples of 'philosophical' abstractions which you can manipulate into little structures.[20]

This renouncement of the "fundamental contradiction" in favour of "zap" was perhaps bound not to endure for long. Kennedy's earlier awareness of the inevitable coercion that comes with collective existence and which constantly renders "zap" or "fusion with others" unlikely or impossible remained too strong and gained the upper hand again in his *Critique of Adjudication* of 1997. In this work, Kennedy articulates a "modern-postmodern leftist position" characterised by "loss, nostalgia, yearning, depression [and] despair." *A Critique of Adjudication* describes "the way it feels to be *zapless* in a rightsless world."[21] It is not necessary to go into the details of the modern-postmodern (mpm) leftist position elaborated in this formidable work. Suffice it to note that it is "leftist" in the sense of endorsing the typical political sentiments and convictions of the "left" among which opposition to social hierarchies, inequality, racism and patriarchy is central. It nevertheless retreats from any insistence that these political sentiments are correct or "right." In other words, it articulates a conception or political leftism that is infused with a fundamental scepticism that makes the sense of "being right" another enemy to be resisted. Kennedy makes this point with his typical flair for pun and idiom:

> An important strand, a defining strand in the mpm project, is a particular attitude to rightness. . . . This is the attitude that the demand for agreement and commitment on the basis of representations with the pretension of objectivity is *an enemy*. The specific enemies have been the central ethical/ theoretical concepts of bourgeois culture, including autonomous individual choosing self, conventional morality, the family, manhood and womanhood,

19 Kennedy, 1979, p. 212.
20 Gabel and Kennedy, 1984, pp. 15–16.
21 Kennedy, 1997, p. 346 (emphasis added).

the nation state, humanity. But the central ethical/theoretical concepts of the left have also been targets, including the proletariat, class solidarity, party discipline and socialist realism, and more recently, sexual and racial identity. . . . The mpm impulse is to counter the producers of these artefacts with others. The transgressive artefacts are supposed to put into question the claims of rightness and, at the same time, induce a set of emotions – irony, despair, ecstasy, and so on – they are crushed or blocked when we experience the text or representation as 'right'. If we define the left project as the struggle for a more egalitarian and communitarian society, it is not intrinsically connected to rightness in any particular form. But within the left project it has always been true that rightness has played a central role. Leftism has been a bourgeois cultural project within which many leaders and many followers have believed that they were not just left but also right, in the strong sense of possessing coherent and complete ('totalising') descriptive and prescriptive analyses of the social order.[22]

When one reads this 1997 passage against the background of Kennedy's enthusiastic 2001 endorsement of Schmitt's friend-enemy conception of the political, one must note the rather unique friend-enemy that is emerging from the mpm position articulated in *A Critiqique of Adjudication*. The enemy that is singled out in this passage is "rightness" and the pretension of "objectivity." If the drawing of the line concerns the serious case, the *Ernstfall*, as Schmitt calls it, then one must conclude that "objectivity" and "pretension of objectivity" constitute the serious case for Kennedy, irrespective of whether this rightness and objectivity accompany the bourgeois concepts of "autonomous individual choosing self, conventional morality, the family, manhood and womanhood, the nation state, humanity," or the left's conceptions of "proletariat, class solidarity, party discipline and socialist realism, and more recently, sexual and racial identity." One wonders whether this "rightness" can really become an adversary serious enough to be called an enemy. The question that lurks here reminds one of the story of the quarrel between two Russians about the correct understanding of Kant's philosophy that ended with the one pulling a gun and shooting the other.[23]

The question is this: Can one really have a serious enemy – arrive at serious animosity – without considering oneself right enough and your adversary wrong enough to warrant hostility? Schmitt clearly suggests one can. His understanding of the political expressly dismisses the role of rightness in politics. This is not only clear from his enthused exposition of the *hostis iustus* in *Der Nomos der Erde* (see Chapter 2), but also from *Der Begriff des Politischen* itself. The latter text underlines Schmitt's view of the political as an existential act and experience – an intensification (*Intensivierung*) – that at best has an indirect bearing on any normative or epistemic consideration. A situation may have begun to heat up because of some

22  Kennedy, 1997, p. 341 (emphasis added).
23  See Charlton 2013.

normative or epistemic disagreement. But the political moment, the drawing of the line, remains an independent phenomenon that must be understood independently from whatever consideration may have, initially, precipitated a disagreement that eventually slipped into the unique zone of political conflict.[24] In this sense politics is truthless for Schmitt. Kennedy's stance is fully consistent with Schmitt's when he declares "rightness" his enemy.

One wonders, however, whether any serious enmity and animosity remain possible when convictions about right and wrong no longer play any role in the encounter between the potential enemies. It is not hard to see that this question would not have bothered Schmitt. *Der Nomos der Erde* eulogises the duel, the playful contest between equal sovereigns – big men with an appetite for big politics, Schmitt calls them – who experience the need to measure their strength from time to time (see Chapter 2). It is doubtful, however, whether Kennedy has this kind politics in mind in *A Critique of Adjudication*. For if he does, his professed "leftism" would be reduced to a ruse for picking a fight. Does he really have Schmitt's amoral politics in mind, the playful politics in terms of which the sovereign can at worst sin against his own conscience – *[er] sündigt höchstens gegen sein Gewissen*[25] – when he picks a fight for which there is no real ground.

It is doubtful, however, whether Kennedy would really want to qualify his leftism in terms of the sovereignty that just finds some sort of sellable reason – in which he does not really believe – for picking a fight. The mpm leftism that he describes in *A Critique of Adjudication* appears all too normative – too decidedly leftist, however mpm – to be reduced to a playful invitation to a duel. It is surely not Schmitt's "complete amoralism" (as Smend referred to it – see Chapter 9, Section 2) that is at work in Kennedy's mpm leftism. What is Kennedy getting at then, when he declares "rightness" an enemy? This is not at all clear and one can only guess. Here is one plausible guess: He was searching for a different formulation in the passage above, and just did not arrive at it. "Rightness" was not really the enemy he had in mind, but a certain attitude to rightness, the attitude to rightness that Castoriadis describes with regard to Antigone: Thinking only about your own sense of rightness already makes you wrong – *"[m]ême si l'on a raison, n'écouter que la raison qu'on a, c'est déjà avoir tort"* (see Chapter 3, Section 3). If this is correct, if this is the phrase Kennedy was looking for in the passage above, it would be fair to impute to him the wish to articulate something along the lines of the programmatic statement of the liberal democratic ethic in the Introduction of this book. We repeated this statement almost fully towards the end of Chapter 8 (pp. 196–197) and will return to it again in Chapter 11 (p. 243). Let us therefore only highlight its most essential lines here:

By all means believe that the principles and convictions by which you act are the correct ones. You have to do so. *But, do not succumb to the temptation to*

24 See Schmitt 1996a, p. 39.
25 See Schmitt 1997, p. 138.

*insist that those who evidently and adamantly disagree with you have good reasons to agree with you. The moment you do this, you begin the descent into a dogmatic liberalism that ultimately risks becoming as illiberal as any adversary of liberal democracy imaginable.*

If it is correct to assume on Kennedy's behalf that this is the thought that he sought to communicate in the passage above, we should feel compelled to consider him, along with Hart and Kelsen, another pioneer of the concept of liberal democratic law that we have pursued in the chapters of this book. If not, we shall have to leave him behind with Schmitt and Smend and Dworkin, that is, with all those who either did not care about liberal democracy, or simply failed to understand what it means. The notion of the fundamental contradiction to which Kennedy alerted Anglo-American jurisprudence evidently resonates firmly with Hart's call for a legal theory that duly registers the reality that law is always caught up in a tension between those who have internal and those who have external perspectives on the law. It therefore also resonates firmly with the insistence developed in this book that law cannot be rooted in life, because law, which must always end up by reducing the concerns of life to univocal and simple answers, cannot account for the complexity and plurality of life.

Whether Kennedy can indeed be taken as another pioneer of the concept of liberal democracy developed in this book will in the final analysis depend on the way he contemplates law's response to the complexity of life, the complexity of life in which it cannot be rooted, but to which it is always exposed and must always respond. One must recall that Hegel also started off with a profound regard for the dividedness of life, but ended up with a conception of life that is fully reconciled with itself (see Chapter 7, Section 2). Whether Kennedy can avoid this Hegelian termination of an interminable – and interminably frustrating and often traumatic – dialectic depends largely on more specific aspects of his theory of adjudication that we cannot address here.[26] Those aspects will also reveal how Schmittian or un-Schmittian Kennedy is in the final analysis. Suffice it to observe that his retreat from the notion of "intersubjective zap" is a promising sign in this regard. Schmitt's concept of sovereignty and the political can be considered a vision of "intersubjective zap" writ large. Liberal democracy cannot stomach this kind of thing.[27]

Let us therefore conclude for now: Although the jury is still out on some aspects of his work, Kennedy may well be another pioneer of the concept of liberal democracy pursued in this book. It is quite possible that he himself may have difficulty with this association of his work with liberal democracy. The Crits generally reserve the term "liberalism" for the bourgeois and capitalist legal culture that their scholarship seeks to resist. Some of them would probably be horrified to be considered

---

26 This question will be explored further in the follow up to this book that will deal more specifically with the theory of adjudication.

27 The classic and still most incisive description and explanation of "this kind of thing" can be found in Freud 1999.

"liberals." There is, however, a huge difference between bourgeois and/or capitalist liberalism, and liberal democracy or democratic liberalism. Apart from the brief endorsement of C. B. Macpherson's assessment of liberal democracy in the opening pages (see Introduction, Section 7) and the affirmative reference to Alain Supiot's invocation of the "total market" (in Chapter 7, Section 1), this difference has not been addressed in this book and it would certainly be important and worthwhile to do so on another occasion. The only aim of this book was to distil the concept of liberal democratic law from the history of Western metaphysics that cradled it, but also smothered and distorted it for much too long. Let us turn now to the last chapter of this book to see what we have come up with. Perhaps it is not that far removed from the "superliberalism" that Roberto Unger believes can be modelled on the "[narrow and traditional definition] of liberal democratic politics" as "a series of conflicts and deals among more or less transitory and fragmentary groups."[28]

28  See Unger 1986, p. 41.

# 11

# THE DISTILLED CONCEPT

## 1 Two concepts of Nature and Spirit

We have seen from the first three chapters of this book that the standard reference to the *nomos-physis* debate in late fifth and early fourth century Athens leads one astray. At stake in the debate was not so much an opposition between *nomos* and *physis*, but two different concepts of *nomos*, namely, *nomos* conceived as *physis* and *nomos* conceived as *kosmos*. Since then, and perhaps even before then, two conceptions of nature dominated Western metaphysics, nature conceived as cosmic order and nature conceived as the anarchic reign of physical forces. From these two concepts of nature followed two concepts of natural law, natural law understood as a normative reflection of the intrinsic order of things (Aristotle, Aquinas and Roman law), and natural law understood as the forceful imposition of arbitrary order on natural anarchy (arguably Thucydides and Pindar, definitely Hobbes). In the modern age, these conceptions of nature and natural law became historicised and spiritualised. Savigny's *Volksgeist* and Hegel's *Weltgeist* became two of the most prominent versions of this historicised and spiritualised recasting of ancient natural law theories in modern philosophical and legal thought. Both of them basically continued the cosmological pretensions of ancient natural law theories, notwithstanding their reliance on elements of Kant's philosophy that were not in the least reconcilable with cosmological pretensions of any kind. They both deemed it possible to reconceive natural order on the basis of the modern recognition of subjective autonomy or freedom (Hegel) and subjective rights (Savigny).

Savigny's and Hegel's respective conceptions of *Spirit* had two vastly different political orientations, the one liberal and progressive (Hegel), the other conservative, restorative and reactionary (Savigny), but the radicalism with which they both endeavoured to re-root law in nature and life, albeit spiritualised and historicised nature and life, turned them both into modern representatives of an ancient mentality. The elements of this ancient and modern-ancient mentality are heavy, enduring and persistent. They have been put on the burner of many critical revisions, but they do not come to boil and evaporate, as the enduring history of Western metaphysics underlines. Conceptions of cosmic order, nature, life and Spirit just come back again and again. Hence also, the persistent invocation of life as the foundation of law in Western legal thought right into the twenty first century. Hegel's introduction to the *Grundlinien der Philosophie des Rechts*, we saw in Chapter 7, gave us a glimpse of the possible separation of law from life, but that glimpse was short-lived. The *Grundlinien* itself soon found its way back to the old link between law and life, and legal theorists after Hegel again followed suit, as Schmitt's conception of *Lebensrecht* (see Chapter 5), Smend's invocation of *rechtes, gutes Leben* (see Chapter 9), Ehrlich's concept of *living law* and the general insistence on a close link between life and law stressed by Pound and the American Realists (see Chapter 7) made abundantly clear. And if there was any doubt that Dworkin's link between law and political morality was another chapter in this ancient narrative, that doubt was certainly removed by the massive argument that law is ultimately based on a conception of the good life that he published in 2011.

The political and legal theory of Carl Schmitt – as presented in Chapter 10 – can plausibly be understood as a twentieth century restatement of the *physis* line of thinking in Western metaphysics, but we also noted in Chapters 2, 5 and 10 that Schmitt vacillated between this physicalist line of thinking, and another line to which he referred as *Ortungsdenken*. The latter line has many features in common with the Aristotelian and cosmological line.

## 2 Distilling law from the metaphysics of life

It is from this long history of the metaphysics of law and life that the chapters of this book have sought to distil the concept of liberal democratic law. This concept did not fall from the air. It did not have a separate history. It has its roots in this ancient metaphysics. However, a rigorous understanding of the concept of liberal democratic law requires that one uproot and extract it from the history in which it is rooted. Moreover, only in its pure – uprooted, extracted – form can it serve the purpose that it could be expected to serve. What purpose, other than life, can it be expected to serve, one may well ask. The question is pertinent and the answer must be clear: life, nothing but life. There is a big difference, however, between being rooted in life, and serving life. And the condition of life that demands legal service at the beginning of the twenty first century – not for the first time, to be sure – requires a concept of law that is very definitely not rooted in life. This is so because life that requires legal service is never one, but always two or more, always fundamentally divided in itself and separated from itself. When life turns to law, it demands that law serve the irreconcilable demands that result from its divided and unreconciled state. If the law, in response, imagines life reconciled and undivided, as it has been assumed to do throughout the long history of the metaphysics of life and law, it will not serve the irreconcilable demands of divided life well. It will only aggravate and deepen life's division, for it will raise the expectation and demand that the law be rooted in one of the unreconciled parts of life, rather than the other, thereby exacerbating the conflict that it was called to resolve. Thus do legal disputes end up as the clash between unforgiving attempts to get the law on one's side, and thus does the law lose its ability and claim to serve the concerns of all parties to the dispute.

Can this situation be avoided? Not completely. There is no magic formula that will render all parties that exit litigation or arbitration equally content with the outcome. Decisions will always hurt in the one or the other direction. But the situation can be ameliorated in two important ways. One can avoid identifying the law with the decision that allocates gain to the one party and loss to the other. And one can narrow the scope of the decision that allocates gain and loss. Neither of these ameliorations require significant institutional change. But they do require a change in judicial practice that I have begun to describe elsewhere,[1] and to which one must return to work out the full implications of the change proposed. This could not be done here.[2] In what follows, we will only describe the theoretical under-pinnings of the proposed change in view of the extraction of law from life that we have pursued in this book.

The theoretical underpinnings of concern here have five distinct elements. The first involves a complete debunking of all conceptions of *nomos*, natural law and natural essence in the language of law. It may well be quite in order to talk about these things elsewhere, but not when we talk about law. The second involves a similarly complete debunking of *demos* – the People written with a capital P discussed in Chapters 6 and 7 – as a foundation of liberal democracy. The third embraces the point that we have made about divided life as a transcendental condition of all law. The fourth involves the refusal to view the application of law as its realisation, that is, as the actualisation of its potentiality. And the fifth involves understanding law-making as a procedural mechanism that is not rooted in life but designed to uproot law from life. That is why all law should be considered legislation, and why the Roman law and even the common law conception of law-making in terms of organic historical growth and the spontaneous development of societal life should be dismissed as a harmful myth. Let us look more closely at each of these five elements.

## 3 Debunking *nomos*

The Greeks lost their ability to elevate *nomos* to *kosmos* in fifth century Athens, assuming for argument's sake that they had this ability during an earlier age of innocence (see Chapter 3, Section 2). Since then, Western civilisations has never managed to restore the link between *nomos* and *kosmos*.

---

1 See Van der Walt 2014b, pp. 361–400.
2 This will be done in a monograph that will follow this one under the (provisional) title of *Liberal Democratic Judicial Review*.

Schmitt, we saw in Chapter 2, begs to differ. It is a widespread mistake to consider medieval political organisation anarchic and chaotic, he claims in *Der Nomos der Erde – es ist eine weitverbreitete Irrtum, von der Anarchie des Mittelalters zu sprechen.* In another statement earlier on in the text (that may well have been added later) he changed his tune somewhat. Here he conceded to the anarchy and chaos of medieval politics, but insisted on the pillar of meaningful order that prevailed throughout the Middle Ages. In this respect, he contends, the Middle Ages have to be distinguished from the nihilism that descended upon the world in the twentieth century – *ist es notwendig, die Anarchie des Mittelalters von dem Nihilismus des 20. Jahrhunderts in aller Deutlichkeit abzusetzen.* The medieval *nomos* – organised as it was around the idea of Rome as the *katechon* that fended off the Antichrist and the end of time – prevailed until Modernity introduced a new *nomos*, avers the narrative in *Der Nomos der Erde.* The Investiture debacle and the depths of bare physical existence and circumstantial contingency into which an obviously unruly conflict between secular and religious power descended in the tenth and eleventh centuries, and again in the fourteenth – when Boniface VIII contested the supremacy of the secular power of Philip IV of France in his *Unam sanctam* bull of 1302, only to end up manhandled and thrown into prison by Philip's soldiers and dying some weeks later – surely do not testify in favour of Schmitt's assessment of the *nomos* of the Middle Ages. What came to pass between Pope John II and Emperor Otto I in the tenth century, between King Henry IV of Germany and Pope Gregory VII towards the end of the eleventh and beginning of the twelfth and again between Boniface VIII and Philip IV in the fourteenth (see again Chapter 5, Section 2) reflects much more than incidental lapses in the otherwise enduringly grand political order of the Middle Ages that Schmitt invokes in *Nomos der Erde.* These incidents underline the precariousness to which the medieval political order was generally exposed, and how easily it slipped into sordid physical conflict.

From this perspective, Villey's description of the medieval political system as a crude regime of kings, lords and vassals constructed on the ruins of the Roman Empire – see Chapter 5, Section 4 – would appear to be much more accurate. But Villey's adoration of Roman law would seem to also render him inattentive to the sordidness into which the political and social reality of Rome descended rather frequently. The idea of an eternal natural order that depends on sound historical legislation and positive law for its dialectic completion runs like a golden thread through his apology of Aristotelian and Thomist natural law. The straight question that one should ask with regard to Villey's plausible assessment of the medieval decay of ancient Roman law is this one: On what grounds can one base the contention that classical and post-classical Roman law was a true reflection of an eternal natural order that sadly fell into decay during the Middle Ages? On what grounds could one possibly argue that the Roman legal system was at any time anything more than an incidental ingredient of political orders that happened to survive for some centuries by force of highly temporal and contingent constellations of power?

The Roman jurists and magistrates undoubtedly constructed a remarkably rational system of law in a time that myth still played a substantial role in the regulation of life. It thus produced a method of legal thinking that understandably and justifiably earned it the status of the foundation of all Western law. This status certainly need not be denied, but it must also be understood as having been fundamentally conditioned by contingent constellations of power that never reflected the natural order of things, if this natural order is taken to be something qualitatively different from the ancient natural order that the Athenian envoys invoked in their discourse with the Melesians (see Chapter 2, Section 1). Political organization in both ancient Greece and Rome turned on unforgiving domination of commoners by small groups of noble families until the exigencies of battle power (the need for bigger numbers of foot soldiers) broke down the ancient distinction between nobility and common people to some extent (surely not entirely). The Greek and Roman civil wars erased the boundaries between civil order and military decree, thereby introducing the conditions for imperial rule. And persistent conditions of famine and irredeemable debt in ancient republican Rome also render dubious any claim that Roman law was, at any time, the illustrious example of wise distributive and redistributive justice that Villey makes it out to be. Emperor Augustus was the first ruler to alleviate the conditions of famine in ancient Rome, and he did so on the basis of personal largesse, not on the basis of the inherently redistributive faculties of Roman law (Augustus paid for huge importations of grain out of his personal wealth).

Viewed from this perspective, any suggestion that ancient Greece and Rome were actually governed by the notions of *nomos* or natural law contemplated by illustrious philosophers must be considered fictitious. The historical reality never lived up to the idealisations of philosophy. Or, to the extent that it did, it was because these idealisations often served as justifications of oppressive social and class relations, as Aristotle's postulation of the "natural distinction" between slaves and masters underlined. In short, the theory of liberal democratic law is not convinced by Villey's or any other natural law narrative that entertains a naturalistic vision of ethical and legal norms. It is therefore not from Villey's champions of *nomos* and natural law – Aristotle and Saint Thomas – that the contemplation of liberal democratic law takes instruction, but from their Augustinian and nominalist antagonists, William of Ockham most notable among them. It is indeed from the nominalists and Gersonists that modernity learned that law-making is an exercise of sovereignty and it is crucial that one's understanding of liberal democratic legislation – to which we turn below – sustains itself consciously as a nominalist enterprise.

The portrayal of the *nomos* and *Jus Publicum Europaeum* of the modern age (sixteenth to nineteenth centuries) that Schmitt unpacks with his typically candid and "complete amorality" (as Smend called it – see Chapter 9, Section 2) contains another myth that the theory of liberal democratic law must debunk. Civil order was achieved in Europe, argues Schmitt unflinchingly, on the back of the unleashed barbarism that Europeans were free to perpetrate on the far side of the amity line (see Chapter 2, Section 5). This is how Schmitt manages to pair *nomos* and *physis* like a pair of gloves in *Der Nomos der Erde*: *physis* on the far side of the amity line, *nomos* on Europe's side of the line. From the perspective of liberal democracy, which is of course not Schmitt's perspective, this narrative appears to constitute a masterful but unwonted self-debunking of *nomos*. One could simply conclude: If Schmitt's rendition of the modern *Jus Publicum Europaeum* is accurate, he more than anyone else makes it abundantly clear why this *Jus Publicum Europaeum* has fallen into long due obsolescence. After having read *Der Nomos der Erde*, one knows, or at least liberal democrats know, why the self-imagination of old Europe had to come to an end. Resorting to this rather facile way of debunking Schmitt's portrayal of the *nomos* of the *Jus Publicum Europaeum* between the sixteenth and seventeenth centuries nevertheless runs the double risk of not discerning the acute insight articulated in this narrative, and of not discerning the deeper obfuscation and equivocation that underpins its debunkable myth.

The acute insight of concern here is one that the theory of liberal democratic law can only ignore at its peril and we return to it in the last section of this chapter. It is the problem of deeper obfuscation and equivocation to which we turn first now, for this obfuscation and equivocation perform the essential move on which Western metaphysics has pivoted ever since Aristotle. It is this move that also explains why this metaphysics was bound to be caught up in a dichotomous concept of nature that would repeatedly vacillate between conceptions of nature as either *kosmos* or *physis*. The contention that Schmitt's portrayal of the amity line helps him to separate *kosmos* and *physis* for purposes of construing a "quasi-cosmological" European *nomos* is accurate enough at one level, but it also renders inconspicuous the deeper metaphysical equivocation that is afoot in his work.

On the one hand, Schmitt's *Ortungsdenken* is adamantly concerned with constellations of historical facts that manifest intrinsic spatial-normative qualities that are independent of the subjective fiat that one associates with the arbitrariness of sovereign legislation. On the other hand, Schmitt is also remarkably perceptive with regard to the performativity that conditions the link between *Ortung* and *Ordnung* that constitutes *nomos*, as is clear from the way he stresses the fundamental historical act – *historischer Grundvorgang* – on which *nomos* depends. It would seem that Schmitt contemplates a conception of *nomos* that is conditioned by a grand historical performative act, but which nevertheless remains capable of absorbing this performativity again so as to allow for a stable constellation of place and order – *Ortung* and *Ordnung* – with transcendent or quasi-transcendent qualities.

This is the tension that comes to a head in Schmitt's notion of great politics or *grosse Politik*. And it leaves him with no choice but to attribute to it deep secrets, that is, the grand *arcana* of politics that intrigued him incessantly.[3] For it is only under the impenetrable shadows of these grand *arcana* that the contradictory status of his grand political concerns can be obfuscated and edified with recourse to mystical notions such as *ordo ordinans* and *ordo ordinata*.[4] *Ordo ordinans* and *ordo ordinata* – this is the new pair of terms with which *Der Nomos der Erde* embellishes

---

3 Schmitt 1997, pp. 104–105, 127, 261.
4 See Schmitt 1997, p. 50.

the *natura naturans* and *natura naturata* distinction of the *Verfassungslehre*. It is the new pair of terms with which Schmitt endeavours to have his cake of enduring and non-arbitrary order, on the one hand, and the unconstrained historical feast at which sovereignty consumes this order at will, on the other. We noted in Chapter 5 the observation of Ernst Rudolf Huber that Schmitt never made a clear choice between *Ortungsdenken* and the grand interventionism that his concern with the sovereign decision demanded. Considered from this perspective, Schmitt's recourse to political mysticism and mystification should not come as a surprise to anyone. The authoritative appeal to the *arcana* of grand politics is the only way in which he could reconcile the irreconcilable pair of *Ortungsdenken* and *Dezisionismus* in his theory of politics and law. It is here, at this deep level of equivocation that the theory of liberal democratic law should focus its debunking of Schmitt's *nomos*, and of *nomos* as such, for it is at this level that it becomes clear to what extent his thought endeavours to carry the whole burden of a metaphysical tradition that could never decide between *nomos* conceived as *kosmos* and nomos conceived as *physis*. In his twisted way, Schmitt provides one with one of the most revealing versions of this whole metaphysical tradition from which the theory of liberal democratic law needs to take leave. This metaphysics, we saw in Chapter 4, began when Aristotle endeavoured to keep his heavenly piece of Platonic cake, while making a fabulous pastoral picnic of it on Earth.

## 4 Debunking *demos*

In an important late twentieth century debate between Jürgen Habermas and Dieter Grimm, Grimm argued that Europe cannot have a constitution because it does not have a *demos*.[5] If Grimm's later work can be taken as a further elaboration of what he meant with "demos" in this exchange with Habermas, he only had in mind Europe's lack of adequate democratic procedures, that is, the absence of truly functional parliamentary representation at EU level and of effective EU-wide opinion-making media regarding EU affairs.[6] In this respect Grimm's intervention in the debate is surely not at odds with the pursuit of the concept of liberal democratic law in this book. It must in fact be commended for pointing out how desperate and shallow Habermas' formalistic attempt to find an adequate foundation for popular sovereignty in the EU treatises has become.[7] However, a rigorous concept of liberal democratic law requires utmost caution with regard to all invocations of the absence or presence of "the" or "a" people. This caution must remain liberal democracy's relentless register of the crucial imperative to take leave of any invocation of demos that alludes to a People with a capital P.

That modernity's invocation of the People as the foundation of democratic government has from the beginning been steeped in theologico-political myth-making

5 Grimm 1995, pp. 282–302.
6 Grimm 2016, pp. 95–146.
7 See ibid, pp. 58–63.

was shown in Chapter 6 with reference to Claude Lefort's and Pierre Rosanvallon's reflections on revolutionary and post-revolutionary France. That this political myth-making ultimately concerned an economical myth-making is especially clear from Rosanvallon's account of the way in which the problem of political representation in the early nineteenth century – in the wake of a revolutionary event that was essentially and unconditionally non-representable – was resolved with reference to an economic criterion: Ownership of property. The staging of private property as a universal concern thus became the epochal political-economic ruse of this bourgeois century. That this political economic ruse was another instance of theologico-political myth-making – despite Bentham's best efforts to sever economic or utilitarian from theological concerns – became especially clear when, a century later, the Freiburg School of economic thinking began to present free market economies as the realisation of the order God contemplated for the universe.

The essence of this new theologico-political or rather theologico-economic myth-making lay in the presentation of particular class interests as universal social interests. It considered all members of society – and, consequently, society itself – maximisers of economic interest. Ronald Coase's brilliant 1960 article, "The Problem of Social Cost," articulates the essential mechanism of this market society with the suggestion that an accurate assessment of externalities – which is crucial for a sound conception of Kaldor-Hicks efficiency (see Chapter 7, Section 1 again) – can be achieved through merging individuals with conflicting interests into one individual, given that the internal calculation of interests by one individual can be assumed to be free of inadmissible transaction costs. If Smith the rancher and Jones the cropper can be considered united into Smith-Jones the ranching cropper, we saw Coase arguing, he can be trusted to weigh the values of ranching and cropping accurately, considering that any other transaction costs that might interfere with pure economic bargaining between two persons will thus have been eliminated in advance.

However, in making this ingenious move, Coase makes two metaphysical assumptions. He first postulates the possibility of pure economic transactions. And he then reduces social cost to the economic costs that can be identified in pure economic transactions. The problem is that neither of these conditions generally prevail on Earth. If there are individuals whose whole existence can be reduced to economic maximisation, they are surely the exception. Under real life conditions, different individuals may well perform very different "economic" calculations with very different results under the very same circumstances. Some Smith-Joneses may well opt for privileging their comparatively uneconomical crop-farming for non-economic reasons that they consider non-negotiable.

Can one bring Coase's Platonic calculation of economic cost back to Earth as an Aristotelian economist might want to do, without ruining it?[8] That is unthinkable.

---

8 Coase (1960, p. 43) himself suggests this celestial economic abstraction must be brought back to Earth by supplementing the considerations of welfare economics with the study of morals and aesthetics, but does not stop to consider the reality that such a supplementation must ruin the analytical abstraction

Bringing the pure economic transaction back to Earth would require readmitting transaction costs that the heavenly experiment banished. An Aristotelian Coase may want to hang on to the memory of his celestial vision by insisting on the possibility of distinguishing between pure and impure transaction costs. This, however, will only reopen the whole can of obfuscating and equivocating metaphysics that Aristotle bequeathed to Western civilisation. Either you proceed Platonically and reduce everyone to economic maximisers, or you recognise the singularity of personality that enters every transaction and ruin the idea of pure economic cost. Anything in between will be Aristotelian equivocations at the behest of the powerful.

The significance of this engagement with Coase in the pursuit of a pure concept of liberal democratic law concerns the way in which it points out the fundamental error of all political and legal theoretical endeavours that approach the analysis of politics and law on the back of an assumption that all members of society endorse the same set of values in the same way, thus making it completely plausible to unite society into one person, as Coase did with Smith and Jones. This is the essential move in the theoretical frameworks of Dworkin and Smend discussed in Chapters 8 and 9. In the case of Dworkin, it pivots on his mystifying invocation of a concept-conception distinction that transforms this endorsement of "the same values in the same way" into an endorsement of "the same values in different ways." This "personification of society" that expressly underpins both Dworkin's and Smend's theoretical frameworks can be traced back all the way to the nineteenth century construction of the people as one People representable by bourgeois property interests. The concept of liberal democratic law takes leave of this unification and personification of society as decisively and incisively as possible, by making the fundamental divisions and differences between people its unwavering point of departure. Liberal democracy begins with an adequate regard for the irredeemable social divisions that result from the sheer dividedness of life. It begins, in other words, with an adequate regard for the divided condition of life.

## 5  Divided life

Hegel was most likely the first philosopher in the history of Western metaphysics to pay serious attention to the perception that life is divided in itself, and against itself. His *Differenz Schrift* of 1801 articulated this insight with staggering lucidity. The need for philosophy arises when life has lost the power to unite and overcome its division, he observed – *[w]enn die Macht der Vereinigung . . . aus dem Leben der Menschen verschwindet . . . entsteht das Bedürfnis der Philosophie* (see Chapter Seven, section 2). However, this recognition of the dividedness of life was not the concluding statement of his philosophy. This philosophy answered *too* well the need for philosophy pointed out in the *Differenz Schrift*. Or that is the way, it appears,

---

with which he commences, unless one assumes that the moral and aesthetic studies envisaged here will – with parallel celestial vision – also turn Smith and Jones into a moral and aesthetic Smith-Jones.

Hegel understood his philosophical achievement. According to him, his philosophy of Spirit and freedom effectively overcame the torn and divided state – the *Entzweiung* and *Zerissenheit* – of life.

One could, however, also interpret the philosophical overcoming of the divided condition of life differently. A philosophical overcoming of the torn and divided status of life could also be *nothing but* a philosophical overcoming, that is, *nothing more* than a philosophical (Stoic) acceptance of this torn and divided status. The elegiac statement in the Introduction to the *Grundlinien* regarding life that has become too old to renew itself would appear to confirm this less than triumphant understanding of the philosophical overcoming of life's divided and torn status. It is probably impossible to know exactly where Hegel stood with regard to this triumphant and less triumphant "philosophical overcoming." Our engagement with his thought after Chapter 7 ultimately attributed to him a more triumphant conception of this "overcoming." However, if the pursuit of the concept of liberal democratic law stands to learn anything from Hegel, it would be from the less triumphant Hegel, the one who saw or can be imagined to have seen – with eyes that still look out warily and wearily from the well-known portrait of Jakob Schlesinger of 1831 – that life is irredeemably split and cannot be restored to fullness and unity.

Analytical jurisprudence would become alert to the irreparably torn status of life only much later, most likely for reasons of having gone out of its way to ignore Hegel's legacy, as Franz Wieacker observed (see Chapter 7, Section 2). But it finally got a chance to do so in 1961, when Herbert Hart – surely no Hegelian himself – published *The Concept of Law*. The crucial statement in this book that recognised the split social reality with which law always has to contend concerns Hart's recognition of the need for jurisprudence that does justice to the complex reality of the law, namely, the fact that "at any given moment the life of any society which lives by rules . . . is likely to consist in a tension between those who . . . accept and voluntarily cooperate in maintaining the rules . . . and those who . . . reject them and attend to them only from the external point of view as a sign of possible punishment." This statement contains the most crucial insight that the pursuit of the concept of liberal democratic law can draw from the history of analytical jurisprudence. It is only paralleled by Hans Kelsen's articulation of the founding principle of liberal democracy in terms of the sustenance of *majority-minority* relationships. These two pairs of concepts – external and internal perspectives, majority and minority relations – are the four cornerstones of liberal democratic law, for they testify to the recognition that the life that law serves is irreparably divided and torn. There is a good chance that Duncan Kennedy's regard for the fundamental contradiction that permeates all social relationships also strengthens this construction, but the conclusion as to whether or not it does so will have to be reconsidered on another occasion.

## 6 Potentiality and actuality

Divided life has no potentiality that can be actualised. It has no essence that can be realised. It hangs suspended in the perpetual postponement of fulfilment. There may be instances of fulfilled life outside the law (one would sincerely hope that at least some people have this experience sometimes), but life that turns to law for "answers" is already defined by the radical lack of essence that comes from division. Aristotle discerned such a vision of unfulfilled life – life that never realises its essence – in the writings of the pre-Socratic philosophers. Whatever potentiality the pre-Socratics may have contemplated, he observed, was evidently an unfulfilled potential, sheer potentiality incapable of actualisation – ἦν ὁμοῦ πάντα δυνάμει, ἐνεργείᾳ δ' οὔ. Dworkin echoed this Aristotelian insight powerfully when he observed that life that is deprived of a reflected sense of a fulfilled or good life becomes just "one damn thing after another."[9] Heraclitus would probably have conceded the point. The weeping philosopher knew well that the best thing that can be expected from life that issues from the eternal warfare of the elements – Πόλεμος πάντων μὲν πατήρ ἐστι – is the immortality of those who have died young on the battlefield: ἀρηιφάτους θεοὶ τιμῶσι καὶ ἄνθρωποι.[10] This is the best that we can hope for, considering that we are born to die and to have children so that they can also die – γενόμενοι ζώειν ἐθέλουσι μόρους τ' ἔχειν . . . καὶ παῖδας καταλείπουσι μόρους γενέσθαι.[11]

The experience that the reign of justice and the law is just another such battlefield in which nothing comes to fruition is endorsed by a famous statement about justice – δίκη – by another pre-Socratic philosopher, Anaxagoras. Justice ensures that nothing wrongfully occupies the infinite stage of life for too long, that's all – διδόναι γὰρ αὐτὰ δίκην καὶ τίσιν ἀλλήλοις τῆς ἀδικίας κατὰ τὴν τοῦ χρόνου τάξιν. . . ."[12] The understanding of justice that issues from the pure concept of liberal democratic law resonates in many respects with this tragic experience of existence. But it also resonates with a very different experience of existence, to which we shall turn presently. Before we do so, however, let us take a last look at how Aristotle endeavoured to retreat from this tragic vision.

Aristotle "saved the phenomena" from the anarchic and aimless "ups and downs" of the pre-Socratic philosophers, we saw in Chapter 2. He did so through a distinction between potentiality and actuality that endowed reality with intrinsic and essential potentialities. These essential potentialities allowed them and caused them to become what they must become. This is how Aristotle "turned" futile anarchic existence into the good order of which good law – *nomos* – is the natural governmental reflection. He also did so, we saw, in the hope of saving Athens from the ruin it faced at the hands of the Sophists, a group of philosophers whom he may well have considered new representatives of the old pre-Socratic way of thinking in terms of which all becoming was determined by external causation or the playing out of superior forces.

9 Dworkin 2011, p. 419.
10 Heraclitus, frag. 24 in Diels 1912, I, p. 82.
11 Heraclitus, frag. 20 in Diels 1912, I, p. 82.
12 Aniximandros, frag. 9 in Diels 1912, I, p. 15.

Did it work? Did Aristotle save the phenomena, and did he save Athens, Athens' eternal virtue and law? Perhaps right now is not a good time to ask the question. After the total disaster of the first half of the twentieth century, it would appear that the human race has used the couple of decades of relative sanity that followed mostly for purposes of greedily ruining the ecological system on which it depends. If there is a goal or *telos* that would seem reasonable to attribute to a common humanity, saving the Earth from the human being's insatiable preferential ethics would surely seem to be the strongest contender. However, sincere, dedicated and determined endorsement of this one arguably "common" human aspiration and interest is not even remotely on the cards, as things stand towards the end of the second decade of the twenty first century. It does not make much sense to talk about "saved phenomena" when the disaster that threatens the "phenomena" is not even commonly recognised. And Athens? Athens delivered itself into the hands of a foreign emperor not long after Aristotle died, and many Greeks will confirm to this very day that that fateful development has never been significantly reversed.

It is against this bleak background that Agamben's suggestion that Aristotle's potentiality-actuality distinction must be re-thought fundamentally (quoted in full in Chapter 4, Section 3) appears highly justified. It is not always totally clear where Agamben aims to go with his undoubtedly profound and original insights and observations. His little book *State of Exception* makes a strong case that the murder-ous totalitarianisms of the twentieth century can be linked to the collapse of the potentiality-actuality distinction, that is, to the collapse of its political theoreti-cal equivalent, the *auctoritas-potestas* distinction. This argument should certainly be considered seriously. However, it is in his commentary on Saint Paul that one finds, from the perspective of the pursuit developed in this book, the most suggestive articulation of how the potentiality-actuality distinction should be re-articulated. It is here that Agamben develops the Pauline thought regarding the way the Christian community should live under the law, as if not – *hōs mē* – under the law.

This thought is highly suggestive for the concept of liberal democratic law, the contours of which must have become manifest by now. If the law is to be con-sidered a reflection of divided life, of life that is not embodied in any substantive *nomos* or natural law, living by the law – accepting its constraints, doing what it commands – can no longer be considered the destiny of life. Saint Paul's *hōs mē* articulates a dual relation to law. It recognises the law's constraints on life, but does not consider those constraints to affect the deep freedom of life not to identify itself with them. This then is what one gets when one severs the link between law and life: Life that is essentially free from law, despite being constrained by it.

This dual relation between law and life can of course only be sustained as long as the law respects it. The law can only do this as long as it respects the boundary between the inner and outer freedom of the legal subject, as Kant put it in his gen-eral definition of law. In this definition of law, Kant himself articulated the divided nature of life – or freedom – in clear terms. And as we saw in Chapter 7, this is exactly where visions of reconciled and unified life begins to gain the upper hand in Hegel's *Grundlinien*. This is where this formidable text starts retreating from the profound insights articulated in its sublime Introduction. This is also where the concept of liberal democratic law decisively takes leave of Hegel and returns to the Kant that he honoured so brilliantly in so many other respects. And this is, of course, why it also considers Hart's rule theory of law as one of the most profound inspirations for the concept of liberal democratic law. We saw in Chapter 8 that Hart considered the rule theory of law – for sound reasons – applicable to any system of law that functioned as a system of primary and secondary rules, even non-democratic and non-liberal legal systems. However, his insistence on the distinction between law and morality, and on the need for jurisprudence to recognise the complex reality of law – the reality that the law is always suspended in a tension between internal and external perspectives on it – surely constitutes two of the core insights that inform the concept of liberal democratic law. The resonance between Kant and Hart's conceptions of law on both these points is abundantly evident. This is what makes them the pioneering champions of the concept of liberal democratic law that they have been made out to be in this book. And here we must once more add Hans Kelsen, whose conception of liberal democracy in terms of the sustenance of minority and majority opinions – as opposed to truth convictions – goes to the very heart of the concept. In Chapter 6 we also read this Kantian and Kelsenian foundations of liberal democracy into Rousseau's understanding of the social contract.

Rousseau, Kant, Hart and Kelsen must, in view of the reading of them presented here, be considered thinkers who re-articulated Aristotle's potentiality-actuality distinction fundamentally. They did so because of the way their concepts of law pivoted on a regard for the split condition of life that never culminates in fullness; the split condition of human existence that gives rise to endless possibilities – indeed "one damn thing after another" – without any prospect of actualising an intrinsic and essential potentiality. In these theories of law, potentiality becomes a completely undefined and open potentiality that contains nothing that can be actualised. This understanding of life's relation to law has very specific implications for the way law – as a system of rules – relates to its application. Legal rules do not enter their application. They are terminated by their application. Application of the rule is very definitely not its completion, as Gadamer suggests, and for which suggestion Agamben appears to commend him.[13] Legal rules are therefore not determined potentialities that can be actualised. If they are potentialities at all, legal rules are open potentialities – sheer possibilities – that no application can determine for good. That is also why they are interminably amenable to the facilitation and articulation of legal disputes. This is the one point where Hart's conception of the legal rule stands to be corrected, we argued in Chapter 8. A rule does not consist of a clear core and a penumbra of uncertainty, of which the latter requires the judge to resort to discretion. A rule consists of language – usually adequately clear language – that invites disputation and facilitates it.[14]

13 See Gadamer 1975, p. 315; Agamben 2005a, p. 40.
14 See the reference to Lyotard 1983 in Chapter 8, fn. 29.

By inviting and facilitating disputation, the rule gives rise to something that takes place beyond itself. The dispute is about the rule, but the dispute does not enter the rule, and the rule never enters the dispute. There is no communicative transition from the rule to its application. The law does not come alive in its application, as Pound suggests, it dies there, and lives on elsewhere. This "lives on" is only a manner of speaking. The concept of liberal democratic law actually demands that we refrain completely from this biological and vitalistic idiom. It demands that we avoid talking about the "life of the law" and "living law" as far as it is feasible to do so (see the discussion of Ehrlich, Pound and the American Realists in Chapter 7, Section 3). Kelsen's concept of normative validation explains this "continuing elsewhere" of the law beyond legal practice instructively. Of concern is again his methodological distinction between *gesetzt* and *vorausgesetzt*, posited and presupposed. The law is never posited. It is always only presupposed. The law's continuing existence can only be presupposed. "It lives on" in this presupposition. That is why this "living on" is always "elsewhere." The realm of presupposition is a separate realm. It does not mix with the realm of legal application.

This separate existence of the law is undoubtedly *ethereal*, as Hugo Preuß observed with reference to Kelsen and the Austrian School of jurisprudence.[15] It is indeed an ethereal substance – if it can be called that – that we have been distilling from the heavy materials of the West's enduring metaphysics of life and law, this "biological metaphysics," as Macintyre aptly puts it.[16] It is something other than life. We do not really know what it is. Whatever it is, whatever the law is, can only be studied and contemplated in isolation from its applications, as Agamben observes with reference to Kafka (rather contradicting his earlier endorsement of Gadamer's view of legal understanding as application).[17] This profound insight also inspires Kafka's sublime parable *Before the Law*.[18]

Saint Paul's *hōs mē* instruction to the Christians in Rome contemplated a postponement of the reconciliation of law and life to the end of time. It left the reconciliation of the torn state of terrestrial life up to God, and to the return of the Messiah. Put in Aristotelian terms alien to it, the *hōs mē* construction entrusted the actualisation of life's full potential to the Messiah. That is how it stabilised the potentiality-actuality constellation. It took actualisation out of the hands of human beings, hands that are so prone to false actualisation. It thus sidestepped the whole problem of agency and order that we have highlighted with reference to Schmitt. It delivered the full actualisation of order into the hands of God's grace and wisdom. Because of its strong Messianism, it was perhaps significantly more Judaic than Christian. Saint Paul was the one who wrote in Greek but spoke Yiddish, observed Jacob Taubes (see Chapter 4, Section 4).

15 See Chapter 9, fn. 18.
16 See Macintyre 1985, pp. 58, 148, 162, 196.
17 Agamben 2005a, p. 63. See fn. 13 above.
18 See Chapter 8, fn. 32.

Given that we have premised the concept of liberal democratic law on a secure separation of potentiality and actuality, one should consider it poised between the two historical examples that could inform this separation, the pre-Socratic and the Judaeo-Christian. The long history of the latter from which it will never be able to extract itself fully, prevents it from contemplating a return to the former, should it ever wish to do so. The historical entrenchment of typical human rights values such as the inviolability of the dignity and integrity of the person that liberal democracy inherited from the Judaeo-Christian tradition,[19] and from which it will in all likelihood not withdraw its commitment in the foreseeable future, prevents it from returning to the innocent cruelty that the Greeks still displayed with relish, not long before Socrates.

Liberal democracy's Christian history will not allow it to return to the heroic age of the Greeks, but it is highly unlikely that its long and continuing immersion in Christianity will ever erase its memory of the singular beauty of the unforgiving world that once was Homer's. An example of Homer's cruel imagination had already been cited in Chapter 3. For good measure, consider also the following description of the death of Sarpedon in the *Iliad*, as translated by one whom Jürgen Habermas once called "a real Greek":

> Patroklos then made his second cast, and the weapon left his hand with flawless aim. He hit his enemy on the diaphragm, the broad muscle on which throbs the human soul. Sarpedon fell like an oak falls, like the tall pine to the sharp axe he toppled and just his hands fluttered like small wings clutching at the bloodied earth.[20]

It is, however, not only liberal democracy's immersion in Christian values that prevents it from returning to Homer's cruel world. Modern technology has turned warfare into a mechanism of mindless mass murder and maiming that forbids any sane person from contemplating it as a scene of heroic beauty. Here lies one more disconcerting question that the long engagement with Schmitt's narrative in *Der Nomos der Erde* in Chapter 2 has not yet addressed. Towards the end of the book, Schmitt addresses the phenomenon of weapons of mass destruction, but does so by inverting the problematic of modern military conflict with another astounding mystification. He attributes the sudden availability of weapons of mass destruction to the criminalisation of war in the wake of World War I. The fact that enemies would henceforth consider one another criminally responsible for the war, instead of considering one another reciprocally as *just* enemies in a *just* conflict that conceptually eliminates all questions of fault, demanded from them the total destruction of the other. This total destruction, in turn, demanded the development of

---

19 See Moyn 2015, p. 9; 2012, pp. 25–26.
20 Translated into English by Emilios Christodoulidis from Homer and Maronitis 2010, p. 99. The translation is taken with gracious permission from an unpublished essay by Christodoulidis on Simone Weil.

weapons of mass destruction. This is Schmitt's clear suggestion when he asks rhetorically with reference to Hegel:

> We recall one of Hegel's claims, namely that during the transition from feudalism to absolutism humanity needed gunpowder, *and immediately it was there*. Should modern means of destruction also be there because modern man needs them?[21]

If this construal of Schmitt's thinking is right, he was evidently purposefully blind to the possibility that the inverse of the causal relation invoked here provides a much more plausible explanation for the development of international law in the wake of World War I. Warfare was criminalised then because of the mind-shattering realisation that modern technology had turned warfare into practices of indiscriminate slaughter that had nothing in common with anything that warfare may have meant before the age of mechanisation. We have it from Huizinga that warfare is an expression of the human being's need to play.[22] This may or may not have been true for wars fought before the nineteenth century, but it is very definitely no longer true for wars fought since then. Anyone who still considers warfare a game must be contemplating a game for techno-psychopaths, and not for heroic warriors of whom "[the broad muscle of the diaphragm still throbbed with a human soul]." This is one of the most important reasons why the liberal democratic severance of the link between potentiality and actuality can no longer take instruction from the ancient Greek version of this separation.

There is, moreover, another crucial reason for not contemplating the heroic age of the Greeks as an option in this day and age. The Earth can no longer sustain the sheer hubris that conditioned the heroic ethics of the Homeric age. A similar hubris has for much too long driven the capitalist economies of the world to ravage the Earth. The planet that hosts us is in dire need of intensive care, something akin to Judaeo-Christian care,[23] something akin to the very *katechon* that Schmitt identified as the *nomos* of the Middle Ages, but never really contemplated as the careful and caring fending off of evil and dismal death for as long possible. As Chapter 5 made crystal clear, the *katechon* that Schmitt contemplated was little more than a justification of the heroic antics of medieval kings and princes. The *katechon* that liberal democracy contemplates does not entail or concern a *nomos*. It does not have a truth to protect. It does not consider the *katechon* of care a new truth or a new *nomos*. It cannot furnish it with any scientific proof or theological or cosmological argument. But it surely considers it a sound and worthy foundational presupposition. So it just

21 Schmitt 2006b, p. 321.
22 See Huizinga 2016, pp. 89–104.
23 There may well be several other religions that also contemplate this elementary imperative of care as its key concern, and the economical reference to Judaeo-Christian care is not meant to exclude any of them.

cares, cares for the sake of giving everyone as much time as possible for holding on to whatever *nomos* or truth they happen to fancy.[24]

## 7 Law as legislation

It is another consequence of the split condition of life that *presupposed law* – ethereal as it is – *requires positing*, multiple acts of positing, in fact. The relation between presupposed and positive or posited law does not concern either a transition, or an incarnation or embodiment. It concerns the design and insertion of an artifice (for and into a gap that cannot be closed).[25] Just as the legal rule does not enter its application, presupposed law does not enter posited law. Positive law is the register of presupposed law, but it is the register of its non-entry, and non-entries. The format of this register is *legislation*. From the perspective of liberal democratic law, legislation is the principal format of law, and all law is in principle legislation. The key point here is that all non-legislative forms of law – customary law and judicial decisions – only remain law as long as positive legislation tolerates them as law. This recognition of the legislative status of all positive law has vast significance for judicial methodology which we cannot explore further in what follows.[26] It is the legal theoretical understanding of legislation as the register of the gap between life and law that concerns us here. Two key features of liberal democratic legislation – which is typically parliamentary legislation – testify to the gap between law and life. The first is its irreducible reversibility. The second concerns the procedure of promulgation.

The reversibility of ordinary legislation testifies to a principled recognition that legislative measures have no ontological depth. They are nominalist constructions. They have and can have no pretension to effect definitive and enduring connections between law and life, not even for the duration of their validity. Enduring validity is not a sign of deep legitimacy.[27] It is a function of the length of time that the disconnection between legislation and life remains inconspicuous enough not to irritate.

Liberal democratic promulgation of legislation ensures legislation's disconnectedness from life. The liberal democratic demand that legislation remains an outcome of rational majority-minority relations precludes the comprehensive legislative enactment of any specific instance of life at the complete cost of another. Called upon to adequately represent both majorities and minorities, liberal democratic legislation

---

24  See Van der Walt 2019.
25  This phrase is indebted to insightful comments on this point by Frank Michelman, Cambridge, Massachusetts, 27 March 2019. See in this regard also the reference to Lyotard 1983 in Chapter 8, fn. 30.
26  For a previous engagement with the implications with the methodological insistence that all law is legislation, see Van der Walt 2014b, pp. 366–367.
27  Hence the argument that liberal constitutional review does not concern a legitimation but a de-legitimation of legislation. See Van der Walt 2015a.

must betray both. This is what was meant by the statement – in Chapter 9, Section 1 – that legislation is not the actualisation or teleological fulfilment of any truth claim or conviction. It is not the fulfilment of anyone's truth, but the compromise that constantly displaces, dislodges and uproots all comprehensive truth claims.

That this is so is underlined by the astoundingly arbitrary voting procedures that conclude democratic legislation. Despite what one may think at first, these voting procedures do not link law to life, but delink it from life. We vote on something when it has become clear that our intuitions and convictions about matters that concern everyone are not shared by everyone. We vote when we cannot identify the correct or true way to deal with the issues of life that we need to settle. Seen from this perspective, the voting procedures that conclude liberal democratic legislation effectively confirm the gap that opens up between the reality of life and the intuitions or convictions regarding this reality that become manifest in the face of division. Anyone who considers incidental majority positions that come out of a voting procedure (which experience has shown to be irredeemably vulnerable to rapid reversal) the correct assessment of what is to be done is deeply deluded about the dynamics of voting procedures and surely not a liberal democrat. Liberal democrats do not consider majorities "right" and minorities "wrong." They find the idea that a highly contingent majority vote can restore the link with life ridiculous. The liberal democratic demand that majorities and minorities remain equally worthy of respect exacts an unwavering regard for the irreducible ignorance of both.

It should now be clear why the great stand-off between Hegel and Savigny constitutes an exceptional point of reference in the distillation procedure from which we extracted the pure concept of liberal democratic law. On the one count it takes sides entirely with Hegel's endorsement of legislation as the principal format of modern law. This, in any case, is how it understands his epochal rebuke of Savigny's resistance to the codification of German law. The Pandectist conception of the law was premised on the historical and national-spiritual (*volksgeistliche*) embodiment and incarnation of law. This "historical conception" of law was deeply organic and naturalistic, much more so than it was "historical." From the perspective of liberal democratic law, history – or the instance of history – is better understood as the moment of diffraction that reveals the gap between life and law which the metaphysics of life and law covers up (without ever closing it). This diffraction appeared to be upfront in Hegel's mind when he worked on his *Differenz Schrift* and on the Introduction to the *Grundlinien*, as we have pointed out above. But this was just one side of his thinking. On the other side, history was no longer the history of diffraction, but the history of a sweeping spiritual reconciliation that overcame and erased diffraction. From the latter perspective, he must have considered legislation the vehicle for this grand historical reconciliation. It is on this count that liberal democracy lost Hegel, notwithstanding his spirited objection to an anti-democratic revival of Roman law that was hopelessly out of touch with the great historical diffraction of the nineteenth century that was ripping the bourgeois conception of modernity into pieces (see Chapter 6, Section 4).

It is also on this point that liberal democracy lost Hermann Heller, who attributed the decay of the *Rechtsstaat* during the Weimar Republic to the rise of a technical understanding of legislation that severed its relation with the "Absolute . . . foundation and abyss of life" – *seine Beziehung zum Absolutem, zum tragenden Grund und Abgrund des Lebens.* Kelsen's pure theory of law – and the depleted nomocracy *(entleerte Nomokratie)* for which it stands – was once again the handy scapegoat. This empty nomocracy contributed significantly, contended Heller, to the rising fascination with dictatorship among the youth of his time, searching as they were for reality and ethical rootedness – *einer nach sittlichen Begründungen suchenden und wirlickkeitshungrigen Jugend.*[28] The concept of legislation envisaged in Heller's melancholic yearning for a time replete with deeper meaning is not the concept of liberal democratic legislation contemplated in this book. The legislation contemplated here is all too aware of its Protagorian unrootedness (see Chapter 3, Section 4), all too aware that it is nothing but the invention of a human measure in the absence of any other available measures. Liberal democratic legislation is a human and humane measure taken in response to insurmountable political differences that render invocations of the "absolute foundation of life" meaningless.

Put in terms that we have developed with reference to Claude Lefort (see Introduction, Section 3 and Chapter 6, Section 2), liberal democratic legislation is nothing but an intelligent response to irresolvable differences of opinion. It ignores appeals to deeper convictions. It offers no response to the difference between the symbolic and the real. Liberal democratic legislation does not tell anyone that he or she is wrong for having opinions and preferences that conflict with its coercive terms. It simply asks everyone to respect those coercive terms as the outcome of a legitimate legislative procedure and a "legitimately" won right to govern. This also explains why liberal democratic legislation is in principle accompanied by judicial review procedures that unflinchingly respect the right to govern and to pass coercive legislation, but nevertheless prevent the coercive terms of legislation from intruding more than is rationally necessary into the right to think, prefer and exist differently. The liberal democratic legislation envisaged here can learn much from the acute insights that Jeremy Waldron develops in this regard.[29]

## 8 The distilled concept defined

We have arrived at the point where we can proceed to define the concept of liberal democratic law. We shall do so now by first offering a provisional definition, then stepping back to reflect on it, and then stepping forward again to offer a conclusive definition that registers also these last round of reflections. So let's begin with the provisional definition:

> *Liberal democratic law consists of an anomic, unnatural, inorganic, nominalist and non-spiritual system of non-actualisable legislative rules that govern, reflect and sustain the divided life of the societies that they serve.*

28  Heller 1992, pp. 450–451.
29  Waldron 1999a, 1999b.

Stepping back now to see what we have really been up to in the chapters of this book, we should immediately feel struck by considerable incredulity. This thing is not going to fly. Ethereal as it undoubtedly is, it may just drift off and evaporate. If an elixir is to be salvaged from it – the Merriam Webster defines "elixir" as "a substance held capable of prolonging life indefinitely"[30] – some compensation for its lifelessness and other-worldliness would have to be contemplated and duly registered in the definition itself. The first thing that comes to mind in this regard concerns the basic needs of life. This ethereal "substance" or notion will evaporate instantly in any society where the basic demands and expectations of physical life are not served adequately. Widespread hunger and physical neediness invariably feed a range of unforgiving political reactions that claim to be "rooted in the life of the people." These reactions are bound to crush the liberal democracy we are contemplating with little delay. Our concern with uprooting liberal democratic law from life dare not turn us into Arendtians who consider politics unconcerned with the needs and demands of life.[31] We must therefore include a reference to "adequate provision of socio economic needs" in our definition if we want it to fly.[32]

Socio-economic needs, however, are not the only nagging aspect of life that can wreck the ethereal concept of liberal democratic law that we have distilled from the heavy materials of metaphysics. The undeniable and often dismal reality of sheer human cruelty, aggression and obsessiveness that invariably underpins all illiberal politics of truth and conviction are often linked to socio-economic pressures. This reality, however, cannot be explained exhaustively with reference to socio-economic pressures. It also has a separate existence that the theory of liberal democratic law must take seriously on its own terms.[33] It is in this regard that we need to return to the acute insight in Schmitt's *Der Nomos der Erde* alluded to above. That insight is contained in the disconcerting "unburdening" or *Entlastung* function that he attributes to the amity line. According to Schmitt, the amity line cured European warfare of unruly aggression and cruelty by allowing for the complete unleashing of this cruelty of aggression on non-European peoples, and even on fellow Europeans, on the far side of the amity line. This exportation of aggression and cruelty to far away war zones may very well still be the banal reality of many military conflicts

---

30 https://www.merriam-webster.com/dictionary/elixir
31 See Christodoulidis 2011, Van der Walt 2012. For a firm counter-argument that Arendt recognised the political significance of socio-economic concerns, see Gündoğdu 2015, pp. 126–163.
32 See Van der Walt 2014b, pp. 390–400 and 2015b, pp. 307–309 for further discussions of this concern. The position that I have taken up to now, against the earlier Michelman and later Rawls and with the earlier Rawls and later Michelman position (they both took leave of their own and took over one another's earlier positions in their later work) was that a court should not adjudicate social economic rights unless the case "self-evidently" calls for judicial intervention. This "self-evidently" has been left rather undefined up to now and it is one of the points that will have to be worked out further in the planned monograph on *Liberal Democratic Judicial Review* (see fn. 2 above). Here, however, is a point of self-evidence with which one can begin: If socio-economic pressures become an obvious and overwhelming threat to the dis-embodied liberal democracy that we have described here, it may well be time – as long as there is still time – for the judiciary to call the government to order.
33 See Van der Walt 2019.

today, but the normative order associated with liberal democracy no longer permits acknowledgement of this reality as an essential constitutive factor of the civil order that liberal democracy envisages. To the extent that it aspires to never again permit itself to rely on the perpetration of atrocity as a transcendental condition of its civility, liberal democracy would need to duly consider all remaining instances of such atrocity as aberrations that demand eradication, however hypocritical this demand will often appear.[34]

The critical challenge that liberal democracy faces in this regard is, however, much more daunting than the mere eradication of "military indiscipline" that violates the rules of "civilised warfare" by "foot soldiers" on foreign shores. Several factors have to be considered in this regard. The first concerns the very real likelihood of major military operations conducted by supposedly "civilised" and "gentlemanly" commanders in chief falling prey to "military indiscipline." John Rawls' discussion of the bombings of Dresden, Hiroshima and Nagasaki alerts one to a case in point.[35] The generals that fought Europe's "gentlemanly" wars between equal sovereigns from the sixteenth to the nineteenth centuries cannot be assumed to have always been thoroughly disciplined in their strategies and commands. But the state of the art of military technology surely contributed significantly to the containment or *Hegung* of these wars that Schmitt stressed so ceaselessly in *Der Nomos der Erde*. The state of contemporary military technology has, on the contrary, turned the slightest military indiscipline into potential humanitarian disasters. Liberal democracy cannot convincingly continue to assimilate such disasters under the heading of incidental "collateral damage" in the way the gentlemanly generals of the sixteenth to nineteenth century may have been able to. It is for this reason that warfare as such, and not just some of its practices, has become a dimension of human conduct that liberal democracy should basically consider proscribed as far as it is feasible to do so.

This "feasibility" has obvious limits that will indefinitely burden the normative claims of liberal democracies with their own sets of equivocations and functional hypocrisies. However, predictable constraints on the human being's ability to avoid war are not the main predicament that the theory of liberal democracy faces in this regard. The main predicament is this: Both the successful abolition of war and the continuation of war under conditions of mechanised and computerised warfare will deprive human existence of the libidinal release that ritual warfare may have offered it in earlier times. That this is so in the case of abolition speaks for itself, but it is also true with regard to the mechanisation and computerisation of war. Mechanisation and computerisation increasingly turn military action into ultra-long-distance and on-screen elimination and destruction practices. Wars fought in this manner deprive societies of the effective export channels for human cruelty and aggression that earlier societies can plausibly be argued to have found in war. If war was an important game for earlier societies,

34 Let us in this regard never forget John Le Carré's poignant observation that "hypocrisy is the tribute that vice pays to virtue." See Le Carré 2013, p. 54.
35 Rawls 1999, p. 99–101.

as Huizinga (and Smend![36]) claims, it has now become a game that is either too destructive to play, on the one hand, or too devoid of the characteristics of gaming and playing, on the other. Under these circumstances, liberal democracies may well be in dire need of cultural practices that can substitute the constitutive role that the bravery of ancient warriors played in the effective separation of military and civilian order, the separation that rendered not only the former but also the latter possible (see the discussion in Chapter 3, Section 2).

Heller, we saw above, explained the rising fascination with dictatorship among the Weimar youth with reference to their "search for reality and ethical rootedness." In the paragraph that follows this explanation, he also referred to a civil society that is betraying its spiritual essence and throwing itself into the arms of an irrational neo-feudalism – *es verleugnet sein geistiges Sein und wirft sich einem irrationalistischen Neo-Feudalismus in die Arme*. At this point a profound insight struck him from which the theory of liberal democracy can and must take instruction. He started to describe this irrational neo-feudalism in terms of Nietzsche's "supermen" who, from time to time, have to conduct themselves like predators set free to commit the worst of atrocities as if they were student pranks, so that poets would have new material for their poetry and songs of praise – *daß die Dichter für lange nun wieder etwas zu singen und rühmen haben.*[37]

The question with which Heller's vision of a return of an irrational and cruel neo-feudalism in the time of the Weimar Republic leaves the theory of liberal democracy is this one: Will the liberal democracy of the future have to rely on poetry and literature, not to record the great deeds of warriors, but to literally take their place? Can we sidestep the neo-feudalism by just having the poetry? May poetry itself become "the diaphragm, the broad muscle on which throbs the human soul," able to take and absorb the blow of Patroklos so as to sustain the liberal democratic state in which there will no longer be heroes, as Hegel already observed in the *Grundlinien*? Must societies that aspire to be or become liberal democracies sever the political and the poetic, so that poetry would henceforth no longer burden politics with a need for reality, as in Heller's constellation, but unburden it? And if so, would one not then need to understand this severance of the poetic from the political along the lines of the distinction between the poetic and the political drawn with reference to Sophocles and Protagoras in Chapter 3, Sections 3 and 4? Might poetry (in a wide range of versions ranging from the avant garde to the most popular that cannot be explored here[38]) thus come to figure as a zone of absolute freedom – the only zone of absolute freedom – that could unburden liberal democracy from liberty's taste for chaos and cruelty?

---

36 Smend 2010, pp. 151, 161, emphasising the play element of conflict and criticising the naïve pacifism articulated during the negotiation of the Treaty of Versailles in a way that brings him quite close to Schmitt's "just war" arguments in *Der Nomos der Erde*.

37 Heller 1992, pp. 451–452.

38 This will be part of the future work envisaged in fn. 42 below.

That the answer to this question – in all the variations that we have put it – may well be affirmative is the clear suggestion that one draws from Johan Huizinga's description of the insurmountable limits that attach to the feudal celebration of war as a noble and sacred game. Huizinga writes:

> The noble life is seen as an exhilarating game of courage and honour. Unfortunately, even in archaic surroundings, war with its grimness and bitterness offers but scant occasion for this noble game to become a reality. Bloody violence cannot be caught in any great extent in truly noble form; hence the game can only be fully experienced and enjoyed as a social and aesthetic fiction.[39]

Huizinga's suggestion is evidently that poetry – aesthetic fiction – can serve life's yearning for an ennobled reality better than any melancholic political pursuit of this reality can ever hope to do. A parallel insight can be drawn from Agamben's description of messianic yearning in *The Time that Remains*. The Christian community, he suggests, awaits the compensation for a postponed life in the form of God's justice. God's justice will redeem the faithful at the end of time. The wait, however, is terribly long and in need of interim relief. The *hōs mē*, this *living as if not living*, is a divided life, a half-life that cannot be lived fully. It can wait until God fulfils life at the end of time, but it needs interim redemption and interim fulfilment. The only interim redemption plausible, Agamben appears to suggest with reference to Dostoyevsky's *The Idiot*, is poetry.[40] This poetic relief, however, is not only a relief from the *hōs mē*. It also sustains it. It sustains this half-life that cannot be lived fully.[41]

We have passed over these thoughts all too quickly. They pose more questions than they answer, questions that will remain unanswered until we have studied the relation between liberal democracy and aesthetic fiction more incisively.[42] They can nevertheless no longer be ignored and we shall therefore allow them to inform the definition of the concept of liberal democratic law at which we have arrived for now. Therefore, in view of the reflections we have added in the wake of our preliminary definition ventured above, we must now conclude our distillation process with this one:

> *Liberal democratic law consists of an anomic, unnatural, inorganic, nominalist and non-spiritual system of non-actualisable but adequately socialist legislative rules that govern, reflect and sustain the divided life of societies that manage to sustain sufficiently forceful poetic fictions to compensate for the grey lack of heroism that they will have to endure during the time that remains.*

---

39  Huizinga 2016, p. 101.
40  Agamben 2005b, pp. 39–40.
41  Agamben 2011, pp. 234–239.
42  I aim to do this in a third monograph on liberal democracy with the envisaged title *Law, Literature and Liberal Democracy*. See Van der Walt 2014a and 2015b for preliminary studies.

The question is no longer whether or not this thing will ever fly. It probably won't. It has never really flown in the past. To the extent that it may become or remain airborne, it will probably just drift up and away like it has always done. This is what Böckenförde and Lefort have been telling us all along. Liberal democracy is an ethereal vapour that cannot be salvaged. The concept of liberal democratic law may be reasonably well distilled now, but the distilled concept remains the concept of something that resists distillation.

So the question is not whether this thing will fly or not. The question is only whether the concept is well distilled and accurately defined. For if it is, it surely underlines the insurmountable odds that one would always be facing were one to commit oneself to liberal democracy and liberal democratic law in the time that remains to do so. True liberal democrats will probably not be daunted by these odds. They will just face them. They will entertain no illusions of realisable glory. They will just press on, and even soldier on if they must, like the *Soldiers of Salamis*.[43] Perhaps some of them will just be thankful that there are other things that can be distilled.

43 The reference is to Cercas 2004.

# BIBLIOGRAPHY[1]

Adkins, A. W. H. (1973). 'ἀρετή, τέχνη, Democracy and Sophists: Protagoras 316b–328d', *The Journal of Hellenic Studies*, 3–12.

Adorno, T. et al. (1984). *Positivismusstreit in der deutschen Soziologie,* Darmstadt: Luchterhand.

Agamben, G. (1998). *Homo Sacer: Sovereign Power and Bare Life*, Stanford, CA: Stanford University Press.

Agamben, G. (1999). *Potentialities*, Stanford, CA: Stanford University Press.

Agamben, G. (2005a). *State of Exception*, Chicago: University of Chicago Press.

Agamben, G. (2005b). *The Time that Remains*, Stanford, CA: Stanford University Press.

Agamben, G. (2011). *The Kingdom and the Glory*, Stanford, CA: Stanford University Press.

Anouilh, J. (2000). *Antigone*, London: Methuen.

Aquinas, T. (1975). *Summa Theologiae 38*, Cambridge: Blackfriars.

Arato, A. (2000). *Civil Society, Constitution, and Legitimacy*, Lanham, MD: Rowman & Littlefield.

Arato, A. (2010). 'Post-Sovereign Constitution-Making in Hungary: After Success, Partial Failure and now What?', *South African Journal on Human Rights* 26(1), 19–44.

Arendt, H. (1958). *The Human Condition*, Chicago: University of Chicago Press.

Arendt, H. (1963). *On Revolution*, New York: Penguin Books.

Arendt, H. (1970). *On Violence*, San Diego, New York and London: Harcourt Brace & Company.

Arendt, H. (1972). *Crises of the Republic*, New York: Harcourt Brace Jovanovich.

Aristotle. (1932[350]). *Politics*, Cambridge, MA: Harvard University Press.

Aristotle. (1933[350]). *Metaphysics Books I–IX (translation Hugh Tredennick)*, Cambridge, MA: Harvard University Press.

Aristotle. (1935[350]), *Metaphysics Books X–XIV*, Cambridge, MA: Harvard University Press.

Aristotle. (1938), *Categories*, Cambridge, MA: Harvard University Press.

Aristotle. (1989[340]). *Nicomachean Ethics*, Cambridge, MA: Harvard University Press.

Artaud, A. (1964). *Le Théâtre et son double*, Paris: Folio

---

1 When the date of the publication is followed by another date between square brackets, the latter date indicates the date or approximate date of the original publication.

Augustine. (1962[391]). *De Vera Religione*, Editores Pontifici.

Augustine. (1960[426]). *City of God*, Cambridge, MA: Harvard University Press.

Austin, J. (1861). *The Province of Jurisprudence Determined*, London: John Murray.

Behrends, O. (1989). 'Von der Freirechtsschule zum konkreten Ordnungsdenken', in Dreier, R. and Sellert, W. (eds), *Recht und Justiz im "Dritten Reich"*, pp. 34–79, Frankfurt am Main: Suhrkamp.

Benjamin, W. (1977[1921]). 'Kritik der Gewalt', in Benjamin, W., *Gesammelte Schriften II.1*, pp. 179–203, Frankfurt am Main: Suhrkamp.

Bentham, J. (1948[1789]), 'An Introduction to the Principles of Morals and Legislation', in Bentham, J., *A Fragment on Government with an Introduction to the Principles of Morals and Legislation*, Oxford: Basil Blackwell.

Bentham, J. (2002[1816]), 'Nonsense upon Stilts', in Schofield, P. et al. (eds), *The Collected Works of Jeremy Bentham*, Oxford: Oxford University Press.

Bentham, J. (2008), *A Comment on the Commentaries* [1928] *and A Fragment on Government* [1776], Oxford: Oxford University Press.

Blanchot, M. (1980), *L'Ecriture du désastre*, Paris: Gallimard.

Böckenförde, E-W., M. (1991). *Staat, Verfassung, Demokratie: Studien zur Verfassungstheorie und zum Verfassungsrecht*, Frankfurt am Main: Suhrkamp.

Böckenförde, E-W. (2016[1976]). *Staat, Gesellschaft, Freiheit. Studien zur Staatstheorie und zum Verfassungsrecht*, Frankfurt: Suhrkamp.

Bodin, J. (1986[1576]). *Les Six Livres de la République I*, Paris: Fayard.

Boyarin, D. (2012). 'Deadly Dialogue: Thucydides with Plato', *Representations* 117(1), 59–85.

Brandeis, L. (1916). 'The Living Law', *Illinois Law Review* X(7), 461–471.

Brophy, R., 1978, 'Deaths in the Pan-Hellenic Games: Arrachion and Creugas', *The American Journal of Philology* 99, 363–390.

Brophy, R. and Brophy M. (1985). 'Deaths in the Pan-Hellenic Games II: All Combative Sports', *The American Journal of Philology* 106(2), 171–198.

Calabresi, G. and Melamed, D. (1972), 'Property Rules, Liability Rules, and Inalienability: One View of the Cathedral', *Harvard Law Review* 85(6), 1089–1128.

Canning, J. (1996), *A History of Medieval Thought 300–1450*, London: Routledge.

Castoriadis, C. (2004). *Ce qui fait la Grèce, 1. D'Homère à Héraclite*, Paris: Seuil.

Castoriadis, C. (2008), *Ce que fait la Grèce, 2. La Cité et les lois*, Paris: Seuil.

Celan, P. (1983). 'Der Meridian', in Celan, *Gesammelte Werke III*, Frankfurt am Main: Suhrkamp,.

Cercas, J. (2004), *Soldiers of Salamis*, London: Bloomsbury Publishing.

Charlton, J. (2013). 'Russian man shot in quarrel over Immanuel Kant's philosophy', 17 September. Accessed January 2019. https://www.independent.co.uk/news/world/europe/russian-manshot-in-quarrel-over-immanuel-kant-s-philosophy-8820327.html.

Chiassoni, P. (2013). 'Wiener Realism', in Duarte d'Almeida, L. et al. (eds), *Kelsen Revisited*, Oxford and Portland, OR: Hart Publishing.

Christensen, R. and Fischer-Lescano, A. (2007). *Das Ganze des Rechts – Vom hierarchischen zum reflexiven Verstandnis deutscher und europaischer Grundrechte*, Berlin: Duncker & Humblot.

Christodoulidis, E. (2011). 'Depoliticising Poverty: Arendt in South Africa', *Stellenbosch Law Review* 22(3), 501–520.

Coase, R. (1960). 'The Problem of Social Cost', *The Journal of Law and Economics* 3, 1–44.

Cohen, F. (1935). 'Transcendental Nonsense and the Functional Approach', *Columbia Law Review* 35(6), 809–849.

Coing, H. (1962). *Zur Geschichte des Privatrechtsystems*, Frankfurt am Main: Vittorio Klostermann.

Coleman, J. (1984). 'Economics and the Law: A Critical Review of the Foundations of the Economic Approach to Law', *Ethics* 94(4), 649–679.

Coplestone, F. (1972). *A History of Medieval Philosophy*, London: Methuen & Co.

Cornell, D. et al., (eds). (1991). *Hegel and Legal Theory*, New York and London: Routledge.

Crimmins, J. (1986), 'Bentham on Religion: Atheism and the Secular Society', *Journal of the History of Ideas* 47(1), 95–110.

Crimmins, J. (1990). *Secular Utilitarianism. Social Science and the Critique of Religion in the Thought of Jeremy Bentham*, Oxford: Oxford University Press.

Derrida, J. (1985). 'PRÉJUGES. Devant la loi', in Derrida, J. et al., *La Faculté de juger*, pp. 87–139, Paris: Les Editions de Minuit.

Diels, H. (1912). *Die Fragmente der Vorsokratiker I, II, III*, Berlin: Weidmannsche Buchhandlung.

Drees, L. (1968), *Olympia. Gods, Artists and Athletes*, London: Pall Mall Press.

Durfee, H. (1976). 'Austin and Phenomenology', in Durfee H. (ed.), *Analytic Philosophy and Phenomenology. American University Publications in Philosophy, Vol 2.*, Dordrecht: Springer.

Dworkin, R . (1978). *Taking Rights Seriously*, Cambridge, MA: Harvard University Press.

Dworkin, R. (1986). *Law's Empire*, Cambridge, MA: Harvard University Press.

Dworkin, R. (2011). *Justice for Hedgehogs*, Cambridge, MA and London: Harvard University Press.

Dyzenhaus, D. (2000). 'The Gorgon Head of Power: Heller and Kelsen on the Rule of Law', in Caldwell, P. and Scheuerman, W. (eds), *From Liberal Democracy to Fascism: Legal and Political Thought in the Weimar Republic,* pp. 20–46, Boston, Leiden and Cologne: Humanities Press.

Eder, W. (2005). 'The Political Significance of the Codification of Law in Archaic Societies: An Unconventional Hypothesis', in Raaflaub, K. (ed), *New Perspectives on the Conflict of the Orders*, pp. 239–267, Oxford: Blackwell Publishing.

Ehrlich, E. (1888). 'Ueber Lücken im Rechte', *Juristische Blatter* 17(38–53), 447–630.

Ehrlich, E. (1903). *Freie Rechtsfindung und freie Rechtswissenschaft,* Leipzig: Hirschfeld.

Ehrlich, E. (1916), 'Montesquieu and Sociological Jurisprudence', *Harvard Law Review* 29(6), 582–600.

Ehrlich, E. (1989[1913]). *Grundlegung der Soziologie des Rechts*, Berlin: Duncker & Humblot.

Ehrlich, E. (2002[1936]). *Fundamental Principles of the Sociology of Law,* London/New Brunswick: Transaction Publishers.

Eucken, W. (1952). *Grundsätze der Wirtschaftspolitik,* Tübingen: Mohr Siebeck.

Everett, F. (2003). *Backgrounds of Early Christianity*, Grand Rapids, MI: William B. Eerdmans Publishing.

Figgis, J. (1896). *The Theory of the Divine Right of Kings*, Cambridge: Cambridge University Press.

Forsythe, G. (2005). *A Critical History of Early Rome*, Berkeley and Los Angeles: University of California Press.

Freud, S. (1999[1921]). *Massenpsychologie und Ich-Analyse,* in Freud, S., *Gesammelte Werke XIII*, Frankfurt am Main: Fischer Taschenbuch Verlag.

Fuller, L. (1958). 'Positivism and Fidelity to Law – A Reply to Professor Hart', *Harvard Law Review* 71(4), 630–672.

Gabel, P. and Kennedy, D. (1984). 'Roll over Beethoven', *Stanford Law Review* 36, 1–55.

Gadamer, H-G. (1975). *Wahrheit und Methode,* Tübingen: JCB Mohr (Paul Siebeck).

Gardiner, E. (1930), *Athletics of the Ancient World*, Oxford: Oxford University Press.

Gény, F. (1932[1919]). *Méthode d'interprétation et sources en droit privé positif*, Paris: Librarie Générale du Droit et de Jurisprudence.

Geyer, C. (1982), 'Das Jahrhundert der Theodizee', *Kant-Studien* 73, 393–405.

Greene, W. (1936). 'Fate, Good, and Evil in Pre-Socratic Philosophy', *Harvard Studies in Classical Philology* 47, 85–129.

Grey, T. (1989). 'Holmes and Legal Pragmatism', *Stanford Law Review* 41(4), 787–870.

Grimm, D. (1995). 'Does Europe Need a Constitution?', *European Law Journal* 1(3), 282–302.

Grimm, D. (2016). *Europa ja – aber welches? Zur Verfassung der europäischen Demokratie*, München: C.H. Beck.

Grimm, D. (2017). *The Constitution of European Democracy*, Oxford: Oxford University Press.

Grotius, H. (1886). *De Iure Praedae*, The Hague: Martinum Nijhof.

Gündoğdu, A. (2015). *Rightlessness in an Age of Rights. Hannah Arendt and the Contemporary Struggles of Migrants*, New York: Oxford University Press.

Günther, F. (2005), 'Ein Jahrzehnt der Ruckbesinnung. Die bundesdeutsche Staatsrechtslehre zwischen Dezision und Integration in den funftiger Jahren', in Henne, T. and Riedlinger, A. (eds), *Das Lüth-Urteil aus (rechts-) historischer Sicht – Die Konflikte um Veit Harlan und die Grundrechtsjudikatur des Bundesverfassungsgerichts*, pp. 301–314, Berlin: Berliner Wissenschafts-Verlag.

Hart, H. L. A. (1958). 'Positivism and the Separation of Law and Morals', *Harvard Law Review* 71(4), 593–629.

Hart, H. L. A. (1961). *The Concept of Law*, Oxford: Clarendon Press.

Hart, H. L. A. (1968). *Punishment and Responsibility, Essays in the Philosophy of Law*, Oxford: Oxford University Press.

Hart, H. L. A. (1983). *Essays in Jurisprudence and Philosophy*, Oxford: Oxford University Press.

Hart, H. L. A. (2013). 'Discretion', *Harvard Law Review* 127(2), 652–665.

Hart, H. M. and Sacks, A. (1994). *The Legal Process* (ed. by Eskridge, W. and Frickey, P.), New York: Westbury.

Havelock, E. (1957). *The Liberal Temper in Greek Politics*, New Haven, CT: Yale University Press.

Hegel, G. (1970)'. *Werke in 20 Bänden*, Frankfurt am Main: Suhrkamp.

Heidegger, M. (1978). *Holzwege*, Frankfurt am Main: Vittorio Klostermann.

Heidegger, M. (1979[1927]). *Sein und Zeit*, Tubingen: Max Niemeyer Verlag.

Heidel, W. (1910). 'Περὶ Φύσεως. A Study of the Conception of Nature among the Pre-Socratics', *Proceedings of the American Academy of Arts and Sciences* 45(4), 79–133.

Heller, H. (1992). 'Recht, Staat, Macht', in Heller, H., *Gesammelte Schriften II*, Tübingen: J.C.B. Mohr (Paul Siebeck).

Herget, J. and Wallace, S. (1987). 'The German Free Law Movement as the Source of American Legal Realism', *Virginia Law Review* 73(2), 399–455.

Hirzel, R. (1907). *Themis, Dike und Verwandtes, ein Beitrag zur Geschichte der Rechtsidee bei den Griechen*, Leipzig: Verlag von S. Hirzel.

Hobbes, T. (1839). *Leviathan*, in Molesworth, W. (ed.), *The English Works of Thomas Hobbes of Malmesbury III*, London: John Bohn.

Homer. 1950[ca. 850]. *The Illiad (translation by E. V. Rieu)*, Harmondsworth and New York: Penguin Classics.

Homer. (2010). *Homer's Iliad, Vol II (translation into Modern Greek by D. N. Maronitis)*, Athens: Agra.

Horwitz, M. (1977). *The Transformation of American Law 1780–1860*, Cambridge, MA: Harvard University Press.

Horwitz, M . (1997). 'Why is Anglo-American Jurisprudence Unhistorical?', *Oxford Journal of Legal Studies* 17(4), 551–586.

Huber, E. (1951). 'Positionen und Begriffe: Eine Auseinandersetzung mit Carl Schmitt', *Zeitschrift fur die gesamte Staatswissenschaft* 101, 1–44.

Huizinga, J. (2016[1949]). *Homo Ludens. A Study of the Play-Element in Culture*, Kettering: Angelico Press.

Jaeger, W. (1936, 1944, 1947). *Paideia. Die Formung des griechischen Menschen I, II, III*, Berlin and Leipzig: Walter de Gruyter.

Jaeger, W. (1948). *Aristotle*, Oxford: Oxford University Press.

Jhering, R. von. (1894). *Geist des römischen Rechts auf den verschiedenen Stufen seiner Entwicklung II*, Leipzig: Breitkopf & Hartel.

Jhering, R. von. (1916[1877/1883]). *Der Zweck im Recht I,II*, Leipzig: Breitkopf & Hartel.

Jhering, R. von. (1924[1884]). *Scherz und Ernst in der Jurisprudenz*, Leipzig: Breitkopf & Hartel.

Jouanjan, O. (2018). 'Between Carl Schmitt, the Catholic Church, and Hermann Heller: On the Foundations of Democratic Theory in the Work of Ernst-Wolfgang Böckenförde', *Constellations* 25(2), 184–195.

Justinian. (2010[532]). *Corpus Iuris Civilis*. Clark: The Law Book Exchange.

Kafka, F. (2012). 'Vor dem Gesetz', in Kafka, F., *Gesammelte Werke*, pp. 154–155, Köln: Anaconda Verlag.

Kant, I. (1983). *Werke in 10 Bänden*, Darmstadt: Wissenschaftliche Buchgesellschaft.

Kantorowicz, E. (1997[1957]). *The King's Two Bodies: A Study in Mediaeval Political Theology*, Princeton, NJ: Princeton University Press.

Kantorowizc, H. (G. Flavius). (1906). *Der Kampf um die Rechtswissenschaft*, Heidelberg: Carl Winter's Universitätsbuchhandlung.

Kaser, M. (1971). *Das Römische Privatrecht I*, Munchen: C.H. Beck.

Kaupa, C. (2013). 'Maybe not Activist Enough? On the Court's Alleged Neoliberal Bias in its Recent Labor Cases', in Dawson, M. et al. (eds), *Judicial Activism at the European Court of Justice*, pp. 56–75, Cheltenham and Northampton: Edward Elgar.

Kelley, D. (1979). 'Gaius Noster: Substructures of Western Social Thought', *The American Historical Review* 84(3), 619–648.

Kelley, D. (1990). *The Human Measure*, Cambridge, MA: Harvard University Press.

Kelsen, H. (1927). 'Aussprach Über Erich Kaufmann "Die Gleichheit vor dem Gesetz im Sinne des Art. 109 der Reichsverfassung"', in *Veröffentlichungen der Vereinigung der Deutschen Staatsrechtslehrer III*, pp. 1–62 (at 53–55).

Kelsen, H. 1981[1929]. *Vom Wesen und Wert der Demokratie*, Scientia Verlag, Aalen.

Kelsen, H. 1994[1934]. *Reine Rechtslehre*, Scientia Verlag, Aalen.

Kelsen, H. 2008[1911]. Hauptprobleme der Staatsrechtslehre entwickelt aus der Lehre vom Rechtssatze, in Kelsen, H., *Werke 2(I and II)*, Tubingen: Mohr Siebeck.

Kelsen, H. (2010[1914]), 'Über Staatsunrecht. Zugleich ein Beitrag zur Frage der Deliktsfähigkeit juristischer Personen und zum Lehre vom fehlerhaften Staatsakt', in Kelsen, H., *Werke 3*, pp. 439–531, Tübingen: Mohr Siebeck.

Kelsen, H. (2017[1949]), *General Theory of the State*, New York: Routledge.

Kennedy, D. (1976). 'Form and Substance in Private Law Adjudication', *Harvard Law Review*, 89(8), 1685–1778.

Kennedy, D. (1979). 'The Structure of Blackstone's Commentaries', *Buffalo Law Review* 28, 205–382.

Kennedy, D. (1997). *A Critique of Adjudication*, Cambridge, MA: Harvard University Press.

Kennedy, D. (2001). 'A Semiotics of Critique', *Cardozo Law Review* 22, 1162–1190.

Kerferd, G. (1953). 'Protagoras' Doctrine of Justice and Virtue in the "Protagoras" of Plato', *The Journal of Hellenic Studies* 73, 42–45.

Kiefner, H. (1969). 'Der Einfluss Kants auf die Theorie und Praxis des Zivilrechts im 19. Jahrhundert', in Blühdorn, J. and Ritter, J. (eds), *Philosophie und Rechtswissenschaft: Zum Problem ihrer Beziehung im 19. Jahrhundert*, Frankfurt am Main: Vittorio Klostermann.

Kitto, H. (1951). *The Greeks*, Harmondsworth and New York: Penguin Books.

Kohler, J. (1886). 'Ueber die Interpretation der Gesetze', *Zeitschrift fur das Privat- und öffentliche Recht* 13(1), 1–61.

Kojeve, A. (1947). *Introduction à la lecture de Hegel*, Paris: Gallimard.

Krastev, I. (2017), *After Europe*, Philadelphia: University of Pennsylvania Press.

Kroger, J. (2004). 'The Philosophical Foundations of Roman Law: Aristotle, the Stoics, and Roman Theories of Natural Law', *Wisconsin Law Review*, 905–944.

Kyriakou, P. (2002). 'The Violence of Nomos in Pindar fr. 169a', *Materiali e discussioni per l'analisi dei testi classici* 48, 195–206.

Lacey, A., 1965, 'The Eleatics and Aristotle on Some Problems of Change', *Journal of the History of Ideas* 26(4), 451–468.

Lacey, N. (2006), *A Life of H.L.A. Hart*, Oxford: Oxford University Press.

Lacey, N . (2013), 'The Path not Taken: H. L. A. Hart's Harvard Essay on Discretion', *Harvard Law Review* 127(2), 636–651.

Laertius, D. (1925). *Lives of Eminent Philosophers II*, Cambridge, MA. Harvard University Press.

Lahusen, B. (2013). *Alles Recht geht vom Volksgeist aus*, Berlin: Nicolai.

Le Carré, J. (2013). *A Delicate Truth*, London: Penguin Books.

Lee, D. (2016). *Popular Sovereignty in Early Modern Constitutional Thought*, Oxford: Oxford University Press.

Lee, M. (2005), *Epistemology of Protagoras*, Oxford: Oxford University Press.

Lefort, C. (1986a). '*Permanence du theologico-politique?*", in Lefort, C., *Essais sur le politique*, pp. 275–329, Paris: Editions du Seuil.

Lefort, C. (1986b), 'Permanence of the Theological-Political', in De Vries, H. and Lawrence, S. (eds), *Political Theologies*, New York: Fordham University Press.

Lefort, C . 1994, *L'invention democratique: les limites de la domination totalitaire*, Paris: Fayard.

Levi, A., 1940, 'The Ethical and Social Thought of Protagoras', *Mind* 49, 284–302.

Litt, T. (1948). *Mensch und Welt. Grundlinien einer Philosophie des Geistes*, München: Federmann Verlag.

Litt, T. (1953). *Hegel. Versuch einer kritischen Erneuerung*, Heidelberg: Quelle & Meyer.

Loughlin, M. (2010). *Foundations of Public Law*, Oxford: Oxford University Press.

Lyotard, J-F. (1983). *Le Différend*, Paris: Les Editions de Minuit.

MacCormick, N. (1979). *Legal Reasoning and Legal Theory*, Oxford: Oxford University Press.

MacCormick, N. (1981). *H.L.A. Hart*, Stanford, CA: Stanford University Press.

Macintyre, A. (1967). *A Short History of Ethics*, London: Routledge.

Macintyre, A. (1985). *After Virtue*, London: Duckworth.

Macintyre, A. (1988). *Whose Justice? Which Rationality?* London: Duckworth.

Macpherson, C. (1962). *The Political Theory of Possessive Individualism*, Oxford: Oxford University Press.

Macpherson, C. (1977). *The Life and Times of Liberal Democracy*, Oxford: Oxford University Press.

Macpherson, C. (1987). *The Rise and Fall of Economic Justice and Other Essays*, Oxford: Oxford University Press.

Manow, P. (2001). 'Ordoliberalismus als ökonomische Ordnungstheologie', *Leviathan* 2, 179–198.

Marchart, O. (2007). *Political Difference in Nancy, Lefort, Badiou and Laclau*, Edinburgh: Edinburgh University Press.

Marquard, O. (1958). *Skeptische Methode im Blick auf Kant*, Freiburg and Munchen: Alber.

Marquard, O. (1982). *Schwierigkeiten mit der Geschichtsphilosophie*, Frankfurt am Main: Suhrkamp.

Martin, M. (2017). *City of the Sun: Development and Popular Resistance in the Pre-Modern West*, New York: Algora Publishing.

Martin, T. (2012). *Ancient Rome*, New Haven, CT and London: Yale University Press.

Marvin, F. (1965). *Comte. The Founder of Sociology*, New York: Russell & Russell.

Marx, K. (1978[1888]). 'Thesen über Feuerbach', in Marx, K. and Engels, F., *Werke III*, Berlin: Dietz Verlag.

Mauss, I. (1989). '"Gesetzesbindung" der Justiz, und die Struktur der nationalsozialistischen Rechtsnormen', in Dreier, R. and Sellert, W. (eds), *Recht und Justiz im "Dritten Reich"*, pp. 81–103, Frankfurt am Main: Suhrkamp .

Mauss, I. (1992). *Zur Aufklärung der Demokratietheorie. Rechts - und demokratietheoretische Überlegungen im Anschluss an Kant*, Frankfurt am Main: Suhrkamp.

Mehring, R. (2012). *Auf der gefahrenvollen Straße des öffentlichen Rechts' – Briefwechsel Carl Schmitt–Rudolf Smend 1921–1961*, Berlin: Duncker & Humblot.

Menke, C. (1996). *Tragödie im Sittlichen. Gerechtigkeit und Freiheit nach Hegel*, Frankfurt am Main: Suhrkamp.

Michelman, F. (1995). 'Always under Law? (Constitutional Democracy)', *Constitutional Commentary* 12, 227–247.

Michelman, F. (1996). 'Can Constitutional Democrats be Legal Positivists? Or Why Constitutionalism?', *Constellations* 2(3), 292–308.

Michelman, F. (2003). Ida's Way: Constructing the Respect-Worthy Governmental System (2003)', *Fordham Law Review* 72, 345–365.

Michelman, F. (2012). 'The Interplay of Constitutional and Ordinary Jurisdiction', in Ginsburg, T. and Dixon, R. (eds), *Comparative Constitutional Law*, pp. 278–297, Cheltenham and Northampton, MA: Edward Elgar Publishing, .

Mill, J. (1996), *Utilitarianism*, London: J.M. Dent.

Moyn, S. (2012). *The Last Utopia*, Cambridge, MA: Harvard University Press.

Moyn, S. (2015). *Christian Human Rights*, Philadelphia: University of Pennsylvania Press.

Müller, J-W. (2018). 'What the Dictum Really Meant—and What It Could Mean for Us', *Constellations* 25(2), 196–206.

Navarro, P. (2013). 'The Efficacy of Constitutional Norms', in Duarte d'Almeida, L. et al. (eds), *Kelsen Revisited*, Oxford and Portland, OR: Hart Publishing.

Neumann, A. (1938). 'Die Problematik des Homo-Mensura Satzes', *Classical Philology* 33(4), 368–379.

Nietzsche, F. (1999). *Samtliche Werke, Kritische Studienausgabe*, Berlin: Walter de Gruyter.

Nussbaum, M. (1986). *The Fragility of Goodness*, Cambridge: Cambridge University Press.

Oakley, F. (1961a). 'Christian Theology and the Newtonian Science: The Rise of the Concept of the Laws of Nature', *Church History* 6, 433–457.

Oakley, F . (1961b), 'Medieval Theories of Natural Law: William of Ockham and the Significance of the Voluntarist Tradition', *Natural Law Forum* 6, 65–83.

Ockham, W. (1974[1333]. Opus nonaginta dierum in Offler, H.S. (ed) *Guillelmi de Ockham Opera Politica 2*, Manchester : Manchester University Press.

O'Sullivan, N. (1995). 'Pericles and Protagoras', *Greece & Rome* 42(1), 15–23.

Owen, G. (1966). 'The Platonism of Aristotle', *Proceedings of the British Academy*, pp. 125–150.

Pindar. (2012[498–452 BC]), *Olympian and Pythian Odes*, Cambridge, MA: Harvard University Press.

Pinker, S. (2012). *The Better Angels of our Nature*, London: Penguin Books.

Plato. (1921[ca. 339]). *Theaetetus*, Cambridge, MA: Harvard University Press.

Plato. (1924[ca. 390]). *Protagoras*, Cambridge, MA: Harvard University Press.

Plato. (1925[ca. 380]). *Gorgias*, Cambridge, MA: Harvard University Press.

Plato. (1930/1935[ca. 380]). *Republic*, Cambridge, MA: Harvard University Press.

Pocock, J. (1975). *The Machiavellian Moment: Florentine Political Thought and the Atlantic Republican in the Seventeenth Century*, Cambridge: Cambridge University Press.

Pocock, J. (1987). *The Ancient Constitution and the Feudal Law. A Study of English Historical Thought Tradition*, Princeton, NJ: Princeton University Press.

Pound, R. (1907). 'The Need for a Sociological Jurisprudence', *Green Bag* 19, 607–615.

Pound, R. (1908). 'Mechanical Jurisprudence', *Columbia Law Review* 8, 605–623.

Pound, R. (1910). 'Law in Books and Law in Action', *American Law Review* 44, 12–36.

Pound, R. (1911/1912). 'The Scope and Purpose of Sociological Jurisprudence', *Harvard Law Review* 24/25(8/2/6), 591–619, 140–168, 489–516.

Pound, R. (1940/1941). 'Life as the Guide of Philosophy', *The American Scholar* 10(1), 102–119.

Preuß, H. (1900). 'Zur Methode juristischer Begriffskonstruktion', *Jahrbuch fur Gesetzgebung, Verwaltung und Volkswirtschaft im Deutschen Reich* 24, 359–372.

Preuss, U. (1993). 'Vater der Verfassungsväter – Carl Schmitts Verfassungslehre und die verfassungspolitische Diskussion der Gegenwart', in Gerhardt, V. et al. (eds), *Politisches Denken Jahrbuch 1993*, Stuttgart: Metzler.

Priest, S. (2007). *The British Empiricists*, Abingdon: Routledge.

Puchta, G. (1862). *Vorlesungen über das heutige römische Recht*, Leipzig: Bernhard Tauchnitz.

Pugliese, G. (1954). '"Res Corporalis," res incorporales' e il problema del diritto soggetivo', in *Studi in onore di Vicenzo Arangio-Ruiz III*, Naples: Jovene,.

Raaflaub, K. (2005). 'From Protection and Defense to Offense and Participation: Stages in the Conflict of the Orders', in Raaflaub, K. (ed.), *Social Struggles in Archaic Rome. New Perspectives on the Conflict of the Orders*, pp. 185–222, Oxford: Blackwell Publishing.

Radbruch, G. (1946). 'Gesetzliches Unrecht und Übergesetliches Recht', *Suddeutsche Juristen-Zeitung* 5, 105–108.

Rawls, J. (1973). *A Theory of Justice*, Oxford: Oxford University Press.

Rawls, J. (1985). 'Justice as Fairness: Political not Metaphysical', *Philosophy and Public Affairs* 14(3), 223–251.

Rawls, J. (1996). *Political Liberalism*, New York: Columbia University Press.

Rawls, J. (1999). *The Law of Peoples*, Cambridge, MA: Harvard University Press.

Raz, J. (1979). *The Authority of Law. Essays on Law and Morality*, Oxford: Oxford University Press.

Raz, J. (1980). *The Concept of a Legal System*, Oxford: Oxford University Press.

Rials, S. (2000). *Villey et les idoles*, Paris: Quadrige, Presses Universitaires de France.

Riedel, M. (1975). 'Hegels Begriff der bürgerlichen Gesellschaft und das Problem seines geschichtlichen Ursprungs', in Riedel, M. (ed.), *Materialien zu Hegels Rechtsphilosophie 2*, pp. 247–275, Frankfurt am Main: Suhrkamp.

Riesenfeld, S. (1989). 'The Influence of German Legal Theory on American Law: The Heritage of Savigny and His Disciples', *The American Journal of Comparative Law* 37, 1–7.

Ritter, J. (1975). 'Moralität und Sittlichkeit. Zu Hegels Auseinandersetzung mit der Kantischen Ethik', in Riedel, M. (ed.), *Materialien zu Hegels Rechtsphilosophie*, pp. 217–246, Frankfurt am Main: Suhrkamp .

Ritter, J. (2003). *Metaphysik und Politik*, Frankfurt am Main: Suhrkamp.

Rosanvallon, P. (1998). *Le Peuple introuvable – histoire de la représentation démocratique en France*, Paris: Gallimard.

Rose, G. (2009). *Hegel Contra Sociology*, London: Verso.

Rousseau, J-J. (1992[1754]). *Discours sur l'origine et les fondements de l'inégalité parmi les hommes*, Paris: GF Flammarion.

Rousseau, J-J. (1964[1762]). *Du Contract social*, Paris: Editions Gallimard.

Rückert, J. (1984). *Idealismus, Jurisprudenz und Politik bei Friedrich Carl von Savigny*, Ebelsbach: Verlag Rolf Gremer.

Ruppert, S. (2005). 'Geschlossene Wertordnung? Zur Grundrechtstheorie Rudolf Smends', in Henne, T. and Riedlinger, A. (eds), *Das Lüth-Urteil aus (rechts-)historischer Sicht – Die Konflikte um Veit Harlan und die Grundrechtsjudikatur des Bundesverfassungsgerichts*, pp. 327–348, Berlin: Berliner Wissenschafts-Verlag.

Savigny, F. von. (1815). 'Ueber den Zweck dieser Zeitschrift', *Zeitschrift fur geschichtliche Rechtswissenschaft* 1, 1–17.

Savigny, F. von. (1840a). *System des heutigen romischen Rechts I*, Deit & Company, Berlin.

Savigny, F. von. (1840b[1814]). *Vom Beruf Unsrer Zeit Fur Gesetzgebung und Rechtswissenschaft*, Heidelberg: J.C.B. Mohr.

Schönberger, C. (2008). 'Hans Kelsens "Hauptprobleme der Staatsrechtslehre." Der Übergang vom Staat als Substanz zum Staat als Funktion', in Kelsen, H., *Werke*, pp. 23–35, Tubingen: Mohr Siebeck.

Scharpf, F. (2010). 'The Asymmetry of European Integration, or Why the EU cannot be a "Social Market Economy"', *Socio-economic Review* 8(2), 211–250.

Schmitt, C. (1933). *Staat, Bewegung, Volk: die Dreigliederung der politischen Einheit.* Hamburg: Hanseatische Verlagsanstalt.

Schmitt, C. (1958). *Verfassungsrechtliche Aufsatze aus den Jahren 1924–1954*, Berlin: Duncker & Humblot.

Schmitt, C. (1982[1938]). *Der Leviathan*, Stuttgart: Klett-Cotta.

Schmitt, C. (1994[1940]). *Positionen und Begriffe: im Kampf mit Weimar– Genf–Versailles*, Berlin: Duncker & Humblot.

Schmitt, C. (1996a[1932]). *Der Begriff des Politischen*, Berlin: Duncker & Humblot.

Schmitt, C. (1996b[1931]). *Der Hüter der Verfassung*, Berlin: Duncker & Humblot.

Schmitt, C. (1996c[1922]). *Politisiche Theologie. Vier Kapitel zur Lehre von der Souveranität*, Berlin: Duncker & Humblot.

Schmitt, C. (1997[1950]). *Der Nomos der Erde*, Berlin: Duncker & Humblot.

Schmitt, C. (2003[1928]). *Verfassungslehre*, Berlin: Duncker & Humblot.

Schmitt, C. (2006a[1921]), *Die Diktatur*, Berlin: Duncker & Humblot.

Schmitt, C. (2006b). *The Nomos of the Earth.* Candor, NY: Telos Press Publishing.

Schmitt, C. (2006c[1934]). *Über die drei Arten des rechtswissenschaftlichen Denkens*, Berlin: Duncker & Humblot.

Schrage, E. (1977). *Actio and Subjectief Recht. Over Romeinse en Middeleeuse Wortels van een Moderne Begrip*, Amsterdam: Vrije Universiteit Amsterdam.

Schulte, M. (1992). *Die "Tragödie im Sittlichen" – Zur Dramentheorie Hegels*, München: Wilhelm Fink Verlag.

Schultz, F. (1992). *Classical Roman Law*, Aalen: Scientia Verlag.

Shorey, P. (1922). '"Coming-to-Be" and "Passing Away"', *Classical Philology* 17(4), 334–352.

Singh, S. (2010). 'Eugen Ehrlich's 'Living Law' and Its Legacy for Legal Pluralism'. Available at: SSRN: https://ssrn.com/abstract=1660606 or http://dx.doi.org/10.2139/ssrn.1660606. Accessed 2019, https://papers.ssrn.com/sol3/papers.cfm?abstract_id=1660606.

Smend, R. (2010). *Staatsrechtliche Abhandelungen und andere Aufsätze*, Berlin: Duncker & Humblot.

Solmsen, F. (1960). *Aristotle's System of the Physical World*, Ithaca, NY: Cornell University Press.

Supiot, A. (2007). *Homo Juridicus*, London and New York: Verso.

Supiot, A. (2010). *L'Ésprit de Philadelphie*, Paris: Seuil.

Supiot, A. (2013). 'The Public–Private Relation in the Context of Today's Refeudalization', *International Journal of Constitutional Law* 11(1), 129–145.

Tamanaha, B. (2001). 'Postivism and a General Jurisprudence', *Oxford Legal Studies* 21, 1–32.

Tamanaha, B. (2011). 'A Vision of Social-Legal Change: Rescuing Ehrlich from "Living Law"', *Law & Social Inquiry* 36(1), 297–318.

Taylor, C. (1975). *Hegel*, Cambridge: Cambridge University Press.

Taylor, C. (1989). *Sources of the Self. The Making of the Modern Identity*, Cambridge, MA: Harvard University Press.

Teubner, G. (2013). 'The Law Before Its Law: Franz Kafka on the (Im)possibility of Law's Self-Reflection', *German Law Journal* 14(2), 405–422.

Thibaut, A. (1814). *Ueber die Nothwendigkeit eines allgemeinen bürgerlichen Rechts für Deutschland*, Heidelberg: Mohr und Zimmer.

Thijssen, H. (2013). 'Condemnation of 1277', *Stanford Encyclopedia of Philosophy* Available at: https://plato.stanford.edu/entries/condemnation.

Thornhill, C. (2011). *A Sociology of Constitutions: Constitutions and State Legitimacy in Historical-Sociological Perspective*, Cambridge: Cambridge University Press.

Thucydides. (1921/1928). *History of the Peloponnesian War*, Cambridge, MA: Harvard University Press.

Tierney, B. (1988). 'Villey, Ockham and the Origin of Individual Rights', in Witte, J. and Alexander, F. (eds), *Weightier Matters of the Law: Essays on Law and Religion: A Tribute to Harold J Berman*, pp. 1–31, Atlanta, GA: Scholars Press.

Ullmann, W. (1946). *The Medieval Idea of Law as Presented by Lucas de Penna: A Study in Fourteenth-Century Legal Scholarship*, London: Methuen.

Ullmann, W. (1975). *Law and Politics in the Middle Ages*, London: Hodder & Stoughton.

Unger, R. (1986). *The Critical Legal Studies Movement*, Cambridge, MA: Harvard University Press.

Vaihinger, H. (1988[1911]). *Die Philosophie des Als Ob: System der theoretischen, praktischen und religiösen Fiktionen der Menschheit auf Grund eines idealistischen Positivismus*, Aalen: Scientia Verlag.

Van der Walt, J. (2005). *Law and Sacrifice. Towards a Post-Apartheid Theory of Law*, London and Johannesburg: Birkbeck Law Press/Wits University Press.

Van der Walt, J. (2012). 'Law and the Space of Appearance in Arendt's Thought', in Goldoni, M. and McCorkindale, C. (eds), *Hannah Arendt and the Law*, pp. 63–88, Oxford: Hart Publishing.

Van der Walt, J. (2014a). 'Law, Utopia, Event: A Constellation of Two Trajectories', in Sarat, A. et al. (eds), *Law and the Utopian Imagination*, pp. 60–100, Stanford, CA: Stanford University Press.

Van der Walt, J. (2014b), *The Horizontal Effect Revolution and the Question of Sovereignty*, Berlin and Boston: Walter de Gruyter.

Van der Walt, J. (2015a). 'Delegitimation by Constition? Liberal Democratic Experimentalism and the Question of Socio-Economic Rights', *Critical Quarterly for Legislation and Law* 15(3), 303–333.

Van der Walt, J. (2015b). 'The Literary Exception: Reflections on Agamben's "Liberal Democratic" Political Theology and the Religious Destabilisation of the Political in Our Time', *New Perspectives. Interdisciplinary Journal of Central & East European Politics and International Relations* 23(1), 15–44.

Van der Walt, J. (2016). 'When One Religious Extremism Unmasks Another: Reflections on Europe's States of Emergency as a Legacy of Ordo-Liberal Dehermeneuticisation', *New Perspectives. Interdisciplinary Journal of Central & East European Politics and International Relations* 24(1), 79–102.

Van der Walt, J. (2018). 'The Origin of Obligations: Towards a Fundamental Phenomenology of Legal and Moral Obligation', in Matthews, D. and Veitch, S. (eds), *Law Obligation Community*, pp. 35–70, London: Routledge.

Van der Walt, J. (2019). 'The Gift of Time and the Hour of Sacrifice', in Nail, B. and Ellsworth, J. (eds), *Sacrifice in Law and Literature*, pp. 113–149, London: Routledge.

Van Steenberghen, F. (1980). *Thomas Aquinas and Radical Aristotelianism*, Washington, DC: Catholic University of America Press,

Versenyi, L. (1962). 'Protagoras' Man-Measure Fragment', *The American Journal of Philology* 83(2), 178–184.

Villey, M. (1946). 'L'idée du droit subjectif et les systèmes juridiques romains', *Revue Historique de Droit Francais et Etranger* 24, 201–227.

Villey, M. (2003[1975]). *La formation de la pensée juridique moderne*, Paris: Presses Universitaires de France.

Van Ooyen, R. (2008). 'Editor's Introduction: Die Funktion der Verfassungsgerichtsbarkeit in der pluralistischen Demokratie und die Kontroverse um den "Hüter der Verfassung"', in Kelsen, H., *Wer soll der Hüter der Verfassung sein?*, Tübingen: Mohr Siebeck.

Volk, C. (2015), *Arendtian Constitutionalism. Law Politics and the Order of Freedom*, Oxford: Hart Publishing.

Waldron, J. (1999a). *Law and Disagreement*, Oxford University Press, Oxford.

Waldron, J. (1999b). *The Dignity of Legislation*, Cambridge: Cambridge University Press.

Walther, M. (1989). 'Hat der juristische Positivismus die deutschen Juristen im "Dritten Reich" Wehrlos gemacht?', in Dreier, R. and Sellert, W. (eds), *Recht und Justiz im "Dritten Reich"*, pp. 323–354, Frankfurt am Main: Suhrkamp.

Waluchow, W. (1994). *Inclusive Legal Positivism*, Oxford: Oxford University Press.

Watson, A. (1995). *The Spirit of Roman Law*, Athens and London: The University of Georgia Press.

Watson, J. (1898). 'The Metaphysic of Aristotle', *The Philosophical Review* 7(4), 337–354.

Wieacker, F. (1996[1967]). *Privatrechtsgeschichte der Neuzeit*. Göttingen: Vandenhoeck & Ruprecht.

Williams, B. (1973). 'A Critique of Utilitarianism', in Smart, J. J. C. and Williams, B. (eds), *Utilitarianism, For and Against*, pp. 96–100, 110–117, Cambridge: Cambridge University Press.

Williams, J. (1987). 'Critical Legal Studies: The Death of Transcendence and the Rise of the New Langdells', *New York University Law Review* 62(3), 429–496.

Williams, J. (2003). *Augustus*, London: Vintage Books.

Windscheid, B. (1963[1856]). *Lehrbuch des Pandektenrechts*, Aalen: Scientia Verlag.

Zartaloudis, T. (2018). *The Birth of Nomos*, Edinburgh: Edinburgh University Press.

Zilioli, U. (2007). *Protagoras and the Challenge of Relativism. Plato's Subtlest Enemy*, Aldershot and Burlington, VT: Ashgate.

Zimmermann, R. (2015). 'Roman Law in the Modern World', in Johnston, D. (ed.), *Roman Law*, pp. 452–480, Cambridge: Cambridge University Press.

Zimmermann, R. (2001). *Roman Law, Contemporary Law, European Law*, Oxford: Oxford University Press.

# INDEX

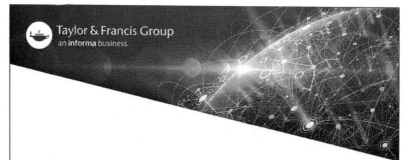